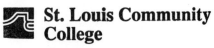

INTERACTIVE INSTRUCTION AND FEEDBACK

INTERACTIVE INSTRUCTION AND FEEDBACK

John V. Dempsey
University of South Alabama

Gregory C. Sales
University of Minnesota

EDITORS

Educational Technology Publications
Englewood Cliffs, New Jersey 07632

Library of Congress Cataloging-in-Publication Data

Interactive instruction and feedback / John V. Dempsey, Gregory C.
Sales, editors.
    p.   cm.
    Includes bibliographical references and indexes.
    ISBN 0-87778-260-1
    1. Educational technology.   2. Instructional systems—Design.
3. Interactive media.   4. Programmed instruction.   5. Feedback
(Psychology)   6. Learning, Psychology of.   I. Dempsey, John V.
II. Sales, Gregory Colin.
    LB1028.3.I5655   1993   92-47430
    371.3'3—dc20   CIP

Printed in the United States of America.

Library of Congress Catalog Card Number:
92-47430.

International Standard Book Number:
0-87778-260-1.

First Printing: April, 1993.

Preface

This book came rather naturally out of our mutual interest in interactive instruction and feedback. One afternoon, as we took a break from sessions at the annual meeting of the Association for Educational Communications and Technology, we discussed all the individuals we knew who were also interested in this topic. As our discussion continued, we decided to try to put together an edited volume of chapters by some of those talented people.

In coordinating a book on this topic, we looked to scholars in the field from diverse institutions around the country. Twenty-one authors are involved in composing these thirteen chapters. Many of these individuals are well-known in the areas of instructional design and educational psychology and are interested in feedback, particularly as it relates to the new interactive technologies of the 1990's and beyond. All agreed that nothing like the proposed book existed in the field and that a collection of chapters in this area was long overdue.

The nature of the chapters grew from the authors' areas of research expertise. A special feature of the book is the "teaming" of authors in most chapters. This was a purposeful decision intended to enrich the breadth of the material presented by linking theorists and researchers with related interests. Our goal was to offer research summaries, methods, techniques, or forecasts for incorporating feedback strategies into interactive instruction. Our hope was that practitioners would find useful guidelines and fresh perspectives for design, development, research, and planning.

In preparing the present volume, we have relied heavily on the cooperation of Lawrence Lipsitz of Educational Technology Publications. From our first contact with him, he has been enthusiastic about this project and has offered us excellent advice throughout its completion. In addition, we wish to thank our respective deans and department chairpersons at the University of South Alabama and the University of Minnesota for supporting our work on this project.

John V. Dempsey
Gregory C. Sales

Table of Contents

INTERACTIVE INSTRUCTION AND FEEDBACK

Chapter One

Feedback in Programmed Instruction: Historical Context and Implications for Practice

Raymond W. Kulhavy
Arizona State University

and

Walter Wager
Florida State University

In this chapter we are interested in examining the effects of feedback within the context of programmed instruction. As we view it, the term "feedback" designates any information that follows a response and allows a student to evaluate the adequacy of the response itself. The definition of "programmed instruction" is lifted directly from B.F. Skinner's initial conception (e.g., 1958). Typically, programmed instruction is distinguished by sequences of individual "frames" which contain the elements shown below.

Elements Within a Frame of Programmed Instruction

1. Instructional Text.
2. Question over Text.
3. Student Response Requirement.
4. Feedback on the Response.

The amount of new instructional information presented in step (1) is kept very small in order to prevent error responses. The question (2) deals

3

specifically with the text, and is heavily prompted if the material has not already been answered correctly in an earlier frame. The student response in step (3) must be overt (for Skinner), and derive directly from the text. Finally, the feedback (4) directly matches the form and content of the expected response. Programs were first designed for presentation on early teaching machines (Skinner, 1961), later printed for use as regular textbooks (Lumsdaine & Glaser, 1960), and finally transferred intact to the computer screen (Coulson, 1962), where they remain to this day (Steinberg, 1991).

In the sections that follow we will attempt to trace the pedagogical view of feedback as it developed within the framework of programmed instruction. Such a journey is of more than historical value, since most education (and a great many psychology) textbooks still define feedback as a "reinforcer," and treat it much as a hungry pigeon treats a pellet of food. The feedback-as-reinforcer position has been highly resistant to extinction, in spite of the fact that it is basically illogical, supported by virtually no data, and has rarely been directly espoused by Skinner himself.

In the first section of the chapter we will overview the historical factors associated with the concept of feedback in instruction, concluding with its identification as an operant reinforcer in the early 1960s. The second section deals directly with research on programmed instruction in the Skinnerian tradition. The third section considers alternate approaches to feedback as a unit of information. This section ends with a review of research on the timing of feedback presentations. We conclude the chapter with a summary of implications for practice which we hope our readers will find useful.

Feedback as a Pedagogical Device: An Historical Overview

During the first half of the twentieth century, there was confusion regarding the role that feedback played in the learning process. By and large, feedback was viewed as (a) a motivator or incentive for increasing the rate or accuracy of performance; (b) a "satisfying state of affairs," which according to E.L. Thorndike's Law of Effect automatically "connected" responses to preceding stimuli; (c) as information which learners could use to validate or change a previous response. As we shall see, this same triad of definitions remains to this day.

The motivational approach to feedback was (and is) based in the belief that letting people know how well they are performing a task acts as an incentive for greater effort in the future. In most early research, "motivation" was generally achieved by providing overall indications of progress at various points during task performance. For example, informing students periodically about their gross performance increased rate of responding for arithmetic (Brown, 1932) and grammar tasks (Symonds & Chase, 1929). The one thing that such studies had in common was their attempt to influence the effort expended by the subject in responding to tasks already learned previously. Although there were numerous attempts to resolve the confusion between rate of responding and actual learning (e.g., Hull, 1935; MacPherson, Dees, & Grindley, 1948–49; Wallach & Henle, 1941), the motivation vs. learning issue continued to be a stumbling block for those interested in conceptualizing how feedback works.

Early on, feedback became identified with concepts like reward and connection-formation through the Law of Effect. It was Thorndike, of course, who laid out the template for much of the early research involving the use of post-response information (Thorndike, 1911, 1913). Near the turn of the century he had specified his "Laws of Learning," and both the Law of Exercise and the Law of Effect had a marked influence on how most data gatherers designed, conducted, and interpreted feedback experiments. Ultimately the Law of Effect (or some version of it) became the dominant view, simply because unadorned practice (exercise) has little explanatory power (e.g., Arps, 1920; Judd, 1905–06; Thorndike, 1927).

There are really two Laws of Effect. In his initial formulation, Thorndike stated that when a response is followed by a "satisfying state of affairs," it is likely to be repeated again; and when it is followed by an "annoying state of affairs," there is an identical likelihood that it will *not* be repeated (Thorndike, 1913). The second, or Truncated Law of Effect, was developed after extensive experimentation (Thorndike, 1932; Trowbridge & Cason, 1932), and essentially removed the influence of annoying states of affairs, leaving the "effect" of satisfying states on responding as the primary mechanism of learning. This is the parent concept of the reinforcement position developed by Skinner, and reinforcement in the operant setting is often said to follow the "Empirical Law of Effect."

The final member of the feedback triad is information. The major difference between information approaches and the motivation/connection positions just described lies in the treatment of error responses. Information-processing theories view human beings as adaptive organisms who are capable of adjusting their behavior according to exterior task demands. For instance, when one produces an error, response feedback allows the error to be corrected. On the other hand, feedback after correct responses is seen as doing little more than verifying that the response was the right one. Implicit in information-processing models is the active participation of the student in the act of learning.

In the context of developing his teaching machine, Sidney Pressey was probably the first to clearly identify feedback as a unit of information. In 1926 he proposed that the right answers following multiple-choice questions on his machine allowed students to correct errors as they moved through the test. Interestingly, although Pressey emphasized error correction, he was careful to include the prevailing wisdom of Thorndike by invoking the "Laws" in a footnote, and having the machine deliver a piece of candy (for effect!) when a lesson was completed. In a later paper (1927), he again implicated correction of errors as the primary teaching act of his machine (which it is, since the student must learn the correct response), but he now viewed correction in Thorndikian terms, as punishment for errors. Actually, Pressey's work provides a good example of confusion regarding feedback's role, since his machine simultaneously "connects" item-stems to right alternatives, and corrects errors (but punishes them, by 1927), and maintains the student's motivation with the candy (1926) and coupons (1927).

Although there were other studies emphasizing the informational nature of feedback (e.g., Angell, 1949; Curtis & Woods, 1929; Peterson, 1931), Pressey's work was classic, and by far the most influential. In 1950 he anticipated many of the current approaches to feedback in an article which tested a punchboard that identified right and wrong multiple-choice responses. In this paper he hit upon both error correction, "The big effect of the punchboard was in the correction of errors" (p. 426), and the fact that students tended to adapt their response to fit the feedback message, ". . . as the automatic pilot on a plane adjusts the flight . . . such devices spot each learner's weakness and assure their correction . . ." (p. 418). Unfortunately for Pressey, the *Zeitgeist* embraced the Law of Effect, and he again did his best to include it in a footnote: "Readers familiar with the methods of Thorndike and others in the study of the law of effect will recognize that repetition of a test using the punchboard involves the 'retained situation' . . ." (p. 429).

The table below relates the three conceptualizations of how feedback works to the major variables of interest to researchers. Although the distinction may be blurred in some cases, most research done with programmed instruction falls into one of these categories.

Feedback Treated as:

	Motivator	Reward or Reinforcement	Information
Variable of Interest	Rate or Accuracy	Correct Responses	Error Responses

This brief examination of the approaches to feedback, and the confusion among them, introduces our review of similar research within the context of programmed instruction. From the mid-1950s through the 1960s the dominant figure in this research was B.F. Skinner, and it is to work based on his approach that we now turn.

Research on Programmed Instruction in the Skinnerian Tradition

In 1954 Skinner published his first article dealing with the educational process, and it had a tremendous influence on thinking in the field of instruction. Here, he offered a solution to the ills plaguing education, by suggesting that his version of the Law of Effect could be applied directly to classroom materials. He then discussed the application of reinforcement principles to children, making it clear that, although such principles were derived from animal work, they would work equally well with people: "In all this work, the species of the organism has made suprisingly little difference" (Skinner, 1954, p. 89). Of course, it was this unquestioning transfer of principles, from rats and pigeons to humans, that helped lesson feedback and alfalfa pellets to be exchanged as common currency in instructional research.

By 1960 Skinner and his advocates (Skinner, 1958; Skinner & Holland, 1960) had not only developed the programmed learning principles we described earlier, but also had succeeded in making them the primary research focus in the field (cf. Lumsdaine & Glaser, 1960; Glaser, 1965). At this point, feedback in programmed instruction had assumed its status not only as a reinforcer, but also as a motivator, thereby maintaining the confusion between learning and incentive. In discussing the use of his teaching machines, Skinner set the stage for the coming decade when he said:

> . . . of course, the machine, like the private tutor, reinforces the student for every correct response, using this immediate feedback not only to shape his behavior most efficiently but to maintain it in strength in a manner which the layman would describe as holding the student's interest. (Skinner, 1958, p. 971)

With few exceptions (e.g., Crowder, 1960), research in the 1960s concentrated on promoting and measuring correct responding. Instructional errors were either ignored, or described as "aversive consequences" to be avoided at all costs (Skinner, 1968). In some cases, the "aversive" nature of errors was further implicated by assuming that feedback following errors was detrimental to students, and led to their being "emotionally upset"

(Ferster & Sapon, 1958). Later, this same line of reasoning was adapted from Terrace's (Terrace, 1963, 1964) work on discrimination learning with pigeons, and wrong answers were looked upon as causing distress and low self-concept—an approach which remains in its original form to current times (e.g., Fischer & Mandl, 1988). The addition of an emotional component to feedback is linked to the "motivational" dimension described earlier. However, to the authors' knowledge, there has been no research supporting the concept that feedback following errors causes students the same distress seen in pigeons pecking colored keys. The interests of instructional design would probably be better served if "motivational" variables, be they rate of response or self-concept, were separated from the feedback message itself, and treated as variables extrinsic to the lesson content. In this way, it seems possible to at last remove the confusion between the content of feedback and other variables that affect learner performance.

Not everyone was as certain as Skinner about the relation between feedback and reinforcement. For example, in reviewing the literature on teaching machine research, Douglas Porter (1957) pointed out that in accepting "knowledge of results" as reinforcement, people commit a logical error, since, "... knowledge of results is a descriptive term which refers solely to a particular kind of sensory feedback, not to the reinforcing value of the feedback" (p. 135). In 1960, Amsel went as far as to suggest that partial reinforcement schedules should be used to eliminate errors, as opposed to simply increasing the rate of correct responding. The confusion surrounding the function of feedback was apparent when Ammons (1956) attributed error correction and reinforcing properties to feedback, and then concluded: "The most common effect of knowledge of performance is to increase motivation" (p. 285). However, so strong had the feedback-as-reinforcement position become, due to Skinner's compelling prose and his appeal to "scientific" theory, that dissenting voices were ignored, and feedback, reinforcement, and motivation became as one in programmed instruction. It is to research in this tradition that we now turn our attention.

Programmed Instruction: The Operant Approach

During the 1960s a large number of studies attempted to test directly operant principles within the context of programmed instruction. Such research made use of books, machines, and occasionally computers, as presentation devices, but the overriding objective was to replicate Skinner's laboratory findings with programs. In order to accomplish this task, programs were constructed to "shape" the student's responses, and shaping took the form of presenting material in very small, highly redundant increments. Each small frame of material required a response, and the correct form of that response (feedback) was made immediately available to the learner, generally by having the student move a paper mask down to reveal it, or simply turn the page (in the programmed book formats). For example, *The Analysis of Behavior* by Holland and Skinner (1961) teaches basic principles of conditioning by having the student produce about 2,000 individual responses, with correct answers printed on the page following each such response. Programs constructed in this manner certainly followed operant doctrine (shaping of responses, few errors, immediate reinforcement): however, the basic design led to unanticipated problems, especially in the conduct of research.

As data accumulated in the literature, it became apparent that programs (at least in book format) were not working as expected. Not only did the linear form developed by Skinner occasionally fail to out-perform "branching" versions (cf. Crowder, 1960; Glaser, 1965), but the "immediate reinforcement" provided by feedback often made little difference in terms of student learning (Feldhusen & Brit, 1962; Hough & Revsin, 1963; Krumboltz & Weisman, 1962; McDonald & Allen, 1962; Moore & Smith, 1961, 1964; O'Day, Kulhavy, Anderson, & Malczynski, 1971; Rosenstock, Moore, & Smith, 1965; Sullivan, Baker, & Schutz, 1967; Sullivan, Schutz, & Baker, 1971). To further complicate the matter, there were even occasional studies where students who saw no feedback outperformed those who did (e.g., Lublin, 1965). The lack of effect for "reinforcement" presented something of a dilemma for Skinnerian programmers, since explanations based on sheer practice (the old Law of Exercise) were unsatisfactory.

The solution to the lack-of-effect problem turned out to be a surprisingly simple one. Recall that linear programs are highly redundant; correct answers are highly prompted by frame content; and the correct-answer feedback is in close proximity to the response itself. Although such a design meets operant canons, it also has two undesirable side-effects with human learners who are reading programs. First, the heavy prompting of correct responses allows students to bypass the actual reading of frame material and still produce the desired answer (Anderson & Faust, 1967). Second, since the correct answer is readily available, students find it easier to copy the feedback instead of reading the text (Anderson, Kulhavy, & Andre, 1971, 1972). Under these conditions, students make few errors on frames, progress rapidly through the program (both desirable from an operant point of view), and learn very little of the content because they do not bother to read it! Such results indicated that the promise of directly transferring laboratory principles to human instruction were unlikely to be fulfilled. There are vast differences between people reading texts and rats pushing bars, not the least of which is a tendency on the part of students to find the path of least resistance (i.e., copying instead of reading), and to take it.

Research in the Skinnerian tradition also tackled the question of partial, or scheduled, reinforcement in programs. In these studies, correct-answer feedback followed frame responses on either a fixed or variable ration schedule, ranging from 10 to 66 percent of the total frames (Krumboltz & Weisman, 1962; Lublin, 1965; Rosenstock, Moore, & Smith, 1965). In general, not one such study produced an effect consistent with laboratory experiments on intermittent reinforcement. Actually, there is no reason to expect such replication, since students are rarely under powerful contingency control, and the stimulus-response relations in a program are constantly changing (Anderson, 1967). Once again, the conclusion is that programs designed from an operant base do not work well when people try to learn from them.

Predictably, there was also research conducted on the role of "extrinsic reinforcement" that was similar in nature to the candy and coupons expelled by Pressey's machines (e.g., Moore & Smith, 1964; Sullivan, Baker, & Schutz, 1967; Sullivan, Schutz, & Baker, 1971). Such studies were really motivational in nature, and attempted to influence student effort by providing reinforcers, like money or time off from class, for high lesson performance. In no case did the external rewards interact with the presence of feedback, nor did they consistently meet operant expectations concerning increases in rate of responding.

So what can we conclude from Skinner's attempt to apply his analysis of behavior to the domain of human instruction? There appear to be three main points. First, it seems difficult, if not impossible, to translate operant principles directly into an instructional system that works well with classroom students. Second, the "programming" of information is a far more complex task than Skinner originally imagined, simply because students become bored with small-response increments, and tend to seek a less resistant path if they can find one. The third point is that Skinner was able to gain great support for the concept of instructional design, especially self-instruction. His attempt to tie instructional design to learning theory paved the way for a large volume of related research, and made instructional technology and psychology legitimate areas of investigation within behavioral science. His concept of programmed instruction produced many related lesson designs, and it is to research on such alternate approaches that we now turn.

Alternate Approaches to Feedback in Programmed Instruction

By about 1970, most workers in the field had become disenchanted with the Skinnerian approach to programming. However, given ten years of research in which many experiments had shown no systematic effects for feedback, it was necessary to *re-establish the basic functions served by post-response information*. A series of three studies published by R.C. Anderson and his colleagues was designed to accomplish exactly this objective (Anderson, Kulhavy, & Andre, 1971, 1972).

The Anderson *et al.* research used programmed instruction dealing with the diagnosis of heart disease, and with the fundamentals of human genetics, which were presented on a computer system that allowed control of the point at which the student could see the post-response information. Essentially, the studies made three important points about the use of feedback in programs. First, they clearly demonstrated that when students are able to copy feedback, they will do so, and learn little from the lesson content itself. This finding accounted for the many studies in which feedback in linear programs failed to have a positive effect on instructional performance. The second outcome of this research was to demonstrate that feedback significantly facilitates learning from programmed material—especially when students *must* respond *before* seeing the feedback itself. Finally, the data provided every indication that feedback works primarily to correct errors, and has a much smaller effect on initially correct responses. Such research clarified important issues regarding the role of feedback in programs, and paved the way for the many feedback-as-information studies that followed.

Of course, there had been research in the information tradition all along. Probably the most important example of such an alternate approach can be found in Norman Crowder's concept of "branching" or "intrinsic" programs (Crowder, 1960, 1961). Crowder tied his programming style to the concept that errors are not necessarily detrimental, and that they can be corrected by the presentation of information in addition to simply telling students the correct responses. Using larger segments of content material in his frames, Crowder included multiple-choice items which allowed students to "branch" to correction frames specially designed to correct a specific error choice.

In spite of the fact that Crowder's programs emphasized the informational nature of feedback, people had difficulty showing that they performed better than the linear approach (e.g., Silberman, Melaragno, Coulson, & Estavan, 1961), and still more difficulty in linking instructional performance to the amount of information in the feedback (Kaufman, 1963; Merrill, 1965; Merrill & Stolurow, 1966). Generally, feedback was superior to no feedback in terms of amount of learning: however, variations in the content of the feedback message yielded no systematic differences. The basic information-processing assumption—that increasing the amount of feedback information should yield like increases in error correction—found little consistent support in the research on programs (e.g., Kulhavy, 1977). It is on the question of feedback form and content that we now focus our attention.

Research on Feedback Form and Content

Between the 1960s and the present there have been more than 50 studies comparing various feedback configurations in programs or program-like lessons (Kulhavy & Stock, 1989). Unfortunately, for those who design instruction, the overall verdict has remained the same, and there appears to be no consistent pattern of results in this sizable literature—other than the general finding that some feedback is better than no feedback.

On one hand, research on feedback content shows a decided advantage over more complex feedback messages (e.g., Albertson, 1986; Collins, Carnine, & Gersten, 1987; Grant, McAvoy, & Keenan, 1982; Hannafin, 1983; Roper, 1977). In these studies, feedback forms containing more information generally produce higher instructional performance. On the other hand, there is a counterpoint literature, in which increases in amount of information have no significant effect on lesson performance (e.g., Corbett & Anderson, 1990; Gilman, 1969; Hodes, 1985; Kulhavy, White, Topp, Chan, & Adams, 1985; Merrill, 1987). What these results indicate is that lessons and learners vary so greatly that it may not be possible to specifiy a systematic relation between feedback content and instructional performance prior to the administration of the lesson itself. One implication of this reasoning is that the best match between responses and subsequent feedback may require information about the learner's knowledge state at the time the response is made.

Much of the research done with various styles of programmed lessons in the past 15 years has used some form of computer-assisted presentation. Computers are a natural medium for programmed instruction lessons, since each "screen" of material can be thought of as a frame of information. The processing capacities of computers have allowed development of at least two feedback approaches based on the student's knowledge state at the time of responding.

The first approach has been to perform a detailed analysis of the types of errors made by students, and then attempt to design a feedback strategy aimed at specific error correction (e.g., Anderson, Boyle, & Reiser, 1985; Andrews & Uliano, 1985; Birenbaum & Tatsuoka, 1987; Brown & Burton, 1978; Fischer & Mandl, 1985). The error analysis approach has the advantage of customizing feedback for different types of errors—a more precise tactic that simply adds more information to the feedback for all responses. For example, Birenbaum and Tatsuoka (1987) had eighth-graders complete a lesson on signed numbers and analyzed errors in terms of their "seriousness." Feedback was either straight verification ("OK"/"NO"), the correct response, or a statement of correct and incorrect solutions to problems. In line with information processing assumptions, the more complex the feedback, the greater the likelihood of error correction for "non-serious errors." Serious errors were relatively unaffected by the types of feedback. These results indicate that amount of information interacts with error type, and this raises the possibility of the prescriptive use of feedback based on the type of error produced by the learner.

A second, even more learner-oriented, approach has been proposed by Kulhavy and Stock (1989). In developing a model of feedback processing, Kulhavy and Stock make primary use of response-confidence estimates produced by the learner. This research indicates that a student's confidence in the correctness of a particular response can be used as an index of how well the instruction has been comprehended. Further, confidence estimates yield consistent predictions for both initial error and correct responses. Such predictions apply to both the amount of time a student will spend studying feedback, and to the probability that an initial instructional response will be remembered correctly on a later test (e.g., Kulhavy, Stock, Thornton, Winston, & Behrens, 1990). Since response-confidence measures are relatively easy to obtain, such estimates may have considerable prescriptive value for the design of computer-presented programs.

Both error analysis and response confidence approaches have potential for determining exactly what feedback content will be most effective for a given response. To one degree or another, such measures are linked to the knowledge state of the student at the time the response is made. The interaction of this knowledge state with feedback formats can begin to take advantage of the processing capacity inherent in computer-driven lessons.

Research on the Timing of Feedback

Recall that one of the canons of Skinnerian programmed instruction is that the reinforcement (feedback) must follow the instructional response as closely in time as possible. As Skinner himself put it, in discussing applications of his system to education: "... the lapse of only a few seconds between response and reinforcement destroys most of the effect" (Skinner, 1954, p. 91). This was a direct laboratory analogy, since delay of reinforcement for hungry rats severely reduces response learning (Renner, 1964). Research on delayed feedback has been a constant problem for those who advocate the operant approach to programmed instruction.

Over the past decade and a half a sizable literature has appeared on the subject of feedback timing (see Kulik & Kulik, 1988). Unfortunately, for the current discussion, many of the studies performed with delayed feedback have not used typical programming approaches, but have confined themselves to multiple-choice items, with or without preceding blocks of instruction (e.g., Sturges, 1972; Surber & Anderson, 1975). However, the results with items and prose have been replicated with programs (e.g., Rankin & Trepper, 1978), and with similar devices, such as Pressey's punchboard-like response cards (English & Kinzer, 1966). In fact, Kulik and Kulik (1988) conclude that delayed feedback has its most prominent effect in cases where there is a high degree of control over the instructional presentation and subsequent responding—cases much like the typical program. Hence, we will frame our discussion below in terms of the general conclusions reached in the feedback timing literature.

The main question in the timing research has been whether or not immediate feedback produces better performance than delayed. Without question the most important work in this area has involved the "delay-retention effect" (DRE), a phenomenon first identified by Yvonne Brackbill and her colleagues (Brackbill & Kappy, 1962; Brackbill, Wagner, & Wilson, 1964). Essentially, what Brackbill *et al.* discovered was that a delay in presenting feedback increased scores on a later test of retention. This particular effect for feedback timing was replicated numerous times, and became an embarrassment to those who favored Law of Effect explanations (e.g., Moore, 1969; Phye & Baller, 1970; Rankin & Trepper, 1978; Sassenrath & Yonge, 1968, 1969; Sturges, 1969, 1972).

No reasonable explanation rooted in operant theory could account for the DRE, and it ultimately became necessary to turn to information-processing concepts based in error correction. In 1972, Kulhavy and Anderson proposed a theoretical framework for the DRE which they labeled the "interference-perseveration" hypothesis. Interference-perseveration assumes that initial error responses perseverate to the feedback stage, and tend to proactively interfere with the student's ability to acquire the correct answer from immediate feedback. However, when feedback is delayed, inital errors are less well remembered, and the likelihood of substituting the correct response increases because errors are less interfering. In addition, students who see delayed feedback tend to spend more time studying it, probably because they are less fatigued following a delay. Interestingly, the positive effects of feedback delay have been rediscovered in the cognitive science literature, and the "working memory" explanation appearing there is conceptually very similar to interference-perseveration (Schooler & Anderson, 1990).

The interference-perseveration model has held up over the past fifteen years (Bradwell, 1981; Kulik & Kulik, 1988; Sassenrath, 1975; Surber & Anderson, 1975), although it may need refinement as further data on feedback timing become available (Peeck & Tillema, 1979; Phye & Andre, 1989). What research on the DRE has done is to demonstrate that feedback timing can be of potential use for instructional design, especially when there is reason to believe that relatively high error rates may occur in the lesson.

Summary of Implications for Instruction

Programs, at least as they were originally conceived by Skinner and his associates, are no longer widely used. However, during its heyday the programmed instruction movement provided an empirical forum for evaluating the effects of feedback on learner performance. Because of research using programs, we now know a number of facts about feedback in the instructional environment. First, there is really no question that feedback increases lesson performance, provided that students process the instruction prior to seeing the feedback (Bangert-Drowns, Kulik, Kulik, & Morgan, 1991). Second, feedback primarily acts as a unit of information, and has its greatest effect when it follows an *incorrect* response. Feedback allows students to correct errors; confirms right responses; and generally assists learners in adapting to the requirements of the instruction on which they are working.

Research with programs indicates that both the content of feedback and the timing of its presentation influence learner performance. However, such data provide no clear-cut prescription concerning how content and time interact with specific instructional sequences. The literature does suggest that feedback is more effective when it restates the correct answer, instead of simply verifying ("right" vs. "wrong") the learner's initial response (Hancock, Stock, & Kulhavy, in press). However, adding further information to the feedback message has no consistent effect on instructional performance.

Advances in the prescriptive use of feedback may depend on using measures of the learner's knowledge state at the time of responding. Adapting feedback content to the types of errors produced by students (e.g., Birenbaum & Tatsuoka, 1987), or to the learners' confidence in their response (e.g., Kulhavy & Stock, 1989) are two possible ways in which the successful prescription of feedback formats might be accomplished.

References

Albertson, L.M. (1986). Personalized feedback and cognitive achievement in computer-assisted instruction. *Journal of Instructional Psychology, 13,* 55–57.

Ammons, R.B. (1956). Effects of knowledge of performance: A survey and tentative theoretical formulation. *Journal of General Psychology, 54,* 279–299.

Amsel, A. (1960). Error responses and reinforcement schedules in self-instructional devices. In A. A. Lumsdaine & R. Glaser (Eds.), *Teaching machines and programmed learning.* Washington, DC: National Education Association, 506–516.

Anderson, J.R., Boyle, C.F., & Reiser, B.J. (1985). Intelligent tutoring systems. *Science, 228,* 456-462.

Anderson, R.C. (1967). Educational psychology. *Annual Review of Psychology, 18,* 129-164.

Anderson, R.C., & Faust, G.W. (1967). The effects of strong formal prompts in programmed instruction. *American Educational Research Journal, 4,* 345-352.

Anderson, R.C., Kulhavy, R.W., & Andre, T. (1971). Feedback procedures in programmed instruction. *Journal of Educational Psychology, 62,* 148–156.

Anderson, R.C., Kulhavy, R.W., & Andre, T. (1972). Conditions under which feedback facilitates learning from a programmed lesson. *Journal of Educational Psychology, 63,* 186–188.

Andrews, D.H., & Uliano, K.C. (1985, April). *An instructor's diagnostic aid for feedback in training.* Paper presented at the American Educational Research Association, Chicago.

Angell, G.W. (1949). The effect of immediate knowledge of quiz results on final examination scores in freshman chemistry. *Journal of Educational Research, 42,* 391–394.

Arps, G.F. (1920). Work with vs. without knowledge of results. *Psychological Monographs, 28,* No. 3, Whole #25.

Bangert-Drowns, R.L., Kulik, C.C., Kulik, J.A., & Morgan, M. (1991). The instructional effect of feedback in test-like events. *Review of Educational Research, 61,* 213–238.

Birenbaum, M., & Tatsuoka, K.K. (1987). Effects of "on-line" feedback on the seriousness of subsequent errors. *Journal of Educational Measurement, 24,* 145–155.

Brackbill, Y., & Kappy, M.S. (1962). Delay of reinforcement and retention. *Journal of Comparative and Physiological Psychology, 55,* 14–18.

Brackbill, Y., Wagner, J.E., & Wilson, D. (1964). Feedback delay and the teaching machine. *Psychology in the Schools, 1,* 148–156.

Bradwell, R. (1981). Feedback: How does it function? *Journal of Experimental Education, 50,* 4–9.

Brown, F.J. (1932). Knowledge of results as an incentive in school room practice. *Journal of Educational Psychology, 23,* 532–552.

Brown, J.S., & Burton, R.R. (1978). Diagnostic models for procedural bugs in basic mathematical skills. *Cognitive Science, 2,* 155–192.

Collins, M., Carnine, D., & Gersten, R. (1987). Elaborated corrective feedback and the acquistion of reasoning skills: A study of computer-assisted instruction. *Exceptional Children, 54,* 254–262.

Corbett, A.T., & Anderson, J.R. (1990). The effect of feedback control on learning to program with the Lisp tutor. *Proceedings: Twelfth Annual Conference of the Cognitive Science Society.* Hillsdale, NJ: Lawrence Erlbaum Associates, 796–803.

Coulson, J.E. (1962). *Programmed learning and computer-based instruction.* New York: John Wiley & Sons.

Crowder, N.A. (1960). *The arithmetic of computers.* Santa Barbara, CA: Western Design.

Crowder, N.A. (1961). Intrinsic and extrinsic programming. In J.E. Coulson (Ed.), *Programmed learning and computer-based instruction.* New York: John Wiley & Sons, 58–66.

Curtis, F.D., & Woods, G.G. (1929). A study of the relative teaching values of four common practices in correcting examination papers. *The School Review, 37,* 615–623.

English, R.A., & Kinzer, J.R. (1966). The effect of immediate and delayed feedback on retention of subject matter. *Psychology in the Schools, 3,* 143–147.

Feldhusen, J.F., & Brit, A. (1962). A study of nine methods of presentation of programmed learning material. *Journal of Educational Research, 55,* 461-466.

Ferster, C.B., & Sapon, S.M. (1958). An application of recent developments in psychology to the teaching of German. *Harvard Educational Review, 28,* 58–69.

Fischer, P.M., & Mandl, H. (1985). Function and efficiency of contingent instrumental feedback. In G. d'Ydewalle (Ed.), *Cognition, information-processing, and motivation.* Amsterdam: Elsevier Science Publishers, 587–598.

Fischer, P.M., & Mandl, H. (1988). Knowledge acquisition by computerized audiovisual feedback. *European Journal of Psychology of Education, 111,* 217–233.

Gilman, D.A. (1969). The effect of feedback on learners' certainty of response and attitude toward instruction in a computer-assisted instruction program for teaching science concepts. *Journal of Research in Science Teaching, 6,* 171–184.

Glaser, R. (1965). *Teaching machines and programmed learning, II: Data and directions.* Washington, DC: National Education Association.

Grant, L., McAvoy, R., & Keenan, J.B. (1982). Prompting and feedback variables in concept programming. *Teaching of Psychology, 9,* 173–177.

Hancock, T.E., Stock, W.A., & Kulhavy, R.W. (in press). Predicting feedback effects from response certitude estimates. *Bulletin of the Psychonomic Society.*

Hannafin, M.J. (1983). The effects of systematized feedback on learning in natural classroom settings. *Educational Research Quarterly, 7,* 22–29.

Hodes, C.L. (1985). Relative effectiveness of corrective and noncorrective feedback in computer assisted instruction on learning and achievement. *Journal of Education Technology Systems, 13,* 249–254.

Holland, J.G., & Skinner, B.F. (1961). *The analysis of behavior.* New York: McGraw-Hill.

Hough, J.B., & Revsin, B. (1963). Programmed instruction at the college level: A study of several factors influencing learning. *Phi Delta Kappan, 44,* 286–291.

Hull, C.L. (1935). Thorndike's fundamentals of learning. *Psychological Bulletin, 32,* 807–823.

Judd, C.H. (1905-06). Practice without knowledge of results. *Psychological Review Monographs Supplement, 7,* 185–198.

Kaufman, R.A. (1963). An experimental evaluation of the role of remedial feedback in an intrinsic program. *Journal of Programed Instruction, 4,* 21–30.

Krumboltz, J.E., & Weisman, R.G. (1962). The effect of intermittent confirmation in programmed instruction. *Journal of Educational Psychology, 53,* 250–253.

Kulhavy, R.W. (1977). Feedback in written instruction. *Review of Educational Research, 47,* 211–232.

Kulhavy, R.W., & Anderson, R.C. (1972). Delay-retention effect with multiple-choice tests. *Journal of Educational Psychology, 63,* 505–512.

Kulhavy, R.W., & Stock, W.A. (1989). Feedback in written instruction: The place of response certitude. *Educational Psychology Review, 1*, 279–308.

Kulhavy, R.W., Stock, W.A., Thornton, N.E., Winston, K.S., & Behrens, J.T. (1990). Response feedback, certitude and learning from text. *British Journal of Educational Psychology, 60*, 161–170.

Kulhavy, R.W., White, M.T., Topp, B.W., Chan, A., & Adams, J. (1985). Feedback complexity and corrective efficiency. *Contemporary Educational Psychology, 10*, 285–291.

Kulik, J.A., & Kulik, C.C. (1988). Timing of feedback and verbal learning. *Review of Educational Research, 58*, 79–97.

Lublin, S.C. (1965). Reinforcement schedules, scholastic aptitude, autonomy need, and achievement in a programmed course. *Journal of Educational Psychology, 56*, 295–302.

Lumsdaine, A.A., & Glaser, R. (1960). *Teaching machines and programmed learning.* Washington, DC: National Education Association.

MacPherson, S.J., Dees, V., & Grindley, G.C. (1948-49). The effect of knowledge of results on learning and performance. *Quarterly Journal of Experimental Psychology, 1*, 68–78.

McDonald, F.J., & Allen, D. (1962). An investigation of presentation, response, and correction factors in programmed instruction. *Journal of Educational Research, 55*, 502–507.

Merrill, J. (1987). Levels of questioning and forms of feedback: Instructional factors in courseware design. *Journal of Computer-Based Instruction, 14*, 18–22.

Merrill, M.D. (1965). Correction and review on successive parts in learning a hierarchical task. *Journal of Educational Psychology, 56*, 225–234.

Merrill, M.D., & Stolurow, L.M. (1966). Hierarchical preview vs. problem oriented review in learning an imaginary science. *American Educational Research Journal, 3*, 251–261.

Moore, A.J. (1969). Delay of feedback and the acquisition and retention of verbal materials in the classroom. *Journal of Educational Psychology, 60*, 339–342.

Moore, J.W., & Smith, W.I. (1961). Knowledge of results in self-teaching spelling. *Psychological Reports, 9*, 717–726.

Moore, J.W., & Smith, W.I. (1964). Role of knowledge of results in programmed instruction. *Psychological Reports, 14*, 407-423.

O'Day, E.F., Kulhavy, R.W., Anderson, J.W., & Malczynski, R. (1971). *Programmed instruction: Techniques and trends.* New York: Appleton-Century-Crofts (Psychology Series).

Peeck, J., & Tillema, H.H. (1979). Delay of feedback and retention of correct and incorrect responses. *Journal of Experimental Education, 47*, 171–178.

Peterson, J.C. (1931). The value of guidance in reading information. *Transactions of the Kansas Academy of Science, 33*, 41–47.

Phye, G.D., & Andre, T. (1989). Delay retention effect: Attention, perseveration, or both? *Contemporary Educational Psychology, 14*, 173–185.

Phye, G.D., & Baller, W. (1970). Verbal retention as a function of the informativeness and delay of informative feedback. *Journal of Educational Psychology, 61*, 380–381.

Porter, D. (1957). A critical review of a portion of the literature on teaching devices. *Harvard Educational Review, 27*, 126–147.

Pressey, S.L., (1926). A simple device which gives tests and scores—and teaches. *School and Society, 23*, 373–376.

Pressey, S.L. (1927). A machine for automatic teaching of drill material. *School and Society, 25,* 549–552.

Pressey, S.L. (1950). Development and appraisal of devices providing immediate automatic scoring of objective tests and concomitant self-instruction. *Journal of Psychology, 29,* 417–447.

Rankin, R.J., & Trepper, T. (1978). Retention and delay of feedback in a computer-assisted instruction. *Journal of Experimental Education, 46,* 67–70.

Renner, K.E. (1964). Delay of reinforcement: A historical review. *Psychological Bulletin, 61,* 341–361.

Roper, W.J. (1977). Feedback in computer assisted instruction. *Programed Learning and Educational Technology, 14,* 43–49.

Rosenstock, E.H., Moore, J.W., & Smith, W.I. (1965). Effects of several schedules of knowledge of results on mathematics achievement. *Psychological Reports, 17,* 535–541.

Sassenrath, J.M. (1975). Theory and results on feedback and retention. *Journal of Educational Psychology, 67,* 894–899.

Sassenrath, J.M., & Yonge, G.D. (1968). Delayed information feedback, feedback cues, retention set, and delayed retention. *Journal of Educational Psychology, 59,* 69–73.

Sassenrath, J.M., & Yonge, G.D. (1969). Effects of delayed information feedback and feedback cues in learning and retention. *Journal of Educational Psychology, 60,* 174–177.

Schooler, L.J., & Anderson, J.R. (1990). The disruptive potential of immediate feedback. *Proceedings of the Twelfth Annual Conference of the Cognitive Science Society.* Hillsdale, NJ: Lawrence Erlbaum Associates, 702–708.

Silberman, H.F., Melaragno, R.J., Coulson, J.E., & Estavan, D. (1961). Fixed sequence versus branching autoinstructional methods. *Journal of Educational Psychology, 52,* 166–172.

Skinner, B.F. (1954). The science of learning and the art of teaching. *Harvard Educational Review, 24,* 86–97.

Skinner, B.F. (1958). Teaching machines. *Science, 128,* 969–977.

Skinner, B.F. (1961). Why we need teaching machines. *Harvard Educational Review, 31,* 377–398.

Skinner, B.F. (1968). *The technology of teaching.* New York: Appleton-Century-Crofts.

Skinner, B.F., & Holland, J.G. (1960). The use of teaching machines in college instruction. In A.A. Lumsdaine & R. Glaser (Eds.), *Teaching machines and programmed learning.* Washington, DC: National Educational Association.

Steinberg, E.R. (1991). *Computer-assisted instruction: A synthesis of theory, practice, and technology.* Hillsdale, NJ: Lawrence Erlbaum Associates.

Sturges, P.T. (1969). Verbal retention as a function of the informativeness and delay of information feedback. *Journal of Educational Psychology, 60,* 11–14.

Sturges, P.T. (1972). Information delay and retention: Effect of information in feedback and tests. *Journal of Educational Psychology, 63,* 32–43.

Sullivan, H.J., Baker, R.L., & Schutz, R.E. (1967). Effect of intrinsic and extrinsic reinforcement contingencies on learner performance. *Journal of Eductional Psychology, 58,* 165–169.

Sullivan, H.J., Schutz, R.E., & Baker, R.L. (1971). Effects of systematic variations in reinforcement contingencies on learner performance. *American Educational Research Journal, 8,* 135–142.

Surber, J.R., & Anderson, R.C. (1975). Delay-retention effect in natural classroom settings. *Journal of Educational Psychology, 67,* 170–173.

Symonds, P.M., & Chase, D.H. (1929). Practice vs. motivation. *Journal of Educational Psychology, 20,* 19–35.

Terrace, H.S. (1963). Discrimination learning with and·without errors. *Journal of the Experimental Analysis of Behavior, 6,* 1–27.

Terrace, H.S. (1964). Wavelength generalization after discrimination learning with and without errors. *Science, 144,* 78–80.

Thorndike, E.L. (1911). *Animal intelligence.* New York: Macmillan.

Thorndike, E.L. (1913). *Educational psychology: The psychology of learning.* Vol. 2. New York: Teachers College Press.

Thorndike, E.L. (1927). The law of effect. *American Journal of Psychology, 39,* 212–222.

Thorndike, E.L. (1932). *The fundamentals of learning.* New York: Teachers College Press.

Trowbridge, M.H., & Cason, H. (1932). An experimental study of Thorndike's theory of learning. *Journal of General Psychology, 7,* 245–260.

Wallach, H., & Henle, M. (1941). An experimental analysis of the Law of Effect. *Journal of Experimental Psychology, 28,* 340–349.

Chapter Two

Text-Based Feedback

John V. Dempsey
University of South Alabama

Marcy P. Driscoll
Arizona State University

and

Linda K. Swindell
University of Mississippi

This chapter focuses on feedback as it is used to promote learning from written instruction other than printed programmed materials. Research over the last decade has established a view of feedback that is firmly rooted within a cognitive paradigm, and our discussion of text-based feedback is consistent with this view. In addition, we concentrate on feedback delivered by more advanced technologies, such as computer-based instruction (CBI).

Mediating Factors in Feedback Effects

Even before the 1970s, when cognitive psychology was clearly in its ascendancy, many educational psychologists and instructional designers had shifted from a behavioral to a cognitive view of feedback. Less concerned about the external "mechanics" of feedback, they became interested in how feedback influenced central cognitive and metacognitive processes within a learner (Briggs & Hamilton, 1964). In essence, this shift was from the *primarily reinforcing* function characteristic of behavioral psychology to a *primarily informational* function which is in the purview of cognitive theories of learning. The informational function is emphasized in a definition of feedback offered by Kulhavy (1977): "...feedback is used in a generic sense to describe any of the numerous procedures that are used to tell a learner if an instructional response is right or wrong" (p. 211).

The effect of this information on whether and how a learner corrects errors or misconceptions, however, is less than straightforward. In this chapter, we examine factors that appear to mediate feedback effects in learning. Because this chapter is part of a larger effort, certain relevant variables covered in other chapters (e.g., motivation) are de-emphasized to some extent. Moreover, the approach we take in considering factors of interest is not meant to detach the individual learner from the process of learning. Our effort is aimed at providing an organizing structure within which prescriptive instructional feedback may be appraised.

Before we proceed, a word of caution is appropriate. In much of the available literature concerned with text-based feedback, four tendencies can be noted that are particularly disturbing. First, there is very little agreement on terminology. Second, researchers frequently generalize studies conducted in testing environments to learning environments. Along this line, researchers fail to distinguish between studies that incorporate instruction and those that do not. Third, learning outcomes are often unspecifed. Finally, sweeping claims regarding the implications of experimental studies are proposed by some experimenters and promoted by literature reviewers. We urge the reader to keep these problems in mind when appraising the effects and implications of feedback studies.

Timing of Feedback

The lack of agreement in terminology is perhaps nowhere more apparent than in the literature related to the timing of feedback. In order to clarify the research in the area of timing of feedback with CBI, Dempsey and Wager (1988) proposed operational definitions for immediate and delayed feedback. They also endorsed a taxonomy which considered context (learning vs. testing and immediate vs. delayed) within Gagné's (1985) domains and subdomains of learning (see Figure 2.1). All the types of feedback resulting from Dempsey and Wager's categories are currently in use, although rarely are the contexts or types of feedback agreed upon or carefully described by researchers.

A more crucial issue, however, concerns the argument over the use of immediate versus delayed feedback. In his classic article "Feedback in Written Instruction," Kulhavy (1977) supported the use of delayed feedback because of a phenomenon referred to as the Delay-Retention Effect (DRE). The delay-retention effect first defined by Brackbill and associates

Immediate feedback is informative corrective feedback given to a learner or examinee as quickly as the computer's hardware and software will allow during instruction or testing.

Types of immediate feedback are:

(1) item-by-item

(2) learner-controlled

(3) logical content break

(4) end-of-module (end of session)

(5) break by learner

(6) time-controlled (end of session)

Delayed feedback is informative, corrective feedback given to a learner or examinee after a specified programming delay interval during instruction or testing.

Types of delayed feedback are:

(1) item-by-item

(2) logical content break

(3) less than 1 hour (end-of-session)

(4) 1–24 hours (end of session)

(5) 1–7 days (end-of-session)

(6) extended delay (end-of-session)

(7) before next session

Figure 2.1. Immediate and delayed feedback with CBI: Definitions and categories (from Dempsey & Wager, 1988).

(Brackbill, Bravos, & Starr, 1962; Brackbill & Kappy, 1962) occurred in studies concerned with multiple-choice testing. Specifically, delaying the presentation of feedback for a day or more appeared to increase what a student remembered on a retention test. In experimental studies reviewed by Kulhavy (e.g., Kulhavy & Anderson, 1972), the most widely accepted explanation offered for the DRE was that initial error responses interfered proactively with the acquisition of the correct answer when the student saw feedback immediately after responding. This hypothesis, referred to as the interference-perseveration hypothesis, is the most popular explanation for the DRE. Since Kulhavy's review, DRE and the interference-perseveration hypothesis have been the impetus for many experimental studies seeking to prove that delayed feedback "is better" or that the hypothesis is not an adequate explanation for the effect (e.g., Peeck & Tillema, 1979).

In 1988, the immediate versus delayed feedback controversy took a new turn with the findings of a meta-analysis conducted Kulik and Kulik. They reported that applied studies using actual classroom quizzes and materials usually found immediate feedback to be more effective than delayed feedback. Delayed feedback was typically effective only in experimental situations such as learning lists that repeated the stimulus word or test content. The conclusion of this meta-analysis, that immediate feedback facilitates learning better than delayed feedback in applied settings, challenges the use of delayed feedback in practical learning situations. Moreover, Kulik and Kulik's findings also called into question the adequacy of the interference-perseveration hypothesis as an explanation for feedback effects in most actual learning environments.

Kulik and Kulik's findings point to the formative nature of immediate feedback, especially in mastering intellectual skills. On the other hand, the success some researchers have had using delayed feedback in testing situations and the lack of effect in actual instructional situations suggests the summative nature of this method. Does this suggest that immediate feedback is always better than delayed feedback in instructional situations? No, that is too simple a rule. Rather, we suggest that delayed feedback, in many instructional contexts, is tantamount to withholding information from the learner that the learner can use. Under most circumstances, there would seem to be little reason to withhold feedback. On the other hand, it makes at least intuitive sense to withhold feedback from or repeat feedback to learners in those cases where delay is purposeful and not punitive.

From a different perspective, Tosti (1978) and Keller (1983) have proposed that it may be effective to present feedback about key elements of a learner's prior performance with a skill *before* the next occasion when the learner is attempting to acquire that skill. This amounts to what has often been referred to as "the teachable moment."

As new instructional technologies become more commonplace, the use of text-based feedback will become less commonplace. Technology has given instructional developers ever-widening feedback delivery options, which include more sophisticated text processing and delivery of feedback using multiple modalities. The controversy over immediate versus delayed feedback types likewise becomes more complex and less settled. Nevertheless, we suggest, in most "real" instructional settings employing text-based feedback, immediate feedback should be prescribed unless the feedback is delayed systematically and for a specialized purpose.

Complexity of Feedback
One of the most common independent variables in the research literature related to text-based feedback is type of feedback as it refers to how

much and what information should be contained in the feedback message. Arguments over the relative merits of simple or complex feedback continue to be a problem for practitioners, who want a simple answer to what is a rather knotty question. In our discussion of this variable, we will concentrate on five common text-based feedback types, emphasize corrective feedback studies, and, for purposes of clarity, use the nomenclature which follows.

1. *No feedback* presents a question and requires a response, but does not indicate whether the learner's response is correct.
2. *Simple verification feedback or knowledge of results* (KR) simply informs the learner of a correct or incorrect response.
3. *Correct response feedback or knowledge of correct response* (KCR) informs the learner what the correct response to the question should be.
4. *Elaborated feedback* provides an explanation for why the learner's response is correct or incorrect or allows the learner to review material relevant to the attributes of a correct response.
5. *Try-again feedback* informs the learner when an incorrect response has been made and allows the learner to make one or more additional attempts to answer correctly.

Naturally, there are many possible variations and combinations of these feedback types.

An early CBI study that considered type of feedback was conducted by Gilman (1969), who compared five feedback types. An important finding in this study was that undergraduate science students who received knowledge of correct results performed significantly better than those not receiving knowledge of correct results. It is noteworthy that there were no significant differences among the KCR groups regardless of the information quality of the feedback. "Apparently," Gilman interpreted, "the factor which accelerated the learning of Ss was being informed as to which response was the correct one" (p. 507). Another interesting finding of this study was that it took the KCR-only group significantly less time to reach criterion than any of the other feedback conditions.

A study by Roper (1977) confirmed Gilman's conclusion that KCR feedback is more effective than KR feedback (notwithstanding Roper's criticism of Gilman for failing to discuss how this conclusion differed between correct and incorrect answers). In addition, Roper substantiated the prior finding by Guthrie (1971) with evidence that correction of errors rather than strengthening of responses was the major effect of the feedback. The number of topics that students answered incorrectly in the instructional program and those subsequently answered correctly on the posttest was significantly higher for the KCR group than either the KR or the no feedback group.

A comparison of three types of feedback in a computer-based concept learning task by Waldrop, Justin and Adams (1986) also supported similar findings in Gilman's and Roper's studies that knowledge of correct response with elaborated feedback is superior to simple knowledge of results feedback on an immediate posttest. Although the study by Waldrop *et al.* is interesting, their conclusions are limited by at least three factors typical of many feedback studies. Similar to Gilman's study, the independent variable, types of feedback, is applied to both affirmative and corrective feedback, instead of separating these obvious dichotomies. Second, no attempt was made in either to monitor the number of error responses or the pattern of error responses made during the instructional treatment. Last, as with Gilman's and Roper's studies, delayed posttests were not employed, so readers are unable to judge the extent to which various feedback methods reduce forgetting.

Providing a learner with a second attempt following an error is a design feature in many CBI programs, yet until recently this has been the subject of little controlled empirical investigation. Some studies (e.g., Lasoff, 1981) which use multiple tries after an incorrect response fail to recognize the importance of this condition or control for its effects. Noonan (1984) manipulated the presence or position of KR, KCR, elaborated, and try-again feedback. Interestingly, knowledge of results with an explanation and a second attempt was no less effective than giving KCR and moving on or giving KCR and a subsequent second attempt. One explanation for this finding is that Noonan's process explanations depended more on the correct answer than the type of error made by the learner. Noonan speculated that a more sophisticated procedure would involve analysis of common errors or error patterns based on a computer record of the type of error made by the learner (p. 26).

Two recent studies have looked more closely at try-again feedback. In the first, Clariana (1990) compared the effects of KCR and try-again feedback on learning of social science materials being learned by low ability eleventh graders. Clariana found that the learners in the KCR treatment performed significantly better on a posttest. The KCR condition was also found to be more efficient.

A second study by Clariana, Ross, and Morrison (1991) found that the relative benefits of try-again feedback increased as the wording of posttest items became less similar to the questions in the lesson. Results of this study also showed (once again) significant benefits for feedback over no feedback.

Another common debate in computer-based instruction concerns whether or not students should be required to make an overt correction response after an error. Some instructional design theorists (e.g., Wager & Wager, 1985; Siegel & Misselt, 1984) suggest that an overt response is unnecessary unless the student is forced to make a connection between the correct answer and the question. Other educators presume that overt responding is better than no responding and may assist students to more actively process information. Hundreds of CBI modules espousing both philosophies are available. A common sense solution is to tie the question of typing in the correct answer more directly to learning outcomes.

Overt correction after error was supported by an experiment by Suppes and Ginsberg (1962) in which 48 five- and six-year-old children were required to learn concepts of the binary number system. One group was required to make an overt correction response after an incorrect answer. A second group was informed at the end of a trial whether each response was correct or incorrect. The children who were required to make an overt correction response (as a result of feedback) learned significantly faster than those who were not.

Overt responding was also studied by Tait, Hartley, and Anderson (1973) in a CBI math lesson. Results failed to confirm a hypothesis that suggested active feedback (overt correction after an incorrect response) would be more beneficial to students than passive feedback. As expected, both feedback groups performed better than the no feedback group. Furthermore, the hypothesis that feedback would have its greatest effect on the least advanced pupils was strongly confirmed. Although the study by Tait *et al.* showed no difference between the active and passive response groups on a posttest, the performance of the two groups was markedly distinct during practice sessions. The active group attempted a mean number of 143 problems and averaged 113 correct responses on the first try (79%). The passive group, on the other hand, attempted a mean number of 209 problems but only answered an average of 126 correctly on the first try (60%). The efficiency with which the overt corrective response group performed during instruction merits further examination.

Expectancy and Feedback

Feedback has been assigned both a reinforcing and an informational purpose. Some literature considers the role of feedback in relation to one or the other of these functions, but seldom are they mentioned in the same prescriptive context. Increasingly, it has become clear that the reinforcing function of instructional feedback is dependent on factors related to the information that learners consider to be important. Briggs and Hamilton (1964) stated:

Reinforcement by reward or punishment is distinguished from informational feedback which may bring correction, confirmation, or other guidance of learning. Reinforcing functions of feedback may be those that relieve anxiety about achievement and encourage the learner to persist with the task. (p. 557)

This view contradicts a common presumption which contrasts motivational feedback (which from this primarily behaviorist perspective would be affirmative feedback) with corrective feedback. This view of feedback, common in earlier studies (e.g., Payne & Hauty, 1955), suggests that persistence is related to what Locke, Cartledge, and Koeppel (1968) refer to as the incentive function (affirmative feedback), not the directive function (corrective feedback).

There are numerous studies which reveal that the greatest facilitative effect of feedback is its ability to correct inaccurate information where the learner has comprehended the text information (e.g., Anderson, Kulhavy, & Andre, 1971; Kulhavy & Anderson, 1972; Tait, Hartley, & Anderson, 1973). In a series of studies on concept acquisition, Buss and his associates found that informing subjects of their errors yielded higher criterion performance than did confirming correct responses (Buss, Braden, Orgel, & Buss, 1956; Buss & Buss, 1956; Buss, Weiner, & Buss, 1954). Similar results were obtained in a verbal information study (German words) by Travers, Wagenen, Haygood, and McCormick (1964). In this study, there was a significant advantage for students who received the correct answer in addition to the knowledge that an incorrect response had been made.

In a chapter concerned with the use of the ARCS Motivational Model in computer-based instruction, Keller and Suzuki (1986) propose that, "People evaluate outcomes against their own expectations" (p. 34). A good deal of research by Kulhavy and his associates provides a basis for hypothesis that corrective feedback should be personally relevant to the learner and tailored to the learner's expectancy for success. Linkage between a learner's expectancy and corrective feedback has substantial implications for both motivational and instructional designs.

Typically, in most instruction, a given response is scored in a dichotomous fashion. That is, the response is either right or wrong. For learners this dichotomy is often counterintuitive. In the first of eight "empirical generalizations" Ammons (1956) stated, "The performer usually has a hypothesis about what he is to do and how he is to do it, and these interact with knowledge of performance" (p. 281). Similarly, trial data reported by Kulhavy, Yekovich, and Dyer (1976) and Kulhavy (1977) indicate that:

... what students do is create a hierarchy of confidence in the correctness of possible choices and then make their response selection based on what they believe to be the most probable right answer. Consequently, when an error is made the reaction to it could range from surprise when confidence is high to acceptance when confidence is low. (1976, p. 522)

Based on their research and personal observations, Kulhavy (1977) incorporated learner confidence into a model by relating feedback to response confidence. This model predicts that high confidence correct answers yield the shortest study times, high confidence errors yield the longest time, and low confidence answers fall somewhere in between. These observations were validated by several experimental studies beginning with two by Kulhavy, Yekovich, and Dyer (1976; 1979). An additional finding of the Kulhavy *et al.* (1979) study endorses a marked interplay between corrective feedback and the main body of text attached to a question.

The consequence of Kulhavy's "right/wrong" model suggests simply that text-based instructional feedback is most important when an anticipated right answer is in fact wrong. That is, the learner seeks in the feedback a reason for why the answer is wrong. This may be especially true when the main body of the question remains visible for the learner as a guide to finding the correct response. Conversely, once the learner has responded correctly, affirmative or correct answer feedback serves the primary function of simple confirmation and, therefore, need not be elaborated.

A study by Guthrie (1971) bears out Kulhavy's assertion that corrective feedback which informs students of the right response aids in error correction. In this inquiry, 90 adult students were required to read a passage from an encyclopedia chapter on magnetism. After each sentence, Guthrie presented students with a completion question (cloze item). On posttest questions matched to items answered correctly during learning, students who had received correct answer feedback did no better than students who had not received affirmative feedback. In other words, there was no indication that correct answer feedback strengthened tendencies to give correct answers. In contrast, posttest performance was significantly increased by corrective feedback on items initially answered incorrectly.

Feedback Complexity and Learner Expectancy

Studies which concern themselves with both feedback complexity and learner expectancy are rare indeed. One exception is a study by Kulhavy, White, Topp, Chan, and Adams (1985). In this experiment, the researchers used a print-based reading task with 120 college students to consider feedback complexity and corrective efficiency. Subjects read a 2400-word passage, responded to 16 multiple-choice questions, and received one of four types of feedback following their responses. Instructional efficiency was calculated by dividing the total correct posttest responses by the time required to either read the instruction or process the feedback.

Results of this study indicated that complexity of feedback was inversely related to both error correctability and criterion efficiency. Although feedback study time was significantly greater for more complex feedback conditions, raw posttest differences were not significantly different. Moreover, the experimenters found the less complex forms of feedback to be more efficient in terms of posttest yield per unit of study time invested. Mean feedback efficiencies were also plotted as a function of response confidence. This study supports prior findings of Kulhavy and his associates which assume that high confidence ratings indicate that the reader has no trouble in comprehending the instructional content.

A computer-based study by Spock (1987) involved a computer literacy rule learning task. In addition to affirmative feedback, two forms of corrective feedback were used, knowledge of correct results and explanatory feedback. The type of feedback presented to each of the four feedback groups in the study varied by the correctness of the response and the confidence that the learner had in the response. Spock found that the explanatory feedback group required significantly more time than the group receiving KCR feedback. No significant differences, however, were found on achievement or retention for any feedback treatment. One explanation for this may be the difficulty of instruction, with an average posttest score of about 50% correct.

The poor overall performance of the subjects prompted Spock to note that, "A paradox exists in which effective feedback requires a situation where (a) learners have not completely mastered the content so that they do have some need for the information in the feedback, yet (b) learners are not so helplessly lost in the instruction that the feedback makes no sense to them" (1987, p. 15). Kulhavy (1977) phrased it differently: "If learners fail to comprehend the material in the first place, feedback will have nothing more than a cursory effect on performance" (p. 224).

Error Type and Expectancy

For quite some time studies have found that written corrective feedback which supplies the right answer corrects errors. This has been supported recently in the meta-analytic study by Bangert-Drowns *et al.* (1991). What is less clear however is how the type of error a learner makes will interact with error correction and a learner's expectancy for success.

Research and theoretical work involving the use of rational sets of concepts and simple rules (Driscoll & Tessmer, 1985; Klausmeier & Feldman, 1975; Markle & Tiemann, 1971) have established a method by which errors of fine and gross discrimination in concept learning may be predicted. This method was adapted to the computer (Dempsey, 1986) and refined (Dempsey, Driscoll, & Litchfield, in press) by comparing actual on-task observations made during instruction. Prior experiments involving some of these authors (e.g., Driscoll & Tessmer, 1985; Litchfield, Driscoll, & Dempsey,

1988; Tessmer & Driscoll, 1987) have indicated that learners make a higher number of incorrect answers that are fine discrimination errors than gross discrimination errors. The types of errors measured in these studies were ascertained through content analysis (Litchfield *et al.*, 1988). A related finding (Dempsey *et al.*, in press) was that learners who made fewer fine discrimination errors during instruction scored higher on a retention test.

Another important indicator of how engaged learners are in the instruction is the amount of time they spend studying corrective feedback. In one study (Dempsey *et al.*, in press), for example, learners used almost twice as much time when they made fine discrimination errors regardless of the complexity of the text-based feedback given them. Feedback study time was measured directly by the computer for incorrect responses only. Using self-report measures of certitude, Kulhavy and his associates (Kulhavy *et al.*, 1976, 1979; Kulhavy, White, Topp, Chan, & Adams, 1985) for years have asserted also that students' expectancy for success is related to the amount of time they spend studying feedback. In other words, students who incorrectly respond to a question, but think they got the right answer will spend more time studying the corrective feedback than students who have less confidence that they answered correctly.

Although there are both common sense and empirical support for Kulhavy's theory, the findings of a recent study by Dempsey and Driscoll (1992) called into question the simple direct relationship between confidence of response and feedback study time. In this experiment, we attempted to link fine discrimination errors (based on content analysis and trial data) with high confidence errors (based on learner's self-reports).

In this study, 63 university students enrolled in a biology class responded to multiple interrogatory exemplars in a module related to substance abuse. The adaptive computer-based module varied the difficulty of the questions depending on the subject's on-task responses. Fine and gross errors were determined using a two-step approach of analysis employing content experts' judgement and trial data. Students' confidence of response was measured on a five-point self-report scale in a similar manner to that proposed by Kulhvay *et al.* (1979). The results of the study indicated that, as expected, feedback study time was directly correlated with fine discrimination errors ($r = .456$). In contrast, feedback study time was inversely correlated with confidence of response ($r = -.469$).

Although these findings are far from conclusive, two possible explanations could explain the negative relationship between fine discrimination errors and confidence of response. These are: (1) inconsistencies with the learners' self-reports of their confidence of response, and (2) the relationship between high confidence errors and effort.

In the Kulhavy studies (as well as the present study) learners stopped after each response and rated their confidence of response. One wonders how often learners accurately portray the response hierarchy with which the question was answered. We would suppose, for example, that there would be a great difference in the reliability of self-reported confidence measures among sophisticated learners versus those with less ability—or older versus younger learners. In discussing self-reports, Borg and Gall (1983) observed, "People often bias the information they offer about themselves, and sometimes they cannot accurately recall events and aspects of their behavior in which the researcher is interested" (p. 465). An initial investigation by Swindell, Greenway and Peterson (1992) upholds our suppositions. In a study with 4th- and 6th-grade students, these researchers found that 6th graders were more reliable in estimating response confidence than were 4th graders. They also found that the response patterns of the 6th graders were similar to those of college students (Kulhavy, Stock, Hancock, Swindell, & Hammrich, 1990), but response patterns of the 4th-grade students were distinctly different. In addition, self-report measures during instruction are distracting. Essentially, learners are asked two questions, one constant related and one not. Thus, the practical value of self-report as an instructional or motivational design measurement tool is reduced.

Secondly, the findings of Dempsey and Driscoll's (1992) study, considered in respect to the exisiting text-based feedback literature, indicate a more complex relationship between the type of error made (determined via content analysis), expectancy (measured by confidence of response scales), and the amount of effort a learner makes (as measured by feedback study time) than had been suspected. In addition to other factors, we suspect that confidence of response measures is greatly influenced by specific learning outcomes, the difficulty of material to be learned, the learner's prior knowledge, and the relevance of the material to the learner (see Figure 2.2).

From another perspective, certitude measures intrinsically linked to specific program activities, especially those which the learner feels are relevant, may be an effective metacognitive tool. A recently developed middle school science interactive videodisc program, entitled *Ergomotion* (Scarth & Litchfield, 1990), may serve as an illustration. In a physics activity game, a student is presented a problem and can choose an answer offered by one of two physics consultants. The student "wagers" a point value representing her confidence of response. If the student's response is correct, points are added to the score. Incorrect responses deduct whatever certitude value is wagered. In this way the student becomes overtly aware of her confidence of response on particular items. The activity is arranged as a humorous competition and, thus, the measures of certitude are integral, relevant, and linked to the informational feedback offered the learner.

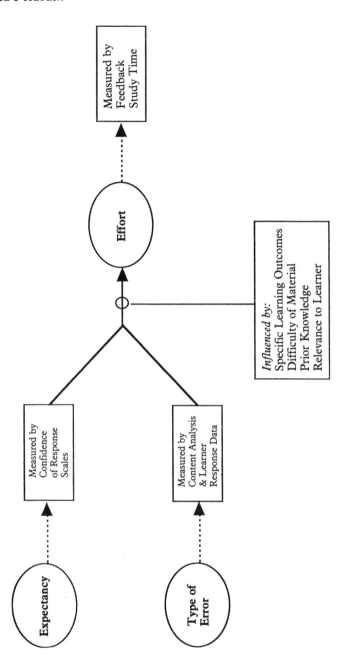

Figure 2.2. Hypothesized relationship among expectancy, type of error, and effort.

Feedback and Adaptive Structures

For computer-based, response-contingent concept and rule-learning exercises which have been subjected to content anyalysis (Merrill & Tennyson, 1977), it may be difficult to differentiate between feedback and branching strategies. In one study, for example, Park and Tennyson (1986) investigated the effect of presentation form (adaptive and fixed) and sequencing of concept examples (discrimination rule and generalization rule) on performance of a classification task involving 72 high school students divided into four experimental groups. The adaptive presentation form presented the learner with another interrogatory (questioning) example following a correct classification of a defined concept, but for an incorrect response presented an example in an expository (telling) form. In the fixed presentation form, all examples were presented in an interrogatory form. The "sequencing of examples" variable involved whether the next example after an incorrect response should be from a concept related to the discrimination error (discrimination rule) or from the same concept that the learner incorrectly classified (generalization rule). Results indicated an interaction effect where the adaptive selection/generalization rule group had the highest performance on a posttest and a retention test. In other words, the group with the best performance in this experiment received knowledge of results and a worked example (i.e., expository example) of the correct concept after an error, a process akin to elaborated corrective feedback. Following this "feedback," another example was randomly selected from the rational set of examples and presented in an interrogatory form.

One may see from Park and Tennyson's research that some researchers involved with adaptive instruction choose to avoid studying or even mentioning corrective feedback which they do not consider to be related to a learner's specific problem. According to Tennyson (1987), "the important concern is to design a system that can identify possible specific errors rather than the typical CAI method of feedback and branching" (p. 27). The emphasis on corrective error analysis by Tennyson and his associates has been very consistent and has been an important influence on many instructional designers involved with computer-based instruction. Less clear is why this research should not be connected to corrective feedback. In their review of the concept-teaching literature, Tennyson and Cocchiarella (1986) called for additional research "on feedback elaboration strategies during interrogatory presentation forms" (p. 65) but failed to discuss how these strategies would be more efficient than corrective feedback. A study by Park and Roberts addresses this enigma.

Park and Roberts (1985) studied three guided instructional strategies to see their effect on retention and time-on-task. In this experiment, 47 college students were taught psychology concepts using computer-based instruction. A full-guidance (FG) strategy was a three-step procedure designed to minimize the possibility of error-making during instruction. A non-guidance (NG) strategy was designed for error correction through feedback. The third strategy, diminishing-guidance (DG), gradually progressed from the FG to the NG procedure. A second independent variable, learners' field-independent and field-dependent cognitive styles (as determined by learners' scores on the Group Embedded Figure Test), was also investigated in order to observe a possible interaction effect with the guided instructional strategies. It was hypothesized that field-dependent students would perform better with the DG procedure than either the FG or the NG procedure. For field-independent students, however, the experimenters felt that none of the three instructional strategies would make a significant difference on achievement. Results indicated that, regardless of their learning styles, students benefited more from the NG (affirmative and corrective feedback) procedure than either of the other two adaptive guidance strategies. The students in the feedback (NG) group made substantially more errors during instruction, and needed a significantly greater amount of time, and more examples to reach criterion during instruction than did the full-guidance (FG) group. On the retention test, however, the feedback (NG) condition resulted in better student performance. To explain this finding, Park and Roberts admit, "It is possible that incorrect responses made by the student facilitate learning by serving as comparative information for understanding correct answers that are usually presented in feedback" (1985, p. 22).

Other researchers involved with adaptive instruction more readily avow the value of corrective feedback. Siegel and Misselt (1984) randomly assigned 102 college undergraduates to one of six drill-treatment groups related to their Corrective Feedback Paradigm (CFP) in order to study the effect of these conditions on discrimination errors and instructional time. Subjects were assigned to learn 20 English-Japanese (transliterated) word pairs on the PLATO computer system.

Features of the CFP under study included adaptive feedback, discrimination training, and increasing ratio review. Results of this study found no significant differences in time to mastery, but demonstrated a main effect for increasing ratio review and for adaptive feedback with training. The last result is of particular interest. In the adaptive feedback condition, the type of feedback depended on the type of error made by the learner. This adaptive feedback condition separated two types of errors: (1) discrimination errors (responses that are answers to another item on the drill list) and (2) out-of-list errors (responses that are not an answer to another item on the drill list). Discrimination training, which was applied to discrimination errors only, gave new examples of both new and miscued items (i.e., the correct response was compared to the incorrect response). The outcomes of this study suggest that it is worthwhile to anticipate wrong answers made by learners and to tailor the feedback to discrimination problems made by the learner.

A weakness of this inquiry is the kind of learning chosen for the experiment. The experimenters suggest that "the most important instructional implication of the CFP is that it allows the use of a drill format to teach generalizable concepts" (p. 316). Unfortunately, this experiment involved verbal information, not concepts. Second, as described in this article, the paradigm would seem to promote memorization rather than concept learning, which relies on being able to classify new instances. Even so, the effective use of adaptive feedback is an impressive feature of this study that may well be applicable to concept and rule learning.

A recent science concept and rule-using study which concentrated on four of the most common feedback types in an adaptive CBI environment was conducted by Dempsey, Driscoll, and Litchfield (in press). In this study 153 students enrolled in an undergraduate biology class were randomly assigned to one of four immediate corrective feedback conditions: (1) KCR; (2) KCR + Forced CR (the student was required to enter the correct response after being told the correct response); (3) elaborated feedback; and (4) try-again feedback. Results indicated the group which received simple KCR feedback used significantly less time to achieve the same score and, therefore, KCR was more efficient than any other condition. (Efficiency was computed, based on Kulhavy, White, Topp, Chan, & Adams, 1985, by dividing the retention percentage score by the square root of the feedback study time.) Consistent with prior studies, the adaptive design strategy overcame any differences in the retention scores themselves that may have occurred using a fixed number of interrogatory examples. In essence, these findings suggest that, at least within an adaptive environment, complex feedback forms of corrective feedback are no more effective and are less efficient for both the learner and the developer of instruction.

Goals

It is common sense that feedback given in response to learner goal-driven efforts can affect both a learner's motivation and self-esteem. We all remember as children critical situations in which we were encouraged or discouraged in our efforts to perform a task. Feedback of this type regulated our sustained efforts and probably our future. It would seem worthwhile, therefore, to consider the learner's goal orientation, when designing instruction, particularly with those media that do not involve human interaction. Unfortunately, with a few exceptions (see Derry, Jacobs, & Murphy, 1987) instructional designers fail to develop feedback which considers the goals which the learner has adopted or generated.

Feedback enters into the goal-setting process as a basis for evaluating assigned goals and for forming personal goals (Erez & Zidon, 1984; Locke, Shaw, Saari, & Latham, 1981). Goals are also thought to take an essential element of challenge in intrinisically motivating instruction. Goals which challenge the learner are thought to have three attributes. First, they should be personally meaningful. Second, they should be obvious (easily under-standable) or, alternately, should be easily generated by the learner. Finally, according to Malone (1981), in order to be motivated by a goal, learners usually need some kind of performance feedback to tell whether they are achieving their goals.

Assigned goals, and feedback regarding these goals, may be accepted or rejected. Some researchers (e.g., Locke *et al.*, 1981) contend that goals enhance performance only when the learner conscientiously accepts them. This contention has been supported by Erez and Zidon (1984), who found a linear decrease in performance after assigned goals were rejected. Realizing that assigned goals may be unclear to the learner or rejected, Malone's (1981) caveat that goals must be personally meaningful becomes all the more important.

A recent study by Vance and Coella (1990) examined the effects of goal discrepancy feedback (GDF) and past-performance discrepancy feedback (PDF) on acceptance of assigned goals and personal goal levels. GDF indi-cated whether subjects were performing above or below the assigned goal, and by how much. PDF indicated whether the subject's performance was increasing or decreasing from one trial to the next. The study was designed so that the assigned goals became increasingly difficult over given trials. Goal discrepancy feedback, accordingly, became increasingly negative and goal acceptance became increasingly less likely. Subjects were expected to (and did) switch over to performance-discrepancy feedback as a basis for evaluating assigned goals and for selecting new goals. Before each trial, subjects also were urged to set personal goals that could differ from the assigned goals. Unexpectedly to the authors, personal goals and perform-ance remained high even after assigned goals were rejected.

An important implication of this and related studies (e.g., Ashford & Cummings, 1983) is that performance feedback should be varied according to the on-task acceptance by the learner of the instructional goals, both assigned and personal. Considering the technological power available, par-ticularly with adaptive computer-controlled instruction, goal-based per-formance feedback is both possible and practical. Furthermore, overtly varying feedback type and adapting goal states according to instructional strategies and a learner's personal goals should contribute positively to a learner's feelings of competence. Likewise, this method of adaptive feedback may positively affect other indicators of on-task learning such as certitude and persistence.

Mindfulness

One of the more interesting recent additions to the literature involving text-based feedback is a meta-analysis by Bangert-Drowns, Kulik, Kulik, and Morgan (1991). In this study, the researchers reviewed 58 effect sizes from 40 reports, most of which took place at the college level. Some of the findings of this study were as follows.

1. Feedback does not always increase achievement and, in some cases, is associated with decreases in achievement.
2. Uncontrolled presearch availability (i.e., the learner can easily locate correct answers without searching through or reading the lesson) significantly diminishes the instructional effects of feedback. [This further supports Kulhavy's (1977) assertion.]
3. Feedback that indicated only that a response was correct or incorrect resulted in a lower effect than when feedback informed the learner of the correct answer in some fashion. [The authors here suggest that in test-like events, feedback's primary importance is in correcting errors.]
4. Using pretests produced significantly lower effect sizes. [Here the authors suggest, for good or ill, that pretests act as primitive advance organizers, influence learner expectations, pre-review instructional content, and provide practice in test item formats.]
5. Feedback in programmed and computer-based instruction was less effective than in those studies concerned with text comprehension and conventional testing situations. [The authors assert that feedback is more important with complex content, particularly when fewer cues, organizers, and instructional supports are provided.]

This last finding allows the authors to state:

> When students are informed of correct answers after responding with relatively little prompting to questions on relatively complex presentations, their ability to accurately retrieve information is greatly improved. In less optimal conditions, however, feedback's performance diminishes. More specifically, feedback is most effective under conditions that encourage learner's mindful reception. (p. 233)

The construct of mindfulness (Salomon & Globerson, 1987) may be portrayed as a reflective process in which the learner explores situational cues and underlying meanings relevant to the task involved. It is one in which alternative information-gathering strategies are generated or adopted, outcomes are examined, and new connections and structures are constructed. Bangert-Drowns *et al.* propose a five-stage model of learning that stresses the importance of mindfulness in the operation of text-based feedback (see Figure 2.3).

In the first stage, the learner's *initial state* is characterized by prior knowledge, experience with instruction (including questions/feedback sequences), goal orientation, interests, and self-efficacy.

In the second stage, *search and retrieval strategies* are activated by a question. This stage requires a minimum presearch availability. The information related to the question should be stored in an elaborate context which would provide multiple pathways to alternate responses.

In the third stage of the model, the *learner responds* to the question. Given the richer context assumed in the model, the learner perceives a degree of certainty about the response. Therefore, the learner should have some expectations about the feedback which will follow.

Next, the *learner evaluates* the response in light of the informational feedback. Here, the degree of certitude likely influences the way feedback is used to evaluate response. The authors appear to support the certitude model proposed by Kulhavy and his associates (Kulhavy, 1977; Kulhavy & Stock, 1989) which is discussed in a later section of this chapter. Even so, they caution that the findings of their meta-analysis show no clear relation between initial confidence, confirming or disconfirming feedback, and posttest performance.

The final stage of the model involves *adjustments of the learner's cognitive state*. As a result of the response evaluation, the learner's relevant knowledge, self-efficacy, interests, and goals are changed. Along with the learner's subsequent experiences, these adjusted states construct the next initial state.

The model of mindfulness discussed here is an important framework for future research involving text-based feedback. Although the meta-analysis from which the model grew considered instructional programs which the authors suggest "may be too simple or specific" (Bangert-Drowns *et al.*, 1991, p. 234), it points to a shift to study feedback in more complex textual environments with higher-level learning outcomes. The authors are careful to state that the meta-analysis was unable to pinpoint the cognitive processes involved in response evaluation or identify the characteristics of feedback that influence the evaluation process. Even so, the model proposed by Bangert-Drowns and his associates extends the careful examination of prior feedback studies conducted by Kulik and Kulik (1988) and calls for more research in complex learning environments where it may be most critical.

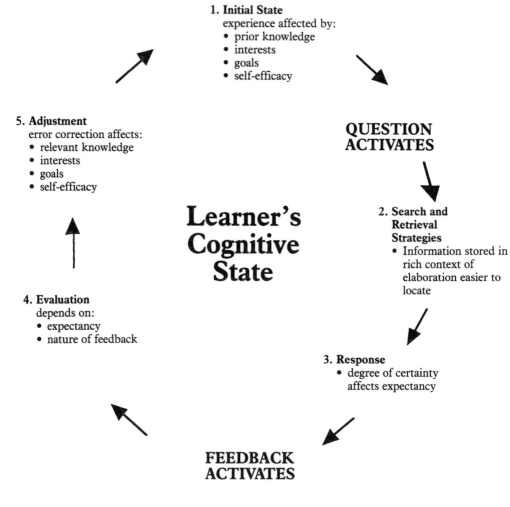

Figure 2.3. The state of the learner receiving mediated intentional feedback for retrieval accuracy (based on Bangert-Drowns *et al.*, 1991).

A Certitude Model of Feedback in Written Instruction

It is one thing to identify the variables that are important to an understanding of how feedback influences learning, as we have done in the first part of this chapter. It is quite another to construct a model that takes these variables into account, proposes testable predictions, and offers theoretical explanations for the predicted results.

As described earlier, Bangert-Drowns *et al.* (1991) proffered a five-stage "model," which relates the state of the learner to the information contained in feedback. Although this model serves as an effective heuristic for organizing current findings regarding feedback, it is perhaps too general to do much more. In other words, its stages can hardly be argued. Without specific predictions, the model cannot be subjected to empirical verification (or disconfirmation).

By contrast, Kulhavy and Stock (1989) proposed a model of feedback in written instruction that not only attempts to make sense of previous findings but also makes specific predictions of feedback effects. As it is currently being tested, this model integrates the factors of learner confidence, complexity (or elaboration) of feedback, and effort devoted to error correction. In addition, it has been investigated under different feedback presentation modes (e.g., aural vs. written) and under different timing conditions (e.g., immediate vs. delayed feedback). Without question, Kulhavy and Stock's model is the most comprehensive treatment in existence of feedback as it facilitates learning from written instruction.

In this section of the chapter, then, we describe the Kulhavy and Stock (1989) model, together with evidence of its validity as well as its limitations.

A Three-Cycle Feedback Paradigm

Similar to the stages of the model proposed by Bangert-Drowns and his associates (1991), Kulhavy and Stock (1989) conceived of three cycles (constituting one act of instruction) within which feedback was assumed to exert an influence. As shown in Figure 2.4, these cycles consist of a practice question that a learner encounters in the instruction, the feedback he receives following a response to the question, and the corresponding posttest item assessing criterion performance on the target information. In each cycle, the learner responds in both covert and overt ways. Covertly, the learner engages in some mental activity aimed at processing the input and preparing an appropriate response. Overtly, the learner performs that response. The crux of the Kulhavy-Stock model has to do with the cognitive evaluations a learner performs in determining how to respond.

As noted earlier, Kulhavy's work has increasingly emphasized the importance of learner response confidence in understanding how learners will

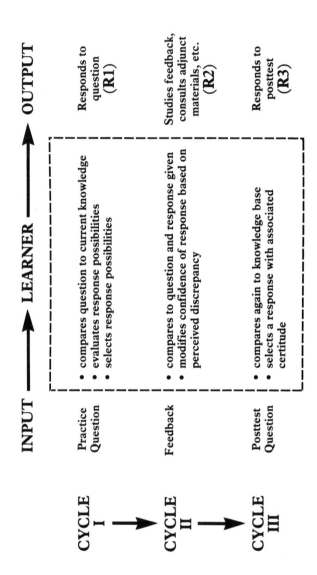

Figure 2.4. A simplified representation of Kulhavy and Stock's (1989) certitude model of text-based feedback.

approach the feedback that follows their response. In their model, Kulhavy and Stock suggest that response confidence first appears as a mental product of Cycle I. That is, learners compare the demands of the instructional question to their prior knowledge and current understanding of the instructional situation. If the perceived match is reasonably good, they will select a response with some degree of confidence. The worse the match, the lower their confidence in whatever response is finally selected.

When feedback is provided to learners in Cycle II, they again conduct a cognitive evaluation, this time to compare their answer to what is given as correct. This process is what Kulhavy and Stock refer to as verification. When verification is combined with initial response confidence, perceived discrepancy results. For example, no discrepancy occurs when a student receives verification of a correct answer that she was certain would be correct. In that case, the student is simply reinforced, and the certainty of correctness is deepened. Conversely, discrepancy will be high for learners who are told by the feedback that their answer was wrong when they were confident it would be right. In this case, response certainty is likely to drop slightly while the learners scramble to determine why the answer was wrong.

Kulhavy and Stock (1989) postulated that discrepancy is a major factor influencing the time and effort students will spend in processing feedback. That being so, it must also mediate effects of different types of feedback (in terms of complexity or elaboration). In the low discrepancy case described above, for example, learners have no need for extensive or elaborated feedback, nor are they likely to pay attention to it. In the case of high discrepancy, however, feedback must, at the least, provide sufficient information for the learner to correct whatever error was made.

What about cases of low discrepancy that are caused by low response confidence, regardless of whether verification indicated a right or wrong answer? Kulhavy and his associates speculated that low confidence may be a sign of complete bewilderment or misconception on the part of the learner and should therefore signal a need for feedback that essentially amounts to new instruction.

The "ultimate test of the effect of feedback," according to Kulhavy and Stock (1989, p. 295), is the output from Cycle III of the model. By comparing initial responses (R1) to posttest responses (R3), one has a measure of what effect feedback had in the previous Cycle II. An initially correct answer that remains correct, for instance, indicates that feedback served to verify and strengthen the response, strengthening its durability. Similarly, an error made initially but changed to a correct answer on the posttest indicates a facilitative effect of feedback. That is, the learner is assumed to have used the information provided in the feedback to correct an initial misconception. When an error remains an error, or a correct answer is changed to an error, feedback is thought to have either no effect or a detrimental one.

Supporting Evidence

Predictions made by the Kulhavy-Stock model have so far proven robust under a number of conditions. In the first of three studies reported by Kulhavy and Stock (1989), discrepancy and feedback study times covaried. That is, as predicted, students spent more time studying feedback for incorrect answers that they were certain they got right (high discrepancy). In the second study, Kulhavy and Stock reversed this relationship by falsely telling students their answers were wrong when they were in fact correct, and vice-versa. Thus, so long as students *thought* they got wrong an answer which they were certain would be correct (and in actuality, *was* correct), they spent more time studying feedback, as predicted by the model. Finally, in their third study, Kulhavy and Stock (1989) demonstrated that the probability of correct R3 (posttest) responding increased with the initial response certitude, especially when initial responses were also correct (low discrepancy). In this case, feedback served to increase the durability of initially correct answers. Related to this last finding, Kulhavy, Stock, Hancock, Swindell, and Hammrich (1990) also tested and confirmed the prediction that, in the absence of feedback, response confidence and the probability of correct R3 responding should be positively related.

In other studies conducted by Kulhavy and his associates, predictions of the model have been upheld under a variety of conditions. Swindell (1991), for example, suggested that feedback elaboration should be useful in correcting particularly high certitude errors. Although this turned out to be the case, feedback "elaboration" was operationalized as presenting the stem and all the alternatives listed with the correct alternative starred, a definition of elaborated feedback which differs from that proposed earlier in this chapter. The non-elaborated feedback condition consisted of the stem and the correct alternative only.

Finally, the Kulhavy-Stock model provides a useful framework for explaining past research results. For example, Peeck & Tillema (1979) and Peeck, van den Bosch, and Kreupeling (1985) demonstrated that initially correct responses are better remembered than errors, particularly when feedback is delayed. Assuming that learners are more likely to make higher confidence judgments for correct responses than for incorrect responses, the durability hypothesis of Kulhavy and Stock (1989) provides a theoretical explanation for these results. The basic hypothesis is that high confidence represents better comprehension and therefore will be better remembered. Following this argument, Kulhavy and Stock predict that measures of response certitude and durability should be positively related.

The model also explains the error correction data reported by Peeck and his colleagues (Peeck & Tillema, 1979; Peeck *et al.*, 1985). In a series of studies, learners were not only more likely to recall initially correct responses, they were also more likely to correct initially wrong responses if they could recall their initial response. Once again, the concepts of durability and discrepancy described in the Kulhavy-Stock model account nicely for these data. Initially correct responses are more likely to be recalled as a function of the positive relationship between confidence and durability. Initially incorrect responses associated with high confidence result in maximum discrepancy within the learner system. The learner therefore works to reduce this discrepancy by studying the information provided during feedback, and as a result, the incorrect response is likely to be corrected on a later test. Initially incorrect responses associated with low confidence, however, result in low discrepancy and less effort exerted to correct them. Thus, durability and discrepancy provide a theoretical explanation for empirical results across a continuum of response confidences.

Recent investigations have upheld the predictions of the model. Swindell, Kulhavy, and Stock (1992) directly tested the durability hypothesis and found response patterns closely parallel to those reported by Peeck and his colleagues. Again, the probability of remembering a high confidence error was higher than remembering a low confidence error. These researchers found that for high confidence corrects, the probability of recall was .90. The probability for recalling a high confidence error was .70. Conversely, when students had little confidence in their responses, probability rates fell to .72 and .60 (for corrects and errors, respectively). These trends proved stable over an eight-day period.

Limitations of the Model

The Kulhavy-Stock model suffers from some of the same problems that we cited at the outset of this chapter. For one thing, much of the research investigating its claims has been conducted in testing environments. That is, students are given no instruction at all, but instead respond to multiple choice questions on some topic. In these studies, feedback manipulations included no feedback vs. feedback (right/wrong verification; Kulhavy & Stock, 1989; Kulhavy *et al.*, 1990), simple feedback (verification or KR) vs. elaborated feedback (presentation of correct answer or KCR; Swindell, 1991), and feedback presented via different modes. Although such studies have provided evidence to support the Kulhavy-Stock model, it does not necessarily follow that the model will be supported under true instructional conditions. We agree with Peterson and Swindell (1991) that actual instruction should be part of the feedback model and that the model should be tested under those conditions.

To give Kulhavy and his associates due credit, instruction is a part of some studies. It has typically taken the form of brief paragraphs of information each followed by a single multiple choice question based on the content of the preceding paragraph. The content is largely descriptive, on such topics as the U.S. Navy, ocean science, rattlesnakes, and a mythical tribe called the Himoots. Students are asked to recall factual pieces of information. Although this is instruction of a kind, it does not yet represent very well what happens in actual classrooms or how students read textbooks. For the Kulhavy-Stock model to have practical utility, it must now be tested under more ecologically valid conditions.

The nature of instruction used in the Kulhavy studies raises another issue already touched upon earlier in the chapter, namely, the exclusive focus on verbal information as the learning outcome. There is evidence to suggest that the Kulhavy-Stock model, shown to be a reasonable account of verbal information learning, does not hold for more complex forms of learning. In the Dempsey and Driscoll study described earlier, for example, students were learning concepts, which involved both discriminating among examples of similar concepts and generalizing each concept to new and divergent examples. In that study, response confidence showed an inverse relationship to feedback study time, precisely the opposite of what is predicted by the Kulhavy-Stock model.

Mory (1991) conducted the only study to our knowledge that has simultaneously investigated feedback effects on two different types of learning outcomes. In the study, college-level participants completed a computer-based instructional program presenting information about Gagné's (1985) taxonomy followed by examples of each level in the taxonomy. Embedded questions asked for recall of verbal information or identification of new examples (concept classification). Results indicated that predictions of the Kulhavy-Stock model held for verbal information learning but not for concept acquisition.

Swindell (1991) reported a study that also attempted to determine whether the model would generalize to higher level learning. Half the students were asked to construct a response to each question, and their performance was compared to that of students who answered multiple-choice questions. Feedback effects were similar across the two conditions, which Swindell took as evidence of the model's generalizability. The questions in the study, however, asked for recall of verbal information only, so that constructing a response was no guarantee that any intellectual skill learning occurred. It appears, then, that the jury is still out on whether the Kulhavy-Stock model will explain feedback effects on learning outcomes other than verbal information. This is clearly an area where more investigation is required.

It has already been noted that what Kulhavy and associates mean by elaborated feedback is quite different from what other researchers mean by the same term. So far, the only feedback "elaboration" that seems to have been investigated in the context of the Kulhavy-Stock model is KCR, or presentation of the correct answer. Not surprisingly, in view of the other research reviewed in this chapter, KCR feedback facilitated the correction of high certitude errors. What is still needed, however, is systematic investigation of how other types of feedback elaboration may serve to correct errors, both high certitude and low certitude. In considering questions of feedback efficiency, it will also be necessary to tease out added feedback study time that is caused solely by the extra time it takes to read elaborated feedback.

In addition to increased investigation into intellectual skills, feedback elaboration can certainly function within the purview of learning strategies, and that area, with a few notable exceptions (e.g., Derry & Murphy, 1986), remains relatively unexplored. In its present form, the model makes more precise predictions of learner behaviors for high confidence responses than low confidence responses, and virtually no predictions for mid-range confidence. If the model is to provide useful predictions for tying instructional feedback to confidence estimates, the entire range of metacognitive judgments and learner behaviors will need to be addressed.

Related to this issue is the use of self-report measures in reporting response confidence. There seems little question that these self-reports, by themselves, function as an informal learning strategy. We have mentioned earlier in the chapter that this method can be (and has been) used as an instructional strategy unrelated to research. Explorations to date, with the exception of the introductory study by Dempsey and Driscoll (1992), have not acknowledged the very specialized nature of instructional situations in which confidence self-report measures are applied.

Practical Implications and Future Directions of Research on Text-Based Feedback

What can practitioners take away from this discussion of feedback in written instructional materials? What directions should research follow in the future in order to maximize its practical benefits? These questions provide the focus for this final section of the chapter. As a means of organizing our discussion, we have identified at least three themes by which findings can be integrated. These are: feedback elaboration and response confidence, functions of feedback, and feedback for different learning outcomes.

Feedback Elaboration and Response Confidence

Most findings of studies that investigated various forms of feedback complexity or elaboration offer little hope for the utility of any elaborations beyond a statement of the correct answer. In almost all cases, KCR feedback was superior to KR feedback, but very little difference in performance accrued from KCR feedback versus any other elaborated form. Moreover, KCR feedback, because of its brevity, has been shown to be more efficient than other, elaborated forms. Yet, the Kulhavy-Stock model sheds light on conditions under which greater elaboration should be useful. It also suggests conditions under which KR feedback might be preferred over KCR feedback. The learner's response confidence is the key to these decisions.

For high certitude correct answers, for example, learners need only be told, "Great! You're right," which is an instance of KR feedback. For high certitude wrong answers, more information is required, but only enough to enable the learner to correct his or her mistake. In this case, KCR feedback constitutes the minimum information that should be given. By contrast, for low certitude responses, both right and wrong, additional information must be given in such a way as to increase cognitive processing and comprehension. This could amount to re-teaching, new examples, or additional questions designed to diagnose specific learner misunderstandings.

Bangert-Drowns *et al.* (1991) also made the important point that for feedback elaboration to have the desired effect, learners must attend to it mindfully. They suggested further that emphasis on specific fact retrieval might work to the detriment of mindfulness, because learners become interested only in the right answer, not why that answer is correct. If this is true, then "elaborate feedback may be more important in the building of conceptual frameworks, drawing of inferences, or applying rules in complex situations" (Bangert-Drowns *et al.*, 1991, p. 234). Perhaps, when learner response confidence is tapped in these situations, fine-tuned decisions will be possible concerning what and how much information to include in feedback.

Functions of Feedback

Throughout this chapter we have emphasized the informative function of feedback, as opposed to its reinforcing function. With respect to this informative function, "feedback's primary importance is in correcting errors" (Bangert-Drowns *et al.*, 1991, p. 232). This statement summarizes quite well the current focus of research on feedback effects, but it also illustrates an unnecessary narrowness of focus that should now be broadened.

Peterson and Swindell (1991) distinguished feedback as used to verify comprehension and correct errors from feedback as modeling the kinds of questions learners should ask to determine for themselves whether comprehension has been attained. This is an important distinction, which is echoed in Bangert-Drowns *et al.'s* (1991) call for feedback that triggers "mindful, metacognitively driven knowledge alteration" (p. 234). Such a distinction shifts the responsibility and the control for learning to the learner. The learner becomes proactive in the educative process, rather than reactive. How might such feedback be implemented?

On one hand, feedback for a wrong answer might be strategic in nature, rather than informational in the sense of presenting content information. For instance, the learner might be told, "Your answer was wrong. Go back to the paragraph and try to identify the words you did not understand." Alternatively, for a concept: "You chose the wrong classification for this example. Study its attributes more carefully and see how it is the same or different from other examples provided in the text."

On the other hand, feedback may be generated by the learners themselves, rather than provided them via the instruction. This procedure may be particularly suited to collaborative learning settings, in which pairs or small groups of students work together on a computer program, for example. It may also be uniquely effective for facilitating complex or higher-order learning outcomes. One can easily imagine learners constructing a rationale or chain of reasoning for their responses, as in mathematical or scientific problem solving, for example.

In situations where feedback takes on this modeling, or metacognitive, function, the role of response confidence is likely to increase in complexity, just as we have seen occur with concept acquisition as opposed to information learning. To the extent that learners are confident of their information sources, and in their own reasoning from those sources, they will be certain of their answers. It also seems likely that a host of other variables may affect these judgments. For instance, higher achievers are better monitors of their own performance and are therefore likely to form more accurate certitude judgments than would lower achievers. As a result, lower achievers may require assistance in developing the skills to provide feedback to themselves. Likewise, highly efficacious learners may overestimate their certitude, which could result in inadequate self-feedback.

Although a speculation at this time, feedback that models metacognitive strategies or is generated by the learners themselves may well have significant benefits for higher-level learning. As we have also stated elsewhere in this chapter, some evidence suggests that performance feedback should be varied according to the learner's acceptance of assigned personal goals. This brings us to our final point.

Feedback for Different Learning Outcomes

Elsewhere in the chapter we have made the case for feedback operating differently depending on what learning outcome is being taught and assessed. Most studies to date have concentrated on knowledge level outcomes, and many have used materials that have little, if any, relevance to those who are studying them. Exceptions to this are the studies conducted by Dempsey and Driscoll (e.g., Dempsey, Driscoll, & Litchfield, in press; Dempsey and Driscoll, 1992) and Mory (1991). In these, students tackled learning materials in the context of semester-long courses that emphasized concept understanding and application.

What does the evidence suggest? For knowledge outcomes in classroom settings (as opposed to laboratory experiments), immediate feedback is important, and learner response confidence may be a useful guide for prescribing feedback elaboration. For concept learning, the types of errors learners make can be useful in determining what information to include in feedback that follows anticipated wrong answers. The role of response confidence in concept learning, however, is not yet clear. For higher-level learning, such as problem solving, theoretically sound and empirically verified prescriptions for feedback are tenuous at best. With additional research, however, perhaps the promises of strategic and learner-generated feedback will be realized.

References

Ammons, R.B. (1956). Effects of knowledge of performance: A survey and tentative theoretical formulation. *Journal of General Psychology, 54*, 279–299.

Anderson, J.R. (1990). *Cognitive psychology and its implications* (3rd ed.). New York: W. H. Freeman.

Anderson, R.C., Kulhavy, R.W., & Andre, T. (1971). Feedback procedures in programmed instruction. *Journal of Educational Psychology, 62*, 148–156.

Ashford, S.J., & Cummings, L.L. (1983). Feedback as an individual resource: Personal strategies of creating information. *Organizational Behavior and Human Decision Processes, 38*, 92–113.

Bangert-Drowns, R.L., Kulik, C.C., Kulik, J.A., and Morgan, M.T. (1991). The instructional effect of feedback in test-like events. *Review of Educational Research, 61*(2), 213–238.

Borg, W.R., & Gall, M.D. (1983). *Educational research* (4th ed.). New York: Longman.

Brackbill, Y., Bravos, A., & Starr, R.H. (1962). Delay improved retention of a difficult task. *Journal of Comparative Psychology, 55*, 947–952.

Brackbill, Y., & Kappy, M.S. (1962). Delay of reinforcement and retention. *Journal of Comparative and Physiological Psychology, 55*, 14–18.

Briggs, L.J., & Hamilton, N.R. (1964). Meaningful learning and retention: Practice and feedback variables. *Review of Educational Research, 34*, 545–558.

Buss, A.H., Braden, W., Orgel, A., & Buss, E. (1956). Acquisition and extinction with different verbal reinforcement combination. *Journal of Experimental Psychology, 52,* 288–295.

Buss, A.H., & Buss, E. (1956). The effect of verbal reinforcement combinations on conceptual learning. *Journal of Experimental Psychology, 52,* 283–287.

Buss, A.H., Weiner, M., & Buss, E. (1954). Stimulus generalization as a function of verbal reinforcement combinations. *Journal of Experimental Psychology, 48,* 433–436.

Clariana, R.B. (1990). A comparison of answer until correct feedback and knowledge or correct response feedback under two conditions of contextualization. *Journal of Computer-Based Instruction, 17*(4), 125–129.

Clariana, R.B., Ross, S.M., & Morrison, G.R. (1991). The effects of different feedback strategies using computer-administered multiple-choice questions as instruction. *Educational Technology Research & Development, 39*(2), 5–17.

Dempsey, J. (1986). Using the rational set generator with computer-based instruction for creating concept examples: A template for instructors. *Educational Technology, 26*(4), 43–46.

Dempsey, J.V., & Driscoll, M.P. (1992). *Conceptual error and feedback: The relationship between content analysis and confidence of response.* Manuscript submitted for publication.

Dempsey, J.V., Driscoll, M.P., & Litchfield, B.C. (in press). Feedback, retention, discrimination error, and feedback study time. *Journal of Research on Computing in Education.*

Dempsey, J.V., & Wager, S.U. (1988). A taxonomy for the timing of feedback in computer-based instruction. *Educational Technology, 28*(10), 20–25.

Derry, S.J., & Murphy, D.A. (1986). Designing systems that train learning ability: From theory to practice. *Review of Educational Research, 56,* 1–39.

Derry, S.J., Jacobs, J.W., & Murphy, D.A. (1987). The JSEP learning skills training system. *Journal of Educational Technology Systems, 15*(4), 273–284.

Driscoll, M.P., & Tessmer, M. (1985). The rational set generator: A method for creating concept examples for teaching and testing. *Educational Technology, 25* (2), 29–32.

Erez, M., & Zidon, I. (1984). Effect of goal acceptance on the relationship of goal difficulty to performance. *Journal of Applied Psychology, 69,* 69–78.

Gagné, R.M. (1985). *The conditions of learning and theory of instruction.* (4th ed.). New York: Holt, Rinehart, & Winston.

Gilman, D.A. (1969). Comparison of several feedback methods for correcting errors by computer-assisted instruction. *Journal of Educational Psychology, 60,* 503–508.

Guthrie, J.T. (1971). Feedback and sentence learning. *Journal of Verbal Learning and Verbal Behavior, 10,* 23–28.

Keller, J.M. (1983). Motivational design of instruction. In C.M. Reigeluth (Ed.), *Instructional design theories and models: An overview of their current status* (pp. 383–437). Hillsdale, NJ: Erlbaum.

Keller, J.M., & Suzuki, K. (1989). Use of the ARCS motivational model in courseware design. In D.H. Jonassen (Ed.), *Instructional designs for microcomputer courseware.* Hillsdale, NJ: Erlbaum.

Klausmeier, H.J., & Feldman, K.V. (1975). Effects of a definition and a varying number of examples and nonexamples on concept attainment. *Journal of Educational Psychology, 67,* 174–178.

Kulhavy, R.W. (1977). Feedback in written instruction. *Review of Educational Research, 47,* 211–232.

Kulhavy, R.W., & Anderson, R.C. (1972). Delay-retention effect with multiple-choice tests. *Journal of Educational Psychology, 63,* 505–512.

Kulhavy, R.W., & Stock, W.A. (1989). Feedback in written instruction: The place of response certitude. *Educational Psychology Review, 1,* 279–308.

Kulhavy, R.W., Stock, W.A., Hancock, T.E., Swindell, L.K., & Hammrich, P.L. (1990). Written feedback: Response certitude and durability. *Contemporary Educational Psychology, 15,* 319–332.

Kulhavy, R.W., White, M.T., Topp, B.W., Chan, A.L., & Adams, J. (1985). Feedback complexity and corrective efficiency. *Contemporary Educational Psychology, 10,* 285-291.

Kulhavy, R.W., Yekovich, F.R., & Dyer, J.W. (1976). Feedback and response confidence. *Journal of Educational Psychology, 68,* 522–528.

Kulhavy, R.W., Yekovich, F.R., & Dyer, J.W. (1979). Feedback and content review in programmed instruction. *Contemporary Educational Psychology, 4,* 91–98.

Kulik, J.A., & Kulik, C.C. (1988). Timing of feedback and verbal learning. *Review of Educational Research, 58* (1), 79–97.

Lasoff, E.M. (1981). The effect of feedback in both computer-assisted instruction and programmed instruction on achievement and attitude. *Dissertation Abstracts International, 42,* 1553A.

Litchfield, B.C., Driscoll, M.P., & Dempsey, J.V. (1988). Presentation sequence and example difficulty: Their effect on concept and rule learning in computer-based instruction. *Journal of Computer-Based Instruction, 17*(1), 35–40.

Locke, E.A., Cartledge, N., & Koeppel, J. (1968). Motivational effects of knowledge of results: A goal-setting phenomenon? *Psychological Bulletin, 70,* 474–485.

Locke, E.A., Shaw, K.N., Saari, L.M., & Latham, G.P. (1981). Goal setting and task performance: 1969–1980. *Psychological Bulletin, 90,* 125–152.

Malone, T.W. (1981). Toward a theory of intrinisically motivating instruction. *Cognitive Science, 4,* 333–369.

Markle, S.M., & Tiemann, P.W. (1971). Conceptual learning and instructional design. *British Journal of Educational Technology, 1*(1), 27–33.

Merrill, M.D., & Tennyson, R.D. (1977). *Concept teaching: An instructional design guide.* Englewood Cliffs, NJ: Educational Technology Publications.

Mory, E.H. (1991) *The effects of adaptive feedback on student performance, feedback study time, and learner efficiency within computer-based instruction.* Unpublished doctoral dissertation, Florida State University: Tallahassee.

Noonan, J.V. (1984). *Feedback procedures in computer-assisted instruction: Knowledge-of-results, knowledge-of-correct-response, process explanations, and second attempts after errors.* Unpublished doctoral dissertation. University of Illinois, Urbana-Champaign.

Park, O., & Roberts, F.C. (1985, April). *Effects of guided instructional strategies in computer-based instruction.* Paper presented at the annual meeting of the American Educational Research Association, Chicago, IL.

Park, O., & Tennyson, R.D. (1986). Computer-based adaptive instructional design strategies for response-sensitive sequencing and presentation forms of examples in coordinate concept learning. *Journal of Educational Psychology, 78,* 153–158.

Payne, R.B., & Hauty, G.T. (1955). Effect of psychological feedback upon work decrement. *Journal of Experimental Psychology, 50,* 343–351.

Peeck, J., & Tillema, H.H. (1979). Delay of feedback and retention of correct and incorrect responses. *Journal of Experimental Education, 47*(2), 171–178.

Peeck, J., van den Bosch, A.J., & Kreupeling, W. (1985). The effect of informative feedback in relation to retention for initial responses. *Contemporary Educational Psychology, 10,* 303–313.

Peterson, S.K., & Swindell, L.K. (1991, April). *The role of feedback in written instruction: Recent theoretical advances.* Paper presented at the annual meeting of the American Educational Research Association, Chicago, IL.

Roper, W.J. (1977). Feedback in computer assisted instruction. *Programmed Learning and Educational Technology, 14,* 43–49.

Salomon, G., & Globerson, T. (1987). Skill may not be enough: The role of mindfullness in learning and transfer. *International Journal of Educational Research, 11,* 623–637.

Scarth, G., & Litchfield, B.C. (1990). *Ergomotion.* (Level III Interactive Videodisc). Boston, MA: Houghton-Mifflin.

Siegel, M.A., & Misselt, A.L. (1984). Adaptive feedback and review paradigm for computer-based drills. *Journal of Educational Psychology, 76,* 310–317.

Spock, P.A. (April, 1987). *Feedback and confidence of response for a rule-learning task using computer-assisted instruction.* Paper presented at the annual meeting of the American Educational Research Association, Washington, DC.

Suppes, P., & Ginsberg, R. (1962). Application of a stimulus sampling model to children's concept formation with and without overt correction responses. *Journal of Experimental Psychology, 63,* 330–336.

Swindell, L. (1991, April) *Testing a model of feedback in written instruction.* Paper presented at the annual meeting of the American Educational Research Association, Chicago, IL.

Swindell, L.K., Greenway, R., & Peterson, S.K. (1992). *Children's use of response confidence in the processing of instructional feedback.* Manuscript submitted for publication.

Swindell, L.K., Kulhavy, R.W., & Stock, W.A. (1992). *The role of response confidence in comprehension and memory for written instruction.* Manuscript submitted for publication.

Tait, K., Hartley, J.R., & Anderson, R.C. (1973). Feedback procedures in computer-assisted arithmetic instruction. *British Journal of Educational Psychology, 43,* 161–171.

Tennyson, R.D. (1987). MAIS: An educational alternative of ICAI. *Educational Technology, 27*(5), 22–28.

Tennyson, R.D., & Cocchiarella, M.J. (1986). An empirically based instructional design theory for teaching concepts. *Review of Educational Research, 56,* 40–71.

Tessmer, M., & Driscoll, M.P. (1987). Effects of diagrammatic display of coordinate concept definitions on concept classification performance. *Educational Communications and Technology Journal, 34*(4), 195–206.

Tosti, D.T. (1978). Formative feedback. *NSPI Journal, 13,* 19–21.

Travers, R.M., Wagenen, K.V., Haygood, D.H., & McCormick, M. (1965). Learning as a consequence of the learner's task involvement under different conditions of feedback. *Journal of Educational Psychology, 55,* 167-173.

Vance, R.J., & Coella, A. (1990). Effects of two types of feedback on goal acceptance and personal goals. *Journal of Applied Psychology, 75*(1), 68–76.

Wager, W., & Wager, S. (1985). Presenting questions, processing responses, and providing feedback in CAI. *Journal of Instructional Development, 14,* 2–8.

Waldrop, P.B., Justin, J.E., & Adams, T.M. (1986). A comparison of three types of feedback in a computer-assisted instruction task. *Educational Technology, 26*(2), 43–45.

Chapter Three

The Role of Questions in Learning

Walter Wager
Florida State University

and

Edna Holland Mory
Florida State University

Researchers have been interested in the role of feedback in instruction for many years. Going back to the height of the programmed instruction movement, there have been many studies on the contingencies of performance, how best to schedule reinforcement, and how to increase the probability of continued behavior. Developers of "Skinnerian" programmed instruction realized at that time that there were many different forms of questions that could be presented to the learner, but they believed that only one form of feedback was necessary—that of knowledge of the correct answer or the response the student should have made. Today we embrace cognitive and information processing theories in our study of learning and have a much more sophisticated view of types of feedback. However, it seems that we have not made much progress on how best to use feedback to facilitate learning. In a meta-analysis of 40 studies, Bangert-Drowns *et al.* (1991) found the average effect size in feedback studies to be about .26, raising the average score by about one fourth of a standard deviation. This meta-analysis looked at 16 characteristics for each feedback study, and found only four significantly related to effect size. About the only prescriptive advice we can derive from the combined results of the Bangert-Drowns analysis is: (1) Don't allow the learners to see the answers to a question before they make a response, and (2) provide knowledge of the correct answer along with knowledge of results.

The premise of this chapter is that in order to understand variables affecting feedback, research must ask the question, "Feedback for what?" This question can relate to many things. First is the effect the type of learning outcomes might have on prescriptions for feedback. For example, effective feedback for verbal learning is probably different from effective feedback for concept learning. This is because the performance requirements of these two different types of learning are quite different, one being recall and the other being generalization (Gagné, Briggs, & Wager, 1992).

Secondly, "Feedback for what?" might be asking the question, "Feedback for what stage of information processing?" Information-processing models look at learning as a sequential process where information undergoes stages of transformation (Gagné, 1985). These stages include attention, selective perception, rehearsal, encoding, and retrieval. Similar to the notion that different types of feedback are appropriate for different types of learning, one might hypothesize that different types of feedback are needed at different stages in learning. For example, consider the research paradigm in which three groups of learners are presented with questions; each group is then given a different form of feedback (knowledge of results, knowledge of the correct answer, or an elaboration of the correct answer). Later they are presented with the same questions to see if they know the correct answer. The findings of such research are generally that the groups that received knowledge of the correct answer and elaboration outperform the knowledge of results group. What purpose did the feedback serve for each group? Did it present a new stimulus? Did it correct misunderstandings? The answer, it seems, would depend on both the students and the type of instruction encountered before the question. If the feedback provides a new stimulus, one might expect that knowledge of the correct answer would be more effective than elaborated feedback because simple feedback should require less selective perception. However, the correction of misunderstandings should be facilitated by elaboration, as it provides a richer context for remembering the new information.

However, studies of comparing one form of feedback to another often produce conflicting or non-significant findings. Why? Is theory about learning insufficient, or are other factors determining the outcomes? Bangert-Drowns *et al.* (1991) imply that in many feedback studies the context and content are not well enough controlled to isolate the variance of the feedback treatment. This same problem has been discussed by Carlson (1991) in his review of research on questioning in classrooms.

Feedback studies that look at the effect of different forms of, timing of, or content of feedback are not likely to be productive until other factors are controlled. The learning tasks being presented must be meaningful to the learner if we are to expect a reasonable effort at learning. Likewise, the characteristics of the feedback must be consistent with the requirements of the type of learning task and stage information processing that is being supported by that feedback. The evidence for such an assertion comes from some of the early research findings of Rothkopf (1970) and Frase (1970) in which the addition of adjunct questions added to text passages seemed to serve different purposes depending on where they were placed. Hamaker's (1986) review also supports this assertion.

The Information-Processing Model

A large part of the research on feedback follows from the strong influence of behavioral psychology in the 1960s. However, toward the end of the 1960s and into the 1970s there was a movement toward cognitive psychology and, especially, information-processing models of learning. In an information-processing model, learning is hypothesized to occur in a number of sequential stages (Bangert-Drowns *et al.*, 1991; Kumar, 1971; Gagné, 1985; Atkinson & Shiffrin, 1968). Research on learning has typically investigated the effects of instructional intervention on one or more of these stages. Since questions, and therefore feedback, may occur at any time during instruction, is it reasonable to expect they serve different purposes? For example, research on adjunct questions often focuses on the stages Gagné (1985) refers to as selective attention, whereas pre-instructional strategies such as providing learning objectives focuses on stimulus perception through the arousal of expectations. In fact, Bangert-Drowns *et al.* (1991) found that in studies where pretests were given, feedback effect sizes were smaller. This implies that some of the variance in feedback outcomes was affected by a pre-instructional treatment.

In the remainder of this chapter we will use the Gagné (1985) model of information processing as a framework for analyzing the different roles questions might serve in learning. According to this model, stimuli from the learner's environment activate receptors which transmit information to the central nervous system. After a brief registration in one of the sensory registers, it is transformed by a process called selective perception into recognizable patterns and put into short-term memory. Storage in short-term memory has a relatively brief duration, and is very limited in capacity. In order that information can be remembered for longer periods and in larger quantities, it is semantically encoded to a form that will go into long-term memory. Both information from short-term and long-term memory may be passed to a response generator and transformed into some sort of action.

The message serves to activate effectors which result in a performance that can be observed to occur in the learner's environment (Gagné, Briggs & Wager, 1992).

The model is composed of a number of processes that comprise the internal events that occur in an act of learning. Gagné (1985) suggests that these internal events can be activated by external events—events in the instructional materials. These external events correspond roughly to the stages of information processing as shown in Table 3.1.

It is our contention that questions and feedback may serve different functions according to which event of instruction—that is, to which internal process—they are being used to facilitate. The role of questions within the model and the corresponding role of feedback for each are presented in Table 3.2.

The role of questions in learning has long been a focus of research. From an examination of studies by Anderson (1970), Frase (1970), Gall (1970), Kumar (1971), Bull (1973), and Ladas (1973), it has already been suggested that questions serve three general functions in learning: (1) to establish and maintain attention, (2) to facilitate encoding, and (3) to provide for rehearsal (Wager & Wager, 1985). In addition, there may be other ways that questions function in learning which are not evident from past research paradigms. When examined across the various events of instruction, questions and feedback may serve additional functions which require new research models, such as the response certitude model of Kulhavy and

Learning Process	Instructional Event
1. Reception of stimuli by receptors	Gaining attention
2. Registration of information by sensory registers	Informing learner of the objective
3. Selective perception for storage in short-term memory	Stimulating recall of prerequisite learning
4. Rehearsal to maintain information in short-term memory	Presenting the stimulus material
5. Semantic encoding for storage in long-term memory	Providing learning guidance
6. Retrieval from long-term memory to working memory	Eliciting the performance
7. Response generation to effectors	Providing feedback
8. Performance in the learner's environment	Assessing the performance
9. Control of processes through executive strategies	Enhancing retention and transfer

Table 3.1. Processes of learning and their relationship to the events of instruction.

Gagné's Stages of Information Processing	Role of Questions	Role of Feedback
1. Reception of stimuli by receptors	—To gain attention —Create uncertainty	—Create greater dissonance between what is currently known & information to be taught.
2. Registration of information by sensory registors	—Create expectations for the learning task —Activate a process of executive control (based on the idea that schemas control perception, and that activating schemas through questions affects selective perception) (West, Farmer, & Wolff, 1991)	—Delayed rhetorical feedback in the format of presentation of stimulus.
3. Selective perception for storage in STM	—Recall (retrieve) prerequisites into STM (to enable integration of previously learned information with new information or skills) —Scanning —Selective attention (control process)	—Ensure skills for understanding new information are in place & can be retrieved. —Function is to be sure that new learning builds on relevant previous learning.
4. Rehearsal to maintain information in STM	—Rehearsal - (Kumar, 1971) —Maintains & renews the items stored in STM (has to do with cognitive information load) (Miller, 1956) —Chunking & chaining	—To confirm rehearsal strategies, provide reinforcement.
5. Semantic encoding for storage in LTM	—Coding —Accretion (Ausubel, 1968) —Questions that cause learners to integrate new knowledge into existing structures or create new structures	—Validate the integration, or it may even question links further. —Serves as learning guidance through demonstration of processes. —Elaboration.
6. Retrival from LTM to working memory	—Retrieval, practice generalization —Activating response organization —Test for understanding or misunderstanding	—Remediate misunderstanding. —Provide for reinforcement. —Spaced reinforcement.
7. Response generation to effectors	—Provides cues for future performance —Provides reinforcement —Provides corrective information	—Was the question correctly interpreted? —Was the answer sufficient?
8. Performance in the learner's environment	—Posttest or retention test —Opportunity for reinforcement and/or correction due to variations in context	—Confirms that the skill has been generalized to a range of situations. —Shows the effects of a learner's actions.
9. Control of processes through executive strategies	—Tuning (interpretation) of existing schema	—Serves to elaborate the existing schema building new examples *and* relevance, confidence, and satisfaction with performance.

Table 3.2. Recommendations for the use of feedback considering stages of information processing.

his associates (Kulhavy, 1977; Kulhavy & Stock, 1989), where intervening learner confidence variables are postulated and tested. The next section of this chapter looks at how questions and feedback may facilitate each of the stages in the information processing model.

Gaining Attention: Reception of Stimuli by Receptors

The first stage in the information-processing model is that of reception of stimuli by receptors. The external event which evokes this internal process is that of gaining attention. Questions are one way to gain attention. Questions are motivational stimuli capable of having arousal outcomes (Frase, 1970; Rothkopf, 1970). The role of questions in this case would be to arouse interest or to evoke uncertainty. Indeed, teachers frequently use questions to gain attention (including the question, "May I have your attention?"). While attention usually involves the two processes of (1) orientation of the receptors toward the stimulus and (2) the encoding of the stimulus (Anderson, 1970), only the first of these two processes relates to this first stage of information processing. Although the process of gaining attention is thought of as an initial event, control of attention within the lesson has been found to be important when students are bored, tired, or under pressure to work quickly, as well (cited in Anderson, 1970). Questions presented as a stimulus for attention arousal will not guarantee that what is to follow will be learned. Unless this attention arousal does occur, however, there will not be adequate reception of the stimuli by the receptors to allow for the other processes to occur. Feedback for attention questions is probably rhetorical, if given at all. It may be desirable to allow students to express answers without confirmation of correctness, if the object is to create cognitive dissonance or information search, for example, starting a class by asking, "Why are more men bald than women?"

Informing the Learner of the Objective: Registration of Information by Sensory Registers

The next stage of processing is registration of information by the sensory registers. There is evidence that what is detected depends on what the learner is expecting. In Gagné's list of events of instruction, this would be effected by informing the learner of the objective. Behavioral objectives focus the learner's attention on relevant information in the instruction (Gagné, 1985). Questions, like objectives, can also shape expectations.

Adjunct question studies going back to Washborne (1929) looked at the effects of level (factual or conceptual) and location of questions in text passages. Washborne suggested that placing the questions at the beginning of the text helped to establish an expectancy about what was to be learned. Large effects on learning have been produced by providing students with *instructional objectives* before exposure to text (Rothkopf & Kaplan, 1972). Questions may serve the same purpose as behavioral objectives when they activate a process of executive control. This is supported by the notion that schemas control perception and that activating these schemas through questions can affect selective perception (West, Farmer, and Wolff, 1991).

Sagerman and Meyer (1987) found a learning effect that resulted from the type of adjunct questions presented after a passage of text. Learners given verbatim questions (i.e., questions in which the learner was asked to recognize a sentence presented in the text) seemed to focus on verbatim details for subsequent passages. Learners who received conceptual questions (i.e., questions that require inferring an answer from information in the text), by contrast, did better on posttest conceptual questions than the verbatim group. This effect, which has been referred to as forward transfer, or specific forward effect (Rickards, 1979), is similar to the effect found by researchers of performance objectives. Faw and Waller's (1976) review of the objectives literature found that (specific) objectives focus attention and improve performance on test items related to those objectives but depress performance on incidental items. When combined with Rickards' (1979) findings, it may be that the type of objective (detailed or general) might affect subsequent processing of the passage more than the content, since it is unlikely that the learner will keep all the objectives in mind while reading.

Another effect from type of question is what Rickards (1979) calls a general forward effect, where overall attention to the learning task is increased by the type of question. This effect is noticed when a particular type of question, e.g., conceptual, increases performance on not only conceptual, but on other types of questions as well. Sagerman and Meyer (1987) observed this in their experiment when the conceptual group scored as well as the verbatim group on verbatim questions. Andre (1979) concluded that there was no empirical support for a general effect, where higher-order questions facilitated performance on *unrelated* higher-order questions. However, conceptual questions appear to increase performance on verbatim recall tasks when that information must be used to answer the higher-order question.

Frase (1970) found that pre-questions interact with text to permit the selection of relevant information and the rejection of incidental information. Rehearsed questions that students have in memory also act as pre-questions, even though they may not necessarily appear frequently within a selected text. Pre-questions produce selective attention processes aimed at the information needed to answer the question. For example, a factual pre-question serves to cue responses to specific stimuli (Frase, 1970).

Ausubel (1968) suggests that the use of advance organizers to facilitate the learning and retention of meaningful verbal learning is based on the premise that logically meaningful material is most readily incorporated in the learner's cognitive structure, insofar as it can be subsumed under specifically relevant ideas. Ausubel has confirmed the supposition that increasing the availability of relevant subsumers in cognitive structure through the use of organizers enhances the meaningful learning of such material. Questions can serve the same function. To be effective they should: (1) activate anchoring concepts in the learner's cognitive structure, (2) be presented at an appropriate level of inclusiveness to provide optimal anchorage, and (3) make rote memorization unnecessary, by assuring a sufficient number of anchoring ideas are made available.

Hamaker (1986) cites many studies which show that factual pre-questions depress scores on incidental information. This tends to support the need for pre-questions that are general or global in nature. Several studies have shown that specific levels of questions focus attention to information required by that level question, while others studies have revealed general attention processes consisting of increased attention to text immediately following the adjunct question (cited in Hamilton, 1985). Most pre-questions might be classified as rhetorical, because the learner is not expected to answer them at that time. Feedback would only be available in the text that follows the question, if the learner remembers the question and processes the answer.

Stimulating Recall of Prerequisite Learning: Selective Perception for Storage in Short-Term Memory

After the sensory registers have recorded the information, selective perception takes place for storage in short-term memory. The function of questions during this stage would be to aid the student in recalling prerequisites into short-term memory in order to enable integration of previously learned information with new information or skills.

What is learned, in most instructional situations, depends a great deal on the activities of the student. Rothkopf (1970) calls behaviors that give birth to learning "mathemagenic" behaviors. Similarly, Kumar (1971) points out that which information that is transferred to short-term memory or long-term memory depends on the learner and a set of processes under the learner's control. These processes, termed "control processes" (Atkinson & Shiffrin, 1968) include the process of selective attention. The learner can selectively extract information according to his or her perceived importance of the information. This results in a reduction of the information present at initial registration, since only selected aspects are focused upon (Kumar, 1971).

The response to one or more aspects of a stimulus is an encoding response. Encoding of the stimulus is what Anderson (1970) refers to as the second process in attention. Examples of encoding responses include forming images of verbal or nonverbal stimuli and/or an elaboration of the stimulus (Anderson, 1970). Studies examining cue selection, or selective attention, suggest that students selectively attend to "the strongest, most salient, most meaningful, or most discriminable aspect of a compound stimulus" (Anderson, 1970, p. 350).

Feature extraction is the basic process responsible for the transfer of information. This often is accomplished by *scanning*, in which newly extracted features are compared to information stored in the long-term memory which is then fed into short-term memory (cited in Kumar, 1971). Scanning is referred to as one state within the process of *translation*, in which the first input for learning is created (Rothkopf, 1970). Due to the limited processing capacity of short-term memory, it is necessary for students to selectively scan to begin coding important information. It has been shown that selective scanning can be improved with practice. The improvement of scanning skills should be an important instructional objective (Kumar, 1971).

Questions can be used to help students selectively attend to salient aspects of what they are expected to learn, to know what features to look for when scanning the material, and to retrieve prerequisite knowledge in preparation for new information to build upon. Feedback would ensure that skills for understanding new information are in place and can be retrieved. Feedback to questions about prerequisite skills would serve two functions. First it confirms for the learners their understanding of the prerequisite skills. Second, it assures the information is in short-term memory and contiguous with information which will build upon it.

Presenting the Stimulus Material: Rehearsal to Maintain Information in Short-Term Memory

As previously noted, short-term memory (STM) is very limited both in duration and capacity. It is generally recognized that storage of information lasts no more than 20 seconds (usually less), and capacity consists of about seven units of information at a time (Miller, 1956; Kumar, 1971). However, the duration of information in STM can be increased through rehearsal, and capacity can be increased by chunking.

Kumar (1971) lists three functions of rehearsal. Two of these, recognized by Atkinson and Shiffrin, (1968), are (a) maintaining information in short-term storage and (b) transferring information to long-term storage or accumulation of information about the item in long-term storage. The third function of rehearsal, suggested by Sternberg (1969), is that of making information stored in long-term storage more accessible. These functions suggest that rehearsal acts to strengthen a single memory trace or increase the number of traces (Kumar, 1971).

Some researchers (Rothkopf & Bisbicos, 1967) found that for certain types of information learning, placing questions after the content resulted in overall better retention performance than the corresponding treatments in which experimental questions were placed before relevant text segments. They imply that the questions may have provided some sort of rehearsal function for newly learned material that enabled encoding. But why wouldn't questions placed before the text work equally as well? We offer the hypothesis that questions placed before new material have less effect if students lack an adequate schema for the new information. In this case, learner variables might influence the relative effectiveness of one treatment over another, depending upon the prior knowledge they bring to the learning task.

The format of post-questions (short answer, essay, or multiple-choice) at this stage is probably not very important. Typically short answer format has been shown to be more effective than multiple-choice format on repeated and related questions (Anderson & Biddle, 1975). However, Hamaker (1986) concludes that the *general effect* of post-questions has been overstated.

Research on the effects of post-questions usually does not allow the learner to look back through the stimulus materials. The purpose of preventing look-back is to control for the confounding variable of re-reading to better understand the variance that may be attributed to the questions themselves. Duchastel (1983) disagrees with this approach and labels adjunct question studies that do not allow students to reread the text as ecologically invalid because rereading would be expected from serious students in classroom situations. However, Hamaker's (1986) literature review showed no effects attributable to looking back. Other studies (Mouton & Reigeluth, 1987) have shown rereading to be as facilitating as adjunct questions, so one has to be careful to examine the effect of both adjunct questions and other techniques that may cause the learner to spend a greater amount of time focusing on the material.

Hamaker (1986) concludes that two critical variables affecting the results in adjunct question studies are the amount of time the student is given to process the text and the length of the text. "Relatively short texts in combination with [experimenters] time control were shown to be associated with slightly negative effects of adjunct questions on unrelated test items" (p. 238). This would support the notion that learners change their learning strategy to fit the conditions or, perhaps, that the questions were serving the function of focusing attention rather than providing a context for more information.

In another study (Reynolds & Anderson, 1982), selective attention was not the only factor at work in learning of answers to repeated questions. They did observe a selective attention effect, but when this effect was statistically removed, the variance attributable to questions was still present in a small yet substantial and significant amount. It was evident that another process other than selective attention was responsible for the learning, and they suggest that this other process was rehearsal.

Some researchers make a distinction betwen rehearsal and repetition, reasoning that rehearsal consists primarily of the search for an effective mnemonic of the items (covert rehearsal), while repetition is merely repeating the item over and over (overt rehearsal). Some findings (cited in Kumar, 1971) suggest that covert rehearsal results in better recall over long-term intervals, while overt rehearsal is better over short-term intervals. It has been speculated that the effect of pre-questions is to maximize rehearsal of question-relevant material. In this case, incidental information, which is not rehearsed, decays before it can be encoded into long-term memory (Kumar, 1971).

The small capacity of the short-term memory to process information can also be increased by employing *chunking* strategies (Kumar, 1971; Miller, 1956). By organizing the stimulus into a sequence of chunks, the information is put into more manageable units (Miller, 1956). These chunks can then be remembered separately and chained together. Rothkopf (1970) describes a similar process of *segmentation*, which results in a linkage of terms during reading activities.

Questions at this stage can serve to maintain and renew the items stored in short-term memory. They may also aid learners in organizing information into manageable chunks or propositions. Feedback would serve to confirm the adequacy of rehearsal strategies or the propositions and provide reinforcement. Prompts or cues might be used to aid in the process of chaining and linking various sequential chunks together (Anderson, 1970). These hints could then be faded as the student becomes more proficient in the task. Prompts help the learner respond correctly to a question by focusing attention on relevant stimuli (Wager & Wager, 1985). Two recognized types of prompts include (1) formal prompts, such as spaced blanks in questions which denote the length of the answer, and (2) thematic, contextual, or grammatical cues. Questions with prompts probably work by decreasing cognitive load during early stages of learning, and aid encoding by providing for rehearsal and repetition.

Providing Learner Guidance:
Semantic Encoding for Storage in Long-Term Memory

Information which has successfully been maintained in short-term memory must be semantically encoded for storage in long-term memory. Questions may be used at this stage to encourage learners to integrate new knowledge into existing cognitive structures. Andre (1979) distinguishes two distinct memory stores within long-term memory: (1) episodic memory, which contains a record of events encountered, and (2) semantic memory, which contains abstracted or generalized knowledge such as concepts, principles, rules, and skills that are broader than specific episodes. He suggests that this knowledge is represented as schema in semantic memory and that semantic memory consists of a network of interrelated schema. He also estimates that higher-level questions influence the nature of the representation that is formed when learners acquire new information in semantic memory. Kumar (1971) also suggests that encoding may be the same thing as schematizing. The addition of new knowledge to existing memory schemas is referred to as *accretion*, the most common mode of learning (Norman, 1982).

Semantic encoding includes an internal sensory representation or image of a thing or event named by a word (Anderson, 1970). Coding is a control process exercised by the student that will affect transfer of information from short-term storage to long-term storage. Coding can even allow students to store information as it comes along, without necessarily maintaining it through rehearsal in the short-term storage (cited in Kumar, 1971). But the success of this process may depend on how much existing knowledge there is in long-term storage upon which to build. With more existing knowledge about the incoming information, less rehearsal would be needed (Kumar, 1971). Norman (1982) refers to this process as *tuning*.

> Tuning is the fine adjustment of knowledge to a task. The proper schemas exist and appropriate knowledge is within them. But they are inefficient for the purpose, either because they are too general or because they are mismatched to the particular use that is required of them, so the knowledge must be tuned, continually adjusted to the task. Practice is one way of accomplishing tuning. (p. 81)

Atkinson and Shiffrin (1968) summarize the mechanisms by which coding facilitates performances as (1) making use of strong pre-existing associations, (2) greatly decreasing the effective area of memory to be searched during a test, (3) greatly increasing the amount of information stored, and (4) protecting new associations from interference by succeeding items.

Questions may reduce the variance in processing information, thereby enabling or facilitating rapid encoding (Miller, 1956). For example, in a rote memorization task of memorizing a list of words, the way in which a question is constructed can aid in more rapid encoding of the task. Consider the following list of words:

APPLE	SHIRT
CHAIR	CARROT
PANTS	ORANGE
ONION	PLATE
CHERRY	SHOES
TABLE	POTATO

To successfully memorize the list in 30 seconds may prove somewhat difficult. However if a student is asked to memorize the words as presented in a new list—one in which the words have been put into sets which allow for them to be remembered according to some sort of prior schema—the words are much easier to successfully memorize in the allotted 30 seconds:

Categories

SHIRT	CARROT
PANTS	ONION
SHOES	POTATO
TABLE	APPLE
CHAIR	ORANGE
PLATE	CHERRY

However, the group given the first list with the question, "What four categories of things can the following list be sorted into?" should be able to produce the second list for themselves. Reigeluth (1983) describes this as strategy activation. If questions cause a forward transfer effect, as described by Sagerman and Meyer (1987), these types of questions might build a stronger use of strategies in future learning, at least for students who are able to apply the strategy.

Feedback given in response to questions which serve to aid in semantic encoding can validate the integration of new information with pre-existing knowledge or it may serve to equalize question links between existing structures and new structures even further. Feedback also may serve as learning guidance through the demonstration of processes. Elaboration in feedback provides the opportunty for additional information to be stored. In fact, elaborations provide redundancy in the memory structure which can act as a safeguard against forgetting and as an aid in fast retrieval (Reder, 1980).

Eiliciting Performance:
Retrieval from Long-Term Memory to Working Memory

To see that retrieval from long-term memory to working memory can be successfully accomplished, performance of the task must be elicited from the learner. Questions in this sense will act to retrieve the information and to provide practice in generalization. Although storage in short-term memory is resistant to forgetting, information is not always available for recall (Kumar, 1971). Shiffrin and Atkinson (cited in Kumar) attribute retrieval failure to an inadequate search strategy or possibly to an insufficient storage of information.

Questions can be used to activate response organization. According to Bartlett (cited in Kumar, 1971), "a schema is an active organization of past experiences" (p. 403). Although schemas may be different, they are still interconnected by common factors in an organized way. The process of reconstruction activates a number of relevant schemas to recreate the event (Kumar, 1971). Questions can act to help in this process of reconstruction by cueing these relevant schemas.

Post-questions act as confirmation for important mathemagenic behaviors, maintaining appropriate responses on succeeding portions of text (Frase, 1970). Questions can test for understanding or misunderstanding. Questions can also act to reinforce learning behaviors. Feedback acts to remediate misunderstanding and to provide spaced reinforcement.

Hamaker (1986) suggests that students receiving feedback to adjunct questions may adopt a passive attitude toward the questions because they know the correct answer will eventually be presented. This would imply that feedback would limit the amount of information search engaged in by a student and lead to a lower level of incidental learning.

Providing Feedback: Response Generation

When a response is generated, the learner attempts to confirm the correctness or appropriateness of the response. Feedback serves to provide reinforcement and corrective information to the student which in turn works to provide cues for future performance. Feedback can address whether or not the question was correctly interpreted and whether or not the answer was adequate. Probably the most important role of feedback at this stage is to correct misunderstandings. This may require a significant amount of instructional feedback in the form of remediation. Some learners may be able to self-remediate simply given the correct answer; however, we suspect that poorer learners will not. Correction of misunderstandings would be most important in intellectual skill tasks where the learning of new material is dependent on an adequate cognitive structure of prerequisite skills.

Much research has been done on the timing of this feedback, differences in types of feedback, learner certitude, and many other variables which are the focus of other chapters in this book, so we will not elaborate on it here. However, the most appropriate type of feedback, at this stage, would be confirmation of correct answers and remediation of misunderstandings inferred from incorrect answers.

Assessing the Performance:
Performance in the Learner's Environment

Performance via a posttest or retention test is probably the most common way that questions are used. Assessing whether or not the task can be performed gives the opportunity for reinforcement and/or correction due to variations in context. Feedback is provided to confirm that the skill has been generalized to a range of situations. If the task happens to be a simulation of some sort, feedback occurs as the effects of the learner's chosen actions. Feedback on performance tests serves a much broader purpose than simply telling us our expertise on a particular set of questions. From assessments we receive grades and information about our performance in comparison to others. This leads to the formation of attitudes about our abilities, and may well affect our perceptions of competency and motivations for similar learning tasks. Poorly constructed tests or inappropriate feedback might have long-term effects on future learning.

Enhancing Retention and Transfer:
Control of Processes through Executive Strategies

Norman (1982) suggests that we are constantly tuning existing cognitive structures, adding new information, and reorganizing old structures.

Questions may serve in tuning existing schemas to incorporate differences in interpretations. Feedback functions to support this tuning of schema by building new examples. Also, feedback can serve to build the motivational areas of relevance, confidence, and satisfaction with the performance. If activity during learning improves acquisition, then it seems that activity after acquisition increases retention and accuracy. Spaced practice through the use of questions can serve this role.

Knowledge transfer, at the most general level, involves change in the performance of a task as a result of the prior performance of a different task. The difference between "transfer" and "learning" is that in the case of transfer, the two tasks are said to be "different." In transfer paradigms, the "different" task is usually selected to be novel to the student (Gick & Holyoak, 1987). The encoding of a training task will aid subsequent transfer to the extent that the learner has acquired rules that will apply to a range of different tasks with "structural commonalities." According to Gick and Holyoak (1987), "If the transfer task evokes similar goals and processing mechanisms, or has salient surface resemblances to the training task, these common components then serve as the basis for retrieval of the acquired knowledge in the transfer context" (p. 40).

One important influence cited as affecting the encoding of the training task is direct feedback about performance levels (Gick & Holyoak, 1987). Feedback can provide guidance and cues as to which rule to apply in certain transfer problems. Similarly, questions which invoke certain commonalities to be recognized and appropriately corresponding rules to be applied can serve as a vehicle for transfer.

Summary

Questions and feedback are inextricably related. Recently the process-product paradigm research on questions was compared to a sociolinguistic perspective (Carlson, 1991). Carlson argues that the meaning of questions is dependent on their context in discourse, and that the content of questions cannot be ignored. Some of Carlson's criticisms of research on classroom questions seem pertinent also for research on feedback. Feedback is always related to a response generated by a question. In this sense, the meaning of feedback is dependent upon its context in the instruction.

Feedback effectiveness may also be dependent upon certain learner variables, such as the learner's confidence in his or her answer. But these personal factors influencing feedback's effectiveness may vary according to the type of learning task involved (see Mory, 1991) and may very well have fluctuating influences within each stage of information-processing, as well.

Function of the question	Function and type of feedback
1. Gain Attention	1. Arousal, create cognitive dissonance. Open-ended questions with no feedback.
2. Inform the learner of the objective.	2. Create an expectancy for performance. Rhetorical questions and didactic answers could be used to inform the student of the objectives.
3. Stimulate the recall of prerequisite learning	3. Bring related knowledge into short-term memory and confirm present knowledge. Questions eliciting analogies with right-wrong or conditional feedback could be used to test the understanding of prerequisites. Pretests may serve the same function (with or without feedback).
4. Present the stimulus material	4. Socratic dialogue to have the student deduce what information is needed. Feedback takes the form of confirmation of responses, and probing questions to guide inquiry
5. Provide learning guidance	5. Questions provide for modeling component parts of the skill being learned. Feedback should show correct analysis by the student.
6. Elicit the performance	6. Questions recall learned skill or components of the learned skill to test for misunderstanding. Feedback should be remedial, directed at the misunderstanding if possible.
7. Provide feedback	7. Feedback should be chosen to fit the purpose that the question is serving in the instructional process. It is possible that the type of feedback should vary with the learners performance and confidence. Give knowledge of correctness and remediation for incorrect answers.
8. Assess performance	8. The purpose is to inform the student of progress toward mastery. Feedback should inform the student of the adequacy of his or her performance.
9. Enhance retention and transfer	9. Provide for spaced practice of the newly learned skill in an authentic situation. Immediate feedback as to correctness would seem most appropriate.

Table 3.3. Recommendations for the use of questions and feedback related to stages of information processing.

In this chapter, we have attempted to show that questions serve many different roles in the learning process, and so it is reasonable to postulate that feedback also serves different purposes at different stages in learning. Table 3.3 provides some examples of how the role of the question might determine the appropriate type of feedback. It seems unlikely that we will find any universal agreement on the "best" type of feedback. One has to ask "Feedback for what?" and take into consideration the type of question, the stage of information processing, and conditions within the learner to arrive at an answer.

References

Anderson, R.C. (1970). Control of student mediating processes during verbal learning and instruction. *Review of Educational Research, 40*(3), 349–369.

Anderson, R.C., & Biddle, W.B. (1975). On asking people questions about what they are reading. In G. Bower (Ed.), *The psychology of learning and motivation*, Vol. 9 (pp. 89–132). New York: Academic Press.

Andre, T. (1979). Does answering higher-level questions while reading facilitate productive learning? *Review of Educational Research, 49*(2), 280–318.

Atkinson, R.C., & Shiffrin, R.M. (1968). Human memory: A proposed system and its control processes. In K.W. Spence & J.T. Spence (Eds.), *The psychology of learning and motivation*, Vol. 2. New York: Academic Press.

Ausubel, D.P. (1968). *Educational psychology: A cognitive view.* New York: Holt, Rinehart, & Winston.

Bangert-Drowns, R.L., Kulik, C.C., Kulik, J.A. Morgan, M. (1991). The instructional effect of feedback in test-like events. *Review of Educational Research, 61*(2), 213–238.

Bull, S.G. (1973). The role of questions in maintaining attention to textual material. *Review of Educational Research, 43*, 83–87.

Carlson, W.S. (1991). Questioning in classrooms: A sociolinguistic perspective. *Review of Educational Research, 61*(2).

Duchastel, P. (1983). Interpreting adjunct question research: Processes and ecological validity. *Human Learning, 2*, 1–5.

Faw, H.W., & Waller, T.G. (1976). Mathemagenic behaviors and effiency in learning from prose materials: Review critique and recommendations. *Review of Educational Research, 46*(4), 691–720.

Frase, L.T. (1970). Boundary conditions for mathemagenic behaviors. *Review of Educational Research, 40*(3), 337–347.

Gagné, R.M. (1985). *The conditions of learning* (4th ed.). New York: Holt, Rinehart, & Winston.

Gagné, R.M., Briggs, L.J., & Wager, W.W. (1992). *Principles of instructional design* (4th ed.). New York: Holt, Rinehart, & Winston.

Gall, M.D. (1970). The use of questions in teaching. *Review of Educational Research, 40*(5), 707–721.

Gick, M.L., & Holyoak, K.J. (1987). The cognitive basis of knowledge transfer. In S.M. Cormier & F.D. Hagman (Eds.), *Transfer of learning: Contemporary reasearch and applications* (pp. 9–46). Orlando, FL: Academic Press, Inc.

Hamaker, C. (1986). The effects of adjunct questions on prose learning. *Review of Educational Research, 56*(2), 212–242.

Hamilton, R.J. (1985). A framework for the evaluation of the effectiveness of adjunct questions and objectives. *Review of Educational Research, 55*(1), 47–85.

Kulhavy, R.W. (1977). Feedback in written instruction. *Review of Educational Research, 47*(1), 211–232.

Kulhavy, R.W., & Stock, W.A. (1989). Feedback in written instruction: The place of response certitude. *Educational Psychology Review, 1*(4), 279–308.

Kumar, V.K. (1971). The structure of human memory and some educational implications. *Review of Educational Research, 41*(5), 379–417.

Ladas, H. (1973). The mathemagenic effects of factual review questions on the learning of incidental information: A critical review. *Review of Educational Research, 43*(1), 71–82.

Miller, G.A. (1956). The magical number seven, plus or minus two: Some limits on our capacity for processing information. *The Psychological Review, 63*(2), 81–97.

Mory, E.H. (1991). *The effects of adaptive feedback on student performance, feedback study time, and lesson efficiency within computer-based instruction.* Unpublished doctoral dissertation. Florida State University, Tallahassee.

Mouton, H., & Reigeluth, C.M. (1987). *Adjunct questions and mediated self instruction: Comparisons of lookback and no-lookback procedures, with high or low level questions, massed or inserted in the text.* (IDD&E Working Paper No. 24). Syracuse, NY: Syracuse University, School of Education. (ERIC Document Reproduction Service No. ED 289 471).

Norman, D.A. (1982). *Learning and memory.* New York: W.H. Freeman and Company.

Reder, L.M. (1980). The role of elaboration in the comprehension and retention of prose: A critical review. *Review of Educational Research, 50*(1), 5–53.

Reigeluth, C. (1983). Meaningfulness and instruction: Relating what is being learned to what a student already knows. *Instructional Science, 12,* 197–218.

Reynolds, R.E., & Anderson, R.C. (1982). Influence of questions on the allocation of attention during reading. *Journal of Educational Psychology, 74*(5), 623–632.

Rickards, J.P. (1979). Adjunct postquestions in text: A critical review of methods and processes. *Review of Educational Research, 49*(2), 181–196.

Rothkopf, E.Z. (1970). The concept of mathemagenic activities. *Review of Educational Research, 40*(3), 325–336.

Rothkopf, E.Z., & Bisbicos, E.E. (1967). Selective facilitative effects of interspersed questions on learning from written materials. *Journal of Educational Psychology, 58*(1), 56–61.

Rothkopf, E.Z., & Kaplan, R. (1972). Exploration of the effect of density and specificity of instructional objectives on learning from text. *Journal of Educational Psychology, 63*(4), 295–302.

Sagerman, N., & Meyer, R. (1987). Forward transfer of different reading strategies evoked by adjunct questions in science text. *Journal of Educational Psychology, 79*(2), 189–191.

Sternberg, S. (1969). The discovery of processing stages: Extension of Donder's method. *Acta Psychologica, 30,* 276–315.

Wager, W., & Wager, S. (1985). Presenting questions, processing responses, and providing feedback in CAI. *Journal of Instructional Development, 8*(4), 2–8.

Washborne, J.N. (1929). The use of questions in social science material. *Journal of Educational Psychology, 20,* 321–359.

West, C.K., Farmer, J.A., & Wolff, P.M. (1991). *Instructional design: Implications from cognitive science.* Englewood Cliffs, NJ: Prentice-Hall.

Chapter Four

Designing Instructional Feedback for Different Learning Outcomes

Patricia L. Smith
University of Oklahoma

and

Tillman J. Ragan
University of Oklahoma

Interactivity is the critical instructional design feature of interactive technologies as it is one-half of the interaction loop. Feedback is the instructional system's response to the learner's actions. Some feedback within the system is instructionally trivial, such as the shift from one screen to another with the press of an "enter" key. However, *instructional feedback* is non-trivial and central to the learning process. Instructional feedback provides information to learners about the quality of their responses. This feedback may provide information as to correctness, timeliness, efficiency, accuracy, or precision of a response. It may inform learners of how their performance compares to others or how their performance compares with their own previous performance. Feedback may include motivational elements to encourage perseverance with the instructional task. Along with practice, feedback is among the most instructionally robust experiences that designers can arrange for learners.

As powerful a factor as feedback may be, about the only conclusion that can be drawn with much certitude from research on instructional feedback is that some feedback is better than no feedback (Kulhavy, 1977; Schimmel, 1983). Even this conclusion is not universal (e.g., Steinberg, 1981; Hyman & Tobias, 1981). Instructional designers who seek guidance in making decisions regarding the nature and scheduling of feedback are often disappointed by the seeming ambiguity of the conclusions drawn from feedback research. Reviewers of the feedback research find it confounded by so many factors that drawing conclusions across studies can be impossible. The following factors seem to vary considerably across studies and in many cases are not clearly described so that comparisons and generalizations across studies cannot be made. Confounding variables in research include:

a. Content of feedback and theoretical rationale for that content. Although researchers have attempted to standardize and categorize kinds of feedback such as KCR (knowledge of correct response), KOR (knowledge of response), and explanatory feedback, we find writers attempting to draw conclusions across studies that have misused these terms or used the term "feedback" generically for reinforcement, information, and remediation.

b. Instructional event which feedback follows—pretest, practice, posttest. A number of reviews have attempted to generalize effects of feedback that was presented after a response during a pretest, without exposure to instruction, and feedback presented after a posttest. The information content and scheduling of feedback following tests may need to be quite different from that which follows practice and which may be used as information for the learner in subsequent practice. Instructionally embedded feedback, which follows practice, attempts to meet information needs of the learner that are importantly different from those needs during assessment events.

c. Amount and nature of information available to learners prior to requiring response of learner. Instruction which is highly generative may rely more on feedback than instruction which is highly supplantive. For example, in a highly generative lesson, one which involves learning from exploration in a data-rich environment but with little or no guidance from instruction, feedback from interacting in the environment will be a primary source of whatever learning takes place. In more highly structured, supplantive instruction, in which material is carefully structured, sequenced, presented, and practiced, the information needs which feedback are to provide are more refined and limited.

d. Characteristics of learners. The amount of prior knowledge that learners possess on a topic may greatly influence the amount and content of feedback. Learners with extensive prior knowledge may require only correct/incorrect feedback. Learners with limited prior knowledge may need more extensive information, hints, and guidance that might actually inhibit more informed learners. It is possible that learners with different cognitive styles or personality characteristics may require different amounts and forms of feedback (Nishikawa, 1988). Individual differences among learners in their motivation, anxiety, and self-efficacy also may impact feedback needs.

e. Second try on same or similar question available. An important instructional variable related to feedback is whether feedback is immediately followed by an opportunity to apply corrective information supplied by feedback on a subsequent practice opportunity. Feedback may be used in immediate subsequent practice, or instruction may require that the information provided by the feedback be held in mind for a long period of time before being able to apply it. When a "second try" or other subsequent practice opportunity is not provided in instruction, the utility of feedback and how it is applied may be altered substantially. The research is not entirely clear as to what mechanism is functioning in second-try feedback. Noonan (1984) investigated the learning of procedural rules in high school algebra, providing second tries with variations in feedback. Noonan found no differential effects for second tries. But Nielson (1990), investigating college-age students' learning of navigation skills found that second tries increased performance on both immediate and delayed tests. Siegel and Misselt (1984) found improvements in verbal information learning from information feedback with review of missed items, while Lee, Smith, and Savenye (1991) failed to find such an effect.

f. Learning task. Much of instructional design theory (e.g. Gagné, 1985; Merrill, 1983; Reigeluth, 1983) is based upon the precept that different kinds of learning tasks require different instructional strategies. Gagné (1985) and Anderson (1985) have proposed that different mental processes are demanded of the learner depending upon the type of instructional task. Gagné extended this theory to propose that different types of learning require different "conditions of learning." One of the external events that Gagné proposes provides these conditions of learning is the feedback event, therefore suggesting that feedback characteristics may need to be different for different kinds of learning outcomes. That relationship, between learning task and feedback, is the focus of this chapter.

Instructional researchers have recognized the need to investigate relationships between feedback and learning outcomes. Indeed, Schimmel's (1983) meta-analysis found differences in the value of informative feedback for declarative versus procedural learning. Although research may have suggested that there is a need for different feedback for different types of learning outcomes, there is insufficient information from research to indicate what that difference should be. Until this research is available, we must examine the theoretical cognitive processing requirements of different varieties of learning and estimate the feedback requirements for them in order to suggest the nature of practice and feedback that would best serve those requirements. That theory-based conjecture is the purpose of this chapter.

As we proceed in this chapter, we will note examples of research that have been conducted related to points being discussed. In addition, readers will find many points amenable to further research.

Before discussing specific types of learning and their associated requirements for feedback, it would be helpful to take a look at the event of instruction that immediately proceeds embedded feedback: practice. Following discussion of the practice event, feedback itself will be discussed with particular attention to needs imposed by different types of learning.

Practice as an Instructional Event

Following presentation of content, learners can be given the opportunity to interact actively with the material being learned and see if they are ready to proceed with the next part of the lesson. It is not the purpose of this event to evaluate learners for grading, but rather to (a) provide for learners' active participation in the learning process and (b) assess how learning is "coming along" so that remediation may be provided if learners are not learning. This practice should occur explicitly and across the range of application and difficulty to which learners are expected to transfer their learning.

When operating under the principles of behaviorism, designers created practice that was almost "error-proof," anticipating that a benefit of totally successful practice would be more effective and motivated learners. More recently, following a more cognitive framework, designers have tended to design practice so that it might evoke any misconceptions about the new information the learners might have developed. This direct addressing of common misconceptions actually seems to pique learners' interest even more than successful experience. So, as they design the practice event, designers can consider the ways that learners might go wrong with the content and design practice experiences which will allow them to confront these "bugs" in their learning.

Interactive technologies are particularly good at providing the practice event because they can interact with all learners, asking them to respond and then checking the accuracy of the their responses. Software can be designed so that learners are required to respond in some way, eliminating the possibility of learners "leaning" on other learners' performance, as can happen in group-based interactions. A limitation of interactive technologies, however, is that they are not generally "intelligent." That is, they cannot think or learn on their own. Their lack of intelligence has an impact on practice because the designer must be cautious in the types of questions or other response-eliciting situations the instruction poses. If learners are to be provided with accurate and meaningful feedback, the designer must insure that questions or situations posed will produce responses which can be judged by a computer. Or, they must analyze learners to determine if they are capable of evaluating their open-ended responses with varying degrees of guidance from the system.

Intelligent tutoring systems can be developed to deal with production responses such as short written answers, to some degree. However, these systems can be very expensive and time-consuming to develop, so they will not be easily available across all content areas for some time. For practice in which open-ended responses are required, a teacher or other human may be needed to assess the appropriateness of the learners' responses.

Feedback as an Instructional Event

The purpose of informative feedback is to give learners the opportunity to consider information about the appropriateness of their responses during practice. When learners complete a practice experience they have one or several of the following information needs. Learners may need to know:

(a) If they are correct or incorrect. This type of feedback seems particularly appropriate for verbal information learning.

(b) If they are incorrect, the correct answer. This type of feedback is often used with verbal information and intellectual skills objectives.

(c) Information or hints so they can determine if they are right or wrong and why they were right or wrong. This type of feedback is particularly appropriate for intellectual skills learning.

(d) Information about the faulty solution strategies they are using, with hints for more appropriate strategies, without being explicitly told whether they are correct or incorrect.

(e) The consequences of their responses. This type of feedback can be used for higher-order rule or principle learning, particularly with instruction that is delivered via a simulation.

(f) How to recognize the proprioceptive (internal sensory) feedback that indicates adequate performance. Learners may have to be taught to recognize these sensory cues.

(g) How they have performed over the entire lesson. Learners may be given cumulative information on their progress during practice. For example, they might be told what pattern of errors they are making or how close they are to reaching mastery or a pre-stated criterion of performance.

(h) How their performance compares to their peers or their own previous performance.

(i) Whether their performance was sufficiently efficient or timely.

Feedback may be coupled with second tries with practice items, so that
if learners are incorrect they can use the feedback to correct the error on
that very problem. Except for cases in which feedback provides the correct
answer, feedback may be used in conjunction with several tries so that
learners may have the opportunity to apply the feedback to correct their
own learning. Practice and feedback are formative, not summative, so
learning should continue through practice and feedback.

As you might surmise, the computer is especially good at providing
individualized and immediate feedback to learners. Unlike most other instructional media—other than a human tutor—the feedback learners receive
can be adjusted to the answers they give. In the case of open-ended, production responses in which many answers may be equally correct, learners
may be provided with model answers and/or criteria to employ to judge the
adequacy of their own responses.

In the following sections, we will discuss how the nature of practice and
feedback must vary from one type of learning to another. We will start with
declarative knowledge, continue with three types of intellectual skills—concepts, rules, and problem solving—then consider cognitive strategies, attitudes, and psychomotor skills.

Declarative Knowledge and Feedback

Declarative knowledge involves "knowing that" something is the case
(Anderson, 1985). It is often what we mean when we want learners to "understand" content. Other words that we use to describe declarative knowledge performance are explain, "describe in your own words," label, recite,
summarize, list, etc. Gagné and Briggs (1979) divided declarative knowledge learning, which they termed "verbal information," into three types:
label and names, facts and lists, and organized discourse.

The learning of all declarative knowledge has certain requirements. E.
Gagné (1985) summarizes the process of learning new declarative knowledge as four phases of active mental activity: (1) new knowledge is presented via some medium and apprehended by the learner, (2) the material
presented is translated by the learner into propositions, (3) related propositions in the learner's memory are activated (linking), and (4) elaborations
are generated by the learner as new "connections" stimulate the making of
inferences. When organized discourse is the desired outcome, learners must
often mentally organize the new information.

Practice for Declarative Knowledge Learning

As learners receive new information, they must actively organize it by clumping sets together, separating sets from one another, subordinating, and making relationships among sets. In order to support the mental activities required for learning declarative knowledge, practice should require linking existing knowledge, organizing and elaborating. One consideration in designing practice for declarative knowledge learning is determining whether the learning task requires recall or whether it only requires recognition. Another consideration in determining the amount of practice needed is, if recall is required, whether the recall should be verbatim or if it may be paraphrased. As automaticity may be critical in many declarative knowledge learning tasks, some declarative knowledge performances may require more extended practice than others.

Practice for labels should be presentation of one of the two elements in the association, such as presenting "Na" and requiring the learner to provide the other element—"sodium." Practice for labels can be verbatim recall or recognition.

Practice for connected discourse is most often in the form of paraphrased recall. Learners are asked to explain, summarize, or describe in their own words content that has been provided in the discourse. Occasionally, learners may be asked to recognize paraphrased statements which best represent the content or they may be asked to determine if a single statement accurately reflects the content.

Feedback for Declarative Knowledge Learning

For labels, facts, and lists, the requirements of feedback are relatively straightforward. Feedback for labels and facts should evaluate whether the response that the learner supplied is complete and whether the associations are correct. Richards (1989) found that this feedback (that shows the pairing of an object and its label) is more effective if there is a format that delays the feedback temporarily and requires the learner to covertly respond a second time to the question (a covert second try, *prior* to feedback). Lists may have two elements, completeness and sequence, which must be evaluated. If answers reflect miscombination of associations, the feedback might point out the error. The simple provision of correct/incorrect may be sufficient for this type of learning: are links correct, is organization reasonable, are elaborations appropriate? Schimmel's meta-analysis (1983) concluded that confirmation feedback is more potent than correct answer feedback in verbal learning tasks. Kulhavy, White, Topp, Chan, & Adams (1985) found knowledge of correct response to be more beneficial than more complex feedback. These findings are reinforced by those of Siegel and Misselt

(1984), who also found that simpler feedback was more effective than complex feedback.

For organized discourse, provision of feedback generally requires that instruction either have an "intelligent" evaluator or provide model responses. An "intelligent" evaluator generally is a knowledgeable human; however, some computer-based intelligent tutoring systems (ITS) may incorporate sufficient natural language processing and "intelligence" to assess a constructed answer. A model response should be constructed with attention to modeling organization, links of information, and elaborations that are essential features of an appropriate answer.

Concept Learning and Feedback

Merrill and Tennyson define a concept as "a set of specific objects, symbols, or events which are grouped together on the basis of shared characteristics and which can be referenced by a particular name or symbol" (1977, p. 3). Some conceptual learning can be viewed more as declarative knowledge, however, to be classified in the intellectual skills/procedural learning category, one must be able to classify instances named by a definitional rule.

We say that learners have acquired a concept when they have learned to recognize a "pattern" in their surroundings and consistently respond to that pattern no matter what nonessential features may appear along with that pattern. Learning a concept requires two cognitive processes—generalization and discrimination. When learners are first exposed to a member of a concept they must learn to *generalize* beyond the single instance of that concept they encounter to others which fall into the same category. So concept learners must *discriminate* between examples of the concept and nonexamples which may share some features with the concept but do not share the critical attributes which make one instance a member of the class and another instance not a member of a group.

Cognitive psychologists theorize that concepts are mentally stored in the form of productions, an if-then representation. For example, a generic representation of a concept production might be stored in the form:

IF the instance has attribute A
    and the instance has attribute B
    and the instance has attribute C
    and the instance has attribute D
THEN the instance is a member of concept X.

Practice for Concept Learning

Practice for concepts should involve the application of the concept across the range of difficulty of the concept from the most simple-to-discriminate to the most difficult. Although the practice may be built from simple practice to more difficult discriminations, it is useful if the settings from which the examples and nonexamples are drawn are as random as possible. This practice should include learners' distinguishing between previously unencountered examples and nonexamples of the concept, some of which require the learner's explanation of why a choice was made, which should include the learners' isolating the attributes of the examples and nonexamples that make them so. The examples and nonexamples used should be carefully selected to elicit any misconceptions the learners might have. These examples and nonexamples should provide opportunities for learners to over- and undergeneralize the concept. In addition learners should practice producing their own examples.

Feedback for Concept Learning

Merrill and Tennyson (1977) suggest that feedback provided to the learners should include an explanation of why an instance is classified as an example or nonexample. They suggest that this information isolate and either verbally or visually focus upon the critical attributes of the concept that clarifies why the instance is or is not a member of a concept class. With an interactive medium this "why" explanation may be placed under the learners' control, especially if the learners have high prior knowledge or effective cognitive strategies. If learners have *overgeneralized* the concept, the explanation may provide clear information as to why the nonexamples they said were examples are not actually examples of that concept. They should be informed of what criterial attributes they are overlooking. If learners have *undergeneralized* the concept, they should be encouraged to determine which features of examples they chose are not actually criterial attributes of the concept. These learners have narrowed the concept inappropriately in some way and need to recognize that they have done so. Designers may construct their questions in such a way that that the system may determine whether the learner is over- or undergeneralizing. To provide such feedback, the program may be designed to delay feedback until the learner has responded to a number of instances. Then the program can analyze the responses to determine whether there is a pattern suggesting a misconception (either over- or undergeneralization) and provide hints or direct feedback to aid the learner's remediation of the problem.

Research has provided some insight into beneficial characteristics of feedback for concept learning. Gilman (1969) found that explanation of answers increased learning of science concepts by college students over less informative feedback. In his research with elementary science students, Reigeluth's (1983) data suggested that provision of hints along with correct/incorrect feedback may produce greater learning than correct answer or correct/incorrect feedback alone. Nielson (1990) also found that more informative feedback supports concept learning. His instruction teaching the navigational concept of "basic pilotage" to college students found a significant influence of amount of information in feedback on delayed posttest performance. In contrast to Merrill and Tennyson's expectations, J. Merrill (1987) did not find that attribute isolation feedback enhanced college-age students' skill in recognizing instances of fictitious science concepts more than correct/incorrect feedback accompanied by repetition of relevant instructional passages.

Feedback for open-ended answers—answers in which learners provide their own examples of the concept—generally cannot be evaluated by an interactive system. Feedback for production answers can be provided through guiding questions that are keyed to the criterial attributes of the concept. This information can be used by learners to evaluate the adequacy of their own answers (e.g., "Is the example that you gave of a transparent object an object through which an image can be clearly seen? If so, it is a transparent object.").

Rule Learning and Feedback

Rules may be of two types: relational rules and procedural rules. **Relational rules** prescribe the relationship(s) among two or more concepts. These relationships are often described in the form of an if-then or cause-effect relationship. Other names that have been used for relational rules are propositions, principles, laws, axioms, theorems, and postulates. Equations from mathematics and science are abbreviated forms of relational rules as they state the relationships among concepts.

Gagné (1985) points out that a rule describes the relationship among the concepts in the rule. These concepts are often in the form of variables, factors that can have many values. These rules or principles allow learners to predict, explain, or control the interaction of these variables (Davis, Alexander, & Yelon, 1974). The application of a rule enables learners to *predict* what will happen if one of the concepts (variables) is changed. Rules also allow the learner to *explain* what has happened. Finally, knowing a rule allows you to *control* the effects of variables upon each other.

The processes underlying knowing a relational rule can be identified in the productions associated with them:

IF the situation described involves key concept A

and if the situation described involves key concept B

THEN rule Q applies in this case (concept recognition)

so,

IF concept A changes in direction R with magnitude Z

THEN concept B will change in direction M with a magnitude of N.

Prior knowledge of the concepts represented in the relational rule (in the above production, identified as concepts A and B) is prerequisite to learning a relational rule. One of the main cognitive tasks in learning a rule is learning to recognize the situation in which these two or more concepts are related in a way such that the rule applies. This recognition requires the generalization of the rule to more contexts beyond those instances first encountered. It also requires discrimination in which the learner learns to recognize occasions in which the rule does not apply. The learner must also be able to state, or otherwise symbolically represent, the relationship of these concepts (a verbal information component of the task). Next, the learner must determine which concept or concepts have changed and the magnitude and direction of the change. Finally, the learner must determine what the effect of these changes will have on the other concept(s).

Practice for Relational Rules

When practicing relational rules learners should practice at four levels:

a. Learners should practice verbally or graphically expressing the rule. Although research results are somewhat mixed regarding the *necessity* of actually being able to state a rule to apply it, it is very useful for learners to have practice in stating the principle or rule.

b. Learners should practice recognizing situations in which the rule is applicable. If students have previously learned related rules, that might be easily confused with the application of the current rule; this practice may include questions that require that the learners distinguish among them.

c. Learners should practice applying the rule. Students should have the opportunity to actually practice applying the rule to predict, explain, or control the effects of one concept on another. To a degree, applying the rule requires that the learners be able to perform the skills practiced in (a) and (b) above. This practice should be across the range of difficulty and applicability of the rule, so as with the examples, the learners are exposed to the range of situations in which the rule is applicable. The situations should vary as much as possible on noncritical aspects (i.e., concepts/variables that are not related by the rule). Some of the practice items should require learners to explain their answers. Some items may ask students to generate their own examples of the application of the rule. Learners might be asked to explain their answers by relating their explanations explicitly to the principles that define the relationships of the variables.

d. Learners should practice determining whether a rule has been correctly applied. It is important that they do not practice at this level until they are skilled at applying the rule, as practiced in (c) above, because they should not be confused by incorrect applications of a rule before they are skilled in its correct application. However, it is important that they be able to scan a solution to a situation in which the rule has been applied and determine if the solution is reasonable and appropriate. They must have this skill to ''check'' their own solutions; therefore, it can be helpful for them to be presented with carefully constructed incorrect solutions and be asked if the answers are reasonable and why or why not. The incorrect solutions could represent common misconceptions or errors which learners make when applying a particular rule. After learners have identified whether the rule has been properly applied, they should be asked to explain their decision. This explanation is important in this situation because, with a dichotomous answer (yes/no), learners have a strong possibility of guessing the answer correctly without actually being able to apply the rule. Requiring an explanation insures that to be able to answer the question correctly the learners must truly be able to apply the rule.

Feedback for Relational Rules

Feedback varies for each type of practice question:

a. For items that practice verbalizing or visualizing the rule, feedback should provide information as to whether their statements contain the key concepts of the rule and relate these concepts appropriately. Feedback might also include identification of any extraneous or incorrect information included in the statement of the rule. Certain of these judgments might be operationalized via keyword searches and other algorithms. In other cases, feedback might be limited to a model answer, with an emphasis of critical features of the statement. Such feedback might also include identification of common errors and factors that should not be included in the answer.

b. Items that practice recognizing situations in which the rule is applicable should be followed with feedback that identifies (1) whether the rule under consideration is applicable, and (2) what features of the situation make the rule applicable or not applicable. The explanatory portion of this feedback might, depending upon learners' prior knowledge and cognitive strategy skill, be placed under learner conrol, as Phye (1979) has suggested that explanatory feedback may confuse some learners.

c. For items in which learners actually practice applying the rule, feedback should provide the outcome of the application of the rule. This may be a single answer, or it may describe the direction and magnitude of the change in one concept (variable) when there is a change in another variable. It is also helpful to make available explanatory feedback in the form of a step-by-step solution of the item, a highlighting of critical features in the item that influence the application of the rule, or by illustrating in graphic form how the solution can be drawn by applying the rule to the information given. Lee *et al.* 1991, in their CAI-delivered study of college students' ability to apply rules in computer programming, found a significant superiority of a more informative, explanatory feedback than simple correct/incorrect feedback. A study reported by Hartley and Lovell (1979), which appears to have required principle application by chemistry students, supports the interaction of amount of explanation and learners' aptitude.

d. Feedback for items in which the learners determine whether a rule has been correctly applied should include correct answer feedback (e.g., "yes, the rule has been applied correctly," or "no, it has not been applied correctly"). Additionally, for situations in which the rule has not been correctly applied, the feedback should specifically point out the error in the application, and how the rule should have been applied.

As with concept learning, the system may analyze responses over a series of similar questions to determine a pattern indicating a bug or misconception. In such a case, the system may provide a hint and encourage the learner to modify the response, or the system may provide direct corrective feedback that is tailored to the particular bug the learner manifests.

Procedural rules are a generalizable series of steps initiated in response to a particular class of circumstances to reach a specified goal. Procedures are often strictly defined—all steps are included, with no ambiguity in each step. Many procedural rules are algorithms. For example, mathematics operations can be procedural rules that are algorithmic. Procedural rules may be simple, with only one set of steps which the learner goes through linearly; or they may be complex, with many decision points, with each decision point leading to a different path, or branch, through the algorithm. Decision points are points in a procedure at which the learner must determine which of two (sometimes more) situations exist (a kind of concept recognition, e.g., "is the appliance connected to a power source?"). Based upon this determination, one branch or another of the procedure will be followed.

Just as with relational rules, procedural rules also require that productions be learned. Productions for procedures may follow the general pattern:

IF the situation contains certain distinguishing features X, Y, Z
(usually understood as concepts),
THEN follow procedure P.

An information-processing analysis for procedural rules is somewhat different from that for relational rules:

1. Recognize a situation in which the procedural rule is applicable.
2. Recall the procedural rule.
3. Apply the steps in the procedure.
4. If required, make decisions at the decision points.
5. If required, choose correct branch(es).
6. Complete steps in required branch(es).
7. Ascertain that procedure has been applied appropriately.

Practice for Procedural Rules

Although the ultimate goal of learning a procedure is the ability to perform all four of its components, it is usually helpful to practice each of these components before moving on to learn how to execute the next component.

a. Learning to determine if the procedure is required. This skill, which is prerequisite to performing the entire procedure, may be practiced by presenting or having the learners propose situations in which the procedure might be useful. They should then decide in a yes/no decision whether the procedure should be applied. Learners should justify their answers to ensure that they have truly identified the situation by its critical attributes. This practice should begin with situations that clearly require the procedure and move to situations which are less clear because they are complicated with extraneous detail. If learners have previously learned other procedures that are easily confused with the new procedure, they should be presented with some of these situations so that they have practice in distinguishing between these potentially confusing situations.

b. Learning to complete the steps in the procedure. In general, each individual step of the procedure should be practiced immediately after it is presented. This may consist of practicing a decision step by determining which of two or more conditions exists, or practicing an operation step by completing a performance step in the procedure. Landa (1983) suggests that the first step be demonstrated and practiced, then the next step demonstrated and practiced, then steps one and two practiced together. Next, step three is demonstrated and practiced. Then it is practiced with steps one and two. He proposed that this "snowballing" effect of practicing new steps with previously learned steps will enhance learners' learning the entire procedure as a whole.

After completing the practice of individual steps in the procedure, learners should have practice in completing the entire procedure a number of times. With a complex procedure this practice might, after initial instruction, involve only simplified cases. However, after instruction with more complex cases, the practice should occur with situations across as wide a range as possible of situations that the learner might encounter, including some situations which require the simplest or most common path, some that require a more complex and extensive path, and some that do not require the procedure at all.

The application of procedures may be practiced in a number of ways with an interactive medium. If the procedure involves manipulation of hardware, the hardware or a simplification of the hardware may be interfaced with a computer, so that the computer may request and evaluate responses. In other situations, procedures may be simulated with the learner covertly completing the step and then matching the process or product of the step with options presented within the computer-mediated lesson. Or, learners may respond to an open-ended, production question to which they actually provide evidence of their completion of the step(s).

c. Learning to list the steps in the procedure. After learners have practiced executing the procedure, it is critical that they practice recalling the sequence and nature of the steps in the procedure. If learners are learning to complete a procedure that is supported by a job aid, of course, this type of practice will not be necessary. However, if they will be required to remember the steps of the procedure in the correct order, then they must be provided with ample opportunity to actually recite this order. In addition, they should be able to recall critical keywords that summarize the performance at each step. It will also be useful at some point in practice to require learners to expand upon these keywords to ensure that they do indeed denote the entire step of the procedure to the learner.

d. Learning to check the appropriateness of a completed procedure. Practice should also include an opportunity for learners to view the process and/or product of a procedure and determine whether the procedure was performed correctly. This practice should include their overt reviewing of their own performance, as well as the opportunity to review the performance of others. Reviewing others' performances or products allows the learners' to note errors that they may not have made yet in their executions of the procedure, but might commit later in their performance. As a part of this practice, learners may be encouraged to identify the source of the error and suggest approaches for rectifying the problem.

Feedback for Procedural Rules
a. Learning to determine if the procedure is required. Of course, the first type of feedback for this kind of question is confirmatory feedback as to whether the learner has appropriately identified the situations that require the application of the procedure. In addition, some explanatory feedback should be available, probably under learner control, as to why a particular situation does or does not require the application of the procedure.

This feedback should include a discussion of the critical attributes of the situation that requires the application of the procedure and a mapping of these attributes on to the situation, indicating where the attributes do or do not match.

b. Learning to complete the steps in the procedure. Learners should be provided with feedback as to the accuracy of their completion of each step of the procedure. During initial learning phases, when each step is first learned, this feedback may be more detailed than in later practice of the entire procedure. Feedback on decision steps will include information as to whether the learner correctly assessed the nature of the situation and made the correct decision, leading to choosing the correct path in the procedure.

Feedback on completion of operation steps should include not only dichotomous information as to whether the step was correctly completed, but also qualitative information as to whether the inputs into the operation were appropriately selected, whether the outputs of the operation reached any prescribed criterion, and whether the step was completed with acceptable precision and efficiency. For some procedures, such as completion of mathematical operations, it may be fairly straightforward for interactive systems to provide practice in each step and feedback as to whether the process or product of the step is completed correctly.

Procedures with operation steps that have a significant motor component or require operation of equipment or interaction with humans may require simulation in order to allow a response to be judged and appropriate feedback provided. In more open-ended situations, learners can be provided with criteria by which to judge the adequacy of the completion of individual steps in the procedure, just as they can judge the adequacy of the completion of the entire procedure. For some procedures that have a motor component, learners can also be provided with criteria by which to identify the kinesthetic feedback when an operation step is completed appropriately.

As procedures are algorithmic, interactive systems can be designed to analyze learners' completion of each step and the entire procedure for common "bugs." In some content areas, a degree of "intelligence" is required in the system to identify these bugs. In such cases the system develops a solution and compares the learner's solution path to the system's, identifies/determines whether the differences in the solutions are errors on the learner's part, and provides direct remediation for these errors. Certain procedures, such as mathematical processes, may use fairly simple matching of the learner's and system's outcomes, which do not require system "intelligence." The discrepancies between expected and input values can be further analyzed for common errors. Then the system can respond with fairly specific feedback, such as hints or remediation. Such bug-focused feedback has produced effective learning (Anderson & Reiser, 1985).

c. Learning to list the steps in the procedure. For procedures that must be completed without a job aid, feedback on whether the steps of the procedure were remembered and remembered in the correct order is also useful. In initial practice this feedback may be in response to a verbal information question of "list/number the steps of X procedure in the correct order." Later, when the entire procedure is practiced, feedback as to whether all steps were completed and whether they were executed in the correct order may be included in the feedback in response to the entire procedure. Additional feedback might include such hints as to what characteristics of an antecedent step cued the step that followed.

d. Learning to check the appropriateness of a completed procedure. Feedback for this type of practice should include correct-answer feedback as to whether the given procedure has been correctly completed. The learners can then compare this judgment to their own assessments of whether a demonstrated procedure has been executed properly. This general feedback might be followed with a detailed explanation of why a particular decision was made.

Problem-Solving Learning and Feedback

An "expert" is someone who can apply knowledge to solve problems in a particular field of endeavor. Within the field of instructional design, problem-solving is viewed as a specialized skill within a domain of knowledge, rather than a generalized skill that can apply across a variety of content areas. This type of problem solving is often described as "domain-specific" problem solving (or "semantically rich" problem solving) because it emphasizes learning to utilize rules in a specific content area, or domain, rather than general problem solving. Problem solving differs from rule learning because problem solving requires the selection and combination of *multiple* rules in order to solve a problem, rather than a single rule. Problem solving requires the ability to combine previously learned rules, both relational and procedural, declarative knowledge and cognitive strategies within a domain of content to solve previously unencountered problems (de Jong & Ferguson-Hessler, 1986; Gagné, 1985). In order to be able to select from and apply multiple rules, learners must know those rules. They must be able to identify situations in which the rules can be appropriately applied, they must be able to apply the rules, and they must be able to confirm that the rules have been correctly applied. Declarative knowledge helps the learner to understand the problem and limit the "problem space" (i.e., goal state, starting state, possible solution paths) of the problem. This declarative knowledge may organize the rule productions into meaningful relationships, both hierarchically, as some rules may be superordinate to other rules, and conceptually, as some rules may have similar conditions or similar actions.

Problem solving requires cognitive strategies, in addition to the content knowledge represented as rules and declarative knowledge. In addition to specific cognitive strategies, problem solving also requires metacognitive awareness and monitoring. Cognitive strategies can facilitate the learners' understanding and representing the problem; decomposing the problem into subgoals; searching, selecting, and combining relevant knowledge; sequencing application of knowledge; and monitoring the relative success of solutions.

Although a single approach is not clearly identified in the research or theoretical literature, it seems that it is common in problem-solving conditions that the following stages often occur. They may not occur in the same sequence as described as follows:

1. Clarify the given state, including any obstacles or constraints.
2. Clarify the goal state, including criteria for knowing when the goal is reached.
3. Search for relevant prior knowledge of declarative, rule, or cognitive strategies that will aid in solution.
4. Decompose problem into subproblems with subgoals.
5. Determine a sequence for attacking subproblems.
6. Consider possible solution paths to each subproblem using related prior knowledge.
7. Select solution path and apply production knowledge (rules) in appropriate order.
8. Evaluate to determine if goal is achieved. If not revise by returning to (1) above.

Practice for Problem Solving

Chase and Chi (1980) suggest that thousands of hours of practice may be needed to transform a novice into an expert problem solver. After learners have experienced the solution of example problems, they should have the opportunity to solve problems of similar difficulty. Practice may initially include instructional guidance such as hints, guiding questions, presentation of a data base of rules, and suggestions for strategies. These aids should be gradually phased out. Sufficient practice should be provided so that (a) knowledge can be reorganized and elaborated in a manner that supports problem solving, (b) pattern-recognition skills become automatic even with complex problems, (c) identification of subgoals and related rules becomes automatic, and (d) selection and application of strategies is automatic.

Simulations are a common practice format for interactive problem-solving instruction. Simulations give details about the characteristics of a problem situation and require the learner to solve the problem. Initial practice may involve performance of only one stage of problem solving—such as (a) identifying the goal state, (b) identifying relevant information in the problem, (c) identifying relationships among variables, (d) developing a representation of variables in given and goal states, (e) identifying pertinent rules, and (f) confirming the appropriateness of a solution—followed by feedback, rather than having the learner apply the entire process. Later, learners should practice solving the entire problem before receiving feedback. Hints and helps on identifying the goal, relevant information, representing the problem, etc., may be initially available to the learner. Later these options should be disabled so the learners must practice supplying these themselves. Practice should start with problems which have easily recognizable, distinctive features in given and goal states, with little extraneous detail. Gradually more ill-structured problems should be introduced.

As domain-specific problem-solving is heuristic rather than algorithmic, it is difficult to provide feedback for open-ended, productive responses. Therefore, interactive practice formats often involve simulations that provide options for the learners' responses, rather than open-ended questions. Interactive lessons can provide open-ended response opportunities. However, the quality and accuracy of the feedback may be lower than with response formats with restricted options.

Feedback for Problem Solving

If the learner's solution has gone awry, initial feedback may be in the form of hints or guiding questions. Feedback may also be specific in terms of which information is used or misused. Feedback may include information, not only regarding the appropriateness of the learners' solutions, but but also information about efficiency of the solution process. As learners make the transition from novice to expert, they will evidence more automaticity in their problem solving. Therefore, as learners become more and more expert their approaches to problems, their solutions should be more and more streamlined. Feedback on the efficiency or speed of problem solving is appropriate to the extent that genuine expertise is expected as part of the learning goal (as it often will be in problem-solving goals). Feedback information, especially early in the instructional process, may also include whether the learner has correctly performed individual phases of problem solving.

Simulations often provide feedback in the form of presenting learners with the consequences of their decisions. For example, in a lesson on changing oil in a motorcycle engine, the consequences of failure to remember to put more oil back into the system can be shown as the motorcycle rolls to a smoking halt. The system may provide feedback to open-ended response questions by presenting a model of the solution process. Or, if the solution process produces artifacts of the stages of the solution, such as intermediate written solutions, the learners may be given a written or visual model answer to the solution. A model solution may include a description of how the solution led from the given state to the goal state and how the solution represents the goal state. During initial stages of practice, feedback should be immediately available for intermediate stages when responses are deleterious to an eventual successful solution (Alessi & Trollip, 1985; Jonassen & Hannum, 1987). A study by Anderson, Kulhavy, and Andre (1971) seems to support this recommendation. Their study with college students given the learning task of diagnosing myocardial infarction from electrocardiograms suggested that providing the correct answer after incorrect responses during problem-solving lessons led to superior learning to lessons that provided a confirmatory correct answer after only correct responses. It appears that learners' uncorrected errors early in the lesson lead to poorer responses later in the lesson. Later during practice, however, learners should be allowed to work through to a conclusion. Correct solutions may be available under learner control with explanations of individual stages.

Cognitive Strategy Learning and Feedback

Cognitive strategies are those techniques that learners use to control and monitor their own cognitive processes. Cognitive strategies are mental tactics for attending to, organizing, elaborating, manipulating, and retrieving knowledge. They include tactics that support learning, which are sometimes called ''learning strategies.''

The overarching cognitive processes involved in applying a cognitive strategy may be represented as:

1. Analyze the requirements of the learning task.
2. Analyze one's ability to complete the task, including the predictable demands on and limitations of memory.
3. Select/invent an appropriate strategy.
4. Apply the selected strategy.
5. Evaluate the effectiveness of the strategy use.
6. Revise as required.

This overarching process, which is mentally employed by the learner, strongly resembles the information-processing analysis of traditional problem solving. Selection, application, and evaluation of a cognitive strategy is indeed very similar to problem-solving.

Practice for Cognitive Strategies

Initial practice may require learners to practice analyzing the requirements of the learning task, analyzing their ability to complete tasks, and selecting or inventing an appropriate strategy. Depending upon the age, prior knowledge and cognitive strategies already available to the learners, each of these phases could be practiced separately and then combined and practiced together. Learners can be provided with example situations in which they determine whether the new strategy is appropriate, or not given their own or a simulated student's capabilities. They should be encouraged to substantiate their answers based upon the requirements of the learning task and the utility of the strategy. If learners have learned related strategies, or have other strategies in their repertoire, they should be encouraged to explain why this strategy may be superior to others, as they identify a strategy as appropriate to the situation. As with other "pattern recognition" practice, some of the instances should be very easy and obvious, while others may involve fine discriminations in order to determine that the learners are neither under- nor overgeneralizing the utility of the strategy. The learners might also be provided with an interactive video presentation of an age-appropriate student applying the strategy in a particular context. The learners might be asked to appraise whether the student is appropriately selecting, inventing, and/or applying the strategy and be asked to explain their answers.

The learners now should be given the opportunity to practice applying the strategy. This practice may be supported with a instruction-supplied or learner-generated checklist or flowchart that reminds the learner of the steps to follow.

This practice may begin with learners evaluating a demonstration of an age-appropriate learner, perhaps in an interactive video or audio format, applying an appropriate strategy. The learners should be asked to evaluate whether the strategy (a) has been appropriately applied and (b) the initial task problem that the strategy was to support is solved. This practice may be supported with a checklist or flowchart that reminds the learner of the steps to follow. With interactive media, the practice may involve cooperative learning in which learners are paired on one computer. One learner can demonstrate the strategy with its accompanying metacognition in a think-aloud mode, while the second learner plays the role of a coach-evaluator, using a checklist as a guide. Then the roles can be reversed.

Next, learners should be provided the opportunity to practice the strategy on more naturalistic, complex materials across a variety of contents and tasks. The practice should also include some tasks to which the newly-acquired strategy is not applicable in order for the learners to practice this decision point in the metacognitive process. This practice may extend across several days, or even weeks, depending upon the scope of the application of the strategy, and the complexity of the feedback.

Feedback for Cognitive Strategies

Feedback for simulated cases in which models demonstrated appropriate or inappropriate decisions and performance should explicitly state whether the decisions and performance were adequate or inadequate. The feedback should also explain why the modeled performance is judged so by focusing on the simulated learner's capabilities, the task characteristics, the efficacy, and the application of particular strategy. For open-ended production, practice in which learners actually applied the strategy to a task feedback must generally be presented through a modeled application of the strategy in which attention is directed to specific aspects of the strategy with which the learners frequently evidence difficulties. This feedback may involve reviewing any artifacts of the strategy, such as notes, or good and poor models of the outcomes of strategy application.

Ahmad (1988) reported the reports of a guided discovery lesson in which college-age learners were taught a strategy compatible with their prior strategies, or incongruent with prior strategies. Interestingly, she found that feedback about the effective use of the strategy (and corrective information when the strategy was ineffective) produced better performance when the strategy was compatible with previously employed strategies. Feedback that was limited to whether a solution was correct or incorrect was more effective when the strategy employed was incompatible with prior strategy use.

Psychomotor Learning and Feedback

Psychomotor tasks involve skills which are of a physical nature. We are using the term "psychomotor" rather than "motor" to emphasize the fact that there is a cognitive part to all motor skills. Once we become actually skilled in a psychomotor capability, the cognitive or "thinking" part of the skill becomes automatic and we are no longer conscious of that part of the skill; yet, in learning a psychomotor skill, the cognitive part of the skill is an important object of the learning task. Skills which are of a psychomotor nature have their own particular characteristics. In general, a learning task can be said to be a psychomotor task if it requires learning to perform coordinated muscular movements.

The two components of psychomotor skill are (a) *executive subroutines* to control decisions and supply subordinate skills in a hierarchical organization or plan (Miller, Galanter, & Pribram, 1960; in Robb, 1972) and (b) *temporal patterning* of skills to integrate the sequence of performance over time in which the skilled performer employs *pacing* and *anticipation* to enable the act to be performed with ease and smoothness (Robb, 1972, p. 44–49).

Psychomotor skills are often placed on a continuum from "closed" to "open." Closed skills, such as a tennis serve, are predictable and do not have to radically adapt to the environment. They are usually internally-paced (Singer, 1982). Open skills, such as hitting tennis ground strokes, must be adapted to unpredictable aspects of a changing environment.

Practice for Psychomotor Skills

Practice for a psychomotor skill in an interactive environment may involve practice on (a) recalling the executive subroutine, (b) judging the appropriateness of modeled response, or (c) actually demonstrating the physical activities. The latter practice usually requires specialized equipment that is interfaced with the computer. Practice with the executive subroutine follows much of the same strategy as practicing procedures: (a) identifying the situation that "fires" the subroutine (for psychomotor skills this recognition usually must be within a certain amount of time); (b) remembering the sequence of actions; and (c) making decisions within the optional paths of the procedure.

Practice may involve using graphics or video to present a demonstration of the execution of the skill for the learner to judge its appropriateness. Practice may finally involve the actual completion of the psychomotor task, although to provide feedback for such open-ended performance may require the use of complex input hardware.

Both closed and open skills should be practiced in situations that vary the environmental conditions in ways similar to how they will vary in actual execution. For closed skills this variation is easy to identify and usually is finite. Environments for open skills are more complex to model and may have an infinite number of variations that can only be sampled.

Feedback for Psychomotor Skills

The goal of feedback in psychomotor skills is similar to that of other learning. The goal is to externally provide a surrogate for the learners' own self-evaluation until such time as the learner can take over this role for themselves. In psychomotor learning this transfer is more pronounced. The learners of psychomotor skills can learn to recognize—through their own built-in proprioceptive feedback mechanisms and senses of hearing and vision—when a skill has been properly executed (Oxendine, 1984). As with other types of learning, feedback is critical to learning, although learners can acquire a psychomotor skill without external feedback (Stelmach, 1970).

Feedback for psychomotor skills can take two forms: feedback about product (the quality of the "response outcome" [Magill, 1985]) and feedback about the process (what causes the response outcome). During the initial stages of practice, process feedback may be more critical. During later stages of practice, information about the response outcome may be sufficient. Feedback appears to be more important during the earlier stages of practice. Indeed, learners appear to learn simple motor skills better when feedback is withdrawn or, at least, at a relative frequency (not after every response) (Ho & Shea, 1978; Newell, 1974). Quantitative feedback, in terms of time, distance, or some other measurable criterion (e.g., "you are holding the ball two inches too high during your approach"), appears to be superior to qualitative feedback (e.g., "too high," "too slow") (Smoll, 1972). However, there is an optimal precision (e.g., millimeters vs. centimeters; tenths vs. hundredths of seconds) of this feedback at different points in practice. Too much precision can actually be detrimental to learning (Rogers, 1974).

Graphic representations have been used for some time to provide feedback regarding the quality of psychomotor response. Lindahl reported in 1945 that "kinematic" graphic representations increased both the efficiency and the effectiveness of adults learning to cut tungsten discs. Similarly, Newell, Quinn, Sparrow, and Walter (1983) found that students provided with kinematic feedback learned a lever-moving task better than learners who were given written feedback. This finding was substantiated by Phillips' and Berkout's (1978) study, in which they found that students learning to operate the gear-shift on heavy equipment performed better when presented with continuous, computer-based graphic feedback than when given written end-of-session feedback.

Attitude Learning and Feedback

The basic desired outcome of instruction focused toward attitude learning is that the learner *choose* to behave in a certain way. When a person has an attitude toward something, the most salient influence which that attitude has on the individual's behavior is on choices which the person makes. If the topic is practicing "safe" sex, or practicing conservation, or settling arguments nonviolently, or voting, whether the instruction has had an influence on students' attitudes on these topics will be *evidenced* by what they choose to *do* with regard to them. The goal of much of instruction is to influence what they choose to do (after school or training is completed).

Attitudes, even though they are generally "affective" in nature, have three components: cognitive, behavioral, and affective. If for example, we wanted students to learn the attitude of "safe" sex, the student has more to do than just acquire an affective disposition toward "safe" sex.

1. The *cognitive component* is comprised of "knowing how." Before the student can practice any attitudes about "safe" sex, the student must know how to make sexual behavior "safe." Although it is reasonable to think of the cognitive component as a prerequisite learning, it is a prerequisite that will always be present, as an examples of attitude learning, and therefore something we can think of as being part of the attitude itself.

2. The *behavioral component* of attitude learning is seen in the need to apply the attitude—to engage in behavior. Thus, to actually internalize the attitude of "safe" sex, it will be necessary for the students to respond to opportunities to make decisions and choose "safe" option, either really or vicariously.

3. The *affective component* is the "knowing why," the importance of practicing "safe" sex. The most fundamental condition for achievement of the affective component is provision of a role model that provides the rationale for certain behavioral choices.

Practice for Attitude Learning

Practice should engage students with all three components of attitude formation or change. They should have practice either vicariously or actually in employing the skill or knowledge associated with the attitude, opportunity to explain why the skill/knowledge should be applied, and opportunity to choose to behave in the manner represented by the attitude. Often in interactive environments, designers choose to employ interactive video and simulations in the practice situation in order to make the situation appear as realistic as possible. The expectation is that this realism will encourage transfer of the attitude to actual life circumstances.

Feedback for Attitude Learning

Learners should first be presented with feedback as to whether they have successfully employed the skill or knowledge required by the attitude. They also should be informed as to whether their responses are congruent or incongruent with the desired attitude. Feedback for attitude-mediated performance often should be presented with information as to the anticipatable consequences of choices. This information regarding the consequences of choices should incorporate the affective component of an attitude, explaining why the behavior which reflects the attitude is important. In addition to such informational feedback, the designer may, after some soul searching, decide to employ positive reinforcement through affirming and personalized statements to learners who evidence the desired behavior.

Conclusions and Conjecture

Our review of the theoretical cognitive requirements of different types of learning and available research indicates that, indeed, different types of learning require different feedback content. Research and theory suggest that the simple association cognitive tasks of learning facts, lists, and labels may require only correct-answer feedback, in which learners must compare their own answers to the correct answer (assuming that the designers ensure that both learner's input and the correct answer remain on the screen together). Correct/incorrect feedback also provides adequate information for this type of declarative knowledge. Both types of feedback are relatively easy to provide with an interactive medium. Providing feedback to practice items that require the learner to explain, discuss, summarize, or describe large bodies of declarative knowledge in paraphrased form requires more processing, whether it is provided by a human or a computer. However, it is possible for designers to create practice that asks learners to recognize whether provided summaries and descriptions are appropriate or to provide model answers of criteria by which learners can evaluate their own answers.

Feedback for the other domains of learning—intellectual skills, cognitive strategies, motor skills, and attitudes—because they require application of knowledge to unencountered situations during practice, are somewhat constrained by an interactive format. Learners may be asked to evaluate whether given solutions are correct. Such decisions can be easily judged by a computer. However, if learners are asked to explain their reasoning, a method that we recommend, then most interactive systems may be unable to assess their explanation. Another situation that is difficult for "unintelligent" systems is judging the adequacy and providing feedback to questions that are open-ended, which requires the learner to construct a response. These practice items more truly reflect the criterion performance; however, except for limited numbers of ITS systems, feedback to constructed answers generally provides model answers and/or criteria with which the learners must evaluate their own responses. This comparison and evaluation may be too demanding for some learners at certain points in the learning process. Therefore, we recommend that designers of interactive learning environments use a combination of response formats, and carefully analyze characteristics of the learners and the cognitive demands of the learning task.

Indeed, it appears that questions regarding the optimal content of feedback (as with most other instructional design questions) really revolve around the issue of the match between the cognitive demands of the learning task; the cognitive skills, prior knowledge, and motivations of the learners; and constraints, such as time, within the learning environment. Smith

(1988) has conjectured previously that design of instruction is a balancing act between providing the learners enough support so that they can learn and persevere in the learning task and limiting this support so that learners must engage in the deep processing required for learning. This balancing act seems to apply to the content of feedback at a number of points. Ideally, when learners make an error, they should be provided with only enough information so that they can puzzle through to an identification and correction of their errors. In reality, many learners may be so confused, unmotivated, or rushed that they cannot recognize their errors. In such cases, the system must be able to be more supplantive, providing additional processing support. The principles upon which such a balancing act revolve are still incomplete. Integration of existing research and new studies are needed before designers can make principle-based decisions.

References

Ahmad, M. (1988). The effect of computer-based feedback on using cognitive strategies of problem solving. *Proceedings of selected research papers, Association for Educational Communications and Technology, Research and Theory Division* (pp. 1–22). New Orleans, LA.

Alessi, S.M., & Trollip, S.R. (1985). *Computer-based instruction: Methods and development*. Englewood Cliffs, NJ: Prentice-Hall.

Anderson, J.R. (1985). *Cognitive psychology* (2nd edition). New York: Freeman.

Anderson, J.R., & Reiser, B.J. (1985). The LISP tutor. *BYTE, 10*(4), 159–175.

Anderson, R.C., Kulhavy, R.W., & Andre, T. (1971). Feedback procedures in programmed instruction. *Journal of Educational Psychology, 62*(2), 148–156.

Chase, W.G., & Chi, M.T.H. (1980). Cognitive skill: Implications for spatial skill in large-scale environments. In J. Harvey (Ed.), *Cognition, social behavior, and the environment*. Hillsdale, NJ: Erlbaum.

Davis, R.H., Alexander, L.T., & Yelon, S.L. (1974). *Learning system design*. New York: McGraw-Hill.

de Jong, T. & Ferguson-Hessler, M.G.M. (1986). Cognitive structures of good and poor novice problem solvers in physics. *Journal of Educational Psychology, 78*, 279–288.

Fitts, P.M., & Posner, M.I. (1967) *Human performance*. Belmont, CA: Brooks/Cole.

Gagné, E.D. (1985). *The cognitive psychology of school learning*. Boston: Little, Brown, and Company.

Gagné, R.M. (1985). *The conditions of learning* (4th ed.). New York: Holt, Rinehart, & Winston.

Gagné, R.M, & Briggs, L.J. (1979). *Principles of instructional design* (2nd ed.). New York: Holt, Rinehart, & Winston.

Gephart, W.J., & Ingle, R.B. (1976). Evaluation and the affective domain. *Proceedings of the National Symposium for Professors of Educational Research (NSPER)*, Phoenix, AZ. (ERIC Document Reproduction Service No. ED 157 911.)

Gilman, D.A. (1969). Comparison of several feedback methods for correcting errors by computer-assisted instruction. *Journal of Educational Psychology*, *60*, 503–508.

Hartley, J.R., & Lovell, K. (1979). The psychological principles underlying the design of computer-based systems. In D.F. Walker and R.D. Hess (Eds.), *Instructional software design: Principles and perspectives for design and use* (pp. 38–56). Belmont, CA: Wadsworth.

Ho, L., & Shea, J.B. (1978). Levels of processing and the coding of postion cues in motor short-term memory. *Journal of Motor Behavior*, *10*, 113–121.

Hyman, C., & Tobias, S. (1981). *Feedback and prior achievement*. A paper presented at the annual meeting of the Northeastern Educational Research Association, Ellenville, NY.

Jonassen, D.H., & Hannum, W.H. (1987, December). Research-based principles for designing computer software. *Educational Technology*, *27*(12), 7–14.

Kulhavy, R.W. (1977). Feedback in written instruction. *Review of Educational Research*, *47*(1), 211–232.

Kulhavy, R.W., White, M.T., Topp, B.W., Chan, A.L., & Adams, J. (1985). Feedback complexity and corrective efficiency. *Contemporary Educational Psychology*, *19*, 285–291.

Landa, L.N. (1983). The algo-heuristic theory of instruction. In C.M. Reigeluth, (Ed.), *Instructional design theories and models* (pp. 163–211). Hillsdale, NJ: Erlbaum.

Lee, D., Smith, P.L., & Savenye, W. (1991). The effects of feedback and second try in computer-assisted instruction for rule-learning task (pp. 441–432). *Proceedings of selected research papers, Association for Educational Communications and Technology, Research and Theory Division*, Orlando, FL.

Lindahl, L.G. (1945). Movement analysis as an industrial training method. *Journal of Applied Psychology*, *29*, 420–436.

Magill, R.A. (1985). *Motor learning: Concepts and applications* (2nd ed.). Dubuque, IA: Wm. C. Brown.

Martin, B.L., & Briggs, L.J. (1986). *The affective and cognitive domains: Integration for instruction and research*. Englewood Cliffs, NJ: Educational Technology Publications.

Merrill, J. (1987). Levels of questioning and forms of feedback: Instructional factors in courseware design. *Journal of Computer-based Instruction*, *14*(1), 18–22.

Merrill, M.D. (1983). Component display theory. In C.M. Reigeluth (Ed.), *Instructional design theories and models* (pp. 379–334). Hillsdale, NJ: Erlbaum.

Merrill, M.D., & Tennyson, R.D. (1977). *Teaching concepts: An instructional design guide*. Englewood Cliffs, NJ: Educational Technology Publications.

Newell, K.M. (1974). Knowledge of results and motor learning. *Journal of Motor Behavior*, *1*, 235–244.

Newell, K.M., Quinn, J.T., Sparrow, W.A., & Walter, C.B. (1983). Kinematic information feedback for learning a rapid arm movement. *Human Movement Science*, *2*, 255–269.

Nielson, M.C. (1990). *The impact of informational feedback and a second attempt at practice questions on concept learning in computer-aided instruction*. Unpublished dissertation, University of Texas at Austin.

Nishikawa, S. (1988). Effects of feedback strategies in computer assisted instruction and the influence of locus of control on the performance of junior high students. *Proceedings of selected research papers, Association for Educational Com-*

munications and Technology, Research and Theory Division (pp. 521–539). New Orleans, LA.

Noonan, J.V. (1984). *Feedback procedures in computer-assisted instruction: Knowledge of results, knowledge of correct response: Process explanations and second attempts after errors.* Unpublished doctoral dissertation, University of Illinois.

Oxendine, J.B. (1984). *Psychology of motor learning* (2nd ed.). Englewood Cliffs, NJ: Prentice-Hall.

Phillips, J.R., & Berkout, J. (1978). Uses of feedback in computer-aided instruction in developing psychomotor skills related to heavy machinery operation. *Human Factors, 20*(4), 415–423.

Phye, G.D. (1979). The processing of informative feedback about multiple-choice test performance. *Contemporary Educational Psychology, 4*, 381–394.

Reigeluth, C.M. (1983). The elaboration theory of instruction. In C.M. Reigeluth (Ed.), *Instructional design theories and models* (pp. 335–382). Hillsdale, NJ: Erlbaum.

Richards, D.R. (1989). A comparison of three computer-generated feedback strategies. *Proceedings of selected research papers, Association for Educational Communications and Technology, Research and Theory Division* (pp. 357–368). Dallas, TX.

Robb, M.D. (1972) *The dynamics of motor-skill acquisition.* Englewood Cliffs, NJ: Prentice-Hall.

Rogers, C.A. (1974). Feedback precision and post-feedback interval duration. *Journal of Experimental Psychology, 102*, 604–608.

Schimmel, B.J. (1983). A meta-analysis of feedback to learners in computerized and programmed instruction. Paper presented to Annual Meeting of the American Educational Research Association, Montreal, April 11–14, 1983. (ERIC Document Reproduction Service No. ED 233708.)

Siegel, M.A., & Misselt, A.L. (1984). Adaptive feedback and review paradigm for computer-based drills. *Journal of Educational Psychology, 76*(2), 310–317.

Singer, R.N. (1982). *The learning of motor skills.* New York: Macmillan.

Smith, P.L. (1988). *Toward a taxonomy of feedback: Content and scheduling.* A paper presented at the Annual Meeting of the Association for Educational Communications and Technology, New Orleans, LA.

Smoll, F.L. (1972). Effects of precision of information feedback upon acquisition of a motor skill. *Research Quarterly, 43*, 489–493.

Steinberg, E.R. (1981). *Experience vs. two kinds of feedback in CAI problem solving.* A paper presented to the annual meeting of the American Educational Research Association, Boston, MA.

Stelmach, G.E. (1970). Learning and response consistency with augmented feedback. *Ergonomics, 13*, 421–425.

Chapter Five

Motivating Learners Through CBI Feedback: Developing a Positive Learner Perspective

Dorthy M. Hoska
University of Minnesota

One of the major benefits of computer-based instruction (CBI) is its ability to provide a one-on-one interaction between the learner and a computer program, which functions as a *coach*. Within most lessons, the coaching responsibilities of CBI are provided through feedback, which includes such activities as (1) reacting to learners as they respond to questions or interact with simulations, (2) advising learners about the scope and sequence of lesson assignments, and (3) focusing learners' attention on critical program elements. Most CBI lessons, however, overlook an important responsibility of any coach—to motivate. Yet this seldom explored function of feedback can be critical to the learning situation, because it affects the way learners both perceive and react to learning tasks. What we refer to as *motivation* is potentially a powerful tool for helping learners invest the effort required to gain knowledge and skill. This chapter explores current theory on motivation and provides guidelines for using CBI feedback that, at minimum, does not encourage task avoidance and, at maximum, causes the learner to invest increased effort in the learning task.

What Is *Motivation*?

The dictionary defines motivation as "an impetus to act." We have known for a long time that this impetus is not stable. It varies from individual to individual; for each person, it can vary from one situation to another and even from one moment to another within the same situation. During the last few decades, we have learned that motivation is far more complex than once thought. We now know that the person who sits idle and avoids tasks can be as motivated as the individual who digs in and works hard. The question has changed from "Is John motivated?" to "What is John motivated to do?" The challenge has changed from "How do we motivate John?" to "How do we redirect John's motivation?"

The scope of what we usually refer to as motivation has expanded to include a complex interaction of many factors. Therefore, within education, perhaps a more accurate way of referring to this concept is with the term *learner perspective*. A learner's perspective is the way the learner perceives both the learning task and his or her relation to the task. Learner perspective is based on the learner's:

- Reasons for approaching the task in a particular manner (goals).
- Perceptions of the relative importance of those reasons, or goals (incentives).
- Judgments concerning whether or not he or she has the abilities to meet task requirements (self-efficacy).
- Opinions about whether he or she will complete the task successfully (success expectancy).

Goals, incentives, self-efficacy, and success expectancy are both learner- and task-specific. Learners' personal goals may or may not be related to the goals of the learning task; they can even be counter to successful task completion. Also, two individuals with the same goals can have very different goal incentives. One learner may have strong incentives to avoid failure and only weak incentives to develop a particular skill. For another learner, the opposite may be true. In a similar manner, two individuals who make similar judgments about their abilities to perform a task may have very different expectations. A learner who has few incentives to perform a learning task may decide that the task warrants little or no effort. Therefore, even though the learner may feel capable of successfully performing the task, he or she may have decided not to try and, therefore, expects to fail.

Consider, for example, Tom and Mike, who have equal math abilities and are assigned the same difficult math problem. After 15 minutes of hard work, Tom successfully completes the task. Mike, however, gives up after a few minutes, starts to "fool around," and fails to solve the problem. The difference between these two learners is not ability nor level of motivation. Both Tom and Mike are motivated, but their motivations are not similarly directed. Tom and Mike approached the learning task differently because their learner perspectives, based on their goals, incentives, self-efficacy, and task expectancy, differed. Possible differences are identified in Table 5.1.

In view of their learner perspectives, both Tom and Mike were highly motivated to act in a certain manner. However, only Tom's perspective led to increased knowledge and skill. A clear understanding of how learners respond to tasks can be gained only by understanding the dynamics of the learners' perspectives and the factors that influence those perspectives—goals, incentives, self-efficacy, and success expectancies.

Goals and Incentives

A goal is something that an individual expects to receive as a result of performing a task; it is a desired outcome of an action. An incentive is the individual's impetus, or stimulus, to achieve a goal. The strength of an incentive is influenced by the learner's view of the goal. The greater the perceived importance or attractiveness of the goal, the stronger the learner's incentive to achieve it.

Goals

Goals include those to acquire something (acquisition goals) and those to avoid something (avoidance goals). They can be external or internal. They can also be specific to the situation or result from an intrinsic learner disposition. Typical acquisition and avoidance goals for learning situations are identified in Table 5.2.

A learner's goals are critical because they direct the learner's actions. In educational settings, learners' goals tend to focus on either performing for others (external goals) or learning for themselves (internal goals). Researchers (Dweck, 1986; Dweck & Legget, 1988; Nicholls, 1984; Nolen-Hoeksema, Seligman, & Girgus, 1986; Prawat, 1989) have found that each individual's general orientation toward goals (tendency to choose a specific type of goal over another) falls somewhere on a continuum, which extends from an ego-involved performing-goal orientation on one end to a task-involved learning-goal orientation on the other. (See Figure 5.1.)

Learners with performing goals want to demonstrate high ability and to avoid poor performance, which they consider to be a sign of low ability. These individuals view effort as merely the means to achieve these external goals. They tie success to displaying their abilities, which they measure in reference to the perceived abilities of others. In contrast, individuals with learning goals pursue learning and extend effort to gain skills. They view competence in terms of improved mastery, which is gained through effort.

	Goals	Incentives	Self-Efficacy	Task Expectancy
Tom's Learner Perspective	Select Strategy to Solve Problem	High	Is not sure if he can solve problem; believes that effort will increase his chances of success.	Expects to work hard and solve problem.
	Increase Math Skills	High		
	Demonstrate Ability	Low		
Tom's Response	Strongest goal is to solve the problem. He applies effort, does not give up when he experiences difficulty, and succeeds at his main goal of solving the problem.			
	Goals	Incentives	Self-Efficacy	Task Expectancy
Mike's Learner Perspective	Avoid Failure	High	Is not sure if he can solve the problem.	Does not expect to solve problem; he does not hope to hide his perceived lack of ability.
	Demonstrate Ability	High		
	Increase Math Skills	Low		
Mike's Response	Strongest goal is to avoid failure. He shows disinterest in the task, joking about it being a silly problem. He fails to solve the problem but succeeds at his main goal of avoiding failure. Since he did not try, he did not fail.			

Table 5.1 Differences in learner perspectives.

Effort, therefore, is perceived as beneficial since it is through effort that mastery is gained.

Under success conditions, the goal orientation of a learner may have only a slight outward effect on his or her incentive to perform a learning task. When a learner's goals are being met, the learner has incentive to extend effort, regardless of whether the goal focuses on demonstrating ability (performing goal) or increasing knowledge or skill (learning goal). It is under failure conditions that the two goal orientations produce vastly different performances.

When individuals with learning goals perceive an impending failure,

Acquisition Goals	
Situation Specific	**Intrinsic Disposition**
External Acquire: • Physical Rewards • High Scores • Appearance of Intelligence • Recognition	Acquire: • High Living Standard • Good Grade Average • Social/Professional Relationships • Good Reputation
Internal Acquire: • Understanding of Lesson Relevance • Knowledge of Lesson Content • Temporary Satisfaction • Temporary Confidence	Acquire: • Knowledge • Range of Skills • Control Over Life Situation • High Self-Esteem • Confidence
Avoidance Goals	
Situation Specific	**Intrinsic Disposition**
External Avoid: • Punishment • Low Scores • Appearing Unintelligent • Going Unnoticed	Avoid: • Poverty • Failure • Low Professional/Social Standing • Bad Reputation
Internal Avoid: • Confusion • Dissonance • Disatisfaction • Feelings of Incompetence	Avoid: • Incompetence • Low Self-Esteem • Lack of Understanding • Laziness

Table 5.2 Types of learning goals.

they usually remain task-focused, viewing obstacles as challenges. Because they believe that effort, rather than ability, is the key to success, they search for strategies to overcome the difficulties they encounter. It is by investing effort that they gain satisfaction. These learners have been shown to attain higher mastery scores and produce fifty percent more work than other learners (Dweck, 1986). When encountering difficulties, a high majority of them maintain their level of strategy use—some are able to find and use more effective learning strategies (Dweck & Legget, 1988). In contrast, a

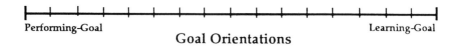

Performing-Goal   Learning-Goal
                              Goal Orientations

Figure 5.1 Goal orientation continuum.

very different behavior pattern emerges when learners with performing
goals sense impending failure.

Learners with strong incentives to perform, even those with high ability, react to obstacles by setting up defenses to protect their sense of self-
worth. One popular tactic is discounting (Kelley, 1973), in which learners
extend effort but have a ready set of excuses for failure. These excuses
include anxiety, disliking the task, and deciding the task is "stupid," too
"difficult," or a "waste of time" (Dweck & Legget, 1988). Other learners
defensively withdraw their effort and implement such self-preservation behaviors as displaying boredom or avoiding the task. These actions provide
them with a low-interest or lack-of-effort rather than a low-ability cause for
an impending failure. In studies conducted by Dweck and Legget (1988),
almost eighty percent of learners with performing goals responded to difficulties by engaging in task-irrelevant actions to bolster their self image (i.e.,
boasting about wealth, possessions, or activities in which which they succeeded); sixty percent regressed to the use of inefficient strategies. Once
engaged in this behavior pattern, referred to as learned helplessness
(Seligman, Maier, & Geer, 1968), this type of learner tends to (1) blame
failures on lack of ability, (2) view difficulties as insurmountable, (3) withdraw from challenging situations, (4) take minimal responsibility for successes and failures, and (5) underestimate both the number and value of any
subsequent successes (Diener & Dweck, 1980; Dweck & Reppucci, 1973).

Incentives

No goal orientation results solely from the type of goals—performing or
learning—the learner sets. Of equal importance are goal incentives. For

each learner, it is the combination of all of his or her goals, each weighted by the strength of its incentive, that yields the learner's general goal orientation. Therefore, a learner who has many strong incentives to perform and weak incentives to learn falls on the performing-goal end of the goal-orientation continuum. Conversely, a learner who has many strong incentives to learn is placed on the continuum closer to the learning-goal end. (See Figure 5.2.)

Modifying Learners' Goals and Incentives

Learners start a task with a predisposition to be either ego-involved, with strong incentives to perform, or task-involved, with strong incentives to learn. In most situations, however, they approach the learning task with two goals: to learn (acquire knowledge and skill) and to perform (maintain or increase their sense of well being). If learners receive no cues to favor one type of goal over another, they act according to their predispositions. However, if a learning situation is structured to foster a particular type of goal, most learners will respond; their goal orientations can be temporarily and, over time, permanently altered.

Lesson feedback has always been viewed as a useful technique to help learners redirect their thought patterns and actions. Feedback designed to influence learners' goal orientations must increase their incentives to learn

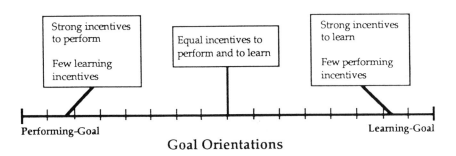

Figure 5.2 Effect of incentives on goal orientations.

and minimize their incentives to perform. Three approaches that have proven successful are (1) modifying the learner's view of intelligence, (2) altering the goal structure of the learning task, and (3) controlling the delivery of learning rewards.

Modifying the Learner's View of Intelligence

One condition that helps determine the goal orientations of learners is their view of intelligence (Dweck and Legget, 1988). Studies have shown (Kangas & Bradway, 1971) that the intelligence quotient (IQ) of individuals can increase as an individual matures, up to and even past mid-adulthood. Olson and Bruner (1974) suggest that ability is skill at decoding various symbol systems—methods of coding information (i.e., language, musical notation, pictures, graphic symbols, mathematics). Individuals vary in the speed and ease with which they learn to use a particular symbol system. Also, the same learner may develop one skill easily but have difficulty learning another. However, most learners, with effort, can gain the necessary skills to be considered able at using one or more of these systems.

In spite of evidence to the contrary, many learners view intelligence as fixed, believing individuals are born with particular abilities, which cannot be altered. These learners tend to have performing goals and blame their failures on lack of ability. Since they feel that their abilities are innate and cannot be increased, they limit the amount of effort they invest in completion of various learning tasks. Their strongest goals are to hide their inabilities and divert attention to those tasks at which they have some success. On the other hand, individuals with learning goals tend to view intelligence as incremental or changeable. They think their abilities can be increased through hard work, and skills can be developed through practice. Therefore, they respond to difficulties by investing increasing amounts of effort.

What is most promising about the hypothesized difference in learners' intelligence theories is that learners' perceptions of intelligence can be modified. If learners are helped to view their intelligence as incremental, they tend to select more learning goals, choose more difficult tasks, and remain on task when encountering difficulty (Dweck and Legget, 1988). Feedback, therefore, should help learners understand that:

- Abilities are skills that can be developed through practice.
- Effort is key to increasing one's skills.
- Mistakes are not failures; rather they are part of the skill-development process.

Altering the Goal Structure

A second condition that can affect goal incentives is the goal structure of the lesson. Common goal structures within learning situations include competitive, cooperative, and individualistic environments. Competitive goal structures cue the learner that performance should carry the most incentive. Competition, with its emphasis on success and failure, causes learners to be ego-involved and usually fosters performing goals (Ames & Ames, 1984). Even learners that enter a learning situation with high learning incentives may reevaluate their goals in a highly competitive environment.

Cooperative goal structures, in contrast, cue the learner that the *task* is important; therefore, they have the capability of fostering learning goals. The more emphasis that is put on the group goal of successfully completing the learning task, the stronger the incentives of the group member's learning goals. Studies by Johnson, Johnson, and Stanne (1985, 1986) suggest that those cooperative environments that stress task completion as a group effort help learners focus on the task; effort is seen as a positive behavior required to meet the group goal of learning lesson content.

Individualized goal structures, such as those found in most CBI learning environments, are usually considered to be noncompetitive. However, this does not guarantee that learners will be task-focused. Whether learners' incentives to learn will be stronger than their incentives to perform is determined by the reward system of the learning experience (Ames & Ames, 1984).

Controlling the Delivery of Learning Rewards

Many of the techniques used by parents and teachers to motivate individuals during their first learning experiences involve providing external personal rewards (e.g., candy, money), offering praise and blame feedback, offering unrequested help to increase chances of success, and comparing the learner's performance to that of others. These techniques tend to foster performing goals because they either focus attention on how the learner is viewed by others or divert the learner's attention away from learning for its own sake.

Providing external rewards. External rewards can undermine any learning goals the learner may have; they often cause learners to select less difficult tasks to increase their probability of success and reward attainment (Deci, 1972; McCullers, Fabes, & Moran, 1987). In research by Newby and Alter (1989), the introduction of external rewards caused learners to start selecting less difficult problems; after removal of the rewards, most learners immediately switched back to increasingly challenging problems. Under competitive conditions, the effects of external rewards are even greater. Because there are not enough rewards to go around, the learners' primary goals become performing well and avoiding failure (Covington & Omelich, 1979). The learners become ego-involved and focus on their abilities; the competition undermines their attempts to focus on the task as they worry about maintaining their self-images (Ames, 1984; Ames, Ames, & Felker, 1977). Also, because rewards are often interpreted as bribes, they affect the learners' perceptions of task difficulty. Learners often think that easy or interesting tasks do not need the added incentive of rewards; only difficult or boring tasks require bribes (McCullers, Fabes, & Moran, 1987).

Within CBI, external rewards are often provided by setting up a gaming atmosphere in which learners earn points. Although a game structure often holds the learners' attention, it reduces the strength of learning goals while it fosters performance goals. Increasingly, achieving a maximum number of points becomes more important than learning lesson content. A better approach is to offer internal rewards by:

1. Emphasizing that the goal of the lesson is to help the learner increase his or her knowledge and skill.
2. Breaking the learning task into small stages and focusing feedback on the skills the learner gains during each stage.
3. Emphasizing that even small increases in skill are valuable.

Offering praise or blame feedback. The use of praise and blame was once thought to be an effective means of providing positive and negative reinforcement. Research, however, has shown that learners often use praise and blame as an indirect estimate of their ability (Deci, 1972; Meyer, 1982). Most learners associate praise as a reward for effort and blame as an admonishment for withholding effort. The tendency to interpret praise and blame feedback as indicators of both ability and success level is especially prevalent in learners with ego-involving performing goals; in competitive learning environments, effort praise can actually produce helplessness in these learners (Koestner, Zuckerman, & Koestner, 1987). Therefore, the effect of praise or blame feedback depends on several factors: whether or not the learner felt the comments were warranted, task difficulty (Meyer, 1982; Meyer *et al.*, 1979), and the goal structure of the learning environment (Koestner, Zuckerman, & Koestner, 1987).

In most situations, praise has the most potential for being misinterpreted.

- *With high praise after successful completion of an easy task:* Learners know that only minimal level effort is needed for completion of easy tasks. If praise is given, they may decide the evaluator thinks they tried hard. The evaluator, therefore, must perceive their ability to be low (e.g., praise-deserving effort would be needed only if ability was low).
- *With minimal praise after successful completion of a hard task:* Learners may interpret this response as belief in their high abilities. High praise was not earned because the evaluator thought that the suc-

cesses were due to high ability rather than great effort.

- *With praise or no reaction after a failure:* Learners may feel this response indicates low ability. Since the evaluator did not think they were capable of succeeding, they should not be blamed for the failure.

Blaming learners for failing at a task can often have a more positive effect than praising them for their successes. Blame, which is perceived to be given only when learners withhold effort, informs the learners that the evaluator considers them capable of success (due to high ability). Blame feedback, however, must be used cautiously. It can be harmful if given to learners who feel they have invested high levels of effort and have achieved some level of success. (They see improvement, even though they may not have met success criteria.) In this case, blame can easily undermine the learners' perceptions of what constitutes a success or failure. If learners feel that only unqualified successes are acceptable, they may give up trying to achieve mastery through small sustained improvements.

Within CBI, learners may have a tendency to ignore praise and blame, especially if it is overstated (i.e., "Fantastic, Great Job") of if it attempts to mimic human statements. Learners know the computer is just a machine. However, learners do respect the ability of computers to gather and process information. Therefore, if praise or blame is used, it must be presented carefully and be coupled with accurate monitoring of learner performance. To help learners consider the computer's advice to be valid, statements must indicate that the computer is collecting information and analyzing their performances. To prevent learners from using praise or blame statements as indicators of their ability, feedback must focus on individual learner responses during lesson interaction rather than overall success levels.

Offering unrequested help. When learners who are encountering difficulty are offered unrequested help, they may interpret it as a sign that the one offering assistance does not think they can succeed on their own. Learners often feel that help is offered to those with low ability; those with high ability are expected to achieve mastery through their own efforts. Therefore, when providing support feedback (remedial sequences) during the initial stages of learning, how learners will respond must be considered. A possible technique to counteract this tendency could be to let the learner control whether or not he or she makes use of available help. Unfortunately, learners often make poor decisions concerning their learning needs (Tennyson & Buttry, 1980). Alternate strategies include:

- Along with offering optional remedial help, advise the learner about the function and usefulness of the help. Learners often follow this type of advice.

- If the learner is performing poorly, provide mandatory help. However, enable the learners to control some feature of the help: when the help is provided (i.e., immediately or after learners try on their own for a while) or the form of the help (i.e., verbal explanation, graphic representation, or additional problems).

Comparing performances. Any lesson that emphasizes how a learner's level or speed of achievement differs from that of others sets up a competitive goal structure, which causes the learner to focus on ability (Dweck, 1986) and reduce interest in the task (Harackiewicz, Abrahams, & Wageman, 1987). The level of effort that learners are willing to invest in learning tasks can decrease under two conditions.

- If low-ability learners receive feedback that indicates lower than average performance, they interpret it as confirmation that their ability is low. In a defensive response, they fall into a helpless pattern and reduce their effort level (Nicholls, 1984).
- If high-ability learners receive feedback that indicates above average performance, they will often lower their effort level (Nicholls, 1984). By lowering effort to the minimum level required for success, these learners feel they demonstrate increased ability levels.

Comparing the successes and failures of learners, however, does not always lead to lower effort levels. The amount of invested effort often increases when (1) high-ability learners receive feedback that indicates below average performance (Weiner & Schneider, 1971) or (2) low-ability learners receive feedback that indicates above average performance (Weiner, 1966). Note that the effect of comparison feedback has opposite effects on low-ability and high-ability learners. Also, even if the feedback results in increased effort levels, it fosters ego-involved performance goals rather than task-involved learning goals.

Providing rewards, unwarranted praise, unrequested help, or performance comparisons within a competitive environment tend to focus a learner's attention on his or her abilities, strengthening performance goals. In contrast, actions within a noncompetitive environment that present effort as a means of gaining knowledge and developing skills can foster a learning-goal orientation. To develop a more task-focused learning environment, CBI feedback should challenge the learner to achieve a certain level of success, which is not referenced to what other learners are doing (Harackiewicz, Abrahams, & Wageman, 1987). Rather than focusing on score attainment, the feedback should concentrate on the learner's increasing knowledge and skill acquisition (Ames & Ames, 1984) and present effort as a valuable investment in the learning process. (See Figure 5.3.)

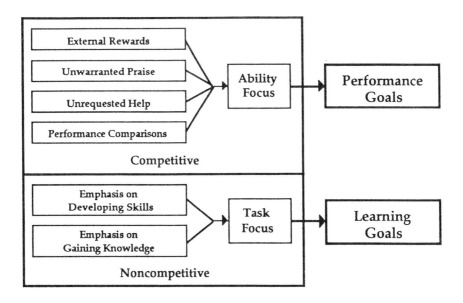

Figure 5.3 Goal development.

Self-Efficacy and Success Expectancy

The goals and incentives that influence a learner's goal orientation are only partially responsible for how he or she responds to a learning task. Equally important are the learner's self-efficacy and task expectancy. Self-efficacy is the learner's perception of how well he or she can execute the tasks required to achieve his or her goals. It helps the learner to select tasks and determine the amount of effort that will be required to achieve success. It also affects the learner's persistence in the face of difficulty. Success expectancy is the learner's view of whether or not he or she will actually complete the learning task. The learner first determines how much effort the task deserves, based his or her incentives to achieve various goals. He or she then decides whether the selected amount of effort will be sufficient for task mastery.

Self Efficacy

Learners derive their general sense of self-efficacy from several information sources (Bandura, 1977).

- *Vicarious experiences:* Viewing others' successes can raise a learner's self-efficacy; viewing others' failures can lower it.

- *Personal performance:* Successes or failures affect how the learner views his or her abilities. The impact of a success or failure, however, is largely determined not by the success or failure itself but by how the learner interprets that outcome (Covington & Omelich, 1979, 1981). Some learners, especially those with performing goals, view level of effort as an indication of their abilities. The more effort they must extend to complete a task successfully, the lower their perceived abilities. Success for these learners does not always enhance self-efficacy. Any success achieved through minimal effort is viewed to indicate high ability and can increase self-efficacy. However, a success that requires high effort suggests low ability and, therefore, can reduce self-efficacy.

- *Verbal persuasions:* Learners listen to and often believe the opinions of their parents, teachers, and peers. Therefore, they can be persuaded that they are either good or poor at performing various tasks. Even learners with an initially high self-efficacy can have their opinions of their abilities lowered by continual exposure to negative criticism. Although positive verbal persuasions do not have as strong an effect as task results, they can increase a learner's confidence and feelings of self worth. In a study by Wilson and Linville (1982), college freshmen who had difficulty during their first semester were shown data indicating that poor grades were typical during the first year and subsequent grade improvement was the norm. They were also given videotaped encouragement from upperclass students, who reinforced the prospect of grade improvement. These learners did better during the next year than others who had not received the verbal persuasion.

The general sense of self-efficacy developed by these three factors (experiences, performances, and persuasions) can be influenced by the situation. A learner's self efficacy can be temporarily affected by:

- *Physiological state:* Feeling physically well can strengthen self-efficacy; feeling physically weak or sick can weaken it (Bandura, 1977).

- *Role assignment:* In learning activities that involve role playing, the prestige of the role can affect a learner's self-efficacy. Subordinate roles can lower self-efficacy; leading or superior roles can strengthen it (Bandura, 1982).

- *Familiarity with the task:* If the learner is unsure of how to approach a new task, his or her self-efficacy can be lowered (Bandura, 1982).

- *Presence of a highly confident individual:* Individuals that demonstrate high confidence in their abilities can cause other less-confident learners to doubt their abilities (Bandura, 1982).

Young learners cannot accurately distinguish between effort and ability (Nicholls, 1978). Therefore, they often misjudge their abilities (Boekaerts, 1988). As a self-protective measure, learners may either overrate themselves, yielding temporary feelings of confidence, or underrate themselves, guaranteeing themselves success when coupled with a certain level of effort (Schunk, 1982). Low-achievers, especially those caught in a helpless pattern, almost always underrate themselves (Boekaerts, 1988). The resulting low self-efficacy feeds itself, causing continuing decrements in confidence and sense of self-worth.

Self-efficacy affects learning because it influences the amount of effort learners invest in tasks. A low self-efficacy can be detrimental because it causes learners to dwell on their personal deficiencies and assess the difficulty level of tasks improperly. It also impairs the learners' performance as their attention is diverted away from strategy use to concern over the possibility of failure (Bandura, 1982). A high self-efficacy, however, does not always result in maximum effort. The amount of effort extended by learners depends not only on their self-efficacy and their goal incentives but also on the perceived demand or load of a task (Salomon, 1984). When learners know that a task is demanding, high self-efficacy usually produces the effort needed for optimal performance. However, when learners are faced with tasks they perceive as easy, high self-efficacy may cause them to feel a minimal need to invest effort.

Success Expectancy

The amount of effort a learner deems as appropriate for a task, based on the learner's goal incentives, determines his or or her success expectancy.

Expectancy has several elements:
- Belief that an outcome, or goal, is possible given the current situation. (Learner must feel that he or she has some control over goal attainment; this goal may or may not be task completion.)
- Belief that an outcome, which can be achieving either an acquisition or an avoidance goal, will have desired consequences. (The consequences of goal achievement must have some value to the learner.)
- Determination of the amount of effort appropriate for goal attainment. (The greater the goal incentive, the more effort the learner is willing to invest to achieve the goal.)
- Determination of whether or not the selected amount of effort will lead to goal attainment.

Moderate expectancies are usually coupled with decisions to invest high levels of effort. They occur when a learner decides that a goal is important enough to invest whatever effort is required to overcome possible challenges and perceived ability deficits; the learner assumes that a high effort level, while not guaranteeing success, will increase his or her chances of achieving it. High and low success expectancies, on the other hand, often reflect low-effort decisions. High expectancies, which usually result from a high self-efficacy, occur when a learner feels that success is probable. Therefore, he or she may decide to extend minimal effort. Low expectancies occur when either the learner's task-related goal has weak incentives or the learner's self-efficacy is low. Under such conditions, the learner may determine that the task requires more effort than task consequences merit. Since the learner feels that the amount of effort he or she has decided to invest will not be sufficient to achieve success, he or she may decide to reduce effort levels even further, perhaps to the point of investing no effort at all.

Modifying Self-Efficacy and Expectancy

A learner's self-efficacy and the strength of his or her task goals influence the level of effort the learner initially decides to invest in the task. That selected effort level then affects the learner's task expectancy, which in turn further influences his or her effort decisions. (See Figure 5.4.)

Learners will invest maximum levels of effort to achieve learning goals only when their goals and self-efficacy enable them to see the benefit of such effort. Two techniques that have proved to increase learner's effort levels are (1) providing positive learning experiences and (2) changing the causes learners attribute to their successes and failures.

Providing Positive Learning Experiences

The effort level of learners can be increased by giving them learning experiences that are positive and internally satisfying. This does not mean providing them with only successes. Rather, learners should experience continually increasing levels of competence. Bandura (1977) suggests the following approach:

1. Provide support and help for the learner when he or she is first learning a new skill. This can include both encouragement and remedial techniques.
2. As the learner becomes skilled, gradually remove the support.
3. After the learner has reached some level or knowledge or skill, allow self-directed study.

As learners see that their effort yields increasing abilities, their self-efficacy will increase. This gradual development of abilities is more effective in increasing learners' self-efficacies than constant levels of achievement.

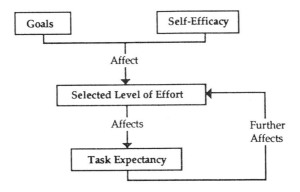

Figure 5.4 Selecting level of effort to invest in a task.

Changing the Causes Learners Attribute to Success and Failure

Another method of increasing a learner's self efficacy is through modifying either the causes that the learner attributes to successes and failures or the dimensions he or she ascribes to those causes (Weiner, 1979, 1985). The causes learners usually cite for their successes and failures are ability, effort, luck, task difficulty, and strategy use. Each of these causes can be dimensioned along several features: locus of causality, globality, stability, and controllability.

The learner determines the dimensions of a cause by posing and answering several questions.

- *For locus of causality, which can be either internal or external:* Does the cause deal with some action or characteristic within myself (internal) or with the actions and characteristics of other things or people (external)?
- *For globality, which can be either specific or global:* Does the cause relate only to this situation (specific) or to most situations (global)?
- *For stability, which can be unstable or stable:* Does the cause relate to conditions that exist at only this moment (unstable), or will the cause always be present in this type of situation (stable)?
- *Controllability, which can be either controllable or uncontrollable:* Do I have control over this cause (controllable) or is the cause beyond my control (uncontrollable)?

The dimensions learners ascribe to causes of successes or failures vary (Weiner, 1985).

- *For ability:* Those who think intelligence is fixed view ability as internal, stable, global, and uncontrollable. In contrast, those who think intelligence is incremental view ability as internal, unstable, specific or global, and controllable.

- *For effort:* Most learners view effort as internal, unstable, specific, and controllable. Some, however, may view it as a stable trait (e.g., a learner is either lazy or industrious).
- *For luck:* Luck is usually viewed as external, unstable, specific, and uncontrollable. However, some learners view luck as stable and global, thinking they are generally lucky or generally unlucky individuals.
- *For task difficulty:* Most learners view task difficulty as external, unstable, specific, and uncontrollable.
- *For strategy use:* Strategy use is viewed by most learners as internal, unstable, and specific. Some learners, especially those who have been trained in strategy use and metacognitive monitoring, think that strategy use is under their control. Others feel they have very limited control over the strategies available to them.

Of these five general causes, ability and effort appear to be the most important in determining a learner perspective. Those with learning-goal orientations usually attribute their track record at gaining knowledge and developing skills to both their abilities (viewed as internal, unstable, controllable, and sometimes specific) and the amount of effort they invest (viewed as internal, controllable, unstable, and specific). Conversely, learners with performance-goal orientations cite only ability (viewed as internal, stable, global, and uncontrollable) as the key to obtaining their goals of obtaining recognition and maintaining a self-image of high ability. These learners view effort only as an indication of their ability—the more effort required, the lower the ability (Covington & Omelich, 1979, 1981). When encountering failure, they try to shift the cause from low ability to low effort (Snyder & Higgins, 1988). Citing high ability/low-effort excuses for failures provides these learners with more control over the situation than is produced with high-ability/high-effort, low-ability/high-effort, or low-ability/low-effort excuses (Covington & Omelich, 1979).

Of the dimensions ascribed to causes, the most important appears to be controllability. Perceived control enables learners to (1) satisfy their need to feel competent, (2) attribute positive outcomes to themselves, and (3) enhance their self-efficacy (Burger, 1989). When learners attribute failure to uncontrollable causes, they often display patterns of helplessness, giving up easily when encountering failure. Learners who feel helpless usually attribute their failures to uncontrollable, internal, stable, and global causes; therefore, they feel unable to take control and turn failures around. Helpless learners also tend to attribute their successes to uncontrollable, external, unstable, and specific causes; hence, they cannot take credit for a success or count on one success leading to another (Butkowsky & Willows, 1980; Nolen-Hoeksema, Seligman, & Girgus, 1986).

An important aspect of controllability is its relation to self-efficacy and expectancy (Bandura and Wood, 1989). The higher the self-efficacy and expectancy of learners, the higher the goals that the learners set for themselves and the stronger the commitment they have to achieving those goals. However, it is only when learners believe that they have some measure of control, over either their actions or their environment, that they are motivated to expend effort to enhance their chances for success. Maximum investment of effort can be achieved if learners:

- Attribute their successes to causes that are internal and controllable; the causes can be stable or unstable, global or specific.
- Attribute their failures to causes that are controllable, unstable, and specific; the causes can be internal or external.

Learners can be helped to change their causal attributions through training, which consists mainly of aiding them to attribute effort, rather than ability causes to their successes and failures (Andrews & Debus, 1978; Dweck, 1975; Dweck & Reppucci, 1973; Fowler & Peterson, 1981; Schunk, 1982). Attribution training is an important and powerful type of feedback. However, because learners tend to interpret feedback on many levels, it must be used carefully. Guidelines for helping learners make effort attributions include the following.

- Provide effort encouragement after a success or failure, not before it (Koestner, Zuckerman, & Koestner, 1987; Schunk, 1982). If the learners are encouraged to try hard before an outcome is reached, they may interpret it as a sign that the task is too difficult for their level of ability. This is especially damaging if the learner perceives the task to be easy. They may say to themselves "If I must try really hard, it must be because I am not good, even at easy tasks."
- When possible, use direct attributions (learners telling themselves they need to try harder) rather than indirect attributions (learners hearing they need to try harder) (Fowler & Peterson, 1981). Within a CBI environment, direct attributions are difficult. However, one technique may be to have the learners select a possible cause for their successes or failures from effort-related options. (i.e., For successes: I read the material carefully; I thought about the question before I answered. For failures: I didn't concentrate when I read the material; I don't understand the information yet and need to review it; I answered the question too quickly, without thinking about it; I did not read all possible answers before I responded.)
- Use attribution training only in noncompetitive, task-focused, learning environments. Competition fosters ability attributions,

while the lack of competition allows learners to make effort attributions. It is only under a task focus that greater competence is associated with effort (Jagacinski & Nicholls, 1984). In task-focused environments, learners demonstrate more self-instruction and more self-monitoring thoughts. They also tend to judge task difficulty in terms of their own abilities rather than the perceived capabilities of others (Ames & Ames, 1984).

- Use attribution training with learning tasks of intermediate difficulty (Nicholls, 1984; Schunk, 1982). Learners gain the most information from their successes or failures at tasks they view of medium difficulty (Meyer, Folkes, & Weiner, 1976). Also, those learners who need the training most—learners with strong performing goals— tend to react negatively to tasks they perceive as especially difficult or easy. If tasks are very difficult, these learners may decide that effort will not be enough to yield success, and that the situation offers only a minimal opportunity to demonstrate high ability. In contrast, if these learners view the task as easy, they may decide that minimal effort is required. If they end up investing some effort, they may interpret it as a demonstration of low ability. The challenge, in using attribution training during tasks of medium difficulty, is that this learning condition is the one most avoided by ego-involved learners who have a low self-efficacy. These learners often invest some effort on easy tasks because some chance of success exists. They may also invest some effort on hard tasks because they have an external, uncontrollable excuse (high task difficulty) for the probable failure (Nicholls, 1984). It is with tasks of medium difficulty that these learners see the greatest chance of ability-caused failures. Therefore, along with attribution training, feedback should help increase the learners' self efficacy.

- Train in the use of strategies, a process that can indirectly help learners make effort attributions (Kurtz & Borkowski, 1984). As learners discover that some strategies work while others do not, they develop a growing sense that they have control over their successes and failures. Effort to find and use the best strategy becomes a useful learning technique.

Modifying a Learner's Perspective Through CBI Feedback

Learners go through a sequence of steps when they select and perform tasks (Weiner, 1979). The goals, current incentives, self-efficacy, and expectancy of a learner interact during each of these steps. Feedback within

CBI can help the learner remain task focused as he or she makes assessments and decisions during each of these steps. (See Figure 5.5.)

Step 1. Learner selects a goal. The goal selected by a learner is influenced by the perceived value of various goal outcomes. This value, in turn, is affected by the learner's goal orientation. Learners with performing goals tend to select goals of obtaining recognition or minimizing the chance of failure; those with learning goals tend to strive for knowledge acquisition or skill development. Feedback, therefore, should cue the learner to the importance of gaining knowledge and developing skills, thereby strengthening the incentives of their learning goals. (See Table 5.3.)

Step 2. Learner evaluates task difficulty. Learners' judgments concerning the difficulty level of learning tasks are based on information from several sources:

• How they performed on similar tasks in the past.

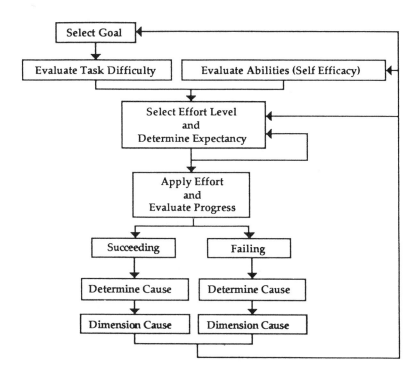

Figure 5.5 Steps in task selection and performance.

Desired Effect	Function of the Feedback	Technique	Cautions
Learner has strong incentives to achieve learning goals.	Help learner view his or her abilities as improvable.	As an introduction to the lesson or as part of feedback presented when a learner has difficulty: • Suggest that abilities are skills that can be developed. • Identify the skills that the lesson is aimed at developing. • Indicate that effort is the main tool for increasing skills. • Treat mistakes as an important part of skill development.	Make certain that the lesson is task-focused and noncompetitive. If learners are working in pairs or small groups, set up a cooperative environment.
	Present a task-focused, noncompetitive learning environment.	When presenting feedback for both correct and incorrect learner responses: • Keep comments task focused. • Have the learner set goals related to completion of small task stages. • Do not tie goals to accuracy rate or the time required for mastery. • Avoid comparisons. Do not rate the learner's progress against the progress of previous lesson users. • Do not offer rewards such as bonus points.	

Table 5.3 Feedback to strengthen the incentive of learning goals.

• How they view the medium of the learning activity. Learners often make judgments concerning lesson difficulty based on the presentation medium. For example, many children in the U.S. think it easier to master information presented on television than information presented in a book (Salomon, 1984). Learners also tend to view the computer as either an entertainment source or a tool (e.g., word processor). They tend not to view it as a learning resource.
• Clues provided by the lesson. Lessons sometimes contain direct statements about the difficulty level of subsequent materials. In other cases, learners develop a sense of the difficulty level through effort statements and the amount of available help.

It is difficult to influence all the factors that help determine a learner's view of lesson difficulty. Also, it may be dangerous to identify a difficulty level; various learners will find the lesson more or less difficult. Therefore, a good tactic may be to help the learner separate difficulty level from task value. (See Table 5.4.)

Desired Effect	Function of the Feedback	Technique	Cautions
Learner sees the value of a learning task as separate from its level of difficulty.	Counteract learner's tendency to view the computer as solely an entertainment source.	As an introduction to the lesson and intermittently within feedback, reinforce the idea that the lesson is designed to help the learner develop skills. During feedback, occassionally stress the importance of paying close attention to presented information.	Do not suggest that the learner needs to work hard before he or she is presented with a learning task. This may cause him or her to overestimate task difficulty.
	Convince learner that difficulties and challenges are positive and do not reflect ability level.	Introduce the idea that the learner may easily complete some parts of the lesson, while having difficulty with others. Present the need for increasing levels of difficulty as a necessary part of skill development.	

Table 5.4 Feedback to minimize the effect of difficulty level.

Step 3. Learner evaluates his or her abilities and develops a level of self-efficacy. A low self-efficacy is always detrimental to the learning process. Although a single lesson cannot overcome the years of experience that resulted in a low sense of worth, it can temporarily increase a learner's confidence about their abilities. At the very least, a lesson and its feedback should not decrease learners' perceptions of their ability levels. (See Table 5.5.)

Step 4. Learner selects an effort level and decides if that level will yield task success. The amount of effort a learner first elects to invest in a task depends on his or her own goals, the perceived task difficulty, and his or her self-efficacy. After an effort level is selected, the learner decides if that level will yield task success. Based on this evaluation, the selected effort level may change.

- If learners are unsure of an outcome but have high self-efficacy, they may increase their effort level.
- If learners expect to succeed easily, they may lower their effort level to the minimum needed for success.
- If learners do not expect to succeed, they may substantially lower their effort levels.

Step 5. Learner invests effort to complete the task and evaluates progress toward task completion. At some point during the completion of a task, the learner decides whether he or she is succeeding or failing.

Desired Effect	Function of the Feedback	Technique	Cautions
Learner feels capable of performing lesson tasks.	Steadily increase the self-efficacy of learners.	To develop a sense of self-efficacy, use the following strategy throughout the lesson: 1. Use feedback that provides support during the early stages of learning a task. Either give the learner some type of advised control over help sequences or attempt to put some aspect of forced support under learner control. 2. As the learner progresses, slowly reduce the amount of available help, letting the learner know that he or she is starting to do well on his or her own. 3. As the learner gains skill, begin to give him or her increasing control over the lesson. Let learners know that they have earned the ability to direct their study. If trackable factors, such as the speed at which the learner selects answers to questions, indicate that poor performance may be due to guessing, suggest to the learner that guessing is a waste of time and lesson mastery is possible if he or she takes time and concentrates.	Do not offer high verbal praise for successes. A learner can easily misinterpret praise as a sign of low ability. Simple verification of a success is usually enough. Do not admonish learners every time they do poorly. If a learner with low self-efficacy is trying, blame may cause him or her to give up. Do not always force help onto a learner. Provide help only when the learner really needs it.

Table 5.5 Feedback to increase a learner's self-efficacy.

Step 6. Learner determines and dimensions the cause of the success or failure.
Learners look for causes (or excuses) for their successes or failures. Typical causes include ability, effort, luck, task difficulty, and selection of learning strategies. After a cause is selected, the learner dimensions the cause along four parameters: locus of causality, globality, stability, and controllability. To keep learners task-focused, they should be helped to gain a sense of control over their learning by making effort attributions. (See Table 5.6.)

Desired Effect	Function of the Feedback	Technique	Cautions
Learner gains a sense of control over his or her learning.	Help learner to attribute his or her successes and failures to effort.	Provide feedback related to effort levels for both successes and failures.. Track the learner's performance, and: • If a learner responds incorrectly to several problems in a row, suggest that the difficulty does not mean failure. Encourage effort and suggest that if the learner tries hard, he or she will achieve success. Follow this advice with a slightly less difficult problem. • If a learner has had difficulty and is now improving, point out the success and suggest that the cause is effort. Encourage continued effort. Follow this advice with a problem the learner has a fairly good chance of answering correctly. • If the learner is having difficulty, guide the learner to select a different, more effective strategy. Relate the search for and use of strategies to effort.	Make certain that the learning environment is task-focused and noncompetitive. Present the effort feedback after the learner responds to a problem, not before. Offer effort-directed feedback only when the learner is working on problems of medium difficulty.

Table 5.6 Feedback to help the learner view effort as the key to success.

Step 7. Learner modifies his or her learner perspective. Finally, the learner uses the causal dimensions of successes or failures to reevaluate his or her goals, self-efficacy, and expectancy. If the change in a learner's perspective is positive, his or her willingness to extend effort to reach difficult learning goals may increase. However, if a learner's perspective becomes more negative, the learner may withdraw from the task in progress and select less difficult tasks in his or her future.

Conclusion

There are no easy answers or guaranteed techniques to providing feedback that will influence all learners to invest effort in a learning task. No two learners are alike, and the process by which each individual decides the *if, when,* and *how much* of extending effort to learn is complex. This chapter is not designed to provide absolute answers. Its goals are first to make you aware that CBI feedback can be an effective agent for helping learners develop task-focused perspectives toward learning, and second to identify some of the factors that should be considered when attempting to influence learner perspectives.

Computer technology has given CBI designers and developers the ability to track data and gain information about the learner. Researchers focusing on motivational theory have presented guidelines for helping various types of learners develop learning goals, become task focused, and increase their self-efficacy. It now becomes the challenge of CBI designers and developers to use these tools to incorporate feedback within lessons that produce positive learner perspectives.

References

Ames, C. (1984). Achievement attributions and self-instructions under competitive and individualistic goal structures. *Journal of Educational Psychology, 76*(3), 478–487.

Ames, C., & Ames, R. (1984). Systems of student and teacher motivation: Toward quantitative definition. *Journal of Educational Psychology, 76*(4), 535–556.

Ames, C., Ames, R., & Felker, D.W. (1977). Effects of competitive reward structure and valence of outcome on children's achievement attributions. *Journal of Educational Psychology, 69*(1), 1–8.

Andrews, G.R., & Debus, R.L. (1978). Persistence and the causal perception of failure: Modifying cognitive attributions: *Journal of Educational Psychology, 70*(2), 154–166.

Bandura, A. (1977). Self-efficacy: Toward a unifying theory of behavior change. *Psychological Review, 84*(2), 191–215.

Bandura, A. (1982). Self-efficacy mechanism in human aging. *American Psychologist, 37*(2), 122–147.

Bandura, A., & Wood, R. (1989). Effect of perceived controllability and performance standards on self-regulation and complex decision making. *Journal of Personality and Social Psychology, 56*(5), 805–814.

Boekaerts, M. (1988). Motivated learning: Bias in appraisals. *International Journal of Educational Research, 12,*267–280.

Burger, J.M. (1989). Negative reactions to increases in perceived personal control. *Journal of Personality and Social Psychology, 56*(2), 246–256.

Butkowsky, I.S., & Willows, D.M. (1980). Cognitive-motivational characteristics of children varying in reading ability: Evidence of learned helplessness in poor readers. *Journal of Educational Research, 72*(3), 408–422.

Covington, M.V., & Omelich, C.L. (1979). Effort: The double-edged sword in school achievement. *Journal of Educational Psychology, 71*(2), 169–182.

Covington, M.V., & Omelich, C.L. (1981). As failures mount: Affective and cognitive consequences of ability demotion in the classroom. *Journal of Educational Psychology, 73*(6), 796–808.

Deci, E.L. (1972). Intrinsic motivation, extrinsic reinforcement, and inequity. *Journal of Personality and Social Psychology, 22*(1), 113–120.

Diener, C.I., & Dweck, C.S. (1980). An analysis of learned helplessness: II. The processing of success. *Journal of Personality and Social Psychology, 39*(5), 940–952.

Dweck, C.S. (1975). The role of expectations and attributions in the alleviation of learned helplessness. *Journal of Personality and Social Psychology, 31*(4), 674–685.

Dweck, C.S. (1986). Motivational processes affecting learning. *American Psychologist, 41*(10), 1040–1048.

Dweck, C.S., & Legget, E.L. (1988). A social-cognitive approach to motivation and personality. *Psychology Review, 95*(2), 256–273.

Dweck, C.S., & Reppucci, N.D. (1973). Learned helplessness and reinforcement responsibility in children. *Journal of Personality and Social Psychology, 25*(1), 109–116.

Fowler, J.W., & Peterson, P. (1981). Increasing reading persistence and altering attributional style of learned helpless children. *Journal of Educational Psychology, 73*(2), 251–260.

Harackiewicz, J.M., Abrahams, S., & Wageman, R. (1987). Performance evaluation and intrinsic motivation: The effects of evaluative focus, rewards, and achievement orientation. *Journal of Personality and Social Psychology, 53*(6), 1015–1023.

Jagacinski, C.M., & Nicholls, J.G. (1984). Conceptions of ability and related affect in task involvement and ego involvement. *Journal of Educational Psychology, 76*, 909–919.

Johnson, R.T., Johnson, J.W., & Stanne, M.B. (1985). Effects of cooperative, competitive, and individualistic goal structures on computer-assisted instruction. *Journal of Educational Psychology, 77*(5), 668–677.

Johnson, R.T., Johnson, J.W., & Stanne, M.B. (1986). Comparison of computer-assisted cooperative, competitive, and individualistic learning. *American Education Research Journal, 23*, 382–392.

Kangas, J., & Bradway, K. (1971). Developmental psychology. *Intelligence at middle age, 5*(2), 333-337.

Kelley, H.H. (1973). The processes of causal attribution. *American Psychologist, 28*, 107–128.

Koestner, R., Zuckerman, M., & Koestner, J. (1987). Praise, involvement, and intrinsic motivation. *Journal of Personality and Social Psychology, 53*(2), 383–390.

Kurtz, B.E., & Borkowski, J.G. (1984). Children's metacognition: Exploring relations among knowledge, process, and motivational variables. *Journal of Experimental Child Development, 37*, 335–354.

McCullers, J.C., Fabes, R.A., & Moran, J.D., III. (1987). Does intrinsic motivation theory explain the adverse effects of rewards on immediate task performance? *Journal of Personality and Social Psychology, 52*(5), 1027-1033.

Meyer, W. (1982). Indirect communications about perceived ability estimates. *Journal of Educational Psychology, 74*(6), 888–897.

Meyer, W., Bachmann, M., Biermann, U., Hemplemann, M., Ploger, F., & Spiller, H. (1979). The informational value of evaluative behavior: Influences of praise and blame on perceptions of ability. *Journal of Educational Psychology, 71*(2), 259–268.

Meyer, W., Folkes, V., & Weiner, B. (1976). The perceived informational value and affective consequences of choice behavior and intermediate difficulty task selection. *Journal of Research in Personality, 1,* 410–423.

Newby, T.J., & Alter, P.A. (1989). Task motivation: Learner selection of intrinsic versus extrinsic orientations. *Educational Technology Research and Development, 37*(2), 77–90.

Nicholls, J.G. (1978). The development of the concepts of effort and ability, perception of academic attainment, and the understanding that difficult tasks require more ability. *Child Development, 49,* 800–814.

Nicholls, J.G. (1984). Achievement motivation: Conceptions of ability, subjective experience, task choice and performance. *Psychological Review, 91*(3), 328–346.

Nolen-Hoeksema, S., Seligman, M.E., & Girgus, J.S. (1986). Learned helplessness in children: A longitudinal study of depression, achievement, and explanatory style. *Journal of Personality and Social Psychology, 51*(2), 435–442.

Olson, D.R., & Bruner, J.S. (1974). Learning through experience and learning through media. In D.R. Olson (Ed.), *Media and symbols: The forms of expressions, communication, and education: The seventy-third yearbook of the National Society for the Study of Education* (pp. 125–150). Chicago: University of Chicago Press.

Prawat, R.S. (1989). Promoting access to knowledge, strategy, and disposition in students: A research synthesis. *Review of Educational Research,* Spring, *51*(1), 1–41.

Salomon, G. (1984). Television is easy and print is tough: The differential investment of mental effort in learning as a function of perceptions and attributions. *Journal of Educational Psychology, 76*(4), 647–658.

Schunk, D.H. (1982). Effects of effort attributional feedback on children's perceived self-efficacy and achievement. *Journal of Educational Psychology, 74*(4), 548–556.

Seligman, M.E., Maier, S.F., & Geer, J.H. (1968). Alleviation of learned helplessness in the dog. *Journal of Abnormal Psychology, 73,* 256–262.

Snyder, C.R., & Higgins, R.L. (1988). Excuses: Their effective role in the negotiation of reality. *Psychological Bulletin, 104*(1), 23–35.

Tennyson, R.D., & Buttry, T. (1980). Advisement and management strategies design variables in computer aided instruction. *Educational Communications and Technology, 28*(3), 169–176.

Weiner, B. (1966). The role of success and failure in the learning of easy and complex tasks. *Journal of Personality and Social Psychology, 3,* 339–343.

Weiner, B. (1979). A theory of motivation for some classroom experiences. *Journal of Educational Psychology, 71*(1), 3–25.

Weiner, B. (1985). An attributional theory of achievement motivation and emotion. *Psychological Review, 92*(4), 548–573.

Weiner, B., & Schneider, K. (1971). Drive versus cognitive theory: A reply to Boot and Hartmen. *Journal of Personality and Social Psychology, 18,* 285–293.

Wilson, T.D., & Linville, P.W. (1982). Improving the academic performance of college freshmen: Attribution therapy revisited. *Journal of Personality and Social Psychology, 48,* 1572–1575.

Chapter Six

Cooperative Learning and Feedback in Technology-Based Instruction

David W. Johnson
University of Minnesota

and

Roger T. Johnson
University of Minnesota

Technology in the Classroom

Harold Innis (1964, 1972) rewrote the history of civilization as a history of media. He claimed that every medium has a bias either toward lasting a long time or traveling easily across distances. Time-based media such as stone hieroglyphics led to small, stable societies because stone was difficult to edit and rewrite and too heavy to distribute over great distances. In contrast, messages on travel-based media such as papyrus enabled the Romans to build and run a large empire. Marshall McLuhan (1964) added the notion that media is an extension of human senses and, therefore, different technologies alter the balance of human senses. The way the technology balances the senses creates its own form of thinking and communicating. Oral communication makes hearing dominant and thought simultaneous and circular. Written communication makes sight dominant and thought linear (one-thing-follows-another), rational (cause-and-effect), and abstract. Electronic technology tends to recreate the village on a global scale through instantaneous and simultaneous communication. Physical distance between people becomes irrelevant. Neil Postman (1985) expressed fears that our ability to reason with rigor and self-discipline is being eroded as fewer people read systematically and more people watch and listen to electronic media. Their thinking may become more reactive and impressionistic.

Not only does the technology alter the balance of the senses and create its own form of thinking, but the use of technology within educational settings becomes more complex as students must concurrently (a) learn how to use the technology, and (b) master the information, skills, procedures, and processes being presented within the technology. Procedural and conceptual learning become intermixed and may either enhance or interfere with each other. While early technological contributions to education, such as telephones, radio, television, and calculators, did not require extensive procedural learning, the emerging hybrid of text, video, sound, image, and computation does. These technologies also frame a different mode of education, human interaction, and cooperation far beyond what previous technological innovations have done. The success of both procedural and conceptual learning depends largely on the social context within which learning takes place. There are three contexts within which technology may be used for educational purposes: competitive, individualistic, and cooperative. The interactive technology being developed can enhance the cooperative context which is essential to successful education.

In this chapter a number of questions are addressed:

1. What is feedback?

2. What are the sources of feedback within a learning situation?

3. What is the context within which feedback has maximal impact on procedural and conceptual learning?

4. What are the essential elements of cooperation that make cooperative relationships ideal settings in which for feedback to occur?

5. What is the actual evidence demonstrating that a cooperative context is essential for feedback to occur effectively?

6. How is feedback institutionalized into cooperative learning groups?

7. What are the advantages of technology-assisted cooperative learning in providing feedback to enhance learning?

8. What are questions concerning the nature of technology-assisted cooperative learning?

9. What practical advice may be given to teachers wishing to utilize technology-assisted cooperative learning?

10. What is the future of technology-assisted cooperative learning?

What Is Feedback?

An important aspect of technology-assisted cooperative learning is the opportunity to both give and receive feedback. Feedback is information made available to individuals that makes possible the comparison of actual performance with some standard of performance. Knowledge of results is information provided to the person about his or her performance on a given effort. Feedback may be in the form of qualitative information in which the person is informed that a performance is either correct or incorrect. Or it may be quantitative information about how much discrepancy exists between the person's response and the correct response. Usually, quantitative information (i.e., process feedback) about the size of the discrepancy existing between actual performance and some standard of performance promotes achievement more effectively than does qualitative information (i.e., terminal feedback) about being right or wrong (Anderson, Evertson, & Brophy, 1979; Lockhead, 1983; Peterson & Janicki, 1979; Peterson, Janicki, & Swing, 1981; Peterson & Swing, 1985; Swing & Peterson, 1982; Webb, 1980). Qualitative feedback helps individuals improve their performance and reinforces them for their work. Both the information and reinforcement inherent in qualitative feedback seem to be most helpful when individuals are not certain about the correctness of their actions. When individuals already know a response is correct, confirming this fact does not increase their information and therefore does not affect subsequent performance.

What Are the Sources of Feedback Within a Learning Situation?

At least three sources of feedback are available in a learning situation: oneself, technology such as computers or videos, and other people. Individuals intrinsically give themselves **personal feedback** through such actions as attending to stimuli produced by the previous response such as the *feel* of swinging a tennis racquet.

Individuals may receive **feedback from technological devices** such as computers. Computers can provide feedback in a number of ways. From tests computers can provide raw score, percentage of items correct, percentile score for each student, items missed, and objectives mastery information. The computer can inform the student when a response is correct. The computer can provide corrective tutorial information for incorrect items. Among the advantages of electronic feedback are continuous monitoring and prompt feedback on performance. Giving students immediate feedback allows them to revise and improve immediately without having to wait—while their interest is still high and while they are still focused on the work. Computers give visual feedback and help students go beyond the literal in understanding what they are reading and writing about. Such multi-dimensional and complex feedback can be quite powerful. Finally, the computer can provide the teacher with feedback on instructional effectiveness by providing summary reports of progress across students.

The most powerful and effective source of feedback is other people. **Interpersonal feedback** has power for a number of reasons. First, receiving personalized feedback from another person increases performance to a greater extent than does receiving impersonal feedback (Acheson, 1964; Fuller *et al.*, 1969; Morse, Kysilka, & Davis, 1970; Steiner, 1967; Tuckman, McCall, & Hyman, 1969). Second, information tends to be weighed in proportion to its vividness (Borgida & Nisbett, 1977; Hamill, Wilson, & Nisbett, 1980; Nisbett, Borgida, Crandall, & Reed, 1976; Taylor & Thompson, 1982). Statistical data summaries and impersonal information sources are less vivid than face-to-face interactions. Third, peers can provide sustained interaction after a student gives an incorrect answer, supportively probing, providing cues, repeating the question, rephrasing the question, or allowing more time for the student to answer, all of which is important for achievement (Webb, 1982). Thus, in order to have maximal impact on performance, attitudes, and behavior, feedback needs to be: (1) received from another person, (2) discussed face-to-face in ways that make vividly clear its personal implications, and (3) offered in a manner to provide sustained followup.

While the optimal situation may be to receive feedback concurrently from oneself, technological devices, and other people, the most powerful source of feedback is from other people. That does not mean, however, that any comment by another person will have positive impact. The context within which interpersonal feedback is given largely determines its effectiveness. Students process the information they receive differently from a collaborator than from a competitor or an indifferent bystander.

Student-Student Interaction

In every classroom, no matter what the subject area, teachers may structure lessons so that students:

1. Engage in a win-lose struggle to see who is best.

2. Work independently on their own learning goals at their own pace and in their own space to achieve a preset criterion of excellence.

3. Work cooperatively in small groups, ensuring that all members master the assigned material.

Feedback takes place within all three of these learning contexts. The balance between feedback from oneself, feedback from technological devices, and interpersonal feedback, however, is different within each context. Both individualistic and competitive learning rely primarily on self feedback and feedback from technological devices such as timers. Interpersonal feedback enhances learning primarily within a cooperative context.

Student-student interaction may be structured in school classes in three ways: competitively, individualistically, and cooperatively. When students are required to **compete** with each other for grades, they work against each other to achieve a goal that only one or a few students can attain. Students are graded on a norm-referenced basis, which requires them to work faster and more accurately than their peers. In doing so, they strive to be better than classmates, work to deprive others (my winning means you lose), to celebrate classmates' failures (your failure makes it easier for me to win), view resources such as grades as limited (only a few of us will get *A*s), recognize their negatively linked fate (the more you gain, the less for me; the more I gain, the less for you), and believe that the more competent and hardworking individuals become *haves* and the less competent and deserving individuals become the *have nots* (only the strong prosper). In **competitive situations,** a negative interdependence exists among goal achievements; students perceive that they can obtain their goals if and only if the other students in the class fail to obtain their goals (Deutsch, 1962; Johnson & Johnson, 1991). Unfortunately, most students perceive school classes as predominantly competitive enterprises. Students either work hard to do better than their classmates, or they do not fully apply themselves because they believe they have no chance of winning.

When students are required to work **individualistically**, on their own, they work by themselves to accomplish learning goals unrelated to those of the other students. Individual goals are assigned and students' efforts are evaluated on a criteria-referenced basis. Each student has his or her own set of materials and works at his or her own speed, ignoring the other students in the class. Students are expected and encouraged to focus on their strict self-interest (how well can I do?), value only their own efforts and own success (if I study hard, I may get a high grade), and ignore as irrelevant the success or failure of others (whether my classmates study or not does not affect me). In **individualistic learning situations,** students' goal achievements are independent; students perceive that the achievement of their learning goals is unrelated to what other students do (Deutsch, 1962; Johnson & Johnson, 1991).

Cooperation is working together to accomplish shared goals. Within cooperative activities, individuals seek outcomes that are beneficial to themselves **and** beneficial to all other group members. **Cooperative learning** is the instructional use of small groups so that students work together to maximize their own and each other's learning. The idea is simple: class members are split into small groups after receiving instruction from the teacher. They then work through the assignment until all group members have successfully understood and completed it. Cooperative efforts result in participants striving for mutual benefit so that all group members benefit from each other's efforts (your success benefits me and my success benefits you), recognizing that all group members share a common fate (we all sink or swim together here), recognizing that one's performance is mutually caused by oneself and one's colleagues (we cannot do it without you), and feeling proud and jointly celebrating when a group member is recognized for achievement (You got an A! That is terrific!). In cooperative learning situations there is a positive interdependence among students' goal attainments; students perceive that they can reach their learning goals if and only if the other students in the learning group also reach their goals (Deutsch, 1962; Johnson & Johnson, 1991).

Technology-assisted cooperative learning exists when the instructional use of technology is combined with the use of cooperative learning groups. Students, for example, may be assigned to cooperative groups of two or three members and given a cooperative assignment to complete a task for which a computer is to be utilized. Positive interdependence is typically established at the terminal so that students are aware of their dependence on other group members in accomplishing their learning goals. In using technology-assisted cooperative learning, the role of technology must be viewed within the whole learning process, not just within achievement.

For interpersonal feedback to enhance both procedural and conceptual learning, it must be given and received within a cooperative context. To structure cooperative learning, five basic elements must be operationalized within the situation.

Basic Elements of Cooperative Learning

Simply placing students in groups and telling them to work together does not mean that they know how to cooperate or that they will do so even if they do know. Group efforts may go wrong in many ways (Johnson & Johnson, 1989). Less able members sometimes "leave it to George" to complete the group's tasks thus creating a **free rider** effect, whereby group members expend decreasing amounts of effort and just go through the team-work motions. At the same time, the more able group member may expend less effort to avoid the **sucker effect** of doing all the work. High-ability group members may be deferred to and may take over the important leadership roles in ways that benefit them at the expense of the other group members (the **rich-get-richer** effect). In a learning group, for example, the more able group member may give all the explanations of what is being learned. Since the amount of time spent explaining correlates highly with the amount learned, the more able member learns a great deal, while the less able members flounder as a captive audience. The time spent listening in group brainstorming can reduce the amount of time any individual may state his or her ideas. Group efforts can be characterized by self-induced helplessness, diffusion of responsibility and social loafing, ganging up against a task, reactance, dysfunctional divisions of labor (''I'm the thinkist and you're the typist''), inappropriate dependence on authority, destructive conflict, and other patterns of behavior that debilitate group performance.

Many teachers believe that they are implementing cooperative learning when in fact they are missing its essence. **Putting students into groups to learn is not the same thing as structuring cooperation among students.** Cooperation is **not:**

1. Having students sit side by side at the same table and talk with each other as they do their individual assignments.

2. Having students do a task individually with instructions that the ones who finish first are to help the slower students.

3. Assigning a report to a group where one student does all the work and others put their names on it.

Cooperation is much more than being physically near other students, discussing material with other students, helping other students, or sharing materials with other students, although each of these is important in cooperative learning.

In order for a lesson to be cooperative, five basic elements must be carefully structured (Johnson, Johnson, & Holubec, 1990). These five elements are what differentiates (a) cooperative learning groups from traditional discussion groups, and (b) a well-structured cooperative learning lesson from a poorly structured one. In a math class, for example, a teacher assigns her students a set of math problems to solve. Students are placed in groups of three. The **instructional task** is for students to solve each story problem correctly and to understand the correct strategy for doing so. The teacher must now implement five basic elements.

The first element of a cooperative lesson is **positive interdependence.** Students must believe that they are linked with others in a way that one cannot succeed unless the other members of the group succeed (and vice versa), that is, they ''sink or swim together.'' Within the math lesson, the teacher creates positive goal interdependence by requiring group members to agree on the answer and the strategies for solving each problem. Positive role interdependence is structured by assigning each student a role. The **reader** reads the problems aloud to the group. The **checker** makes sure that all members can explain how to solve each problem correctly. The **encourager** (in a friendly way) encourages all members of the group to participate in the discussion, sharing their ideas and feelings. Resource interdependence is created by giving each group one copy of the problems to be solved. All students work the problems on scratch paper and share their insights with each other. Positive reward interdependence is structured by giving each group five points if all members score above 90 percent correct on the test given at the end of the unit. The most important factor is goal interdependence. All cooperative learning starts with a mutually shared group goal.

The second element of a cooperative lesson is **face-to-face promotive interaction** among students, which exists when students help, assist, encourage, and support each other's efforts to learn. Students promote each other's learning by orally explaining to each other how to solve problems, discussing with each other the nature of the concepts and strategies being learned, teaching their knowledge to each other, and explaining to each other the connections between present and past learning. In the math lesson, the teacher must provide the time, a knee-to-knee seating arrangement, and teacher encouragement for students to exchange ideas and help each other learn.

The third element is **individual accountability,** which exists when the performance of each individual student is assessed and the results given back to the group and the individual. It is important that group members know (a) who needs more assistance in completing the assignment, and (b) they cannot "hitch-hike" on the work of others. Common ways of structuring individual accountability include giving an individual test to each student and randomly selecting one student's work to represent the efforts of the entire group.

The fourth element is **social skills.** Groups cannot function effectively if students do not have and use the leadership, decision-making, trust-building, communication, and conflict-management skills. These skills have to be taught just as purposefully and precisely as academic skills. Many students have never worked cooperatively in learning situations and, therefore, lack the needed social skills for doing so. In the math lesson the teacher emphasizes the skill of checking to make sure everyone understands. The teacher defines the skill as the phrases and the accompanying nonverbal behaviors to be used by the checker. The group roles are rotated each day. When the teacher sees students engaging in the skill, she verbally praises the group and/or records the instance on an observation sheet. Procedures and strategies for teaching students social skills may be found in Johnson (1990, 1991), Johnson and F. Johnson (1982/1991), and Johnson, Johnson, and Holubec (1990).

Finally, the teacher must ensure that **groups process** how well they are achieving their goals and maintaining effective working relationships among members. At the end of the math period the groups process their functioning by answering two questions: (1) what is something each member did that was helpful for the group, and (2) what is something each member could do to make the group even better tomorrow? Such processing enables learning groups to focus on group maintenance, facilitates the learning of social skills, ensures that members receive feedback on their participation, and reminds students to practice the small group skills required to work cooperatively. Some of the keys to successful processing are: allowing sufficient time for processing to take place, making processing specific rather than vague, varying the format, maintaining student involvement in processing, reminding students to use their social skills while they process, and ensuring that clear expectations of the purpose of processing have been communicated. Often, each group is required to turn in a summary of their processing that is signed by all group members.

The reasons why cooperation is the ideal context for feedback to enhance procedural and conceptual learning may be found in these five elements. The more students believe that they have a stake in each other's success (positive interdependence), the more open they will be to feedback from peers and the teacher. The more students get involved in helping and assisting each other learn, the more precise and accurate their feedback to each other can be. The more accountable students are to do their fair share of the work, the more they will seek out feedback on how their performance can improve. The more socially skilled students are, the better able they are to phrase and time feedback to maximimize its impact. Finally, group processing institutionalizes feedback into the life of the learning group. It is these five elements that make cooperation the ideal setting in which self-feedback, feedback from technological devices, and interpersonal feedback may be most fruitfully integrated.

Given that cooperative learning may be effectively implemented, the next question is whether or not it is a good idea to do so. To address that issue, the research evidence concerning the use of cooperative learning must be examined.

What Do We Know About Cooperative Efforts?

Learning together to complete assignments can have profound effects on students. A great deal of research has been conducted comparing the relative effects of cooperative, competitive, and individualistic efforts on instructional outcomes (Johnson & Johnson, 1989). Over the past 90 years over 575 experimental and 100 correctional studies have been conducted by a wide variety of researchers in different decades with different age subjects, in different subject areas, and in different settings. In our own research program at the Cooperative Learning Center at the University of Minnesota over the past 25 years we have conducted over 85 studies to refine our understanding of how cooperation works. The type of interdependence structured among students determines how they interact with each other, which, in turn, largely determines instructional outcomes. Structuring situations cooperatively results in promotive interaction; structuring situations competitively results in oppositional interaction; and structuring situations individually results in no interaction among students. These interaction patterns affect numerous variables, which may be subsumed within the three broad and interrelated outcomes of effort exerted to achieve quality of relationships among participants and participants' psychological adjustment and social competence (Johnson & Johnson, 1989).

Promotive Interaction

Promotive interaction is characterized by individuals (Johnson & Johnson, 1989):

1. Providing each other with efficient and effective help and assistance.

2. Exchanging needed resources such as information and materials and processing information more efficiently and effectively.

3. Providing each other with feedback in order to improve the subsequent performance of their assigned tasks and responsibilities.

4. Challenging each other's conclusions and reasoning in order to promote higher quality decision making and greater insight into the problems being considered.

5. Advocating the exertion of effort to achieve mutual goals.

6. Influencing each other's efforts to achieve the group's goals.

7. Acting in trusting and trustworthy ways.

8. Being motivated to strive for mutual benefit.

9. Having a moderate level of arousal characterized by low anxiety and stress.

Negative interdependence typically results in students opposing and obstructing each other's learning. **Oppositional interaction** occurs as students discourage and obstruct each other's efforts to achieve. Students focus both on increasing their own achievement **and** on preventing any class-mate from achieving higher than they do. **No interaction** exists when students work independently without any interaction or interchange with each other. Students focus only on increasing their own achievement and ignore as irrelevant the efforts of others. Each of these interaction patterns influences instructional outcomes. Most instructional outcomes may be subsumed within three categories—effort to achieve, interpersonal relationships, and psychological adjustment.

Outcomes

Working together to achieve a common goal produces higher achievement and greater productivity than does working alone. This is so well confirmed by so much research that it stands as one of the strongest principles of social and organizational psychology. Cooperative learning, furthermore, generally results in more higher-level reasoning, more frequent generation of new ideas and solutions (i.e., **process gain**), and greater transfer of what is learned within one situation to another (i.e., **group-to-individual transfer**) than does competitive or individualistic learning. The more conceptual the task, the more problem solving required, the more desirable higher-level reasoning and critical thinking, the more creativity required, and the greater the application required of what is being learned to the real world, the greater the superiority of cooperative over competitive and indivdualistic efforts.

Individuals care more about each other and are more committed to each other's success and well-being when they work together to get the job done than when they work independently from each other and compete to see who is best. This is true when individuals are homogeneous and when individuals differ in intellectual ability, handicapping conditions, ethnic membership, social class, and gender. When individuals are heterogeneous, cooperating on a task results in more realistic and positive views of each other. As relationships become more positive, absenteeism and turnover of membership decrease, member commitment to organizational goals increases, feelings of personal responsibility to the organization increase, willingness to take on difficult tasks increases, motivation and persistence in working toward goal achievement increase, satisfaction and morale increase, willingness to endure pain and frustration on behalf of the organization increases, willingness to defend the organization against external criticism or attack increases, willingness to listen to and be influenced by colleagues increases, commitment to each other's professional growth and success increases, and productivity increases (Johnson & F. Johnson, 1991; Johnson & Johnson, 1989; Watson & Johnson, 1972).

Working cooperatively with peers and valuing cooperation result in

greater psychological health and higher self-esteem than does competing with peers or working independently. Personal ego-strength, self-confidence, independence, and autonomy are all promoted by being involved in cooperative efforts with caring people who are committed to each other's success and well-being and who respect each other as separate and unique individuals. When individuals work together to complete assignments, they interact (mastering social skills and competencies), they promote each other's success (gaining self-worth), and they form personal as well as professional relationships (creating the basis for healthy social development). Individuals' psychological adjustment and health tend to increase when schools are dominated by cooperative efforts. The more individuals work cooperatively with others, the more they see themselves as worthwhile and as having value, the greater their productivity, the greater their acceptance and support of others, and the more autonomous and independent they tend to be. Cooperative experiences are not a luxury: they are an absolute necessity for the healthy development of individuals who can function independently.

Bidirectional relationships exist among efforts to achieve, quality of relationships, and psychological health (Johnson & Johnson, 1989). Each influences the others. **First**, caring and committed friendships come from a sense of mutual accomplishment, mutual pride in joint work, and the bonding that results from joint efforts. The more students care about each other, on the other hand, the harder they will work to achieve mutual learning goals. **Second**, joint efforts to achieve mutual goals promote higher self-esteem, self-efficacy, personal control, and confidence in their competencies. On the other hand, the healthier individuals are psychologically, the better able they are to work with others to achieve mutual goals. **Third**, psychological health is built on the internalization of the caring and respect received from loved ones. Friendships are developmental advantages that promote self-esteem, self-efficacy, and general psychological adjustment. The healthier people are psychologically (i.e., free of psychological pathology such as depression, paranoia, anxiety, fear of failure, repressed anger, hopelessness, and meaninglessness), the more caring and committed their relationships. Since each outcome can induce the others, they are likely to be found together. They are a package with each outcome a door into all three. And together they induce positive interdependence and promotive interaction.

Feedback within cooperative learning groups affects many aspects of students' learning experience. The feedback affects the combination of procedural and conceptual learning that is required for modern technology-assisted instruction. The feedback affects the positive relationships and social support among students. The feedback affects students' psychological adjustment, social competencies, and self-esteem. All aspects of students' life in schools is affected by the feedback received when they work cooperatively with classmates to achieve mutual learning goals. Feedback, furthermore, is inherent within well-structured, cooperative efforts and is institutionalized through both promotive interaction and group processing. Promotive interaction has been discussed previously in this chapter. The research related to group processing is discussed below.

Institutionalized Feedback Through Group Processing

Interpersonal feedback is enhanced when members of cooperative learning groups discuss (i.e., process) how effectively they are working together and what actions are needed to improve the functioning of the group in the future. A **process** is an identifiable sequence of events taking place over time, and **process goals** refer to the sequence of events instrumental in achieving goals. Members engage in **group processing** when they reflect on a group session to (a) describe what member actions were helpful and unhelpful (i.e., give each other specific and concrete feedback about behavior in the group), and (b) make decisions about what actions to continue to change. The purpose of group processing is to clarify and improve the effectiveness of the members in contributing to the collaborative efforts to achieve the group's goals. The group dynamics literature has emphasized the importance of group processing (Cartwright & Zander, 1968; Johnson & F. Johnson, 1991; Napier & Gerschenfeld, 1981; Schmuck & Schmuck, 1974). In terms of group dynamics, in order to be productive, groups must process how well they are working, and take action to resolve any difficulties members have in collaborating together productively.

Almost no direct evidence existed as to whether group processing did in fact improve productivity until a study was conducted by Stuart Yager (Yager, Johnson, & Johnson, 1985). He examined the impact on achievement of (a) cooperative learning in which members discussed how well their group was functioning and how they could improve its effectiveness, (b) cooperative learning without any group processing, and (c) individualistic learning. Eighty-four third-grade students were randomly assigned to three conditions. Subjects studied a transportation unit for 35 minutes a day for 25 instructional days. The results indicated that the high-, medium-, and low-achieving individuals in the cooperation-with-group-processing condition achieved higher on daily achievement, post-instructional achievement, and retention measures than did the individuals in the other two conditions. Subjects in the cooperation-without-group-processing condition, furthermore, achieved higher on all three measures than did the subjects in the individualistic condition.

Johnson, Johnson, Stanne, and Garibaldi (1989) conducted a follow-up study comparing cooperative learning with no processing, cooperative learning with teacher processing (the teacher specified cooperative skills to use, observed, and gave whole-class feedback as to how well individuals were using the skills), cooperative learning with teacher and student processing (the teacher specified cooperative skills to use, observed, gave whole-class feedback as to how well individuals were using the skills, and learning groups discussed how well they interacted as a group), and individualistic learning. Forty-nine high-ability high-school Black American seniors and entering college freshmen at Xavier University participated in the study. A complex computer-assisted problem-solving assignment was given to all individuals. All three cooperative conditions performed higher than did the individualistic condition. The combination of teacher and student processing resulted in greater individual and group problem-solving success than did the other cooperative conditions.

These studies on group processing add to the literature indicating that interpersonal feedback does improve group productivity and individual achievement. The next issue is whether interpersonal feedback and feedback from technological devices such as computers may be used together fruitfully.

Our Research with Computers

Many teachers and software designers automatically assume that all computer-assisted instruction should be structured individualistically. One student to a computer has been the usual rule, and computer programs have been written accordingly. The assumption that learning works best when one student works with one computer remained largely unquestioned for many years. In order to enhance education, however, technology must promote cooperation and the **creation of a shared experience among students** rather than simply helping individuals share their experiences with each other.

We have conducted several studies examining the use of cooperative, competitive, and individualistic learning activities at the computer (Johnson, Johnson, Stanne, & Garibaldi, 1989; Johnson, Johnson, & Stanne, 1985, 1986). The studies included students from the eighth grade through college freshman levels and lasted from 3 to 30 instructional hours. The tasks varied from a computerized navigational and map-reading, problem-solving task to word-processing assignments.

The achievement results paralleled the findings of the previous research. Computer-assisted cooperative learning, compared with competitive and individualistic efforts at the computer, promoted (a) higher quantity of daily achievement, (b) higher quality of daily achievement, (c) greater mastery of factual information, (d) greater ability to apply one's factual knowledge in test questions requiring application of facts, (e) greater ability to use factual information to answer problem-solving questions, and (f) greater success in problem solving. Cooperation at the computer promoted greater motivation to persist on problem-solving tasks. Students in the cooperative condition were more successful in operating the computer programs.

In terms of oral participation, students in the cooperative condition, compared with students in the competitive and individualistic conditions, made fewer statements to the teacher and more to each other, made more task-oriented statements and fewer social statements, and generally engaged in more positive, task-oriented interaction with each other (especially when the social skill responsibilities were specified and group processing was conducted).

Finally, the studies provided evidence that females were perceived to be of higher status in the cooperative than in the competitive or individualistic conditions.

These studies compared the combination of peers and computers with students working only with a computer either individualistically or in competition with classmates. The results support the conclusion that computers are a vehicle that do not in themselves change the consequences of instruction. A *dialogue with peers* promoted more higher-level reasoning and ability to apply learning than did a *dialogue with a computer*.

No evidence existed that the computer in and of itself transformed students' minds. Interaction with peers within a cooperative context led to more successful application of knowledge to test questions requiring higher-level reasoning and problem-solving than did interaction with the computer only.

On the basis of his review of the literature, Richard Clark (1983) concluded that in the 1950s educators urged that the power of radio be applied to the teaching process. Then the 1960s brought nationwide television, which was promoted as a wonderful way to help children learn. Then came the computer, which some educators say should be the most effective way ever to deliver instruction and increase achievement. Each new medium seems to attract its own set of advocates who make claims for improved learning. But Clark concluded that the truth is that media do not influence learning under any conditions. It is the instructional method that affects learning. He stated, "The best current evidence is that media are mere vehicles that deliver instruction but do not influence student achievement any more than the truck that delivers our groceries causes changes in our nutrition.'' (p. 445) The results of our research add some support to Clark's thesis. There are, however, complementary strengths to cooperative learning and technology-assisted instruction.

Complementary Strengths of Cooperative Learning and Computer-Assisted Instruction

Learning as a whole is a social process that involves (a) achievement, insight, understanding, reasoning; (b) caring, committed, supportive relationships; and (c) well-adjusted and socially-skilled individuals. The role of technology must be viewed within the context of learning as a whole process, not just within achievement (especially lower-level achievement). Technology needs to be used in ways that promote positive relationships and psychological adjustment as well as achievement.

A natural partnership exists between cooperative learning and technology-assisted instruction. The more technology is used to teach, the more necessary cooperative learning is. When cooperative learning and computer-assisted instruction are combined, for example, the microcomputer (depending on the software) presents the learning task, provides strategy instructions, controls the flow of activity (e.g., signals when a new task should be initiated), monitors learning activities in an objective and efficient manner, provides reinforcing messages for good performance on all aspects of the task, keeps track of student responses for future analysis, tailors learning activities to the students based on pretraining measures and on responses to tasks within the learning sequence, provides tests over the training materials and, based on students' responses, branches to further strategy instructions, and provides expert content.

In addition, the computer does computations and thus frees members of cooperative groups to be more involved in problem-solving and conceptual learning. For example, it took Johannes Kepler four years to calculate the orbit of Mars. Today students can do this calculation in about four seconds using a microcomputer.

Finally, using a computer helps redefine what is finished and what is still being developed. With the ability to revise writing continually, for example, the computer reduces the resistance to changing one's ideas and work to improve them. Revisions may be made without having to redo an entire report, essay, or theme. A new version is always possible.

The instructional use of technology, however, will not reach its full usefulness unless used with cooperative learning. Cooperative learning structures the positive relationships and efforts to achieve that are key to maximizing the potential of the technology. Computer-assisted cooperative learning has a number of advantages. The first is a sense of joint effort and belonging. The social isolation involved in working alone at a computer can create mood states (such as loneliness, boredom and frustration) that interfere with sustained effort to complete learning tasks. Emotional mood is an important influence on students' achievement motivation and ability to concentrate and persist in learning activities (Showers & Cantor, 1985). Achievement-oriented behavior is often interrupted by emotional mood, which may promote either increased effort or withdrawal from the learning situation. Working cooperatively with classmates (compared with learning individualistically or competitively) increases the positiveness of students' mood states, thereby increasing their motivation to achieve (Johnson & Johnson, 1989).

The second advantage of computer-assisted cooperative learning is that students are given the opportunity to talk through, explain, and summarize the material being learned. Such discussions result in higher level cognitive reasoning, increased achievement and retention, and higher level conceptual understanding (Johnson & Johnson, 1989). Students in cooperative learning groups can assist each other in (a) analyzing and diagnosing problems, and (b) transforming incoming information into an alternate form (such as one's own words, a picture, or an alternative representation system or network). Such transformations allow students to personalize information being learned, test degree of understanding, enter multiple encodings in memory, and "chunk" or network the information being learned. A limitation of computer-assisted individualistic learning is that it denies learners the opportunity to summarize orally and explain what they are learning.

The third is that within cooperative learning groups classmates become social models to be (a) imitated and (b) used for social-comparison purposes. Peer social modeling is one of the most potent methods of teaching learning skills and strategies, and is especially effective when the material to be learned is difficult and complex and when students are learning how to use the computer or run a program. When students work collaboratively on a task involving the use of the computer, they can observe and imitate each other's use of the computer, thereby increasing their speed in mastering both hardware and software. In addition, discussing the material being learned provides opportunities for students to observe and imitate each other's cognitive-processing strategies, thereby increasing their mastery of higher-level reasoning processes. Comparing one's own cognitive-processing strategies with those of other students can increase one's insight into how one's strategies can be improved.

Fourth, experiencing the warmth and approval of a number of classmates is usually much more rewarding than having a computer compliment one on the accuracy and speed of one's work. Approval from a computer is not as potent a reinforcer as encouragement and approval from peers.

Fifth, feedback and evaluation from one's peers are usually more complex and complete than feedback from a computer. Other students can evaluate, diagnose, correct, and give feedback on one's conceptual understanding and oral summary of the material being studied. Feedback from the computer is limited to the evaluation of the literal words or numbers entered through the keyboard.

Sixth, working alone with a computer limits the amount of divergent thinking and creativity students can bring to a problem-solving task. Students tend to generate higher-level reasoning strategies, a greater diversity of ideas and procedures, more critical thinking, and more creative responses when they learn in cooperative learning groups than when they learn individualistically or competitively (Johnson & Johnson, 1983).

Seventh, in cooperative learning, groupmates encourage and support efforts to achieve. Many studies have found more peer regulation, support, and encouragement of task related efforts in cooperative than in competitive or individualistic learning situations (Johnson & Johnson, 1989). Human encouragement is more personal and vivid than is encouragement from a computer. The social support of the cooperative setting is invaluable for persistence and effort on difficult learning tasks and is part of the reason that cooperative groups manage failure more constructively than do individuals working alone. The warmth and approval of one's peers are especially important when tasks are difficult or frustrating. Computer-assisted individualistic learning is limited by the microcomputer not being as effective as classmates in encouraging students to stay on task and exert concentrated effort.

Eight, when cooperative learning is used, fewer computers are required. Even when schools cannot afford a computer for each student, computer-assisted tasks are still possible when cooperative learning is used.

Finally, evidence exists that students *prefer* to work cooperatively at the computer (Hawkins, Sheingold, Gearhart, & Berger, 1982; Levin & Dareev, 1980; Muller & Perlmutter, 1985). Computers provide a learning environment conducive for group work as the introduction of computers into classrooms increases cooperative behavior and task-oriented verbal interaction (Hawkins, Sheingold, Gearhart & Berger, 1982; Levin & Dareev, 1980). Students seem to prefer to work collaboratively with a computer, giving each other suggestions and helping each other over stumbling blocks. Even when students play electronic games, they prefer to have partners and associates. Working at a computer collaboratively with classmates seems to be more fun and enjoyable as well as more effective to most students. Students are more likely to gather at the computer than they normally would for other school work. The computer may not only be a good place to cooperate, but also be a good place to introduce cooperative learning groups in schools.

Since most classrooms lack even a telephone, the possibility of full use of instructional technology seems far away. The potential, however, seems unlimited when used in combination with cooperative learning. We have far more technology and software than we know how to use and certainly more than we are willing to use. Computers are now multimedia devices capable of full motion video, voice recognition, interactive graphics, and touch-sensitive screens. Multimedia or hypermedia information combines moving video, sound, animation, and printed words. With the right software and peripheral devices, computers can now turn a disk of data into a book in a few minutes, making high-quality personalized publishing a reality. Soon we will have self-improving, "thinking" machines. The use of such technology to teach, however, will be limited if it isolates students and makes learning more impersonal. Social, cognitive, and procedural aspects of learning must be recognized in order for technology to be used effectively.

Whenever new technology is introduced into society, a counterbalancing emphasis on human interaction and interpersonal support may be rejected or the technology is rejected. The more technology introduced into schools, the more students and staff will aggregate and want to be with other people. The challenge is to simultaneously increase the use of technology and cooperative learning. Not only will technology be more accepted and used when cooperative learning is concurrently used, but higher achievement and a variety of other instructional outcomes will also be promoted.

Questions About Technology-Assisted Cooperative Learning

Given the powerful effects of cooperation on achievement, relationships, and psychological adjustment, and given the numerous advantages of using technology-assisted cooperative learning, a number of questions about the use of technology may tentatively be answered. **First,** do computers affect achievement, or are they merely a means of delivering instruction? Our results support Clark's (1983) conclusion that computers are merely a means of delivering instruction. A key to achievement in cooperative learning is the confrontation among peers on ideas, opinions, and how things work, and then jointly working to construct a better understanding. Students must discuss, challenge, confront, request and receive rationale, elaborate, and synthesize. Such social interaction is essential for effective learning, for the transformation of the mind, and for the development of expertise.

Second, is a *dialogue* with a computer as effective in promoting achievement, higher-level reasoning, and ability to apply learning as a *dialogue* with a peer? To have a dialogue requires more than the presentation of information. There needs to be an exchange of knowledge that leads to epistemic conflict and intellectual challenge and curiosity. Such an exchange is personal as well as informational. It involves respect for and belief in each other's abilities as well as commitment to each other's learning. Our results indicate that a dialogue with a peer is far more powerful than one with a computer.

The **third** question is, can a computer pass as a person? Our research leads to the tentative conclusion that the dialogues are different so that a person interacts quite differently with a computer and a person. Machines and people are not equally interesting or persuasive. With another person, a commitment exists to his or her learning and well-being. It is rare to feel the same emotions toward a machine.

Fourth, is the effectiveness of a message separate from the medium? Generally, the research on cognitive development indicates that the same information, presented in other formats (especially nonsocial formats), is only marginally effective in promoting genuine cognitive development (Murray, 1983; Johnson & Johnson, 1989).

Fifth, is the computer an amplifier or a transformer of the mind? An **amplifier** serves as a tool function like note-taking or measuring. A **transformer** leads to the discovery and invention of principles. If the computer is a transformer, habitual computer users eventually would be in a new stage of mental functioning—with or without their computers, they would have a way of operating on problems that cannot be explained by the very same cognitive principles that were adequate to explain the workings of the "precomputer mind"? Our research on academic conflicts and the cognitive development research indicate that children confronted by a cognitively more advanced peer develop in the direction of that peer (Johnson & Johnson, 1989). Generally, therefore, it may be concluded that technology such as the computer is a tool to amplify the minds of students. As a tool, the computer (as well as the calculator) can free students from the rote memorization of methods of mathematical formulation and formula-driven science, allowing more time for underlying concepts to be integrated with physical examples. A danger of the computer is that students will know what button to push to get a correct answer without understanding the underlying process or developing the ability to solve the problem on their own without the computer. Expertise is **not** knowing which button to push!

Finally, the **sixth question** is, can technology such as computers prepare a student for the "real world"? Working in a modern organization requires team skills such as leadership and conflict management and the ability to engage in interpersonal problem solving. While clearly cooperative learning is an analog to modern organizational life, experience in using technology in and of itself may not improve employability or job success.

The Future of Technology-Assisted Cooperative Learning

For cooperation to take place, students must have a joint workspace. Collaborators use shared spaces such as blackboards and curriculum materials to work together to create answers. Metal models of gene structures helped two Nobel Prize winners discover the double helix. One of the promises of the computer is to allow students all over the world to create powerful shared spaces—super blackboards and super models. Instead of sharing a blackboard or a worktable, people all over the world can share a computer screen. The future of technology-assisted cooperative learning rests on developing both appropriate software and hardware to create shared workspaces that may be shared by the group, among groups within the same classroom, and among groups throughout the world.

Technology-assisted cooperative learning requires software that supports group work rather than individual work (i.e., **groupware**). In order to write such software, programmers need to understand the nature of cooperation and the five basic elements that mediate its effectiveness. Currently, the people developing the software understand how to write software, but they do not understand how groups work together and the five basic elements that define well-structured cooperative efforts.

What is commonly not understood is that education takes place through relationships, not through the actions of single individuals. Correspondingly, employers hire relationships, not people. Most technology was originally developed to amplify an individual's ability to communicate to other individuals. But in schools and all other organizations, what increases productivity is transforming cooperative efforts. Value is created within joint efforts to achieve mutual goals, not in isolated individual actions. Writing the software to increase the productivity of joint efforts is the current challenge facing programmers.

Given that cooperation among students is an essential aspect of any well-structured learning situation, developers of hardware need to think seriously about how technology can increase human cooperation within education and within the workplace. While more and more work is being done in self-managing teams (perhaps networked electronically with other teams throughout the company and the world) the ability of the hardware to allow or even require people to work cooperatively is an important design issue.

Schools eventually may have to make greater use of appropriate technologies and cooperative learning. Multiple ongoing revolutions in technology and classroom organization require schools to prepare students to make wise choices in the face of an overabundance of information and within a team context. It is technology-assisted cooperative learning that may best prepare students to live in the modern world.

Summary

Feedback is information made available to individuals that makes possible the comparison of actual performance with some standard of performance. There are three sources of feedback—oneself, technological devices such as timers and computers, and other people. In the ideal learning situation, all three sources will occur in an integrated way. Interpersonal feedback is the most powerful of the three sources. It primarily is limited to cooperative situations, where individuals are working together to achieve mutual goals. Technologies traditionally have carried an individualistic bias by assuming that communication contains a sender and receivers who individually try to understand the message. Competitors and indifferent bystanders, however, are not usually acceptable sources for feedback concerning performance. In order for a cooperative relationship to exist, five basic elements must be structured within the learning situation—positive interdependence, face-to-face promotive interaction, individual accountability, social skills, and group processing. These five elements give cooperation its power and provide the context in which interpersonal feedback is sought and utilized.

The research evidence provides strong support for the instructional use of cooperative learning and for the efficacy of technology-assisted cooperative learning. Hundreds of studies have compared the relative effects of cooperative, competitive, and individualistic efforts. Structuring cooperation results in a promotive interaction pattern that has consistent and large effects on effort to achieve, interpersonal relationships, and psychological adjustment. Generally, cooperative efforts result in higher achievement, more positive relationships, and greater psychological health than do competitive or individualistic efforts. Providing each other with feedback is inherent in the group processing of how effective the group is functioning. Our research on computer-assisted cooperative learning, furthermore, provides evidence that to be effective, computers must be used within the context of cooperative learning. Through both promotive interaction and group processing, feedback is institutionalized into the basic structure of cooperative learning.

A number of advantages exist in combining technology-assisted instruction with cooperative learning. The computer, for example, can control the flow of work, monitor accuracy, give electronic feedback, and do calculations. Instructional use of technology, however, will not reach its full usefulness unless it is used with cooperative learning. Cooperative learning provides a sense of belonging, oral explanations of what is being studied, social models, warmth and approval for efforts to achieve, encouragement of divergent thinking, and interpersonal feedback.

When technology is compared with collaborators, current evidence indicates that computers deliver instruction, but they do not affect achievement. The dialogue with the computer is not as effective as a dialogue with another person in promoting achievement and higher-level reasoning. The computer cannot pass as a person. Collaborators are people, not machines. Messages from other people are more powerful and influential than are messages from machines. Technology amplifies communication, while people transform each other's minds.

Technology can either facilitate or obstruct cooperation. The future of technology-assisted cooperative learning depends on the development of software written for cooperative groups and the development of hardware that both requires and facilitates cooperative efforts within the group, among groups in the classroom, and among groups throughout the world.

References

Acheson, K. (1964). *The effects of feedback from television recordings and three types of supervisory treatment on selected teacher behaviors.* (Doctoral Dissertation, Stanford University). Ann Arbor, MI: University Microfilms, No. 64-13542.

Anderson, L., Evertson, C., & Brophy, J. (1979). An experimental study of effective teaching in first-grade reading groups. *The Elementary School Journal, 79,* 193–203.

Borgida, E., & Nisbett, R. (1977). The differential impact of abstract vs. concrete information decision. *Journal of Applied Social Psychology, 7,* 258-271.

Cartwright, D., & Zander, A. (Eds.) (1968). *Group dynamics.* New York: Harper & Row.

Clark, R.E. (1983). Reconsidering research on learning from media. *Review of Educational Research, 53*(4), 445–459.

Deutsch, M. (1962). Cooperation and trust: Some theoretical notes. In M.R. Jones (Ed.), *Nebraska symposium on motivation* (pp. 275–319). Lincoln, NE: University of Nebraska Press.

Fuller, F., Peck, R., Brown, O., Menaker, S., White, M., & Veldman, D. (1969). *Effects of personalized feedback during teacher preparation on teacher personality and teaching behavior.* Austin: University of Texas.

Hamill, R., Wilson, T., & Nisbett, R. (1980). Insensitivity to sample bias: Generalizing from a typical case. *Journal of Personality and Social Psychology, 38,* 578–589.

Hawkins, J., Sheingold, K., Gearhart, M., & Berger, C. (1982). Microcomputers in schools: Impact on the social life of elementary classrooms. *Journal of Applied Developmental Psychology, 3,* 361–373.

Innis, H. (1964). *The bias of communication.* Toronto: University of Toronto Press.

Innis, H. (1972). *Empire and communication.* Toronto: University of Toronto Press.

Johnson, D.W. (1990). *Reaching out: Interpersonal effectiveness and self-actualization* (4th ed.). Englewood Cliffs, NJ: Prentice-Hall.

Johnson, D.W. (1991). *Human relations and your career* (3rd ed.). Englewood Cliffs, NJ: Prentice-Hall.

Johnson, D.W., & Johnson, F. (1991). *Joining together: Group theory and group skills* (2nd/4th ed.). Englewood Cliffs, NJ: Prentice-Hall.

Johnson, D.W., & Johnson, R. (1983). The socialization and achievement crisis: Are cooperative learning experiences the solution? In L. Bickman (Ed.), *Applied Social Psychology Annual 4* (pp. 119–164). Beverly Hills, CA: Sage.

Johnson, D.W., & Johnson, R. (1989). *Cooperation and competition: Theory and research.* Edina, MN: Interaction Book Company.

Johnson, D.W., & Johnson, R. (1991). *Learning together and alone: Cooperative, competitive, and individualistic learning* (4th ed.). Englewood Cliffs, NJ: Prentice-Hall.

Johnson, D.W., Johnson, R., & Holubec, E. (1990). *Circles of learning: Cooperation in the classroom* (3rd ed.). Edina, MN: Interaction Book Company.

Johnson, D.W., Johnson, R.T., Richards, S., & Buckman, L. (1986). The effect of prolonged implementation of cooperative learning on social support within the classroom. *Journal of Psychology, 119,* 405–411.

Johnson, D.W., Johnson, R., Stanne, M., & Garibaldi, A. (1989). The impact of leader and member group processing on achievement in cooperative groups. *The Journal of Social Psychology, 130,* 507–516.

Johnson, R.T., Johnson, D.W., & Stanne, M. (1985). Effects of cooperative, competitive, and individualistic goal structures on computer-assisted instruction. *Journal of Educational Psychology, 77,* 668–677.

Johnson, R.T., Johnson, D.W., & Stanne, M. (1986). A comparison of computer-assisted cooperative, competitive, and individualistic learning. *American Educational Research Journal, 23,* 382–392.

Levin, J., & Dareev, Y. (1980). Problem-solving in everyday situations. *The Quarterly Newsletter of the Laboratory of Comparative Human Cognition, 2,* 47–51.

Lockhead, J. (1983). *Beyond Emile: Misconceptions of education in the twenty-first century.* Paper presented at American Educational Research Association Annual Meeting, Montreal.

McLuhan, M. (1964). *Understanding media: The extensions of man.* New York: New American Library.

Morse, K., Kysilka, M., & Davis, O. (1970). *Effects of different types of supervisory feedback on teacher candidates' development of refocusing behaviors.* (Report Series No. 48). Austin: Research and Development Center for Teacher Education, University of Texas.

Muller, A., & Perlmutter, M. (1985). *Preschool children's problem-solving interactions at computers and jigsaw puzzles.* Manuscript submitted for publication.

Murray, F. (1983). *Cognitive benefits of teaching on the teacher.* Paper presented at

American Educational Research Association Annual Meeting, Montreal, Quebec.

Napier, R., & Gerschenfeld, M. (1981). *Groups: Theory and experience.* Boston: Houghton-Mifflin.

Nisbett, R., Borgida, E., Crandall, R., & Reed, H. (1976). Popular induction: Information is not always informative. In J. Carroll & J. Payne (Eds.), *Cognition and social behavior.* Hillsdale, NJ: Lawrence Erlbaum Associates.

Peterson, P., & Janicki, T. (1979). Individual characteristics and children's learning in large-group and small-group approaches. *Journal of Educational Psychology, 71*(5), 677–687.

Peterson, P., Janicki, T., & Swing, S. (1981). Individual characteristics and children's learning in large-group and small-group approaches: Study II. *American Educational Research Journal, 18,* 453–473.

Peterson, P., & Swing, S. (1985). Students' cognitions as mediators of the effectiveness of small-group learning. *Journal of Educational Psychology, 77*(3), 299–312.

Postman, N. (1985) *Amusing ourselves to death: Public discourse in the age of show business.* New York: Viking Penguin.

Schmuck, R., & Schmuck, P. (1974). *A humanistic psychology of education.* Palo Alto, CA: National Press Books.

Showers, C., & Cantor, N. (1985). Social cognition: A look at motivated strategies. In M. Rosenzweig and L. Porter (Eds.), *Annual Review of Psychology, Volume 36* (pp. 275–306). Palo Alto, CA: Annual Reviews.

Steiner, J. (1967). Observing responses and uncertainty reduction. *Quarterly Journal of Experimental Psychology, 19,* 18–29.

Swing, S., & Peterson, P. (1982). The relationship of student ability and small group interaction to student achievement. *American Educational Research Journal, 19,* 259–274.

Taylor, S., & Thompson, S. (1982). Stalking the elusive "vividness" effect. *Psychological Review, 89,* 155–181.

Tuckman, B., McCall, K., & Hyman, R. (1969). The modification of teacher behavior: Effects of dissonance and coded feedback. *American Educational Research Journal, 6,* 607–619.

Watson, G., & Johnson, D.W. (1972). *Social psychology: Issues and insights.* Philadelphia: Lippincott.

Webb, N. (1980). A process-outcome analysis of learning in group and individual settings. *Educational Psychologist, 15,* 69–83.

Webb, N. (1982). Group composition, group interaction, and achievement in cooperative small groups. *Journal of Educational Psychology, 74*(4), 475–484.

Yager, S., Johnson, D., & Johnson, R. (1985). Oral discussion, group-to-individual transfer, and achievement in cooperative learning groups. *Journal of Educational Psychology, 77*(1), 60–66.

Chapter Seven

Adapted and Adaptive Feedback in Technology-Based Instruction

Gregory C. Sales
University of Minnesota

The term *feedback* is widely used to refer to the communication with a learner to inform him or her of the accuracy of a response to a question (Carter, 1984; Cohen, 1985; Kulhavy, 1977). Under this definition, a learner must be involved in the practice portion of an instructional unit for feedback to be available. Then, depending on the design of the instruction and the mode of delivery, the learner is usually informed of his or her performance after each practice item or following the completion of an entire set of practice items. Several typical examples of the use of feedback follow. As you read these examples, consider the efforts that went into the design and development of the instruction, the factors that govern the role of the feedack, and the feedback's influence on the learner and learning.

(1) After a student completes a worksheet assigned in class, it is turned-in for scoring. When it has been scored and returned to the student, the score and any comments from the teacher serve as feedback on the entire assignment.

(2) Upon completing the chapter review activities in a self-study manual, a student compares his or her responses to the sample responses provided at the back of the manual. In this case, the student's feedback is the degree to which the student-generated responses are perceived to match the ones provided by the author of the instructional material.

(3) Each correct response given during a computer-based lesson is followed by a quickly-played musical scale and the addition of five points to the learner's total score. Each incorrect response results

in the scale being played in reverse order and the loss of five points. Here, both the music and scoring system provide feedback.

(4) A tutor working with a student asks a question designed to help the learner understand the relationship that exists between several of the concepts being studied. As the student responds, the tutor's facial expression changes and she leans back in her seat. When the student has finished, the tutor leans forward and in a quiet, patient tone, asks the student to defend his or her answer, given several specific points that had been discussed earlier. In this example the feedback consisted of the learner's perception and interpretation of the tutor's facial expressions, body language, tone of voice, and the content of her remarks.

In each of the examples above, feedback served a purpose, yet each example reflected a completely different style of feedback and required a different level of design and development effort. The first example provided delayed, massed feedback (the score), as well as specific comments intended to address the individual student's needs. The third example delivered immediate, item-specific feedback. However, the form of this feedback was intended to motivate the student and was identical for each student working through the lesson. Example two required the student to generate his or her own feedback from prepared written material, while example four provided a variety of spontaneously generated visual and auditory cues.

The value of feedback as a tool for motivating students and increasing learning is not a recent revelation. In ancient times, feedback was used to stimulate and motivate learners (see Lysakowski & Walberg, 1981). In modern times, feedback continues to be considered essential to effective instruction and is an integral part of virtually every model of instruction. All too often, however, feedback is designed and delivered in a generic fashion with little attention given to how or when it is used and the impact it may have on the efficiency or effectiveness of the overall instructional process. With a limited investment of resources, the quality of feedback can be enhanced by attending to the needs, interests, and other characteristics of the target learning group.

This chapter examines feedback in technology-assisted instruction. Specifically, the concepts of adapted and adaptive feedback are presented. Particular attention is given to the capability of technology to expand the functional role of feedback and to be optimally efficient in the delivery of feedback, while still being sensitive to the learner's background, instructional performance, educational needs, and the complete instructional environment.

The content of the chapter is presented in four sections. The first section provides a brief introduction to the nature of feedback with an emphasis on the role of feedback in technology-assisted instruction. The section includes an overview of the modes of delivery and functions that feedback may perform. Section two defines adapted or adaptive feedback and elaborates on the positive attributes of each. The criterion variables which provide the motive for adapting feedback and the difference variable on which feedback may be adapted are discussed. The third section is a review and examination of representative literature on adapted and adaptive feedback. Finally, recommendations and guidelines for the design and development of feedback are presented.

Feedback in Technology-Assisted Instruction

The phrase *technology-assisted instruction* is open to many interpretations. As this chapter is intended to provide information to instructional designers who will be using the technologies of today and tomorrow, readers are encouraged to use a broad rather than a narrow definition. Instructional technologies should be viewed as the full range of individual workstations (e.g., personal computers in labs or classrooms, and computer-based multimedia systems in school media centers) and instructional systems for small- and large-group use (e.g., classroom presentation systems, group response systems, spacecraft flight simulators, rides/experiences at EPCOT Center).

Wager and Wager (1986) present a definition of feedback in computer-based instruction that expands its role beyond that found in most non-technology-based instructional situations. They state that feedback in computer-bsed instruction is "any message or display that the computer presents to the learner after a response." Feedback in technology-assisted instruction, then, is information presented to the student after any input. Its purpose is to shape the perceptions of the learner. This reflects the current thinking in cognitive psychology and informaton-processing theory (e.g., Kulhavy & Stock, 1989) and extends the role of feedback across all of the elements of a technology-based lesson rather than restricting it to the area of practice.

This broadened definition of feedback is a double-edged sword for instructional designers. With this expanded role comes not only an increased potential for feedback to influence learners' achievement, but also increased potential for instructional opportunities to be lost through neglect during the design of feedback.

To optimize the effectiveness of feedback, designers may find it helpful to consider feedback to be periodic input to the learner. Such input can be used to aid the learner by providing guidance about instructional decisions, additional instruction, orientation within a lesson or curriculum, procedural support on the operation of an instructional unit, motives for continued effort, or other types of assistance. The following discussion will more fully articulate the range of feedback types and effects. It will also illustrate how feedback can serve an expanded role in technology-assisted instruction.

As technology-assisted instruction continues to evolve, an increasing range of feedback types becomes available. From the late 1970s to the mid-1980s, microcomputer-based instruction consisted largely of text displays with limited graphics and animations. During this time period, the feedback used within such instruction was also restricted to these forms with an occasional beep, click, or simple melody as a supplement. As a result of recent developments in processor speed, memory capacity, disk accessing speed, digital technologies, computer peripherals, and authoring environments, designers now are able to include digital images, high-speed animation, video, audio, and speech in instructional software. Similarly, the modes through which technology-based feedback may be delivered have increased.

Although current instructional technology systems may seem extremely sophisticated, exciting advances are on the horizon. Technologies such as digitized full-motion video and virtual reality will be widely available as instructional environments in the near future, bringing with them opportunities for holistic and multi-sensory forms of feedback. Even with today's more typical instructional technologies, it is possible to utilize any of the following modes, or combinations of modes, as channels for feedback: visual (text, computer graphics, computer animations, digitalized still images, video); auditory (computer-generated sounds: beeps, clicks, simple melodies, digitized audio effects, and digitized speech); tactile (pressing keys and buttons, rolling track balls, moving joysticks, touching the monitor screen, movement), and olfactory (odors, fragrances).

Examples of multi-sensory feedback can be seen in advanced simulations and immersion education experiences. In these environments, learners are exposed to moving instructional platforms, introduction of smoke or plant fragrances, movement of air, an array of sounds and voices, as well as text and visual feedback from display panels. All of these are introduced in response to learner input and decisions made during the instruction. Each is intended to shape the learner's perceptions during the instructional experience.

Many different functions can be attributed to feedback in technology-assisted instruction. A shown in Figure 7.1, by using the delivery modes discussed above, feedback could be presented at various points in a lesson to direct, inform, instruct, motivate, stimulate, advise, or provide summary input for learners (Sales, 1988).

Adapted and Adaptive Feedback

Based on an examination of the technology-assisted instruction products currently available, apparently many software designers and developers devote little time and attention to the role of feedback. Most products contain a generic form of feedback mediated by brief subroutines that have limited capacity to communicate with the learner. Often they present short statements (e.g., Correct or Incorrect) or update a score displayed in response to student input. These feedback routines are designed to function without regard to the individual differences of the specific target group or the demonstrated needs of individual learners. The primary principles behind the development of many of these sub-routines appear to have been (1) that they are easy and inexpensive to develop, and (2) that they can be used repeatedly in response to all user input. Two exceptions to these practices are software products with adapted or adaptive feedback components.

Students of instructional design are aware that a number of factors impact the design of technology-assisted instruction and, therefore, the design of the feedback contained within that instruction. These factors include learner characteristics, the content of the instruction, desired learning outcomes, the environment in which the instruction will be delivered, available instructional support, and others (see Figure 7.2). Adapted and adaptive feedback reflect designers' and developers' efforts to take these factors under consideration and to see that they are effectively addressed throughout the instructional experience.

In one respect, adapted feedback is similar to the generic feedback forms described above—it is *stable* within a software product, meaning each individual using the product will see the same feedback as he or she works through the lesson. However, during the design and development of the software, special attention is given to the role of feedback, and an effort is made to customize the feedback along one or more dimensions. This results in software where the feedback is adapted to capitalize on information about either the instructional setting in which it will be used or the learners who will use it. For example, when it is known that software will be used by pairs of learners, the feedback may be adapted to that instructional situation by incorporating comments that address both learners and encourage cooperation and mutual support during the instruction. Another example of adapted feedback occurs when software capitalizes on a knowledge of the

Role	Explanation	Example
direct	provides information about an action to be taken	"Use the mouse to move the pointer to the item you wish to select, then press the mouse button."
inform	acknowledge the accuracy of input from the learner	"Correct."
instruct	supplemental information intended to improve the learner's understanding of the content being addressed	"Incorrect, as you watch the video, notice that the cells engulf their food source."
motivate	provides a reward or incentive designed to create a motive for continued effort	The needle on a dial (computer graphic) climbs higher with each correct response.
stimulate	arouse the learner to continue	After a period of inactivity, a beep from the computer encourages the user to enter his or her input.
advise	alerts the learner to the status of his or her efforts in relation to the required exit criteria	"You must answer three more items correctly to move to the next lesson."
summarize	a cumulative report of the learner's performance	"You correctly responded to 18 of 20 questions."

Figure 7.1. Roles of feedback in technology-assisted instruction.

Individual Differences
    ability
    aptitude
    attribution
    learning style
    locus of control
    motivation
    personal data (e.g., favorite foods, names of friends, pets, street
        address, favorite activities)
    prior knowledge
    on-task performance

Group
    careers and career objectives (e.g., pilots, engineers, nursing
        students, student teachers)
    common or community data (e.g., state, main street, school,
        principal, teacher, area attractions)
    curriculum (e.g., prerequisite coursework and experiences)
    resources (e.g., individuals, facilities, equipment, books,
        manipulatives)

Content Errors
    number of errors
    pattern of errors (e.g., misspellings, inappropriate responses)
    type of error (e.g., confusion with a similar problem, skipping a
        step in the procedure, calculation error)

Figure 7.2. Listing of selected variables on which to adapt feedback.

availability of specific support materials. In this situation the feedback may be adapted to include specific references to these items. Students may be directed to review a specific table or advised to reread a document.

Adaptive feedback, unlike adapted and generic feedback, is *dynamic*. As they work through the instruction, different learners will receive different information from the computer. The determination of what feedback is provided, when, and to whom, is made by the designer after careful consideration of all available information.

The design and development of adaptive feedback is complex because extensive information must be available for analysis and use before and during the instruction. Required information must be availale for all of the intended learners, or default feedback must be made available. Depending on the adaptive strategy used, the pattern of software use or the environment in which it is used may need to be more carefully controlled. Furthermore, software designers must have a clear understanding of the entire range of desired learning outcomes across the domains of learning (e.g., cognitive, affective, psychomotor) and the effects on each of various adaptive strategies. Information on the influences on learning outcomes of different types of feedback is difficult to gather. It must be gleaned from the literature and validated through personal experience.

Manipulation of the feedback presentation is usually based on an interaction of learners' pre-task or on-task performance and individual difference variables such as ability, learning style, or motivation. (See Figure 7.3.) McCombs and McDaniel (1981) suggest that the most powerful variables on which to adapt instruction are those that have an empirical or hypothesized relationship with the criterion variables of interest (i.e., achievement—success or mastery; motivation—heightened engagement or desire for further instruction; self-efficacy—improved self concept or increased belief in one's ability to influence one's own success). For example, when the criterion variable addressed its motivation, the designer may use gender as the difference variable. Freedman (1989, 1991) found that girls tend to focus on compositional aspects of computer graphics. They prefer to create and view large, static images that use lighter colors. In contrast, boys tend to be more interested in computer graphics that utilize bolder colors and include smaller, animated objects. Using this information, a designer might prepare an adaptive lesson in which young girls view large static images or diagrams as feedback, while young boys see animations where objects move into relative position or collide and explode.

In order to have a positive impact on criterion variables, powerful individual difference variables must be identified (McCombs & McDaniel, 1981). Informed decisions about the potential power of variables can only be made if reliable data about the target audience or specific learner are

Category	Sub-Category	Data Source	Feedback Adaptation
performance	pre-task on-task	test scores, management system records, teacher observation continuous monitoring of student input	Based on a history of errors during regrouping in subtraction problems, a student is given elaborative feedback that illustrates to process.
prior knowledge	skill level coursework completed	records, pre-test (on or off-line) records, questionnaire (on or off-line)	The knowledge of a student's previous coursework allows feedback to directly reference topics, materials, and experiences.
aptitude	mathematics languages mechanical reasoning	test scores	A student with low scores on mechanical reasoning may be shown detailed illustrations as feedback, while a student with high scores receives a simple text response.
personal information	name, name of friends, pets, favorite things, home address, etc.	records, observation, questionnaire (on or off-line)	Motivational feedback may be created by incorporating personal data. For example, "Good work, Mike. The people on Hill St. should be proud of you."
individual characteristics	gender learning style locus of control anxiety	records, observation testing testing	Students with an internal locus of control may be given the opportunity to select a feedback type.

Figure 7.3. Examples of individual difference variables, data sources, and feedback strategies.

available. For many of the variables listed in Figure 7.2, detailed records, perhaps containing multiple measures, must be available. For others, on-line questionnaires would need to be developed to collect and store the data for access as specially-designed lessons were activated. At the present time, this level of data collection and management may be impractical, but systems of computer-managed instruction which have the power and capacity to store and manage all of the data needed are in the marketplace. Now, educational researchers and instructional designers must assume the task of more clearly articulating the relationship and influence of individual difference variables on the range of instructional strategies. Then they can begin to use this knowledge systematically to improve software designs.

Related Research

Researchers have proposed and examined a variety of strategies for increasing the effectiveness of instruction by adapting it to specific difference variables. Many of these strategies involve the creation of adapted or adaptive feedback structures in technology-assisted instruction. The criterion variable, outcomes, or dependent variables researchers study generally fall within three categories:

- achievement—increased learning or decreased time to mastery; higher levels of growth in academic areas when compared to those not exposed to the adapted instruction;
- motivation—increased engagement in an instructional unit or increased desire to continue working through a sequence of instruction; a more positive attitude toward the instruction when compared to those not exposed to the motivational adaptation;
- attribution—changed perception of the causes of success and the factors that influence learning in instructional activities; an increase in acceptance that effort expended on appropriate forms of study will positively impact learning and academic achievement.

The use of these three categories is a convenient vehicle for discussion but should not imply that specific research studies fall into discrete categories. Many studies actually investigate strategies that span two or even all three of these groupings (e.g., Lewis & Cooney, 1987; Mevarech & Ben-Artzi, 1987; Schunk, 1982). The studies discussed below serve only as representative research efforts. Additional examples of research from each category can be found elsewhere in this text.

Achievement as an Outcome

Tobias (1981) states that many methods of adapting instruction lack a foundation in theory or research. He further suggests that understanding the consequences of adapting instruction to individual difference variables is a formidable challenge to basic research. Research addressing this challenge (including numerous interaction studies) has examined the effects of adapted or adaptive feedback on achievement. Difference variables and instructional methods examined include reading and language skills and speech feedback (Olson, Kliegl, Davidson, & Flotz, 1985; Olson, Flotz, & Wise, 1986), learning style degree of elaboration in feedback and locus of control (Sales & Carrier, 1987; Sales & Williams, 1988), anxiety and elaborated feedback (McCombs & McDaniel, 1981), gender and graphic fidelity (Sales & Johnston, 1988), and on-task performance with advisement (Johansen & Tennyson, 1983; Tennyson & Buttrey, 1980).

One example of research with foundation in the literature is that of Sales and associates (Sales & Carrier, 1987; Sales & Williams, 1988). Their work is based on research and theory in the areas of feedback, adaptive instruction, locus of control, and learning styles. In computer-based lessons, college students with different learning styles were exposed to varying levels of elaborative feedback with control of the feedback type being given or withheld based on performance. The studies found that students who perceived the instruction to be difficult selected more elaborative feedback when given the opportunity. Also, findings suggested the need for additional research on the relationship of learning style and locus of control options.

Siegel and Misselt (1984) provide another example of research designed to examine the effects of feedback on achievement. They explored contingent or error-sensitive feedback. This technique adapts feedback presentations based on the type of error represented by an incorrect response rather than a learner characteristic variable. The adaptive strategy investigated was based on direct instruction and feedback literature. It presented different forms of feedback, depending on whether the incorrect response represented a discrimination error among the content being taught, or content not included in the instruction. They found that adaptive feedback with discrimination training was significantly more effective than the other forms studied.

While both areas of research described above attempted to increase students' achievement scores through the use of adaptive feedback strategies, they are dramatically different. One focused on increasing scores by adapting to difference variables, the other to error types. Both studies have added to our knowledge of adaptive feedback and serve to represent the divergent approaches to the study of this topic.

Motivation as an Outcome

A review of the literature on adaptive technology-assisted instruction indicates that many research studies have sought to increase learner motivation or improve learner attitudes toward specific content. While this dependent variable is occasionally the primary focus of research, it is moe often of secondary interest and is investigated because of the links between attitude, effort, time on task, and achievement.

Research on techniques that will increase learners' motives for attending to, or continuing with, instruction is important. Such research, however, must also attend to the power of the variable(s) on which the instruction is adapted. For example, a number of researchers (Ross, 1983; Ross, McCormick, Krisak, & Anand, 1985; Ross & Anand, 1987; Sales & Johnston, 1992) have studied personalizing instruction as a means of increasing learner attention and interest. These studies utilized different strategies for increasing the personal relevance of the instruction. In several studies, Ross and his colleagues (Ross, 1983; Ross et al., 1985) created instruction that matched the interest of students based on their backgrounds. In other studies, Ross and his associates (Ross et al., 1987) integrated into computer-based instruction personal data collected through questionnaires. Both adaptive strategies resulted in increased superior results for those subjects in the intervention treatment groups.

In a recent study, Sales and Johnston (1992) incorporated the face and voice of a teacher known to the subjects into the personalized feedback strategy. The teacher served as the agent who delivered feedback to fith graders as they studied propaganda techniques used in advertising. Feedback informed the students of the accuracy of their responses, and provided corrective statements for errors and praise for correct answers. Subjects in the comparison groups received the same feedback from an unfamiliar agent. The results indicated that students receiving feedback from a known agent were more attentive to the feedback. They achieved at the same level while needing feedback statements repeated only half as often as those working with an unfamiliar agent.

In each of the studies just described, the adaptive design was intended to make the instruction more personally relevant. Yet the extent to which learners might identify with the adaptation is clearly different. Does the influence of a known agent (a teacher) make software more personally relevant than software that includes a learner's name or favorite treats in feedback? Is the motivational effect the same for each strategy? Does the teacher's role in the delivery of feedback cause the learner to attend to instructional aspects, while the use of background data merely provides an incentive for the student to continue with the task?

As effective motivational strategies are identified, research needs to provide clarification as to their relative power in different situations. Guidance needs to be provided as to appropriate and practical application of findings.

Attribution as an Outcome

Attribution theory postulates that learners attribute their success in instructional situations to ability, task difficulty, luck, or effort (Weiner, 1985, 1990). While the first three of these areas can be viewed as fixed, or beyond the control of the learner, effort can be increased or decreased based on a learner's decision to invest resources in a task. Attribution research examines strategies which encourage the learner to see a causal link between the degree of effort and performance on a task. Once the learner accepts this relationship, she or he may be more inclined to work harder, persist, or remain engaged with the task.

Two early studies examining the effect of attributional feedback were conducted by Dweck (1975) and Schunk (1982). Each researcher found that learners' perceptions and performance could be modified through the use of feedback that attributed success to effort. While these studies did not make use of technology delivery systems, because of the ease with which software can be created to effectively deliver customized feedback, they provided a foundation for technology-based research.

Hoska (1991), building on the work of Dweck, Weiner, and others, implemented a computer-based study of attributional feedback designed to explore whether feedback with different attributional content could affect performance. Students were required to select the difficulty of practice items and the amount of elaboration they wished to receive in their feedback as they worked through two lessons in math. Learning orientation feedback, which was more elaborate, was based on the assumption that students are interested in gaining mastery and presented information to help learners determine why their answers were incorrect and how to go about solving problems. The performance-orientation feedback, based on the premise that students have a need to avoid a failure and maintain a positive self-concept, simply informed the learner whether the response was correct or incorrect. Hoska found that students who selected learning orientation feedback treatment were significantly more likely to select difficult practice items than students who selected performance orientation feedback.

A growing body of research and theory related to attribution and student achievement is bringing this topic to the attention of educators. The idea of using feedback to shape students' self-concepts and self-efficacy, while at the same time supporting the mastery of the content being taught, has tremendous intuitive appeal. Additional research that will provide guidance in the design of effective and adaptive strategies is needed.

Recommendations and Guidelines

To achieve the maximum possible benefit from instructional technologies, we must create software that is *sensitive and responsive* to the cognitive and affective needs of the learner. One critical phase in the creation of such software is the development of adaptive feedback. By analyzing the learner's needs and presenting appropriate feedback, perception of instruction can be modified, and motives for engaging the content of the lesson can be heightened.

The seemingly unlimited number of factors with the potential to influence learning may give the impression that instructionally meaningful adaptations of feedback are unlikely to be developed and impossible to predict. McCombs and McDaniel (1981), however, argue that guidance from literature and expert judgment provide a reasonable basis from which to begin the design of adaptive strategies.

Over the past twenty years, a wealth of theoretical work and empirical research related to cognition, learning, and the design of technology-based instruction has been completed. Work on such topics as cooperative and generative learning has yielded guidance on topics ranging from instructional environment and grouping to content presentation and questioning strategies. Research on the interactions among difference variables such as ability, learning style and gender, and instructional methods has produced recommendations for the development of instructional treatments. This information, combined with the expertise of instructional designers, should result in exciting new forms of adaptive instruction.

Obviously, more research is needed. In the selecion of variables to investigate, researchers should be guided by (1) the theory and research that currently exist (Tobias, 1981), (2) the potential power of specific variables (McCombs & McDaniel, 1981) and (3) the potential impact of the findings on future research as well as on application. Researchers should combine efforts, collaborating on research, validating previous work and challenging findings in an effort to provide clear direction to designers and developers of educational materials. Finally, research reports must be clearly and concisely written and disseminated through the most far-reaching mechanisms. Research that cannot be accessed, or that cannot be understood when shared, will have little impact on decisions made during design and development.

In conclusion, the following ideas are offered for consideration by both researchers and designers interested in adaptive instruction. Each has some basis in the literature, yet none has been investigated to the extent that its successful implementation can be guaranteed.

• Care should be taken when implementing adaptive strategies at the group level. Variance within a group will affect the degree to which the adaptation is effective with specific individuals. For example, using audio feedback for low-ability readers and text feedback for high-ability readers may appear to be a reasonable adaptation but may introduce other impediments. The pacing of audio feedback is controlled by the speaker and could slow the progress of the learners at the high end of the low-ability reading group. At the same time, this strategy may deny students in the text group cues given by the speaker's pacing and emphasis.

- Strategies that adapt to the individual learner require specific information about the learner. For these strategies to be most effective, data must be accumulated over an extended period and analyzed frequently. These criteria argue for the development of adaptive instruction in conjunction with computer-management systems.

- New users could opt to complete an on-line questionnaire. The data collected could then be used to personalize both content presentations and feedback. Learners choosing not to complete the questionnaire would receive the default version of the instruction.

- Teacher management sections of software could provide the option to input information used to personalize the instruction to the community or instructional environment. This information would replace the default form.

- Families of products, for example, those produced by a single publisher, could use selected data from a common file. This would allow students or teachers to create a single data file and save it to a hard drive or student data disk for later use with a number of different software packages, thus eliminating the potentially time-consuming task of responding to the same questions each time a specific package or product line is used.

- New and emerging technologies should not be overlooked. For example, software packages could include in the teacher's guide a set of suggested feedback statements that could be read into an audio digitizer and used to replace the pre-programmed feedback. The teacher could personalize these statements.

References

Carter, J. (1984). Instructional learner feedback: A literature review with implications for software development. *The Computing Teacher, 12*(2), 53–55.

Cohen, V.B. (1985). A reexamination of feedback in computer-based instruction: Implications for instructional design. *Educational Technology, 25*(2), 33–37.

Dweck, C.S. (1975). The role expectations and attributions in the alleviation of learned helplessness. *Journal of Personality and Social Psychology, 31*(4), 674–685.

Freedman, K. (1989). Microcomputers and the dynamics of image making and social life in three art classrooms. *Journal of Research on Computing in Education, 21*(3), 290–298.

Freedman, K. (1991). Possibilities of interactive computer graphics for art instruction: A summary of research. *Art Education, 44*(3), 41–47.

Hoska, D.M. (1991). *Modification of learners' goal orientations through motivational feedback in computer-aided instruction.* Unpublished manuscript, University of Minnesota, Curriculum and Instructional Systems.

Johansen, K.J., & Tennyson, R.D. (1983). Effect of adaptive advisement on perception in learner-controlled, computer-based instruction using a rule-learning task. *Educational Communications and Technology Journal, 31*(4), 226–236.

Kulhavy, R.W. (1977). Feedback in written instruction. *Review of Educational Research, 47*, 211–232.

Kulhavy, R.W., & Stock, W.A. (1989). Feedback in written instruction: The place of response certitude. *Educational Psychology Review, 1*(4), 279–308.

Lewis, M.A., & Cooney, J.B. (1987). Attributional and performance effects of competitive and individualistic feedback in computer-assisted mathematics instruction. *Computers in Human Behavior, 3*, 1-13.

Lysakowski, R.S., & Walberg, H.J. (1981). Classroom reinforcement and learning: A quantitative synthesis. *Journal of Educational Research, 75*(2), 69–77.

McCombs, B.L., & McDaniel, M.A. (1981). On the design of adaptive treatments of individualized instructional systems. *Educational Psychologist, 16*(1), 11–22.

Mevarech, Z.R., & Ben-Artzi, S. (1987). Effects of CAI with fixed and adaptive feedback on children's mathematics anxiety and achievement. *Journal of Experimental Education, 56*(1), 42–46.

Olson, R.K., Flotz, G., & Wise, B. (1986). Reading instruction and remediation with the aid of computer speech. *Behavioral Research Methods, Instruments and Computers, 18*, 93–99.

Olson, R.K., Kliegl, R., Davidson, B.J., & Flotz, G. (1985). Individual and developmental differences in reading disabilities. In G.E. MacKinnon & T.G. Waller (Eds.), *Reading research: Advances in theory and practice* (Vol. 4). New York: Academic Press.

Ross, S.M. (1983). Increasing the meaningfulness of quantitative material by adapting context to student background. *Journal of Educational Psychology, 75*(4), 519–529.

Ross, S.M., & Anand, P. (1987). A computer-based strategy for personalizing verbal problems in teaching mathematics. *Educational Communications and Technology Journal, 35*(3), 151–162.

Ross, S.M., McCormick, D., Krisak, N., & Anand, P. (1985). Personalizing context in teaching mathematical concepts: Teacher-managed and computer-assisted models. *Educational Communications and Technology Journal, 33*(3), 169–178.

Sales, G.C. (1988). Designing feedback for CBI: Matching feedback to the learner and learning outcomes. *Computers in the Schools, 5*(1/2), 225–239.

Sales, G.C., & Carrier, C.A. (1987). The effects of learning style and type of feedback on achievement in a computer-based lesson. *International Journal of Instructional Media, 14*(3), 171–185.

Sales, G.C., & Johnston, M.D. (1988). *Graphic fidelity, gender, and performance in computer-based simulations.* (Research Bulletin #1, Improving the Use of Technology in Schools: What We Are Learning.) Minneapolis, MN: MECC/UM Center for the Study of Educational Technology.

Sales, G.C., & Johnston, M.D. (1992). *The effects of familiar voice feedback in computer-based instruction.* Paper presented at the meeting of the Association for Educational Communications and Technology, Washington, D.C.

Sales, G.C., & Williams, M.D. (1988). The effects of adaptive control of feedback in computer-based instruction. *Journal of Research on Computing in Education, 21*(1), 97–111.

Schunk, D.H. (1982). Effects of effort attributional feedback on children's perceived self-efficacy and achievement. *Journal of Educational Psychology, 74*(4), 548–556.

Siegel, M.A., & Misselt, A.L. (1984) Adaptive feedback and review paradigm for computer-based drills. *Journal of Educational Psychology, 76*(2), 310–317.

Stewart, W.J. (1983). Meeting learning styles through the computer. *Journal of Educational Technology Systems, 11*, 291–296.

Tennyson, R.D., & Buttrey, T. (1980). Advisement and management strategies as design variables in computer-assisted instruction. *Educational Communications and Technology Journal, 28*(3), 169–176.

Tobias, S. (1981). Adapting instruction to individual differences among students. *Educational Psychologist 16*(2), 111–120.

Wager, W., & Wager, S. (1986). Presenting questions, processing responses, and providing feedback in CAI. *Journal of Instructional Development, 8*(4), 2–8.

Weiner, B. (1985). An attributional theory of achievement motivation and emotion. *Psychological Review, 92*(4), 548–573.

Weiner, B. (1990). History of motivational research in education. *Journal of Educational Psychology, 82*(4), 616–622.

Chapter Eight

Using Feedback to Adapt Instruction for Individuals

Steven M. Ross
Memphis State University

and

Gary R. Morrison
Memphis State University

Cognitive interpretations of learning stress the importance of being able to relate new information to existing knowledge or *schemata* (Ausubel, 1968; Wittrock, 1989). For instructional designers, this idea encourages efforts to adapt the content of lessons to the backgrounds and needs of individual learners. An exemplary application would be to use different illustrations, explanations, or examples to teach instructional design principles to a class of elementary school teachers and then to a class of corporate trainers. Another would be to diagnose the nature of an individual student's errors in solving a math problem and to provide special feedback to correct that particular response pattern.

As these examples suggest, instructional adaptation can be applied at various phases of the learning process, i.e., during the lesson presentation as well as during feedback presented following answers to embedded questions or test items. However, researchers and designers have given much less attention to the feedback phase. Accordingly, the focus of this chapter is on feedback applications, specifically as provided in computer-based instruction (CBI). As general background for that discussion, major theoretical views and research findings regarding personalized adaptation are reviewed in the first section. Next, the adaptive features of commonly used computer-based feedback strategies, such as knowledge of correct response (KCR) and answer-until-correct (AUC) feedback, are described and analyzed. In a third section, these traditional strategies are compared with *response-sensitive* models that orient the nature of the feedback provided to the particular error response diagnosed. Next, the components of an applied, adaptive CBI model, the *Intelligent Physics Tutor* (Loftin, 1990), are examined. The *Tutor*, which is now being field-tested in high school physics classes, uses a model of individual student performance, error diagnosis, and other special features to provide varied and sophisticated forms of adaptive feedback for students and their teachers. The chapter will conclude with some perspectives and suggested directions for designers who want to increase the adaptive features of CBI lessons.

Personalization as an Adaptive Instructional Strategy

Each student brings a unique set of experiences and knowledge to a learning task (Anderson, Reynolds, Schallert, & Goetz, 1977). The nature of this knowledge base directly influences what information will be attended to during instruction and how that information will be processed (Bransford & Johnson, 1972). *Personalization* is a general term used to describe instructional strategies designed to vary the content of instructional presentations based on information about individual learners (Anand & Ross, 1987; Ross & Anand, 1987).

In our own research, we have used a specific form of personalization, that of embedding material in familiar contexts, to help learners perform better in solving verbal mathematics problems. In an initial study, Ross (1983) adapted the themes of problem applications to college students' majors in either nursing or education. Ross, Morrison, and O'Dell (1989) developed a learner-control strategy in which college students, regardless of major, could select between different problem themes consisting of education, sports, business, and no theme. We are presently conducting a study replicating the latter design with elementary school students, offering them the context options of sports, animals, clothing, and no theme for learning a CBI unit on the metric system.

A second, seemingly more powerful, personalization strategy is to individualize contexts based on information about a particular student. In the Anand and Ross (1987) study, this adaptation was accomplished by using microcomputers to store personal information about the individual (e.g., birth date, names of friends, favorite food, hobbies, etc.) for insertion into standard problem templates. For example, a textbook problem that stated, "23 people had a snack on Monday; 12 people had a snack on Tuesday.

How many more people had a snack on Monday?'' could be personalized in the following manner: *(best friend's name)* gave friends 23 *(favorite candy bar)* on *(student's birthdate)*; he or she gave 12 *(favorite candy bars)* on the next day. How many more *(favorite candy bars)* were given on *(student's birthdate)*?'' Findings indicated that students who received the personalized examples scored higher in achievement and attitudes than did those who received conventional examples.

In a second study (Ross & Anand, 1987), these results were corroborated using print versions of personalization. Interestingly, however, performance benefits were also obtained for a group-personalization strategy, in which the problems incorporated themes and referents that were most frequently conveyed for a class as a whole (see also Lopez, 1990). The group strategy is considered to have practical advantages as a result of eliminating the requirement of developing individualized materials for each student.

Davis-Dorsey, Ross, and Morrison recently completed a study (in press) on how personalization might interact with other types of text modifications. The specific strategies of interest were *rewording* problems to make their meaning more explicit and *personalizing* them using the Anand and Ross (1987) procedure. Results showed that rewording was beneficial for younger students (second-graders) only, whereas personalization improved performance for both the second-graders and older (fifth-grade) students. Interpretations of the personalization effect, as in the earlier studies cited (e.g., Anand & Ross, 1987), stressed the benefits of familiar and personally relevant contexts for generating interest in task and making problem themes more meaningful and thus relatable to existing knowledge.

These results seemingly have the same implications for uses of feedback in instruction as for the design of lesson presentations. To the extent that feedback can appropriately tap individual interests and knowledge structures, it should be more likely attended to, a motivational benefit, and more relatable to existing knowledge, a cognitive benefit. Adapting feedback to learners can take a variety of forms that differ in complexity, sensitivity, and potential impact in accommodating individual differences. These adaptive forms of feedback differ significantly from the earlier behavioral feedback strategies used with programmed instruction. In the following sections, we will analyze different forms of CBI feedback, beginning with those having low adaptability and progressing to other, increasingly adaptive forms.

Conventional CBI Feedback Forms

Feedback, an essential component of the instructional process, is delivered to learners in a variety of forms and modes. The most common delivery mode is from teachers as they interact with students in classroom and training settings. This mode is also potentially the most personalized, due to the ability of teachers to know students individually, analyze their responses, and provide feedback accordingly. Unfortunately, despite this potential, the student-teacher ratio of 25:1 (or higher) in typical classrooms severely limits the frequency and quality of the feedback that a given student will receive (see Stodolsky, 1988).

KOR and KCR Feedback

An alternative means of providing individualized feedback without direct involvement by the teacher is through CBI. Typical uses of CBI feedback occur within the context of multiple-choice testing and encompass one of the following forms: (a) knowledge-of-response feedback (KOR or KR), which indicates that the learner's was correct or incorrect; and (b) knowledge of correct response feedback (KCR), which identifies the correct response. An example of each type is provided in Figure 8.1.

Compared to what can be achieved in print lessons, both forms can be considered adaptive as a result of providing feedback that is contingent on and proximate to the learner's recent (on-task) response. That is, the nature and timing of the specific feedback message depends, respectively, on how and when the learner responds. On the other hand, personalization is minimal in the sense that all individuals who respond to an item correctly or incorrectly receive the identical standard feedback message for that response. Through modifications of these standard feedback forms, as will be discussed in the following paragraphs, higher levels of adaptation can be achieved.

AUC Feedback

KOR can be extended by allowing learners additional tries following an error response item (Clariana, Ross, & Morrison, in press; Dempsey & Driscoll, 1989; Noonan, 1984; Pressey, 1926, 1950). The orientation is conventionally labeled answer-until-correct (AUC) feedback (see Figure 8.1). From an adaptation standpoint, AUC not only provides immediate, response-contingent feedback, as in KOR and KCR, but also varies the learners' degree of contact with items according to the number of trials needed to select the correct responses. Potential advantages are engaging learners in active processing following errors and ensuring that the last response made is the correct one, a long-standing principle of learning (Guthrie, 1935). On

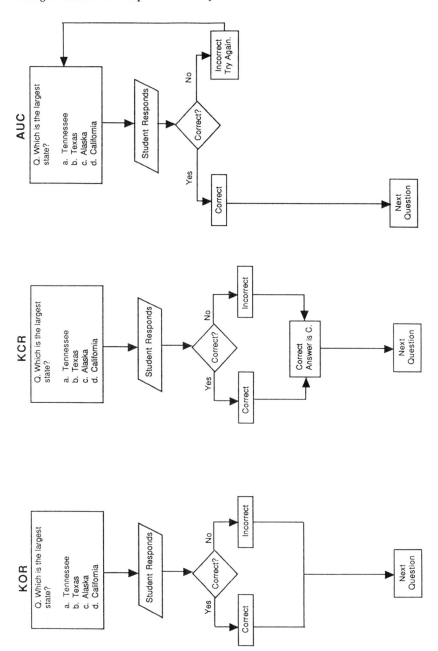

Figure 8.1. The procedure used in three types of feedback.

the other hand, a possible disadvantage of AUC is frustrating learners who do not know how to answer the question but must continue responding until they select the correct alternative (Dick & Latta, 1970).

Delayed Feedback

Another modification of conventional strategies is to delay the provision of feedback in place of or in addition to immediate KOR or KCR. Two alternative explanations of the potential benefits of delayed feedback have been proposed. One, the interference preservation hypothesis (Kulhavy & Anderson, 1972), holds that an incorrect response positively interferes with an immediately-provided correct response. Through the delay of feedback, learners have time to forget their initial (error) responses, thereby decreasing proactive interference. A second, more straightforward interpretation is that delayed feedback repeats the item presentation at the end of the lesson, thereby providing double the exposure of conventional KCR (Kulik & Kulik, 1988). When delayed feedback is presented in conjunction with immediate KCR, increased adaptation can be achieved by displaying in the delayed feedback presentation only those items that were missed (Ross, Morrison, & Barnette, in press). Learners thereby receive unique feedback displays that allow them to concentrate on a reduced, individualized set of items dealing with the content that gave them the most difficulty.

Elaborative Feedback

Kulhavy and Stock (1989) have analyzed the feedback message as consisting of two components, verification and elaboration. Verification is the simple dichotomous information (as provided by KOR, KCR, and AUC) that the answer is correct or incorrect. Elaboration is any information given beyond the initial verification. Three basic types of elaboration are (a) task specific, such as a restatement of the correct answer or inclusion of multiple-choice alternatives (as in KCR); (b) instruction-based, such as an explanation or an excerpt from the lesson text; and (c) extra-instructional, such as examples or analogies not originally part of the instruction. Kulhavy & Stock's (1989) position is that added elaboration by itself may not be sufficient to improve the benefits of feedback. More important is how well feedback properties are adapted to learner needs. In their model, the key variable is degree of discrepancy that learners perceive between their personal knowledge estimates (or *response certitude*) and the information provided by the feedback message. The greater the discrepancy, the greater the dependency on the feedback.

Accordingly, typical uses of elaborative feedback provide richer information (i.e., explanations for answers) than do KCR or KOR (see Merrill, 1985), but are not necessarily more adaptive. As typically structured, the elaborative feedback will uniformly follow the correct response without taking into account the characteristics or performance record of the learner.

Research Findings

In view of their procedural differences, these alternative feedback forms may not be equally effective. Several studies have shown KCR to be superior to KOR, and KOR to be superior to no feedback (see review by Clariana, 1990). However, based on his own research and a meta-analysis of studies, Schimmel (1983, 1988) concluded that this hierarchy of feedback types is not so well established. Evidence also suggests that elaborative forms of feedback often produce no significant improvement over KCR but require a considerable development and implementation cost (Merrill, 1985, 1987). Despite years of research, the types of situations in which different feedback forms tend to operate most effectively are still not understood (Kulhavy & Stock, 1989). Much seems to depend on the complex interaction between learner characteristics, task demands, and the nature of the feedback treatment.

Recently, the present authors, in collaboration with Roy Clariana (Clariana, Ross, & Morrison, in press), conducted an investigation of the relative effectiveness of three different strategies (KCR, AUC, and delayed KCR) used in conjunction with multiple-choice questions on a CBI lesson. Outcomes supported the overall effectiveness of providing feedback, regardless of strategy, compared to a no-feedback control condition. However, feedback in general became less influential as lesson-question and posttest-question similarity decreased. An interesting exception was AUC feedback for which the opposite pattern was evidenced. Also, feedback effects were greater in conditions when the material was taught via questions only rather than via questions and accompanying lesson text.

Our interpretation of the findings stressed the information-processing implications of the different feedback strategies—namely the idea that conventional multiple-choice item feedback (i.e., KCR)—may supplant the natural tendency of questions to stimulate information processing or *mathemagenic activity* (Rothkopf, 1966) as the learner searches memory or the text to find the answers to questions. That is, once the correct answer is identified through KCR, the learner may perceive there to be no need for further processing and resort to rote learning of the answers. Similarly, feedback effects appear to become greater in lesson designs featuring questions only as opposed to text and questions, because of the restriction of the content domain to the specific questions that happen to be included. That is, without supporting text, the opportunity to go beyond the question by seeking further explanation or background is obviously limited.

Based on these perspectives, an important challenge for designers is to use feedback to stimulate more active engagement with learning material. As a result of keeping the learner on the same item until the correct answer is seleced, AUC appears to have greater potential in this regard than do KCR and KOR. However, unless active learning rather than a passive selection of new responses follows, the benefits may be minimal. If feedback information is made directly relevant to individuals' difficulties with the content, it seems more likely that it will be used. The next secion examines approaches designed to achieve this increased level of adaptation.

Adaptive Computer-Based Feedback

An advantage of a computer over print material is the ability to vary feedback on the basis of systematic and timely assessments of learner needs. Such adaptation extends the procedure of presenting standard information frames according to the particular answer selected. Rather, it involves analyzing the student's responses, individually and/or cumulatively, to make an adaptive decision regarding what feedback or new instruction would be optimal for learning at each point. At one level are the intelligent tutoring systems (ITS), which attempt to perform the functions of human tutors. Although ITS work has generated much excitement among instructional technologists, its development is still in its infancy. The tangible products of ITS work to date are largely demonstration models that remain to be validated (Rosenberg, 1987).

Less complex but more practical approaches have used two basic orientations, adaptive instructional modeling (AIM) and response-sensitive analyses. AIM involves generating a quantitative model that uses prior and current performance information to predict the learner's probability of success on a particular learning trial (Hansen, Ross, & Rakow, 1977; Tennyson & Rothen, 1977). Instruction is then adapted accordingly by prescribing increased or decreased instructional support on that trial. One AIM strategy that directly uses feedback adaptively is program *coaching* or *advisement* in which learners are advised to select a certain level of instructional support on the next part of the lesson, based on their level of performance, but are ultimately allowed to make the final choice on their own (Tennyson & Buttrey, 1980; Tennyson, 1981). More practical forms of this procedure, which would not require a formal predictive model, could simply involve monitoring on-task performance and advising selection of additional problems as long as the cumulative score remained below a certain criterion.

Response-sensitive strategies involve adapting feedback information based on inferences regarding what the learner's most recent response implies about his or her current level of understanding. An example is Park and Tennyson's (1986) concept-teaching model in which one strategy (called *discrimination rule*) involved presenting an example of Concept B on the following trial if the learner mistakenly classified a Concept A instance as Concept B. The rationale was to provide information that would best increase the ability to discriminate between the two confused concepts.

Other applications of response-sensitive strategies have used error analysis to provide anticipated wrong answer (AWA) feedback, which is information geared to the type of error made. Such applications have been most common for teaching mathematical concepts (Brown & Van Lehn, 1980; Burton, 1982; Charles, 1980; Cohen & Carpenter, 1980). The basic procedure involves identifying the domain of errors made by students in learning a particular skill. From the errors, inferences are made about the rules that are difficult for the student and, thereby, the type of corrective information needed on the given trial. Schimmel (1988) used the term *bug* to denote a systematic error in the learner's understanding of a procedure. Bug-related feedback attempts to correct the procedural error by providing not only the correct answer, but also an explanation of the error. The challenge of such a system is that, to be fully operational, it must generate all possible errors in a procedure (Brown & Van Lehn, 1980).

A related conception of feedback evolves from *Repair Theory*, which posits that when students are unsuccessful in their response, they will attempt a *repair* by figuring out the correct answer (Brown & Van Lehn, 1980). Repair Theory defines a set of incomplete procedures (responses to the task or problem) and attempts to filter out and correct known error responses. The rationale is to correct the procedure while the student is working and allow him or her to progress.

Currently, one of our graduate students, William Schultz (1990), is conducting his dissertation research on a comparison between adaptive CBI feedback and conventional feedback in teaching mathematical rules (specifically, order of operations). The research design involves varying three conditions of instructional support (rule only; rule and example; and rule, example, and nonexample) with three conditions of feedback (AUC, AUC with response-sensitive feedback, and no feedback).

Schultz's response-sensitive strategy illustrates a practical procedure for making elaborative feedback more adaptive. To implement the strategy, he first constructed a pretest covering the rules taught in the experimental lesson. Next, he administered the pretest to a class that had previously been exposed to the lesson material. He then tabulated the error responses made on the pretest according to frequency. For example, given the problem, $8 + 6/2$, the most frequent error would be to add the 8 and the 6 and divide the sum (14) by 2, resulting in the incorrect answer of 7. Accordingly, students who enter 7 as their answer are almost certainly misapplying the rule that gives division higher priority than addition $[8+6/2 = 8+(6/2) = 8+3 = 11]$. Analyses of other students' work may further suggest, for example, that those who obtain 10 as a final answer are likely to have used the rule correctly, but to have made an addition error. With this information, feedbac can be personalized to address the specific types of error response each learner makes. Schultz is hypothesizing that, as a result of these adaptive properties, the response-sensitive feedback will be more effective for learning than will conventional AUC feedback.

As just reviewed, response-sensitive feedback provides a means of extending conventional KCR and elaborative feedback by incorporating in the instructional strategy a prior or on-task analysis of the learner's knowledge and skills on the task. Specifically, the process may entail identifying (a) the incorrect responses given to test items, (b) the misconceptions or errors likely to account for each incorrect response, and (c) the type of feedback information that will best correct the error while strengthening acquisition of the correct response. Once this analysis (i.e., steps a-c) is made, the basic CBI lesson design is not more complicated operationally than those for KCR and standard elaborated feedback modes. Specifically, the only change is linking appropriate feedback information frames in the program to their corresponding error responses, as in traditional branching designs.

The Intelligent Physics Tutor

A recently developed software package, *The Intelligent Physics Tutor* (IPT) (Loftin, 1990), features varied and powerful adaptive feedback components and encompasses virtually all forms of personalization reviewed in the preceding sections. The IPT project is sponsored by the Software Technology Branch at the NASA/Johnson Space Center and by the Apple Classroom of Tomorrow (ACOT) at Apple Computer, Inc. The purpose is to provide an interactive environment, using the architecture of an intelligent tutoring system, in which students in high school or college physics classes can practice applications of physics concepts while receiving individualized guidance and feedback. Consequently, as students work on the tutor in class, the teacher is freed to give special attention to individuals who need it. The *Tutor* operates on an Apple Macintosh II computer and makes use of high-resolution graphics, color, and sound. A review of how it operates, with special attention to its adaptive feedback properties, is provided in the following sections.

Content

The completed *Tutor* will contain a comprehensive set of *lessons* corresponding to standard topics covered in introductory physics courses. The basic content within lessons consists of problems of increasing complexity that students solve by working interactively with the computer. The instructor is provided the capability of assembling the lessons into an order that fits his or her particular curriculum and of establishing appropriate dependencies between lessons. Instructors may also choose terms and symbols compatible with their textbook and/or preferences.

A sample screen showing the problem presentation and workspace can be seen in Figure 8.2. The calculations in the workspace are the student's. While working the problem, individuals can access, where needed, a calculator, algebraic conversion routines, and Help screens.

Adaptive Model

The basic instructional model used by the *Tutor* involves diagnosing misconceptions that the student experiences in trying to solve particular problems. The identified misconceptions then form the basis for determining the immediate feedback provided on the current problem and for selecting additional problems. This analysis takes place via *local strategy* that records every response (as *student action codes*) that the student makes in

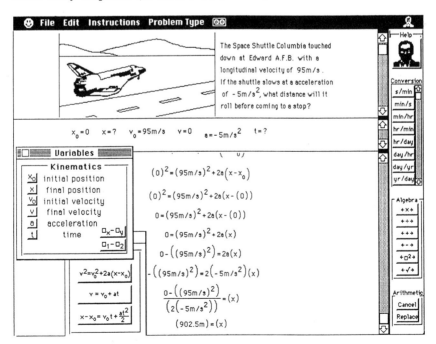

Figure 8.2. Problem presentation and workspace for *Physics Tutor* problem.

solving the problem. At each step a comparison is made between the students' action and the correct or expected action. If a discrepancy is indicated, the most likely misconception for that problem is diagnosed on the basis of the error response and the cumulative action codes. Appropriate feedback, as outlined below, is then provided.

Feedback System

On-task feedback. Students receive on-task feedback messages only when an error is detected. Otherwise, they are allowed to proceed without interruption. The error messages provided are geared to the specific misconception diagnosed, and become increasingly specific as errors reflecting that misconception accumulate. Importantly, by correcting the error at the time it is made, the system prevents the learner from proceeding down an incorrect pathway (and thus losing time and experiencing frustration).

An example of an *early* feedback message is shown in Figure 8.3. It should be noted that the indivdual pictured in the panel is the student's teacher (in this case, the *Tutor* developer, R. Bowen Loftin), thus adding another dimension of personalization. Figure 8.4 shows a *verification* screen which appears with auditory reinforcement (the cry, *Yabba Dabba Do*) when the student successfully completes the entire problem. Based on the cumulative frequencies of misconceptions recorded for the individual across completed problems, the *Tutor's global model* then selects a new problem that requires practicing skills directly related to the diagnosed areas of weaknesses (i.e., the specific misconceptions having the highest frequencies of occurrence).

Performance feedback summaries. Additional feedback systems provide summaries and analyses of performance for both classes and individuals. Figure 8.5 shows an example for a student, *Fred*, who has just completed one of the problem-solving units. The top part of the display shows the misconceptions currently diagnosed while the bottom display suggests a prescription of how many related exercises (or problems) he should be given for strengthening the problem-solving skills for a given misconception. From this display, the teacher receives clear and comprehensive adaptive feedback to direct subsequent planning of remediation activities for the student. Further, as illustrated in Figure 8.6, the teacher also receives parallel feedback for the class as a whole, thus providing useful guidance for whole-group follow-up instruction. For example, the particular class (NASA) appears to be having difficulty in distinguishing acceleration from velocity.

Summary. At the time of this writing, the *Tutor* is being beta-tested and evaluated by the first author in several physics classes. Although its effectiveness in improving the learning of physics has not yet been identified

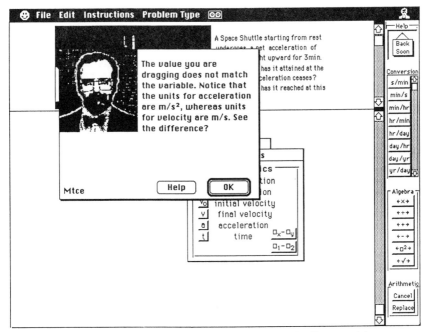

Figure 8.3. Immediate feedback message on *Physics Tutor* problem.

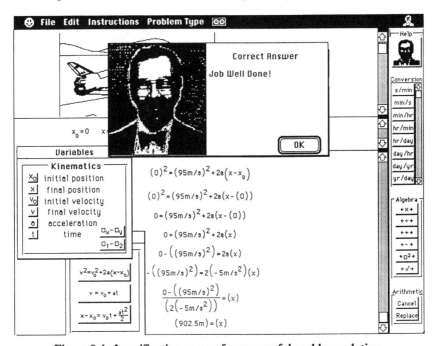

Figure 8.4. A verification screen for successful problem solution.

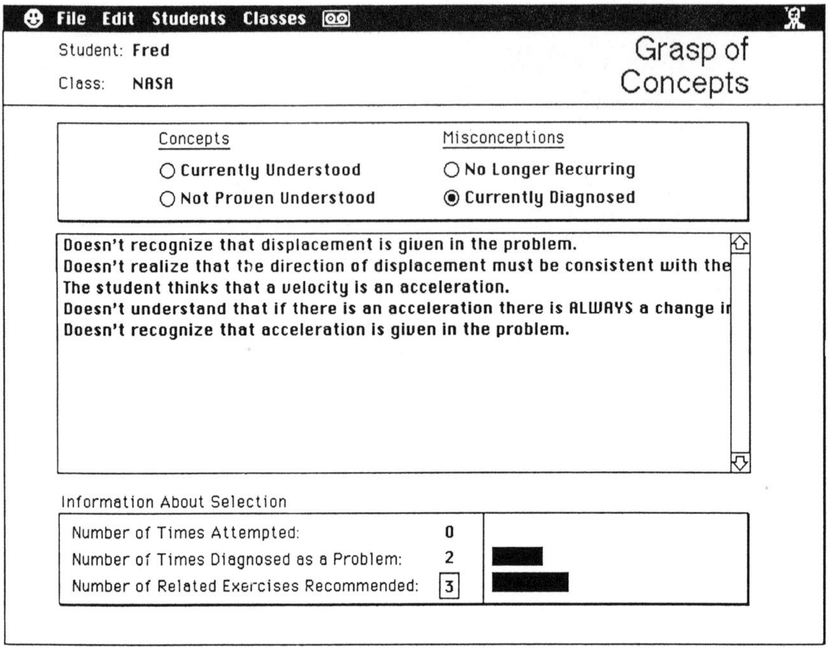

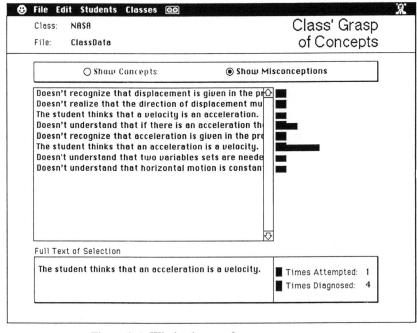

Figure 8.5. Individual student performance summary.

Figure 8.6. Whole class performance summary.

through valid experimental-control group comparisons, preliminary data from over 200 surveys and close to 100 student interviews is highly positive. Specifically, students enjoy working with the *Tutor* and regard it as beneficial to their learning. They especially like the on-line adaptations that provide them with corrective feedback geared to specific errors made while working problems. This immediate feedback component eliminates the considerable frustration often experienced in working textbook problems due to making an error early in the procedure and becoming increasingly lost through the pursuit of incorrect pathways that yield anomalous or uninterpretable outcomes. Teachers especially like the concept of each student receiving problems and feedback geared to his or her specific needs as well as the ablity to monitor and analyze from the performance summaries how individuals and the class are performing on each unit.

Implications for Instructional Design

In this chapter we have taken a cognitive perspective in examining the role of personalization and adaptation in using feedback. This perspective differs from the traditional behavioral orientation of the 1950s and 1960s in which feedback was viewed primarily a reinforcement for correct responses. In our view, although feedback may facilitate learning through its reinforcement properties, its critical role is providing information to learners about the accuracy of their responses and level of understanding of the material in general.

When a student responds correctly and has a high level of understanding, feedback primarily serves the purpose of providing verification. In situations where responses are incorrect and/or a student has low certainty about the material, the need for feedback extends beyond simple verification by helping the learner to correct errors and misconceptions (Kulhavy & Stock, 1989). For this purpose, we see two main challenges facing instructional designers. One is to make appropriate corrective feedback available; the second is ensuring that the feedback information will be attended to and processed actively to enhance learning.

The main theme of this chapter has been that *personalized* or *adaptive* feedback addresses both of these design objectives. First, personalized feedback is more motivating to students. As a result, attention to the feedback message should increase. Second, personalized feedback is directly oriented to the specific learning needs of the individual. As a result, ability to understand and apply the feedback information during learning should increase. The idea of personalizing feedback, however, is much easier to appreciate as a concept than to implement in practice. Obviously, few lesson designs are likely to permit the range and complexity of the adaptations incorporated in the *Intelligent Physics Tutor*, as just reviewed. Yet, it seems reasonable that many of the basic strategies used by the *Tutor* and in some of the research applications previously noted can be employed on a smaller scale in more modest CBI programs. Some examples include:

1. Personalized messages (e.g., greetings, prompts, or instructions that use students' names or describe familiar events and people (Anand & Ross, 1987; Ross & Anand, 1987).

> *Example:* "That is not correct, *Alice*. If you had a liter of your favorite drink, *Coke*, it would be *more* than a quart. How do 2 liters of *Coke*, then, compare to 2 quarts?" (Note: Personalized referents here appear in italics.)

2. AUC-type response routines that do *not* permit the learner to progress to the next step in a problem (or to a new question) until he or she has given the correct answer to the present question (e.g., Clariana, Ross, & Morrison, in press). For students experiencing difficulty (e.g., those who have made multiple errors on the same question or are performing below criteria on the overall lesson), the feedback message might also include (a) special cuing to help narrow the response choices, (b) special help screens that provide explanations or rephrase the question, and/or (c) guidance regarding what concepts to review before continuing.

> *Example A:* "Your response is not correct. It is recommended that you reread the section on helping verbs in the lesson. Press < Return > to review that material."

> *Example B:* "Before answering again, try to remember the distinction between an adverb and an adjective. Which one modifies a noun?"

3. Cumulative performance summaries that provide a description and, if possible, analysis of the errors made on the lesson (e.g., Ross, Morrison, & Barnette, in press).

> *Example A:* The items you missed are as follows:
> Ausubel: Advance Organizer
> Skinner: Operant Conditioning
> Thorndike: Connectionism
> Gagné: Conditions of Learning

> *Example B:* Here is an analysis of your performance on the lesson:

	% Correct	No. of Errors
Motion	100	0
Velocity	92	1
Vectors	80	3
Force	100	0
Overall	93	4

4. Response-sensitive elaborative feedback geared to particular errors made on each problem or question (Schultz, 1990).

Example A: "You are confusing *links* with *lynx*. *Links refer to loops forming a chain. A lynx is a wildcat with a short tail.*"

Example B: "Your answer of 27 is incorrect. It seems as if you are forgetting to consider the effects of friction in your equation. Enter friction as a variable and try again."

5. Advisement regarding how many more practice problems to complete, based on the individual's level of on-task performance (Tennyson & Buttrey, 1980).

Example: "On Unit 12E, it is recommended that you work five problems."

As the above examples suggest, numerous ways exist to personalize feedback to make it more adaptive to individual needs. Although the sophistication of CBI systems and software has advanced considerably over the years, the feedback strategies employed still commonly remain some form of standard KOR and KCR. By making feedback more personalized, designers can increase both its saliency and information value for individual students. As a result, both interest in learning and academic achievement should improve.

References

Anand, P., & Ross, S.M. (1987). Using computer-assisted instruction to personalize math learning materials for elementary school children. *Journal of Educational Psychology, 79,* 72–79.

Anderson, R.C., Reynolds, R.E., Schallert, D.L., & Goetz, E.T. (1977). Frameworks for comprehending discourse. *American Educational Research Journal, 14,* 367–382.

Ausubel, D.P. (1968). *Educational psychology: A cognitive approach.* New York: Holt, Rinehart, & Winston.

Bransford, J.D., & Johnson, M.K. (1972). Contextual prerequisites for understanding: Some investigations of comprehension and recall. *Journal of Verbal Learning and Verbal Behavior, 11,* 717–726.

Brown, J.S., & Van Lehn, K. (1980). Repair theory: A generative theory of bugs in procedural skills. *Cognitive Science, 4,* 379–426.

Burton, R.R. (1982). Diagnosing bugs in a simple procedural skill. In D. Sleeman & J. Brown (Eds.), *Intelligent tutoring systems* (pp. 157–183). New York: Academic Press.

Charles, R. (1980). Some guidelines for teaching geometry concepts. *Arithmetic Teacher, 27*(8), 18–20.

Clariana, R.B. (1990). *An experimental study comparing three forms of feedback across two conditions of acquisition.* Unpublished doctoral dissertation, Memphis State University.

Clariana, R.B., Ross, S.M., & Morrison, G.R. (in press). The effects of different feedback strategies using computer-administered multiple-choice questions as instruction. *Educational Technology Research and Development.*

Cohen, M.P., & Carpenter, J. (1980). The effects of non-examples in geometrical concept acquisition. *International Journal of Math, Education, and Science Teachers, 11*(2), 259–263.

Davis-Dorsey, J., Ross, S.M., & Morrison, G.R. (in press). The role of rewording and context personalization in the solving of mathematics word problems. *Journal of Educational Psychology.*

Dempsey, J.V., & Driscoll, M.P. (1989, March). *The effects of four methods of immediate corrective feedback on retention, discrimination error, and feedback study time in computer-based instruction.* A paper presented at the annual meeting of the American Educational Research Association, San Francisco, CA.

Dick, W., & Latta, R. (1970). Comparative effects of ability and presentation mode in computer-assisted instruction and programmed instruction. *Audio-Visual Communication Review, 18*(3), 34–45.

Guthrie, E.R. (1935). *The psychology of learning* (1st ed.). New York: Harper & Brothers.

Hansen, D.N., Ross, S.M., & Rakow, E.A. (1977). *Adaptive models for computer-based training systems.* Final report for contract No. 1-22890-1903, Navy Personnel Research and Development Center. Memphis, TN: Memphis State University.

Kulhavy, R.W., & Anderson, R.C. (1972). Delay-retention effect with multiple-choice tests. *Journal of Educational Psychology, 68,* 522–528.

Kulhavy, R.W., & Stock, W.A. (1989). Feedback in written instruction: The place of response certitude. *Educational Psychology Review, 1,* 279–308.

Kulik, J.A., & Kulik, C. (1988). Timing of feedback and verbal learning. *Review of Educational Research, 58*(1), 79–97.

Loftin, R.B. (1990). *The intelligent physics tutor: Project description.* Unpublished manuscript, University of Houston-Downtown, Department of Natural Sciences.

Lopez, C.L. (1990, February). *Personalizing math problems.* Paper presented at the annual meeting of the Association for Educational Communications and Technology. Anaheim, CA.

Merrill, J. (1985). *Levels of questioning and forms of feedback: Instructional factors in courseware design.* Paper presented at the Annual Meeting of the American Eduational Research Association, Chicago. (ERIC Document Reproduction Service No. ED 266 755).

Merrill, J. (1987). Levels of questioning and forms of feedback: Instructional factors in courseware design. *Journal of Computer-Based Instruction, 14*(1), 18–22.

Noonan, J.V. (1984). Feedback procedures in computer-assisted instruction: Knowledge-of-results, knowledge-of-correct-response, process explanations, and second attempts after explanations. (Doctoral dissertation, University of Illinois at Urbana-Champaign). *Dissertation Abstracts International, 45*(1), 131.

Park, O., & Tennyson, R.D. (1986). Computer-based adaptive design strategies for response-sensitive sequencing and presentation forms of examples in coordinate concept learning. *Journal of Educational Psychology, 78,* 153–158.

Pressey, S.L. (1926). A simple apparatus which gives tests and scores—and teaches. *School and Society, 23,* 373–376.

Pressey, S.L. (1950). Development and appraisal of devices providing immediate automatic scoring of objective tests and concomitant self-instruction. *The Journal of Psychology, 29,* 417–447.

Rosenberg, R. (1987). A critical analysis of research on intelligent tutoring systems. *Educational Technology, 27*(3), 7–13.

Ross, S.M. (1983). Increasing the meaningfulness of quantitative material by adapting context to student background. *Journal of Educational Psychology, 75,* 519–529.

Ross, S.M., & Anand, P. (1987). A computer-based strategy for personalizing verbal problems in teaching mathematics. *Educational Communications and Technology Journal, 35,* 151–162.

Ross, S.M., Morrison, G.R., & Barnette, J.J. (in press). Using electronic study-guides as instructional aids in college courses. *Journal of Structural Learning.*

Ross, S.M., Morrison, G.R., & O'Dell, J.K. (1989). Uses and effects of learner control of context and instructional support in computer based instruction. *Educational Technology Research and Development, 37,* 29–40.

Rothkopf, E.Z. (1966). Learning from written instructive materials: An exploration of the control of inspection behavior by test-like events. *American Educational Research Journal, 3*(4), 241–249.

Schimmel, G.J. (1983, April). *A meta-analysis of feedback to learners in computerized and programmed instruction.* Paper presented at the annual meeting of the American Educational Research Association, Montreal. (ERIC Document Reproduction No. ED 233 708).

Schimmel, G.J. (1988). Providing meaningful feedback in courseware. In D. Jonassen (Ed.), *Instructional designs for microcomputer courseware* (pp. 183–196). Hillsdale, NJ: Lawrence Erlbaum Associates.

Schultz, C.W. (1990). *The use of examples and nonexamples in procedural learning using computer-based instruction with varying forms of feedback.* Unpublished doctoral prospectus, Memphis State University.

Stodolsky, S.S. (1988). *The subject matters.* Chicago: The University of Chicago Press.

Tennyson, R.D. (1981). Use of adaptive information for advisement in learning concepts and rules using computer-assisted instruction. *American Educational Research Journal, 18,* 425–438.

Tennyson, R.D., & Buttrey (1980). Advisement and management strategies as design variables in computer-assisted instruction. *Educational Communications and Technology Journal, 28,* 169–176.

Tennyson, R.D., & Rothen, W. (1977). Pretask and on-task adaptive design strategies for selecting number of instances in concept acquisition. *Journal of Educational Psychology, 5,* 126–134.

Wittrock, M.C. (1989). Generative processes of comprehension. *Educational Psychologist, 24,* 345–376.

Chapter Nine

Simulation and Gaming: Fidelity, Feedback, and Motivation

John W. Jacobs
Electronic Selection Systems Corporation

and

John V. Dempsey
University of South Alabama

Introduction

Developed in response to advances in computer technology, as well as to the general criticism regarding the lack of motivational features within current computer-based instruction (Dekkers & Donatti, 1981), simulations and games are becoming more prevalent as an instructional format. Computer simulations range from simple games having relatively few overt instructional features, to comprehensive instructional packages designed for a specific content area (e.g., chemistry, micro- and macro-economics, experimental design, or pedestrian safety), to complex systems, as in the case of some aircraft flight simulators.

This chapter takes an applied approach. We set out to answer several basic questions an educational practitioner might ask. These questions concern the nature and use of simulations and games and include the following: What are simulations and games, and how are they used? How does one go about developing a simulation training program? What does the research literature say about how to develop effective simulations and games, and what benefits can be derived from their use? What differences are there between simulation and gaming, and what does gaming add to the instructional environment?

The discussion that follows takes the position that instruction is a form of dialogue between learner and instructional material. An important aspect of this dialogue constitutes what is commonly referred to as the *interactive* component of instruction. In addition to reflecting on instructional content, the learner also responds to questions and prompts designed to facilitate cognitive processing of to-be-learned material. The learner-instruction dialogue continues via feedback concerning the appropriateness of the learner's response and includes information about response correctness. In some cases, feedback would include explanatory information, metacognitive prompts, or clues to help the learner correct wrong or partially correct responses. By facilitating learner involvement via simulation and gaming and incorporating sound instructional features, learning outcomes should show improvements relative to other training methods that are less engaging or that provide less effective means of instructional interaction.

Among other benefits, simulation and gaming have great potential for incorporating metacognitive strategy training into instructional environments. Oxford and Crookall (1988) claim that simulations and games foster the development of many learning strategies, including: organizational strategies (paying attention, self-evaluating, and self-monitoring), affective strategies (anxiety reduction and self-encouragement), memory strategies (grouping, imagery, and structured review), compensatory strategies (guessing meaning intelligently and using synonyms to represent an unknown precise expression), and others. With the once-fantastic technological possibilities now available, simulation and gaming, using instructional feedback where it is needed, may assist learners to become more responsible for their own learning processes.

The use of feedback to enhance instruction has been well documented in the research literature, and its use and benefits are primary foci of this book. A key component that is sometimes overlooked when discussing feedback is the link between feedback and assessment. The learner's ongoing performance must be measured and ultimately evaluated in order for useful feedback to be generated. The benefits provided by interactive technologies, especially computers, include the ability to track (and measure) a wide variety of instructional variables in an ongoing manner (e.g., learning pace, response time/accuracy, or use of prompts). Simulations offer the additional benefit of providing a relevant context for couching performance feedback. The use of gaming in conjunction with training simulations increases learner interest due, in part, to the infusion of competition, and may serve to add to the fidelity of the simulation if competition is an important aspect of the real-life (operational) environment being simulated.

In keeping with the theme of this book, we consider gaming and simulation in those media where interactivity is possible. These media include human-directed, computer-based, interactive video, printed workbook, and others. The key elements of any of these interactive instructional media are provisions for: (1) bi-directional communication, and (2) informational feedback in some form.

What Is Simulation?

According to Morris and Thomas (1976), simulation refers to "the ongoing representation of certain features of a real situation to achieve some training objective," while simulator refers to "the media through which a trainee may experience simulation" (p. 66). When used for training, simulation may provide instruction on a small portion of the total operational task or on the entire task as an integrated unit. Simulators corresponding to these two aspects of instruction are commonly referred to as part-task and whole-task trainers, respectively (Kinkade & Wheaton, 1972; Hays & Singer, 1989).

A simulation, according to Reigeluth and Schwartz (1989), is composed of three major instructional design elements. The *scenario* recreates, to a particular degree, a real-life situation. The *model* reflects the causal relationships which govern the situation. The *instructional overlay* is the design aspect, which seeks to optimize learning and motivation. In addition, the authors have identified three major types of simulations: procedural, process, and causal. Procedural simulation promotes learning of a sequence or steps. Naturally occurring phenomena composed of a specific sequence of events are taught by process simulation. Causal simulation, by contrast, enhances learning of cause and effect relationships.

Historically, simulation has been used as a tool for training, assessment, and planning. Recently, however, simulations have been receiving increased attention due to the possibilities offered by technological innovations (e.g., computer hardware and software, improved graphics and video capabilities, etc.). One area of use having a high degree of visibility is the training and evaluation of pilots. Military flight simulators have been in existence for over 50 years, and there exists a comprehensive literature base describing their use and evaluating their effectiveness. Simulation has also been used extensively for the assessment of managerial skills in business and industry. Developed initially during World War II, "hands-on" simulations were used by the United States Office of Strategic Services to select qualified candidates for dangerous espionage assignments. Now, work simulation exercises are an integral part of what is referred to in the field of

Industrial/Organizational (I/O) Psychology as assessment centers (Thornton & Byham, 1982). Though simulation exercises within assessment centers involve live role play almost exclusively, a great deal of theory and research has been generated by researchers and practitioners attempting to understand and refine the use of simulations for evaluating key managerial skills. Also, there exists a variety of computer-based simulations targeting many aspects of business (from production, to finance, to personnel decision making) which currently are being used to aid instruction on college campuses throughout the country (see Faria, 1987, for a survey of usage).

Developing Effective Simulations

In order for a simulation to be effective, two basic issues must be addressed: (1) what aspects of the operational environment require simulation, and (2) to what extent should they be replicated? The supposition we make is that one only needs to simulate those events or characteristics that allow the learner to perform in a proficient manner when performing in the operational environment, i.e., the real world. This representation of the characteristics of simulation have been characterized by Gagné (1962), and later by Clariana (1989) in the following formula:

Simulation = (Reality) − (Task irrelevant elements)

These questions, involving optimal environment and extent of replication, as well as issues surrounding simulation design, have generated a great deal of discussion and debate within the psychological and educational literature. We agree with Reigeluth and Schwartz (1989) that content is the single most important basis for prescribing variations in a simulation. At the core of this discussion are the concepts of fidelity and transfer of training. In this chapter, we argue for focusing simulation design on capturing the functional aspects of the operational environment rather than solely attempting to re-create the physical aspects. Moreover, in certain instances, we contend that degrading realism by adding sound instructional techniques (e.g., feedback and prompts) serves to increase the effectiveness of training simulations.

Simulation Versus Gaming

The distinction between simulation and the concept of games or gaming is often blurred, and many recent articles in this area refer to a single "simulation game" entity (e.g., Laveault & Corbeil, 1990; Coleman, 1989;

Kryukov & Kryukova, 1986). After all, a game, like a simulation, generally may be assumed to have goals, activities, constraints, and consequences. A distinction could be made between simulations and games in the following way. Where the task-irrelevant elements of a task are removed from reality to create a simulation, other elements are emphasized to create a game. These elements include competition and externally imposed rules, and may include other elements such as fantasy and surprise.

The concept of gaming, for the purpose of this chapter, is viewed as being separate from simulation and is defined, in a basic sense, as any training format that involves competition and is rule-guided, a view which is consistent with that of other authors in the area (e.g., Jones, 1987). A competitive format, as we define it, does not necessarily require two or more participants. For example, if a simulation produces an overall "score," then it is possible for a learner to compete against herself by comparing scores over successive attempts at the simulation. Therefore, the learner may be in a gaming mode. If, however, the focus of the simulation involves the completion of an event (e.g., safely landing an aircraft), then according to our definition the simulation would not be considered a game. This is not to say that a game structure may not be imposed on the simulation from outside. For example, in the flight simulation scenario learners could compete by seeing how many safe landings can be done in a row. The gaming element offers additional characteristics which may be manipulated within the simulation training context, and thus should be treated separately.

The Game Is Up

The use of games in instruction may be more prevalent than some suspect. Based on a mail and telephone survey of approximately 1,500 contacts in four-year colleges, Faria (1987) concluded that 8,755 instructors in 1,900 business schools used business games in their course work. The same author reported that 4,600 of the larger U.S. firms used business or experiential games in training and development.

Gaming, like simulations, is considered to produce a wide range of instructional benefits, although a number of researchers have questioned some claims due to a lack of sufficient empirical support (e.g., Bredemeier & Greenblat, 1981). Other researchers assert that instructional games have been found to improve practical reasoning skills (Wood & Stewart, 1987), result in significantly higher levels of continuing motivation (Malouf, 1988), and reduce training time and instructor load (Allen, Chatelier, Clark, & Sorenson, 1982). Authors have proposed employing gaming strategies in learning activities as diverse as attention-reduction training (Jacobs, Dempsey, & Salisbury, 1990) and complex problem solving (Hayes, 1981).

One important finding in some of the gaming literature is that gaming ability may differ in significant ways from academic abilities, which rely on abstract thinking and verbal fluency (Bredemeier & Greenblat, 1981). Braskamp and Hodgetts (1971), for example, found a negative correlation of −.37 between students' performance on a business simulation game and their grade point average. According to Seigner (1980), gaming ability differs from academic ability in at least three respects: (1) the cognitive processes involved in gaming may include the ability to perceive relationships rather than language command; (2) gaming is more independent from self-perceptions of confidence and control; and (3) gaming is not affected directly by social background (p. 419).

There is also some evidence that games may improve retention of what is learned. Twenty-two research reports that compared the effects of simulation or games with those of conventional instruction on a variety of learning outcomes were reviewed by Pierfy (1977). Only three of the studies showed significant immediate differences in favor of simulation or gaming. An equal number found differences in favor of conventional methods. The majority (15 studies) found no differences. In contrast, 11 of the 22 studies which assessed retention by administering the posttest at a later date had much different findings. Eight of these studies found retention significantly better with simulation and gaming, while three found no difference.

Additionally, the categorization of game types is subject to frequent overlap, making distinctions difficult. Game categories in the literature include adventure games, simulation games, competition games, cooperation games, programming games, puzzle games, and management games—as a sample. It is quite usual to categorize a game as one thing (e.g., a mathematics adventure game) and have it quite legitimately considered to be another type of game (e.g., a puzzle).

Developing Effective Games

Probably the most influential guide available to instructional game designers and researchers is the work of Malone (1980, 1981a, 1981b). Based on prior research and studies of "highly-motivating" computer games, Malone formulated a rudimentary theory of intrinsically motivating instruction. As the author pointed out, his studies focused on what made the games fun, not what made them educational. Most importantly, Malone proposed that a more extensive theory of instructional design might be developed based on three categories: *challenge, fantasy,* and *curiosity*. This theory is so important to the study of effective instructional games that it will be discussed in some detail.

Of the three categories, some recent authors (e.g., Baltra, 1990) consider the most crucial factor to be *challenge*. In analyzing challenge, Malone considered four attributes: goals, uncertain outcome, toys versus tools, and self-esteem. Goals (or objectives) should be clear and personally meaningful to the learner. For a goal to be an effective motivator, learners need some form of performance feedback to tell whether they are achieving their goal. For an environment to be challenging, Malone contended that there must be an uncertain outcome. This may be achieved by varying the level of difficulty, designing multiple level goals, hiding selective information from the learner, and using randomness to heighten interest. Malone also felt that it was important to make a distinction between toys and tools. Toys were defined as systems for their own sake with no external goal (e.g., puzzles). Tools, on the other hand, were defined as systems used as means to achieve an external goal (e.g., a text editor). Their requirements with respect to challenge were dissimilar. Finally, challenge is captivating because it engages a learner's self-esteem by providing success opportunities. Again, varying the difficulty level is an implication. Another implication proposed by Malone is that performance feedback should be presented in a way that minimizes the possibility of damage to a learner's self-esteem. Regarding this issue, Malone states:

> Note that there is a tension here between the need to provide clear performance feedback to enhance challenge and learning, and the need not to reduce self-esteem to the point where the challenge becomes discouraging rather than inviting.(1981a, p. 360)

In addition to challenge, *fantasy* and *curiosity* are central components of Malone's theory. Regarding the former, Malone distinguishes between extrinsic (fantasy depends on the skill but not vice versa) and intrinsic fantasies (fantasy depends on the skill and the skill builds on the fantasy). Malone claims, based on one research study, that, "In general, intrinsic fantasies are both (a) more interesting and (b) more instructional than extrinsic fantasies" (1981a, p. 361). Examples of intrinsic and extrinsic fantasies in instructional gaming and discussed later in this chapter. Malone also points out the cognitive and emotional effects of fantasy. One of his most interesting notions in this regard is that of creating a fantasy of the learner's choice. This notion has additional consequences regarding the nature and quality of feedback presented to the learner as a result of varying scenarios.

Malone distinguishes between sensory curiosity (attention-attracting changes in light, sound, or other sensory stimuli) and cognitive curiosity (which he defines as "a desire to bring better 'form' to one's knowledge structures" (1981a, p. 363). Effects promoting sensory curiosity may be used as a decoration, to enhance fantasy, as a reward, and as a representation system. In order to engage a learner's cognitive curiosity, Malone suggests that insructional designers should provide learners with just enough information to make their existing knowledge seem incomplete, inconsistent, or unparsimonious. Especially relevant in light of technological advances in the last ten years are Malone's prescriptions regarding informative feedback and curiosity. To engage a learner's curiosity and learning, feedback should be both surprising and constructive. Malone points out that curiosity and challenge are very related. Both, "depend on feedback to reduce uncertainty (about one's own ability in the case of challenge and the state of the world in the case of curiosity)" (1981a, p. 363).

Malone's theory provides a practical reference for designing instructional games as well as a solid basis for further research and theory building regarding instructional gaming. Unfortunately, all too often instructional gaming relies too heavily on aspects of sensory curiosity that embellish, rather than embody, instructional and metacognitive goals.

Examples of Low-Cost Instructional Games

At this point, it may be useful to introduce two examples of relatively simple games which incorporate some of Malone's prescriptions. These games are among a dozen or so designed by the second author of this chapter for the Job Skills Education Program (JSEP), an extensive basic skills computer-based instructional (CBI) program developed for the U.S. Army. Because of what are probably the usual problems associated with any large CBI project (i.e., limited computer memory, unsophisticated programmers, and tight deadlines), it was difficult to get any games approved as part of the curriculum. Those that were had to be relatively easy to program and, in most cases, had to be rather generic. In addition, it was important that users were able to learn the rules of the game structure in a very short period in order that scarce instructional time would not be wasted.

One game that met these criteria is called *Round the Track*. This game is an extrinsic fantasy pitting the learner, pictured as a tiny person, against a tiny anthropomorphized computer figure. Around the perimeters of the computer screen is a type of race track with a clearly designed start and finish. The majority of the screen is used as a part of any of a series of lessons (e.g., mathematics) in which a game may be employed. The race-type structure of *Round the Track* encourages the learner to "beat the computer" by responding approximately to random sets of content-relevant questions. Each time the learner responds correctly, the human figure advances. Each incorrect response advances the tiny computer figure. Feedback varies according to the content of the lesson as well as the learner's on-task performance. Although the outcome is uncertain, the learner needs to get only 50% of the question set correct (usually well below mastery) on the first attempt to beat the computer. Special care was taken to design helpful content feedback or prescribe additional remediation for learners performing below mastery. Learners performing above mastery level received feedback intended to enhance self-esteem. Because *Round the Track* was designed to be used with many different content areas, it had the advantages of being cost-efficient and easy to implement across the curriculum. Further, learners who participated in multiple lessons employing this game structure were able to use the game structure immediately without direction.

A second game, called *Over the Hill*, employs an intrinsic fantasy to support instruction related to degree measurement, mil measurement (a military artillery measure similar to degrees), the concepts of clockwise and counterclockwise, and similar goals. This scenario usually is used to tie together an entire instructional module. The goal of the game is for the learner (soldier) to "drive" a truck starting from his or her unit over a 180-degree hill to pick up some emergency supplies from headquarters on the other side of the hill. The scenario makes it clear that other soldiers in the unit badly need the emergency supplies. When the learner correctly answers question items, the truck moves forward (clockwise) in 15-degree increments. Depending on the lesson objectives and the size of the question sets, the learner is required to "drive" the truck back (counterclockwise), do so within a given period to advance, or do so more quickly than was done on the last supply run. In addition to content-related feedback, a small feedback box in the corner of the screen informs the learner at all times how far over the hill the truck has passed (e.g., 45° CW—from a central observation point). The learner can also click on this box to see a graphical representation of the truck's progress over the hill.

The chief advantage of a game like *Over the Hill* as compared to a game like *Round the Track* is that the game structure itself is helping to teach the content. That is, not only are learners responding to question-based examples related to, for instance, degree measurement, they are also participating in a fantasy which requires facility in that particular skill to achieve the goal of the game. The primary disadvantage of intrinsic fantasies like *Over the Hill* is that they are not as generic as extrinsic games and are therefore less easy to integrate into instruction. Even so, these games are intentionally uncomplicated by design, generally resource-efficient to develop, and used as an embodiment of the instruction, rather than as embellishment or pure entertainment. In addition, they incorporate some of the motivational characteristics attributed to effective instructional games, including clear goals, informative feedback, scores that show improved performance, high response rates, uncertain outcomes, visual effects, and fantasy (Malone, 1981a).

Simulation Design: Content Versus Construct Validity

The primary goal when designing simulations is to capture the relevant activities which make up the real-life or operational environment. Is this really true? When designing simulation exercises for evaluating managers, some psychologists have argued that what is truly being measured within the exercises are constructs or skill dimensions, such as leadership, decision making, problem analysis, and communication (see Thornton & Byham, 1982, pp. 117–126). These constructs or skills allow the participant (manager) to perform specified work activities, such as providing performance feedback to a subordinate, in an acceptable manner within the simulation. Thus, in one sense, the simulation is content-valid to the degree that it captures critical aspects of the job position through careful construction of stimulus items. These include pertinent background information and use appropriate measures, such as behavioral ratings, to evaluate a participant's performance (Sackett, 1987). Another view holds that while the identification and simulation of these work activities are important, the level of evaluation should be at the skill or construct level, because skills enable the participant effectively to perform these activities (Thornton & Byham, 1982).

The debate concerning content versus construct validity is equally cogent for the design of training simulations. That is, it may be that the learning taking place within the simulation has limited application outside the simulation. This is true to some degree in all cases because there are a finite number of parameters used to define and control a given simulation. Thus, knowledge and skills acquired through training simulations will always be situationally constrained to a greater or lesser degree (Weitz & Adler, 1973). To the extent the simulation prepares the learner to deal with some, but not all, situational constraints operating in the real-life environment, it may be considered content-valid, yet have limited construct validity. In general, it is more desirable for the simulation to foster general skills and abilities (e.g., to analyze problems or make effective decisions) that are useful in a wide range of situations that arise in the operational environment (e.g., attempting to maximize the value of one's stock portfolio, or to decide on the best course of action when faced with multiple incoming enemy aircraft).

It is interesting to note that some researchers have found that certain types of cognitive strategies differ in their applicability across situations. For example, Newell's (1980) conceptualization of a "weak to strong" approach in training cognitive skills views the strength of a given strategy to be inversely related to its generalizability in use. Thus, weak strategies, like general problem-solving heuristics, trade power for their applicability in a variety of situations and tasks. Conversely, strong strategies are limited in use to a narrow range of specific problem situations, yet may improve performance considerably when employed.

The content versus construct validity issue may never be completely resolved, since the underlying content and activities presented within the context of the simulation will never exactly emulate the operational environment. The simulated or gaming environment, however, can offer distinct advantages over the operational environment during training. This is especially so when the activities being trained are complex or have situational constraints which inhibit the training process in the operational environment (e.g., occur infrequently, or have associated risk, danger, or expense).

In the final analysis, the effectiveness of any training simulation can be expressed in terms of its learning outcomes, the most pertinent being transfer of training (subsequently referred to as transfer). The central importance of transfer to the design and evaluation of simulations, and to training in general, cannot be overstated and will be discussed in more detail later.

Job Analysis and Simulation Design

Let us now focus on the simulation design process and techniques that may be used to facilitate this process. It should be noted that while the focus of this discussion involves simulation design, many of the issues are relevant to the discussion of gaming or game design. For over 50 years, psychologists and personnel practitioners have studied simulation techniques in an effort to select effective managers. A critical step in the simulation design process requires identification of important work activities and duties which serve to "capture" the content of a given job position. Collectively, procedures used to identify these work activities, and subsequently to determine which activities should be the foci of one or more simulations, are referred to as job analysis (Thornton & Byham, 1982). Not surprisingly, in the case of managerial selection, no single method for analyzing a job position can ensure that all critical work activities of the job have been identified. In this case, the term "critical" may be operationally defined as a function of rated importance and frequency of occurrence (Haymaker & Grant, 1982).

Typically, work activities are initially identified using a structured interview, which probes such areas as interactions with other persons within and outside the organization (e.g., face-to-face and phone conversations), decision-making authority, and major job duties or responsibilities. Interviews are conducted with individuals currently in the target position (incumbents) and the incumbents' direct superiors.

The data collected in the interviews are summarized on a questionnaire in the form of multiple work activity statements (sometimes exceedng 100), such as, ''Monitors work processes of subordinates to ensure they are completed in a timely manner and conform with stated policies and procedures.'' This questionnaire, referred to as a task analysis questionnaire or TAQ, lists each activity statement and requires respondents to rate its importance and frequency of occurrence using behaviorally anchored scale values (e.g., daily = 5, weekly = 4, monthly = 3, etc.). A measure of ''criticality'' can then be determined by calculating the product of an activity's mean importance and frequency of occurrence ratings. Once identified using this procedure, activities having the highest ''criticality'' values are those which should be the focus in the simulation design process.

Prior to the simulation design phase, work activities are grouped together into clusters. These clusters form the basis for determining independent skill areas, which are then evaluated during the simulation. For illustrative purposes, Table 9.1 presents a hypothetical clustering of work activities into two skill areas, leadership and problem analysis, for a hypothetical office manager position. To ensure that each skill is independent of the other skills, overlap of work activities across skill areas is held to a minimum. It is desirable, however, to measure a given work activity in more than one assessment center simulation exercise, especially if the activity in question has been determined to have a high criticality value. By measuring individual activities (and skills) in two or more simulation exercises, a multitrait-multimethod measurement methodology is being employed. In other words, multiple skills (traits) are being measured in multiple situations (methods). This methodology is made stronger by having different assessors evaluate the performance of an individual participant in each simulation or game, thereby controlling one source of measurement error or bias.

It is also noteworthy that the importance of a given skill within a simulation or simulation game exercise is not determined by the number of instances the participant has to display the skill. Rather, a skill's importance is a function of whether ineffective performance in the skill results in ineffective performance in the simulation as a whole. For example, the skill of organizing and planning may be critical for processing a set of items (i.e., memos, letters, and reports) that make up an in-basket simulation. That same skill of organizing and planning would be less critical, and certainly secondary to the skill of leadership (defined as influencing or coaching others) in a simulation where the participant (manager) must meet with a subordinate to discuss his or her poor performance.

SKILLS/WORK ACTIVITIES	PRODUCT OF MEAN IMPORTANCE AND FREQUENCY OF OCCURRENCE RATINGS[1] (CRITICALITY)
LEADERSHIP -	
To influence the action and thinking of others. Included here is the ability to delegate, give direction to others, and implement monitoring and follow-up procedures.	
Work Activities -	
1. Monitors subordinates relative to pre-established performance goals and plans to reach these goals.	21.34
2. Adjusts work activities of self and others to optimize work output.	17.68
3. Provides guidance to subordinates concerning specific job assignment (e.g., how to handle specific customer/account, etc.)	13.41
PROBLEM ANALYSIS -	
To determine an appropriate course of action based on available facts or information; to evaluate factors essential to the solution of a problem.	
Work Activities -	
4. Develops and submits operating budget for office.	10.73
5. Conceptualizes and implements new work flow and operating procedures to enhance administrative effectiveness/efficiency.	12.18
6. Monitors actual resource expenditures (e.g., manpower, equipment, space, etc.) relative to planned expenditures.	23.72

Note 1: Criticality values presented here are based on a five point rating scale for determining both importance and frequency of occurrence, thus criticality values can range from 1 to 25.

Table 9.1. Skill areas and related work activity clusters for hypothetical office manager position.

In summary, simulation, and in some instances gaming design take into account several factors. First, all relevant activities that make up the job position (operational environment) should be identified during the initial simulation design phase. Second, the relative "criticality" of the various activities should be determined, and those activities found to be highly critical should be incorporated as the focus of the simulation or game. Third, performance evaluation is an important aspect of establishing content validity and should go beyond simply assessing performance related to individual work activities and focus on skills (e.g., problem analysis, decision making, or communication) required for effective performance of these activities within the simulation or game.

Fidelity Requirements for Designing Simulations and Simulation Games

Mention the word "simulator" and people generally think of a flight simulator. Their metamorphosis from simple box-and-stick mockup devices to extremely complex (and expensive) pieces of equipment offers valuable guidelines for those currently developing simulation-based instructional programs.

Current state-of-the-art simulator cockpits are often physically identical to those of the operational aircraft. Computer systems used to simulate flight-control characteristics are based on complex mathematical algorithms, and in some cases are evaluated by experienced pilots to refine their responsiveness. In addition, sophisticated add-on systems, such as motion platforms, high-definition visual systems, G-seats and G-suits (pneumatically driven G-force simulators), to name a few, are used to match, as closely as possible, those forces experienced by a pilot in the operational aircraft.

In other words, a great deal of time, energy, and money is spent trying to simulate accurately the physical components of the operational environment to as close a degree as the prevailing technology allows. Despite the continued efforts aimed at improving the physical characteristics of the flight simulators, a recent meta-analytic review of the flight simulator training literature suggested that the functional aspects of fidelity are also important to achieving transfer to the operational environment (Hays, Jacobs, Prince, and Salas, 1992; Jacobs, Prince, Hays, and Salas, 1990). These authors cite evidence indicating positive transfer can be accomplished using simulators that only slightly match the physical characteristics of the operational environment, but whose functional requirements (e.g., in the form realistically portrayed mission elements) provide for an effective learning environment (e.g., Caro, Corley, Spears, & Blaiwes, 1984; Prophet & Boyd, 1970).

With this thought in mind, let us explore some of the issues involving fidelity requirements. In their book examining simulation fidelity in the training environment, Hays and Singer (1989) offer a useful definition of simulation fidelity:

> *Simulation fidelity* is the degree of similarity between the training situation and the operational situation which is simulated. It is a two-dimensional measurement of this similarity in terms of: (1) the physical characteristics, for example, visual, spatial, or kinesthetic; and (2) the functional characteristics, for example, the informational, and stimulus and response options of the training situation. (p. 50)

These researchers go on to suggest that functional requirements are often overlooked as a guiding concept during the simulator design phase. Said differently, learning from experience can only happen if the learner is able to benefit from the consequences of his or her actions. These researchers argue that simulation design should optimal fidelity. That is, an effort should be made to determine the minimum acceptable fidelity level that still ensures adequate training outcomes, especially transfer. Other researchers have made similar arguments concerning the need to focus less on physical fidelity when designing simulations. For example, Reigeluth and Schwartz (1989) suggest that only certain aspects of the real-world environment require high fidelity, and state that an "overload" situation may be created by incorporating non-essential components into the simulation, thereby reducing motivation and ultimately reducing the instructional (learning) benefits of the simulation. A similar conclusion was reached by Clariana (1989) when addressing the question of whether to add elements of realism into the simulation environment, concluding ". . . the potential efficiency of a computer simulation depends on the quality and not necessarily the quantity of reality included in the simulation" (p. 15). In a previous study conducted by Weitz and Adler (1973), subjects exposed to over-learning procedures and who were trained using high-fidelity simulation produced lower transfer scores than subjects trained using a lower fidelity simulation.

In summary, it is evident that the need for determining adequate simulation fidelity is an important concern when developing effective simulation exercises. The focus, however, should be on improving instructional outcomes, and in particular on increasing transfer to the operational environment (e.g., work place), rather than attempting to upgrade the physical fidelity of the simulation for no other reason than to faithfully reproduce "reality." In short, simulation designers should guard against treating simulation fidelity as an end in itself. This sentiment is consistent with the views of Hays and Singer (1989), who state:

> It cannot be assumed that an appropriate fidelity specification provides all necessary answers about training. It will still be necessary to develop, analyze and incorporate the best possible instructional strategies into the training program. . . . The most important thing to remember about the concept of fidelity is to use it as a tool, but not to let it dictate to the user how it should be used. The term fidelity does not necessarily imply high (or low) fidelity. It has meaning as a summary concept, but can still be used to advantage by training system developers, especially when carefully delineated in terms of its dimensions and interactions with the myriad other training systems factors. (pp. 45–46)

The question remains as to what should be the guiding impetus driving the development of training simulations. Reigeluth and Schwartz (1989) offer several suggestions concerning what factors should be considered when deciding on the level of fidelity of a simulation, including: (1) the degree of complexity of the real-world environment, (2) the potential for transfer to the operational environment, (3) the motivational consequences of incorporating the high-fidelity characteristics, and (4) the resulting expense involved in upgrading the realism of the simulation (see also Clariana, 1989).

The importance of transfer as a training outcome metric cannot be overstated. Due to the importance of having a unified model of transfer for guiding and interpreting research in this area, important issues surrounding transfer and simulation design will be discussed next.

Models of Transfer and Fidelity

Stated simply, transfer involves the continued appropriate responding of a learner in situations that differ from the original learning context. That is, transfer is said to occur when the learner applies previously learned information to new situations. Differences between the original and transfer environment may be due to changes in setting, materials, performance measurement, or a combination of two or more of these variables. Moreover, training transfer may be either positive, negative, or zero, depending on whether performance in the transfer situation is enhanced, degraded, or stays the same relative to some predetermined baseline performance level (e.g., performance prior to training or performance of a control group).

In their review of flight simulation training, Wheaton and his colleagues (1976) describe several models of training and transfer that prescribe training needs, and in some cases predict transfer. These models are classified into two broad types: task-analytic and micro-analytic. Task-analytic models, they state, ''. . . assume that information about a given task category can be used to indicate the best method for training within that category'' (Wheaton, Rose, Fingerman, Korotkin, Holding, & Mirabella, 1976, p. 6). Taking this one step further, transfer is also assumed to occur for this model when similar tasks are trained in both the simulation and operational environment.

Micro-analytic models are more fine-grained and analyze the operational and training environment by comparing stimuli and responses. Positive transfer may be assumed to occur here if stimulus-response relationships coincide in both environments.

Both models use Osgood's (1949) theory of transfer as the basis of predicted level of transfer. The central premise of the theory is that the amount of transfer is a function of the degree to which there exists common elements between the original and transfer situation or task (see also Thorndike, 1903). It is easy to see why simulation designers may base their design decisions on predominantly physical fidelity requirements, thereby attempting to improve the match between the operational and training (simulation) environment. As a guiding concept for determining simulation design, the search for ever higher physical fidelity can be questioned on conceptual, theoretical, and empirical grounds.

Conceptually, a reliance on physical fidelity as a guide for simulation design is tautological. One can always make the argument that low or unacceptable training transfer is due to the less-than-perfect fidelity or sub-optimal calibration of simulation configuration parameters.

Theoretically, the psychological and educational literatures offer alternative views of transfer that are relevant to simulation training. For example, Royer (1979) describes two general approaches to understanding and explaining transfer. The first is what he termed programmed training, which is identical to the theory of common elements described previously. The second approach is cognitive in nature, and asserts that, ". . . the likelihood that transfer of learning will occur is determined by the probability of retrieving the relevant prior learning during the search process" (Royer, 1979, p. 62; see also Brown and Campione, 1984). This framework is based on the assumption that the human memory storage system is structured and that retrieval of stored information is systematic. Also, memory structures may vary in their "richness" or "elaborateness" due to variations in the number of interconnections between memory units (e.g., nodes or propositions). According to this framework, understanding is a necessary, but not sufficient, condition for transfer to take place.

Empirically, several lines of research can be cited which question the applicability of designing simulations based predominantly on physical fidelity requirements. One area of research that has direct relevance to this issue is referred to as asymmetrical transfer, which refers to a phenomenon where transfer between two related tasks is not equal. As noted by Wheaten *et al.* (1976), ". . . transfer may be greater in one direction than in the reverse direction between two tasks which differ in difficulty" (p. 68). By definition, differences in similarity between the two tasks are identical and thus a theory of common elements would predict transfer in both directions to be identical. In addition, there are examples in the flight simulation evaluation literature indicating that high physical fidelity simulation is not a necessary ingredient to produce positive transfer (see e.g., Caro, Corley, Spears, & Blaiwes, 1984; Waag, 1981). Conversely, there is evidence indicating high fidelity does not ensure positive transfer outcomes (e.g., Martin & Waag, 1978; Pohlman & Reed, 1978).

A Model of Motivation

Historically, motivational theory and research, even in education, focused on behavioral reinforcement and performance issues with less emphasis on increasing learner motivation via instructional means. Recently, John Keller and his associates have presented a useful framework for increasing learner motivation using instructional design strategies via an "ARCS" model (Keller, 1984; 1987a; 1987b; Keller & Kopp, 1987; Keller & Suzuki, 1987). The ARCS model seeks to improve the motivational content of instructional material by incorporating strategies related to four categories: attention, relevance, confidence, and satisfaction (hence the A-R-C-S acronym). Each category has subcategories that help the instructional designer to analyze the instructional material/environment and guide the design process (via use of specified strategies) toward ways to increase learner motivation. Not surprisingly, one subcategory of attention strategies involves increasing learner participation and suggests the use of simulations and games (Keller, 1987a). A review of the ARCS model categories, both in terms of analysis and design strategies, is instructive because it provides a possible explanation for why simulations are motivating and what additional benefits are provided by incorporating a gaming component.

Table 9.2 presents the categories and subcategories described in the ARCS model as they relate to training simulations. A number of strategies were not listed because they did not necessarily pertain to a simulation or gaming format.

Interestingly, the area of relevance offers but three instructional design strategies related to simulations and games. Given the commonly held perception that simulation is synonymous with realism, one would assume that one strategy in this area would be to provide the opportunity for practice in realistic settings. This strategy is considered by Keller to be a satisfaction strategy, and this appears to be a problem for the model. Although the model offers a systematic approach for assessing the motivational content of instruction, the relationships between design strategies and process categories and subcategories are not always readily apparent. Also, there appears to be some overlap within and between subcategories. For instance, two satisfaction strategies related to positive outcomes are: "Give verbal praise for successful progress or accomplishments," and "Provide motivating feedback (praise) immediately following task performance." A similar strategy related to scheduling states, "Provide frequent reinforcement when a student is learning a new task." Finally, there are strategies which may not produce the desired effects, such as the one stating, "Avoid external performance evaluations whenever it is possible to help the student evaluate his or her own work." There is evidence suggesting that learner self-evaluation

Categories & Process Subcategories	Design Subcategories	Suggested Design Strategies	
Attention A. Perceptual Arousal B. Inquiry Arousal C. Variability	1. Incongruity, Conflict 2. Concreteness 3. Variability 4. Humor 5. Inquiry 6. Participation	2(a) 2(b) 2(c) 3(a) 3(b) 5(a) 6(a)	Visually represent important concepts, ideas, relationships Give examples of concepts/principles Use relevant antidotes, case studies, biographies Vary the format of instruction to fit audience attention span Vary instructional medium (e.g., print, computer, video, etc.) Incorporate problem-solving activities Use simulations, role play, and games
Relevance A. Goal Orientation B. Motive Matching C. Familiarity	1. Experience 2. Present Worth 3. Future Usefulness 4. Need Matching 5. Modeling 6. Choice	1(a) 3(a) 4(a)	State how instruction enhances learner skills State how instruction relates to future learning activities Provide positive achievement opportunities
Confidence A. Learning Requirements B. Success Opportunities C. Personal Control	1. Learning Requirements 2. Difficulty 3. Expectations 4. Attributions 5. Self-Confidence	1(a) 1(b) 1(c) 2(a) 3(a) 4(a) 4(b) 5(a) 5(b)	Incorporate unambiguous learning goals Provide self-evaluation related to goals Explain evaluation criteria Provide challenge via increasing difficulty Assist learner in developing useful performance plans/strategies Attribute learner success to effort as opposed to luck or ease of task Encourage learner to verbalize positive attributions (i.e., to effort not luck, etc.) Provide opportunity for independent learning and skill acquisition Provide opportunity for low risk skill acquisition as well as realistic skill practice
Satisfaction A. Natural Consequences B. Positive Consequences C. Equity	1. Natural Consequences 2. Unexpected Rewards 3. Positive Outcomes 4. Negative Influences 5. Scheduling	1(a) 3(a) 3(b) 3(c) 5(a)	Provide realistic setting for skill acquisition/practice Praise successful performance Provide positive attention Provide immediate feedback Schedule the frequency and quantity of reinforcement to promote motivation

General Note: This Table is derived from information presented in two sources: Keller, 1987a, Tables 1-4, pp. 4-5, and Keller, 1987b, Table 1, p. 2. The wording of various strategies has been modified here for the sake of brevity and we apologize if these modifications inadvertently change the meaning or intent of the strategy.

Table 9.2. ARCS model categories/subcategories and accompanying design strategies related to training simulations.

of performance may not be highly accurate or provide comparative criteria, such as is often found in performance evaluations by superiors (Bennett, 1988).

The use of gaming and competition may add to the motivational properties in several areas. First, in the area of attention, games are highly participative and offer an alternative learning format, which may serve to enhance learner attention. Also, they can provide an opportunity for shifting interaction from primarily instructor-student to student-student. In the area of relevance, by setting up competition between groups, affiliation and achievement needs may be met. Learner confidence can be enhanced using a game format by providing a more realistic setting, provided real-world activities are inherently competitive in nature, as is the case for many business and industry situations. Moreover, competition is in itself challenging, and by competing against opponents with varying skill levels, one can in effect vary the level of difficulty of the task. Finally, in the area of learner satisfaction, a game format (as noted above) may provide a realistic setting for skill practice and, depending on the scoring format, offer a varied schedule of reinforcement (e.g., by way of accumulating points and successfully carrying out a plan of action).

While simulations can provide a highly motivating learning format, the specific factors making it more or less effective as a training instrument have yet to be identified. A critical evaluation of the ARCS model has yet to be completed. In general, the ultimate measure of its usefulness is the model's ability to explain and predict performance (i.e., training outcomes). Use of gaming in conjunction with simulation may add to the overall motivational properties of the simulation. The exact nature of the positive effects that competition and gaming have on training simulations requires further study.

Metacognitive Prompting

The use of prompts has been explored as a means to improve training effectiveness. Prompts may take a number of forms. For example, prompts may be given to help the learner respond to a question and take the form of an answer or partial answer. Prompts may be used in a less direct manner, such as providing a rule or mathematical formula. Prompts can also be used to promote the learners' self-awareness or self-monitoring of their cognitive processes. When used in the latter way, prompts are seen as a tool for promoting learning-to-learn activities. Smith (1987) discusses the benefits of computer simulations in classroom settings and notes that prompts can assist the learner by shortening response times. In the area of computer-based training, Derry, Jacobs, and Murphy (1987) report the use of prompts as an integral component of an embedded "learning strategy" curriculum for the Job Skills Education Program (JSEP), mentioned earlier in the chapter. The core JSEP curriculum, consisting of over 600 computer-based lessons using two authoring systems, is aimed at improving low-ability soldiers' basic verbal and math skills, which form the prerequisite competencies required for effective performance in selected military occupations. Learning strategy modules in the areas of reading comprehension, math problem solving, motivation, time management, and test taking comprise an innovative supplementary curriculum designed to improve soldier's learning skills. A module is defined as a related set of lessons. By embedding the learning strategy modules within the core curriculum, learners may practice newly acquired knowledge acquisition skills in a content-relevant context. In theory, such practice should increase the likelihood that learners will transfer the use and application of learning skills within the instructional environment (i.e., as an aid when taking the basic skills course materials).

The prompting system that was developed (although not entirely implemented) in conjunction with the JSEP learning strategy curriculum operates in the manner which follows. Upon completing a learning strategy module, the prompts for that module are turned on or activated within JSEP core lessons. Within the lesson, specific visual symbols or icons are displayed at predetermined intervals. The icons reflect the learning strategy areas they represent. For example, the icon of "SGT Booker," a book figure with arms, legs, helmet, and stripes indicating rank, represents the reading strategies module. When the icon appears, the learner has the opportunity to press a designated key and view the prompt screen. The prompt screen reminds the learner of specific information presented in the learning strategy modules. Prompts from a given module are pre-placed within the lesson according to their proposed function. Specifically, prompts direct the learner to initiate a learner-strategy activity that would help in a particular situation. For example, the time management prompt that deals with goal setting is given in the beginning of a lesson. The motivational skills prompt that explains how to become "re-energized," on the other hand, is given at the middle or end of particularly long lessons. With the exception of the test-taking module, these activities are derived from a general problem solving heuristic or metastrategy. The metastrategy for the reading strategy module, for instance, is called the "4 C's," and consists of (1) clarify the reading situation, (2) come up with a reading strategy, (3) carry out the reading strategy, and (4) check results.

Once the learner's performance improves (i.e., he or she passes a lesson on the first try), prompts for the corresponding learning strategy module become optional, and the learner has the choice of activating them for the next lesson. When four lessons are passed on the first try, the prompts are automatically deactivated until future poor performance warrants their reactivation. Since individual lessons may or may not include prompts from a given learning strategy area, and some lessons include prompts from two or more areas, the status of each area is tracked independently.

Learning strategy modules were prescribed according to need, although it was felt that most or even all learners would benefit from time management. The prompting system was designed to encourage learning-to-learn activities by learners without making them dependent on continuous prompting when applying newly acquired knowledge acquisition skills. As yet, a definitive evaluation of the learning strategies curriculum and corresponding prompting system has yet to be undertaken. The JSEP project, with its embedded, learning strategies curriculum, offers an intriguing view of what can be accomplished by tracking and evaluating a range of performance measures and incorporating a wide range of instructional techniques.

Feedback During Training Simulations

Researchers in the areas of simulation training and computer-based training (CBT) have studied the benefits of using feedback and prompting. For example, Munro, Fehling, and Towne (1985) investigated the use of varying degrees of intrusive feedback in simulation training. Thirty high school and college students were presented simulation training problems involving an air intercept controller task. Half of the students received computer-generated error messages whenever the computer recognized an error, and the remaining students were able to view error messages by pressing a specified computer key. The results were that significantly fewer errors were reported for subjects in the latter group (less intrusive condition). The authors viewed these results as suggesting students benefit more from processing demands inherent in the less intrusive feedback condition.

This finding is interesting because it suggests that feedback, when given on learner performance within the training simulation, should not happen immediately after an individual response, but should be provided after the simulation is completed, or at least be postponed until there is a logical break in the scenario. Allowing learners to exercise control over when they receive feedback may or may not prove beneficial, given that there is evidence suggesting that learners tend to make inaccurate judgments of learning (JOL) while studying (e.g., Nelson, 1984; Vesonder & Voss, 1985; see, Nelson & Dunlosky, 1991, for an alternative view). Results suggesting learners benefit more from less intrusive feedback is also of interest because of its implication regarding the use of prompts. By their nature, prompts are intrusive, and there are questions regarding their beneficial effects when used in simulations or CBT (Derry, Jacobs, & Murphy, 1987).

The source of feedback has also been studied. In their article discussing ways to improve assessment of communication skills within simulations (especially role play), Saunders and Gunn (1990) suggest information from three sources be sought. These three sources include observations from an independent observer, the learner, and co-participants. In a similar vein, Stolovitch (1990) describes a model for debriefing, which if used after interactive training activities, such as simulation and role play, are hypothesized to increase transfer. The model has six elements: (1) general overview, (2) delineating factual information from training activities, (3) generating inferences, (4) discussion of inherent differences of the training (e.g., simulation) environment relative to the operational environment, (5) making generalizations, and (6) discussing ways in which learned material can be applied.

The evaluative component used to generate feedback is as important as the feedback itself. In general, evaluation in the context of training simulations and games can be broken into outcome and process measures. Outcome measures reflect the learner's overall performance in the simulation. Outcome measures may simply document the final status of events, such as knowledge that a safe landing was completed, or may specify some cumulative performance measure, such as the final dollar amount of the stock portfolio being manipulated. Comparative criteria may also be applied to a given outcome measure, thereby providing a relative scaling of performance in relation to others completing the simulation.

Process measures, on the other hand, analyze critical step-by-step actions and decisions that eventually lead to final outcomes. By identifying critical processes, the simulation designer is forced to define operationally what is to be measured and the criteria for effective performance. One way to evaluate process performance in a simulation involves assessing the learner's performance in pre-designated skill categories, such as decision making, problem analysis, adaptability, perception, risk taking, and so on. An effective way to evaluate performance relative to a given skill is to generate comparison statements similar to the one below. Comparison statements juxtapose sample-effective with sample-ineffective behaviors couched in language consistent with activities displayed in the simulation. The following comparison statement could be used for evaluating the skill of adaptability in a hypothetical stock market simulation:

> To what extent did the learner modify his or her buy/sell strategy when economic conditions changed from a bull to bear market *versus* failed to make any

strategy modifications or made inappropriate or maladaptive strategy changes.

A behavioral rating scale can be used in conjunction with the comparison statements making the evaluation process more reliable and easier to use. For example, a relatively simple rating criteria which differentiates between less than acceptable, acceptable, and more than acceptable performance may be all that is required to assess adequately a learner's performance. In order to rate the learner's performance using the above comparison statement, an outside assessor may need to observe directly the learner's ongoing activities as he or she works through the simulation.

To summarize, research suggests that feedback is an important instructional component used in conjunction with training simulations and games, both to improve learner performance within the simulation or game and to promote the transfer of learned skills to the operational environment. Improvements in this area can be made by continuing to explore ways of expanding the number and type of information sources used to generate feedback and of providing this feedback in such a way that it will not disrupt the learning process. Improvements in the evaluation process used to generate feedback are also needed. One approach involves identifying relevant skills that allow learners to successfully perform critical work activities within the simulation. Evaluation of such skills may take the form of comparison statements spelling out both effective and ineffective behaviors and couch the statement within the context of situational parameters making up the simulation. Finally, the issue of learner control of feedback has implications for other instructional techniques, and in particular, the use of prompts.

Evaluation of Simulation Effectiveness

Computer simulations, as noted previously, are often developed partly in response to criticism concerning the general lack of motivational features of computer-based instruction. By adding a dose of "realism" to the instructional environment, learning is less of a chore because it is viewed as being incidental to participating in the simulation. By way of analogy, simulation is the sugar that helps the medicine (learning) go down. Although this discussion deals with simulation training, many of the issues may also be applied to gaming.

Simulation training has numerous benefits, including increased motivation and interest, greater skill development, enhanced knowledge acquisition and retention (Butler, 1988; Fraas, 1980; Hensen, 1982; Saunders & Crookall, 1985; Smith, 1987; Wehrenberg, 1986; and others), and increased transfer to the operational environment (Deluga & Andrews, 1985/86;

Meyers, Strang, & Hall, 1989; Jacobs *et al.*, 1990; Reigeluth & Schwartz, 1989). Moreover, positive training outcomes have been documented for children as young as five years of age (Renaud & Stolovitch, 1988; Renaud & Suissa, 1989), as well as for mentally retarded adults on such diverse behaviors as washer/dryer use (Neef *et al.*, 1990), operation of an automated banking machine (Shafer, Inge, & Hill, 1986), and independent menstrual care skills (Richman, Ponticas, Page, & Epps, 1986).

Despite an accumulation of evidence indicating that the use of simulation results in positive training outcomes, it does not guarantee that training will be effective. The meta-analysis of flight simulation transfer-of-training studies conducted by Jacobs *et al.* (1990) is illustrative in this respect. These researchers found that the use of simulation training was generally more effective than training conducted using the actual aircraft (the mean effect size was .26). Their results indicated, however, that several factors influenced the training results. For example, the type of task involved could produce substantial differences in training results. Normal takeoffs, approaches, and landings, presumably less complex in nature, produced mean effect size outcomes at or above .57, whereas night carrier landings and selected aerobatic maneuvers, thought to be more complex, often produced low or even negative effect size outcomes. Clearly, the effectiveness of simulation training is affected by a number of factors, such as task type. The identification of these factors should be of prime concern to both researchers and practitioners in this area.

Due to the paucity of empirical studies evaluating the effectiveness of simulation training programs outside the flight training area, it is difficult to make any generalizations regarding which factors are important for producing effective training outcomes. What we propose is a model that can be used to guide ongoing research involving simulation training. This model (see Figure 9.1) is adapted from the "meta-model" presented by Jacobs *et al.* (1990) and uses a systems approach. As can be seen from the model, input variables include information about the learner, task, and equipment. It is important to note that the term "equipment" does not necessarily involve something as elaborate as a flight simulator. Simulation training can be accomplished using a variety of media, including computer, video, and videodisc. More recently, heads-up display systems have been developed and used to present what has been come to be known as "virtual reality" scenarios. Technological advances such as this insure that the equipment variable will play an ever increasing role in simulation training. Thus, despite the fact that most training simulations available today are self-contained, computer generated phenomena, the visual representation of information within the simulation will be presented using a variety of different media that may revolutionize the simulation training field. In this context, it is important to remember that, as an input variable, learner characteristics must include basic computer operation skills as a prerequisite competency.

The "simulator design" variable in the throughput stage of the model may also play an increasing role because of the expected reliance on technologically advanced equipment. Factors such as training context and training type, as well as performance measurement, play an important role. As mentioned previously, performance measurement is of particular concern because of its link to feedback. By tracking and evaluating relevant variables associated with both the learning processes (e.g., pace, response to questions or situations, and decision making) and the learner (e.g., self-monitoring of motivation and comprehension), meaningful feedback can be provided that will improve learner performance within the simulation, as well as improve other training outcomes, such as transfer.

In general, the model's utility is dependent on the willingness of researchers to document their research and evaluation efforts. Although meta-analytic techniques have limitations, they offer a unique window through which to summarize and analyze an empirical literature base. It is

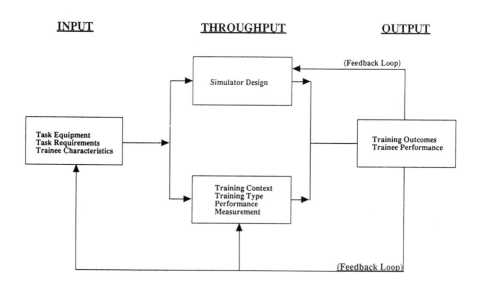

Figure 9.1. Model for evaluating simulation training.
(Adapted from Meta-Model presented in Jacobs *et al.*, 1990)

imperative, however, that adequate documentation of critical design and evaluation factors be provided within individual studies. To guide this effort, Jacobs *et al.* (1990) provide a detailed description of what information should be reported for the benefit of future meta-analytic reviewers (see also Hays *et al.*, 1992).

Some Implications

In this chapter, we have explored some of the many questions concerning the nature and use of simulation and gaming for instructional purposes. In summary, we reiterate some of the key implications of this discussion.

Simulation Training Design

In order to determine *what* to simulate, a detailed analysis should be performed resulting in a listing of all relevant activities that make up the operational environment. Subsequent analyses should then focus on determining the relative criticality of these activities, thereby providing a focus for later simulation design activities.

In order to determine *to what extent* the key characteristics in the operational environment require replication, the training designer should consider the physical as well as the functional aspects. Ultimately, the fidelity level that is chosen should provide adequate transfer to the operational environment while taking into consideration other critical factors (e.g., monetary investment and development time).

Simulation Training Effectiveness

Previous reviews of simulation training have identified several factors as being important moderators of simulation training, among them task type and the use of sound instructional techniques, such as feedback and prompts. With regard to feedback, care must be taken to reduce the intrusiveness of feedback so as not to interrupt ongoing simulation activities.

Determining the effectiveness of simulation training characteristics is ongoing and cumulative process requiring sufficiently detailed documentation. Adequate documentation of critical design and outcome variables provides future reviewers the opportunity to test whether a given factor is responsible for helping or hindering training.

Gaming

Gaming can provide additional benefits to the instructional environment due, in part, to enhanced learner motivation. There is also some evidence that gaming can improve retention. Gaming aspects may be incorporated into simulation training as an inherent part of the instructional program, or externally by incorporating elements of scoring and competition. In general, gaming should be treated as a separate component of simulation training.

Gaming elements can be designed to induce challenge, curiosity, and fantasy. If incorporated into othewise instructionally sound courseware, these elements can positively influence training outcomes. Gaming environments designed for instructional purposes should not be overly complex. Complex rules and scoring require the learner to expend valuable learning time and energy to understand the game. One option is to vary levels of difficulty or complexity based on learners' experience with the gaming structure. In this way, learner interest in the instructional materials can be maintained as their gaming abilities increase.

References

Allen, J.P., Chatelier, P., Clark, H.J., & Sorenson, R. (1982). Behavioral science in the military: Research trends for the eighties. *Professional Psychology, 13,* 918–929.

Baltra, A. (1990). Language learning through computer adventure games. *Simulation and Gaming, 21*(4), 445–451.

Bennett, R.D. (1988). Improving performance without training: A three-step approach. *Performance Improvement Quarterly, 1*(1), 58–68.

Braskamp, D.H., & Hodgetts, E.B. (1971). In K. Edwards (Ed.), *Student evaluations of a business game as a learning experience.* Bethesda, MD: ERIC Document Reproduction Service No. ED 058 142.

Bredemeier, M.E., & Greenblat, C.E. (1981). The educational effectiveness of games: A synthesis of findings. *Simulations and Games, 12*(3), 307–332.

Brown, A.L., & Campione, J.C. (1984). The three faces of transfer: Implications for early competence, individual differences, and instruction. In M. Lamb, A. Brown, & B. Rogoff (Eds.), *Advances in developmental psychology* (Vol. 3, pp. 143–192). Hillsdale, NJ: Lawrence Erlbaum Associates.

Butler, J.T. (1988). Games and simulations: Creative educational alternatives. *Tech Trends, 33,* 20–23.

Byham, W.C. (1980, February). Starting an assessment center the right way. *Personnel Administrator, 25*(2), 27–32.

Caro, P.W., Corley, W.E., Spears, W.D., & Blaiwes, A.S. (1984). *Training effectiveness evaluation and utilization demonstration of a low-cost cockpit procedure trainer* (NAVTRAEQUIPCEN Tech. Rep. 78-C-0113-3). Orlando, FL: Naval Training Equipment Center.

Clariana, R.B. (1989). Computer simulations of laboratory experiences. *Journal of Computers in Mathematics and Science Teaching, 2,* 14–19.

Coleman, J.S. (1989). Simulation games and the development of social theory. *Simulations and Games, 20*(2), 144–164.

Dekkers, J., & Donatti, S. (1981). The interpretation of research studies on the use of simulation as an instructional strategy. *Journal of Educational Research, 74*(6), 424–427.

Deluga, R.J., & Andrews, H.M. (1985/86). A case study investigating the effects of low-cost intervention to reduce three attendance behavior problems in clerical training program. *Journal of Organizational Behavior Management, 7*(3–4), 115–124.

Derry, S.D., Jacobs, J.W., & Murphy, D.A. (1987). The JSEP learning skills training system. *Journal of Educational Technology Systems, 15*(4), 273–284.

Faria, A.J. (1987). A survey of the use of business games in academia and business. *Simulations and Games, 18*(2), 207–224.

Fraas, J.W. (1980). The use of seven simulation games in a college economics course. *Journal of Experimental Education. 48*(4), 264–280.

Gagné, R.M. (1962). *Psychological principles in system development.* New York: Holt, Rinehart, & Winston.

Hayes, J.R. (1981). *The complete problem solver.* Philadelphia: Franklin Institute Press.

Haymaker, J.C., & Grant, D.L. (1982). Development of a model for content validation of assessment centers. *Journal of Assessment Center Technology, 5*(2), 1–7.

Hays, R.T., Jacobs, J.W., Prince, C., & Salas, E. (1992). A meta-analysis of the flight simulation training literature. *Military Psychology, 4*(2), 63–74.

Hays, R.T., Jacobs, J.W., Prince, C., & Salas, E. (in press). Requirements for future research in flight simulation training: Guidance based on a meta-analytic review. *International Journal of Aviation Psychology.*

Hays, R.T., & Singer, M.J. (1989). *Simulation fidelity in training system design: Bridging the gap between reality and training.* New York: Springer-Verlag.

Hensen, K.T. (1982). Simulation games and teaching. *NASSP Bulletin, 66,* 94–98.

Jacobs, J.W., Dempsey, J.V., & Salisbury, D.F. (1990). An attention reduction training model: Educational and technological implications. *Journal of Artificial Intelligence in Education, 1*(4), 41–50.

Jacobs, J.W., Prince, C., Hays, R.T., & Salas, E. (1990). *A meta-analysis of the flight simulation training literature* (NAVTRASYSCEN Tech. Rep. TR89-006). Orlando, FL: Naval Training Systems Center, Human Factors Division.

Jones, K. (1987). *Simulations: A handbook for teachers and trainers.* London: Kogan Page.

Keller, J.M. (1984). The use of the ARCS model of motivation in teacher training. In K.E. Shaw (Ed.), *Aspects of educational technology: Vol. XVII: Staff development and career updating.* London: Kogan Page.

Keller, J.M. (1987a). Development and use of the ARCS model of instructional design. *Journal of Instructional Development, 10*(3), 2–10.

Keller, J.M. (1987b). The systematic process of motivational design. *Performance and Instruction, 26*(9), 1–8.

Keller, J.M., & Kopp, T. (1987). Application of the ARCS model of motivational design. In C.M. Reigeluth (Ed.), *Instructional theories in action: Lessons illustrating selected theories and models (pp. 289–320).* Hillsdale, NJ: Lawrence Erlbaum Associates.

Keller, J.M., & Suzuki, K. (1987). Use of ARCS motivation model in courseware design. In D.H. Jonassen (Ed.), *Instructional designs for microcomputer courseware* (pp. 409–434). Hillsdale, NJ: Lawrence Erlbaum Associates.

Kinkade, R., & Wheaton, G. (1972). Training device design. In H. Vancoff & R. Kinkade (Eds.), *Human engineering guide to equipment design.* Washington, DC: American Institutes for Research.

Kryukov, M.M., & Kryukova, L.I. (1986). Toward a simulation games classification and game dialogue types. *Simulations and Games, 17*(3), 393–402.

Laveault, D., & Corbeil, P. (1990). Assessing the impact of simulation games on learning: A step-by-step approach. *Simulation/Games for Learning, 20*(1), 42–54.

Malone, T.W. (1980). Heuristics for designing enjoyable user interfaces: Lessons from computer games. *Proceedings of the Association for Computing Machinery Symposium on Small and Personal Computer Systems,* Palo Alto, CA, 63–68.

Malone, T.W. (1981a). Toward a theory of intrinsically motivating instruction. *Cognitive Science, 4,* 333–369.

Malone, T.W. (1981b). What makes computer games fun? *Byte, 6,* 258–277.

Malouf, D.B. (1988). The effect of instructional computer games on continuing student motivation. *The Journal of Special Education, 21*(4), 27–38.

Martin, E., & Waag, W. (1978). *Contributions of platform motion to simulator training effectiveness: Study I-basic contact.* (AFHRL Tech. Rep. TR-78-15). Williams Air Force Base, AZ: Air Force Human Resources Laboratory.

Meyers, S.C., Strang, H.R., & Hall, E.L. (1989). Impact of microcomputer simulation training on student-clinicians' ability to effectively intervene with preschool stutterers. *Journal of Fluency Disorders, 14*(2), 135–151.

Morris, R., & Thomas, J. (1976). Simulation in training—part 1. *Industrial Training International, 11*(3), 66–69.

Munro, A., Fehling, M.R., & Towne, D.M. (1985). Instructional intrusiveness in dynamic simulation training. *Journal of Computer-Based Instruction, 12*(2), 50–53.

Neef, N.A. *et al.* (1990). In vivo versus simulation training: An interactional analysis of range and type of training exemplars. *Journal of Applied Behavior Analysis, 23*(4), 447–458.

Nelson, T.O. (1984). A comparison of current measures of the accuracy of feeling-of-knowing predictions. *Psychological Bulletin, 95,* 109–133.

Nelson, T.O., & Dunlosky, J. (1991). When people's judgements of learning (JOLs) are extremely accurate at predicting subsequent recall: The "delayed-JOL effect." *Psychological Science, 2*(4), 267–270.

Newell, A. (1980). One final word. In D.T. Tuma & F. Reif (Eds.), *Problem solving and education* (pp. 184–187). Hillsdale, NJ: Lawrence Erlbaum Associates.

Osgood, C.E. (1949). The similarity paradox in human learning: A resolution. *Psychological Review, 56,* 132–143.

Oxford, R., & Crookall, D. (1988). Simulation/gaming and language learning strategies. *Simulations and Games, 19*(3), 349–353.

Pierfy, D. (1977). Comparative simulation game research: Stumbling blocks and stepping stones. *Simulations and Games, 8,* 341–360.

Pohlman, L., & Reed, J. (1978). *Air to air combat skills: Contributions of platform motion to initial training* (AFHRL Tech. Rep. TR-78-53). Brooks Air Force Base, TX: Air Force Human Resources Laboratory.

Prophet, L., & Boyd, A. (1970). *Device task fidelity and transfer of training: Aircraft cockpit procedures training* (AFHRL Tech. Rep. TR-78-53). Brooks Air Force Base, TX: Air Force Human Resources Laboratory.

Reigeluth, C.M., & Schwartz, E. (1989). An instructional theory for the design of computer-based simulations. *Journal of Computer-Based Instruction, 16*(1), 1–10.

Renaud, L., & Stolovitch, H. (1988). Simulation gaming: An effective strategy for creating appropriate traffic safety behaviors in five-year-old children. *Simulations and Games, 19*, 328–345.

Renaud, L., & Suissa, S. (1989). Evaluation of the efficacy of simulation games in traffic safety education of kindergarten children. *American Journal of Public Health, 79*, 307–309.

Richman, G.S., Ponticas, Y., Page, T.J., & Epps, S. (1986). Simulation procedures for teaching independent menstrual care to mentally retarded persons. *Applied Research in Mental Retardation, 7*(1), 21–35.

Royer, J.M. (1979). Theories of transfer. *Educational Psychologist, 14*, 53–69.

Sackett, P.R. (1987). Assessment centers and content validity: Some neglected issues. *Personnel Psychology, 40*, 13–25.

Saunders, D., & Crookall, D. (1985). Playing with second language. *Simulation/Games for Learning, 15*, 166–172.

Saunders, D., & Gunn, R. (1990). The assessment and evaluation of communication skills associated with simulation/gaming. *Simulation/Games for Learning, 20*, 215–234.

Seigner, R. (1980). Game ability and academic ability: Dependence on SES and psychological mediators. *Simulations and Games, 11*, 403–421.

Shafer, M.S., Inge, K.J., & Hill, J. (1986). Acquisition, generalization, and maintenance of automated banking skills. *Education and Training of the Mentally Retarded, 21*(4), 265–272.

Smith, P.E. (1987). Simulating the classroom with media and computers: Past efforts, future possibilities. *Simulations and Games, 18*(3), 395–413.

Stolovitch, H.D. (1990). A debriefing model. *Performance and Instruction, 29*, 18–19.

Thorndike, E.L. (1903). *Educational psychology.* New York: Lemcke and Buechner.

Thornton, G.C., & Byham, W.C. (1982). *Assessment centers and managerial performance.* Orlando, FL: Academic Press.

Vesonder, G.T., & Voss, J.F. (1985). On the ability to predict one's own responses while learning. *Journal of Memory and Language, 24*, 363–376.

Waag, W. (1981). *Training effectiveness of visual and motion simulation* (AFHRL Tech. Rep. TR-79-72). Brooks Air Force Base, TX: Air Force Human Resources Laboratory.

Wehrenberg, S.B. (1986). Simulations: Capturing the experience of the real thing. *Personnel Journal, 65* (4), 101–102.

Weitz, J., & Adler, S. (1973). The optimal use of simulation. *Journal of Applied Psychology, 58*(2), 219–224.

Wheaton, G., Rose, A., Fingerman, P., Korotkin, A., Holding, D., & Mirabella, A. (1976). *Evaluation of the effectiveness of training devices: Literature review and preliminary model.* (ARI Res. Memo. 76-6). Alexandria, VA: U.S. Army Research Institute).

Wood, L.E., & Stewart, P.W. (1987). Improvement of practical reasoning skills with a computer game. *Journal of Computer-Based Instruction, 14*(2), 49–53.

Chapter Ten

Feedback and Certitude in Interactive Videodisc Programs

Brenda C. Litchfield
University of South Alabama

Introduction

This chapter will address the design of interactive videodisc (IVD) in-structional materials and the implication for feedback and certitude as a result of design. The integration of self-regulated learning as a function of feedback will also be examined. Certitude is defined by Kulhavy and Stock (1989) as how sure a learner is about a particular response that he or she has given. Self-regulated learning processes involve goal-directed activities that students instigate, modify, and sustain (Zimmerman, 1989). Self-regulated learning occurs when students activate and sustain congnitions and behaviors systematically oriented toward attainment of learning goals (Schunk, 1989). With Level III interactive videodiscs it is possible to structure learn-ing to incorporate activities which facilitate these processes.

The majority of studies related to feedback and certitude appear to be with print-based instruction. A few are in the area of computer-based in-struction (CBI) and virtually none in the area of IVD. The feedback options and certitude measures used in print and computer-based formats do not transfer well to most IVD instructional programs because of their unique design. As a result, some of the current feedback design strategies used in print and CBI will require modification to be effective in IVD.

An important instructional design consideration for incorporating feed-back into IVD programs is the amount of interactivity built into the pro-gram. Without a high degree of interactivity, the need for feedback dimin-ishes. The key here is *instructional* interactivity. Many "interactive" programs do require the user to choose, click, move about, read, look, and listen. On close inspection, however, much of the interactivity falls into the realm of navigation. Instructional interactivity requires the learner to manipulate variables, collect data, work in artificial environments, and formulate and operate models. These types of activities require different kinds of feedback.

Two types of feedback for interactive videodisc programs are proposed: "traditional" program-generated feedback (PGF) and "non-traditional" learner-generated feedback (LGF). The goals for learning outcomes influence the design of the programs which, in turn, influence the type of feedback used. Each type of feedback is designed to be used with certain kinds of IVD programs, ranging from games and simulations to higher level discovery and inquiry-based problem-solving instructional materials. Interactive videodisc uses both traditional and non-traditional feedback, but it has especially rich possibilities for using the non-traditional. The integration of self-regulated learning methods and strategies also fits well within the design of interactive videodisc programs. Specific design considerations will be discussed and their implications for research examined.

Interactive Videodisc Technology

Interactive video can be a misleading term. It includes everything from videotape to the most sophisticated Level III laser disc programs. Because each type of interactive program carries distinct implications for instructional design strategies and feedback options, it is important to specify the exact type of interactive program. This chapter will focus on design considerations for Level III interactive laser videodisc instructional programs.

Levels of Interactive Videodisc Programs

IVD programs fall into one of four levels: 0, I, II, or III. Level 0 is an IVD that can be played only from beginning to end, with fast forward or reverse. Many films are now coming out on laser videodisc. Because most films are simply viewed from beginning to end, there really is no reason to select specific frames, although it can be done.

Level I IVD consists of a laser disc player, a color monitor, and a hand-held remote-control keypad. The visuals are stored as stills or moving video, which can be speeded up or slowed down by using the hand-held remote control. Any of the 54,000 possible visuals or 30 minutes of linear play (per side) can be randomly accessed in 1 to 3 seconds. Because a Level I disc is not connected to a microcomputer, the amount of interactivity is limited. Level I programs do not contain any feedback within the program itself. Level I can be thought of as an immense slide tray (almost a football field's length of carousel slide trays laid on their sides).

A level II IVD uses a Level I set-up plus an internal computer controlling the order of visual scenes that appear. The program commands are recorded onto the surface of the disc. Level II programs contain a variety of feedback—textual, visual, sound, or a combination. This feedback is generally question and content specific. For example, a multiple-choice question and answer format is used where there is a specific correct answer. By selecting an answer choice, the learner can be branched to a number of types of feedback. This feedback may be provided in different formats, but there is still just one correct answer.

To be classified as a Level III program, the laser disc player is combined with an external computer. The videodisc instructional sequences are controlled by a program stored on the microcomputer or on a floppy disk. This configuration allows instructional programs to utilize the features of computer programs (word processing, graphing spreadsheets, calculators, video overlays, databases) in combination with the visual aspects of a videodisc. Learners can manipulate audiovisual materials stored on the videodisc in a variety of ways. They can choose to interact with or select visuals, text, audio, or a combination of media. These choices may result in exploration or in a more structured pathway to an answer or answers. This combination of computer and videodisc brings up some interesting possibilities for feedback options within these kinds of interactive instructional programs.

Interactivity and Feedback

The type of feedback designed and incorporated into IVD programs is strongly tied to the level of interactivity. Definitions of interactivity are many and varied. There are no accepted sets of guidelines and no well-defined models for interactivity, especially instructional interactivity. Gery (1989) suggests that good interactivity is a function and integration of the following variables:

- the nature and frequency, along with the placement and repetition, of interactions in relationship to the content, learning activities, and learner population;
- the complexity of the interactions, for example, the number of components, the complexity of the structure, and what it requires of the learner;
- the completeness, sophistication, and appropriateness of the response analysis in relationship to the learner's mindset, the content, and the learning objectives;

- the quality, nature, depth, and completeness of the feedback to the learner; and
- the structure of the program and the flexibility and control offered to the learner within the program itself. (p. 118)

Level III programs, although relatively expensive to implement, provide the highest degree of interactivity with learners. If a program is truly Level III, the degree of interactivity is considered to be high. (See Figure 10.1 for an example of interactivity criteria.) This means learners are actively engaged in manipulating the program's numerous components, such as graphics, visuals, calculations, models, sound, and others. These types of feedback, manipulated by the learner, determine the level of interactivity in an IVD program. As stated earlier, interactivity can be a misleading term. Even programs labeled Level III contain a wide range of interactivity and must be carefully evaluated by the instructor for instructional interactivity before being accepted and used as Level III.

The data-handling and programming capabilities of a microcomputer can provide instruction with a far wider range of learning outcomes. This is an obvious advantage in learning upper-level skills. Accordingly, Level III IVD is becoming more popular with those educators who want to push past lower-level intellectual skills (Litchfield & Dempsey, 1992).

Before beginning to design feedback for an IVD, its instructional interactivity must be firmly established. This is best accomplished during the design stage. Without valid instructional goals and objectives that are checked against interactivity criteria, it is difficult to design meaningful feedback. Criteria for interactivity vary as widely as instructional IVD programs. Some general criteria for evaluating interactivity are included in Figure 10.1. Instructional interactivity will drive the design of feedback.

Current Research on Interactive Videodisc Programs

Most studies in the area of interactive video focus on case-study applications based on the capabilities of the technology (Cameron, 1983). According to Hannafin (1986), most published research on interactive video has focused on prescribing how to design programs, case studies which describe techniques and procedures used during a specific project, and those studies claiming the effectiveness of the medium. Others focus on navigational and representational issues (Gay & Mazur, 1990), teachers' use of interactive videodiscs (Malby, 1987; Carnine, Englemann, Hofmeister, & Kelly, 1987), learner control (Kinzie, 1990; Milheim & Azbell, 1988), and a plethora of media comparison studies which are too numerous to list. Few studies investigating principles of learning using interactive video as the

GENERAL FEATURES

Students are actively involved as participants
One or more goals/objectives for topic is achieved
A problem to be investigated is presented
A conclusion or generalization of results is drawn
Variables can be manipulated
Variables can be manipulated with observable result

PROCESS SKILLS
Does the program provide opportunities for students to develop the following skills?

Observation
Classification
Measurement
Inference
Prediction
Communication
Construct operational definitions
Construct sequences and time/space relationships
Formulate questions and hypotheses
Experimentation
Interpretation of data
Formulation of models

EXPERIMENTAL PROCEDURES
Does program provide opportunities for students to...

Define the problem
Collect information on the problem
Form a hypothesis
Experiment to test the hypothesis
Observe and record data
Draw conclusions or make generalizations about findings

SIMULATION
Does program contain elements of a simulation?

Students are the central figures in the action
Variables or methods for investigation are selected by students
Support and learner guidance is given
Results are performed in real time
Artificial environment/set of circumstances is created
Challenging situation(s) is presented
Students analyze and resolve the situation
Real life forces are manipulated
Forces beyond our power in real life are manipulated
Strategies for managing information are developed
Feedback for each result is provided

FEEDBACK
Does program provide video feedback?

Literal
People-based
Variable based on results
Immediate

INTERACTIVE MEDIA
How does student manual interact with electronic media?

Student workbook is an integral part of the activity
Charts/tables/graphs are constructed to support data
Data interpretation questions help analyze data
Group discussion questions are given for key concepts
Summary questions are given for each key concept

FOLLOW-UP ACTIVITIES

Activities are related to each key concept
Activities provide for transfer of knowledge
Activities are simple with minimal or no equipment
Activities provide a wide variety of choices

Figure 10.1. Criteria for evaluating videodisc interactivity.
From Litchfield, B.C. (1990) Criteria for evaluating videodisc interactivity, *Performance and Instruction, 29*, 25–26.

instructional medium have been reported (Cushall, Harvey, & Brovey, 1988). In addition, only a few applications of interactive video have been based upon learning and cognition influences (Hannafin, Gearhart, Rieber, & Phillips, 1985). Little is known about the effectiveness of the technology as a teaching tool (Marlino, 1990). Little attention has been focused on how the individual learns from interactive video.

Because the lack of studies in the area of instructional interactivity in videodisc instruction, there is an even greater paucity of studies in the area of feedback in this medium. There are, however, many studies of feedback in CBI. According to Schimmel (1988b), despite the wide acceptance of feedback in computer-based instruction, empirical support for particular types of feedback information has been inconsistent or weak, and research provides little guidance for designing feedback. Even if CBI feedback research could provide guidelines for the design and effects of feedback, it would only be applicable to traditional feedback where the learner works toward selecting a predetermined correct answer. This type of feedback (with a predetermined correct answer) will be discussed in subsequent sections as a program-generated feedback.

Instructional Design in IVD Learning Programs

A survey of current interactive videodisc catalogs shows that the majority of IVD programs currently used in education (K-college) are Level I. These programs range from art to zoology, providing learners with a vast array of visuals that can be utilized in a number of ways. Level II are found primarily in business, industry, and training. Over the past several years, Level III programs have begun to appear more often in all areas.

Interactive multimedia implies multiple forms of communications media controlled, coordinated, and integrated by the microcomputer (Lynch, 1991). Hypermedia is another design that has emerged recently. Hypermedia is defined as a tool for linking nonlinear information presented in the form of graphics, animation, video, and sound (Osgood, 1987). Interactive multimedia—the convergence at the computer of print, audio, and video—can be managed by a hypermedia system where the student is the active controller (Gay & Raffensperger, 1989). Both multimedia and hypermedia involve a much more complex structure for designing instruction. They present a new set of challenges for instructional designers when compared to computer-based instruction. Straight CBI tends to fall neatly into familiar design and development procedures because of its generally linear format. Gagné's events of instruction (1977) can all be included and there is a place for text feedback during practice and final assessment. Feedback options for IVDs with low instructional interactivity typically function similar to those used in CBI. Hypertext designs, such as those found in Level III IVD, tend to present a different set of considerations for feedback options and certitude measures.

IVD can vary from simple designs with low instructional interactivity to complex hypertext and hypermedia designs such as the example in Figure 10.2. This disc layout is from Science Vision's Level III disc, *Astrovision* (Kisiah & Litchfield, 1990). With a flexible structure (such as *Astrovision*), learners can move freely through the information in many directions according to their own needs (Nielson, 1990). Various kinds of feedback can be incorporated throughout the program at any number of points.

The problem with many IVD instructional materials is that they continue to use CBI design strategies and feedback options rather than taking full advantage of the newer medium. Even those programs claiming to teach inquiry-based problem-solving, critical-thinking, or decision-making skills, upon close inspection are often closer to a linear presentation than one which facilitates the development of these skills. An interactive videodisc is an excellent medium for teaching higher-order cognitive skills, although it is often not used to its fullest capacity. This medium should not be used to present information to passive learners for rote recall of information. Effectively designed instruction should help students develop learning strategies and metacognitive skills (Jost, 1990). Distinct instructional advantages lie in being able to access numerous components of a lesson in a variety of sequences. Learners can follow a number of pathways to an answer or conclusion and receive relevant feedback. In this way, individual differences can be accounted for within the instructional program.

Individual differences having the most impact on the learning process are: (1) aptitude variables, (2) prior knowledge, (3) cognitive styles, and (4) personality styles (Carrier & Jonassen, 1988). They further state that just knowing how learners differ is not sufficient to design better instructional courseware. It is essential to know how learners' performance differs on various tasks as a function of the kinds of instructional treatments they receive. The interactivity level of IVD programs can provide instructors with insight into both of these factors. Students can be compared with each other for similarities and differences by employing traditional, program-generated feedback. On tasks where performance differences and pathways to an answer can vary widely, the interactive design of learner-generated feedback, with its high degree of learner control, can provide additional information about individual learning processes and strategies.

Design factors influencing the effectiveness of interactive videodisc programs are similar to the overall guidelines for designing effective instruction in most media. In IVD there is the additional consideration in

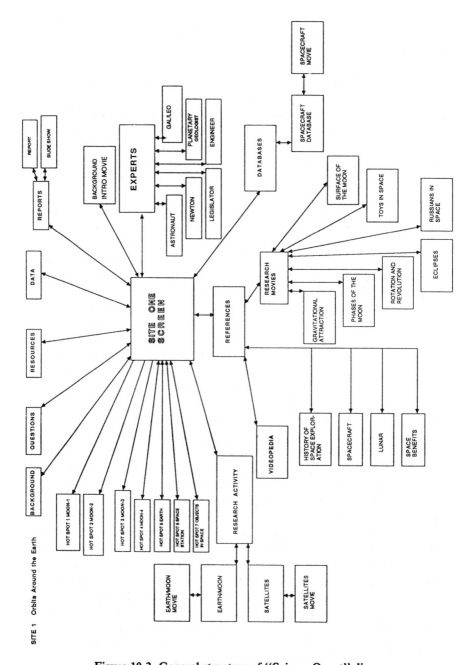

Figure 10.2. General structure of "ScienceQuest" discs.
From "Science Quest: A Multimedia Inquiry-based Videodisc Science Curriculum"
B. C. Litchfield, 1990, *Instruction Delivery Systems, 4*(3), 14-15.

message design of its formats—visuals, stills, and graphics. It is here that the power of feedback lies. Interactive videodisc programs are not limited to text-based feedback, but rather have extended the depth and breadth of feedback by incorporating video.

Central design considerations for Level III IVD programs should be interactivity, motivation, and feedback. All other parts of a program should build on these three components in order to produce a program that is interesting and will hold the learner's attention. An important consideration in the design of IVD is the use of instructional feedback as a feature of the overall design rather than a component of the instructional strategy. Motivation is a function of the integration of all the features and can be addressed in a number of ways throughout the program. With a medium as powerful as IVD, which has the potential to provide exceptional feedback in many forms, it is essential to use this capability. Instructionally effective interactive video should include the factors illustrated in Figure 10.3.

Feedback and Certitude in IVD Programs

Because of the variety of programs designed, it is difficult to specify exactly which type of feedback should be used with IVD instructional programs. Even with Level III programs, variation can be considerable, depending on the desired learning outcome. Programs concentrating on procedural skills require feedback addressing the correctness of actions and sequences. For example, skills involving servicing machinery, assembling equipment, or providing medical treatment may all depend heavily on successful completion of certain steps in sequential order. Feedback accompanying these types of programs needs to be specific and exist within a range of accuracy determined by the developer. It is either an exact match or has slight variability. It assumes the learner's final understanding matches the developer's intent to achieve a correct answer. This type of feedback is program-generated feedback (PGF).

An alternative to program-generated feedback is learner-generated feedback (LGF). Learner-generated feedback is constructed by the learner. It varies with the IVD program resources used by the learner to exhibit how and to what degree instructional material has been mastered. In constructing LGF, students are exhibiting their certitude related to the material they have learned. These students become metacognitively, motivationally, and behaviorally active participants in their own learning. Zimmerman (1986) identifies this as self-regulated learning. Programs designed to increase problem-solving skills and foster independent learning through individualized learning and higher-order cognitive skills can encourage the develop-

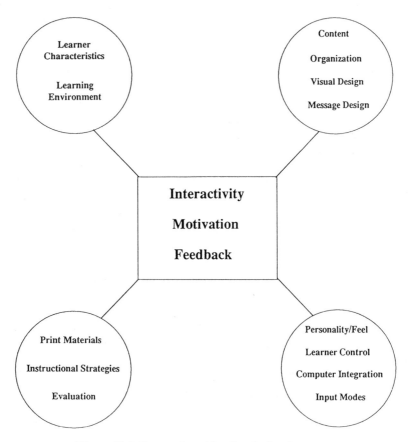

Figure 10.3. Interactive videodisc design features.

ment of self-regulated learners. These self-regulated learning strategies can be employed to achieve desired academic outcomes on the basis of feedback about learning effectiveness and skill (Zimmerman, 1990). Because learner-generated feedback must emanate from IVD programs that allow for individual initiation, interpretation, self-evaluation, and self-monitoring, it requires a completely different type of feedback that is aligned with the nature of the learning goals.

Along with specifying feedback format, it is equally difficult to integrate certitude measures into the dynamic nature of IVD programs. The whole idea of Level III IVD instruction is to provide learners with varied paths through the material and opportunities to construct some of their own knowledge. Why incorporate certitude in the first place? And where do certitude measures fit in? From studies done with written instruction, Kulhavy and Stock (1989) have found that certitude estimates are a useful index of lesson behavior. They may represent judgment incorporating a number of learner characteristics, rather than just knowledge prediction. In addition, low certitudes probably stem from a lack of comprehension. They further suggest that these estimates of personal knowledge can be an important element for determining instructional prescriptions.

Because the design and execution of instructional sequences can be critical in promoting learning and retention, certitude measures may help to define these areas. Transferring these findings to Level III IVD programs, it could be a simple matter of programming to base the degree of feedback on the level of certitude indicated by the learner. A low-certitude estimate could provide expanded feedback. A high estimate of certitude could provide minimal feedback. Used along with an embedded management system, instructors would be able to track learning and pinpoint difficulties in knowledge acquisition.

The remaining issue is how to integrate certitude measures into IVD programs. Integration depends on which type of feedback, program-generated, learner-generated, or both, is designed into the program. With print-based instruction, certitude measures are fairly straightforward. The learner selects an answer to a question, then indicates the level of certitude. In IVD instruction, certitude measures can remain straightforward or become more complex. If the certitude measures do not go beyond those found in printed instruction, it is likely that the full capabilities of the IVD program are not being used. Interactive videodisc programs have the ability to integrate many aspects of a lesson or activity. Certitude measures, therefore, may be most effective if they are designed to not only measure confidence of response, but also allow the learner to see how these measures are integrated with other lesson requirements. This opens up numerous possibilities for games and simulations for individual and groups of learners.

Each of the feedback options and measures of certitude will be discussed in the following sections.

Program-Generated Feedback

Feedback Characteristics

Program-generated feedback (PGF) generally consists of a finite set of answers to a specific question or response from the learner. It can be the result of multiple-choice questions, short answer, or any of the standard question and answer formats currently used in IVD programs for skill or procedural development. This PGF is usually constructed to be tied to quantifiable scores, grades, or evaluations of the learner's progress through the instructional material. The information can be used for grading by calculating scores. It can also be used as a performance measure by assessing how well the learner has performed a set of steps for a given task. In either case, there *is* a correct answer. It must match the developer's answer.

Program-generated feedback is produced by the program itself. It can exist in many presentation formats, depending on the learning objectives. Some PGF does exist as information for the learner and is not tied to any scoring results. This feedback can be selected by the learner as progress is made through a program. It can provide clarification, alternative solutions, or checkpoints where learning can be evaluated by the learner. Its purpose is to allow learners to self-monitor their progress and the instructional material that has been learned. This provides information which can be used to develop a general certitude about learning, content, or skill acquisition in a particular lesson or activity.

Measuring Certitude

There seems to be a consistent trend toward the relationship of certitude and response acquisition and maintenance. Findings by Kulhavy and Stock (1989) on knowledge level items have shown that student responses are generally systematically related to certitude. These studies, however, dealt primarily with print instruction and not IVD. Even so, the same strategies can be applied to program-generated feedback used with IVD instructional programs designed to teach procedural skills, basic training, or instruction in a variety of areas.

While the basic design of feedback options in IVD programs with low instructional interactivity may remain similar to those of print instruction, the question of how to design certitude measures is not quite so clear. IVD programs using PGF usually employ a more structured format of question and answer practice or assessment methods. They operate under a predetermined set of feedback options already incorporated into the design of the program. Many feedback studies have found only trends in the relationship of certitude and various elements of feedback (e.g., study time, elaboration, discrepancy, delay-retention, complexity, and timing). Thousands of hours have been spent investigating what type of feedback works best and why. Based upon research (Spock, 1988; Kulhavy, White, Topp, Chan, and Adams, 1985), although there was a significant difference in the amount of time learners spent studying types of feedback, there was no significant differences were found in posttest achievement. These studies conclude that the most efficient feedback may be simply to inform the learners they were correct or incorrect. Schimmel (1988a) found that after both correct and incorrect answers, the majority of learners chose a simple yes or no feedback rather than the feedback with an explanation. After a correct response, 87% chose the yes-no feedback; and, after an incorrect response, 72% chose the yes-no feedback. This would seem to indicate that students just want to know if the answer is correct or incorrect and that is all. Forget all the certitude measures, reading the feedback, and figuring out why it was wrong. Next question.

Because the real value in certitude measures may lie in instructional diagnosis and not in getting the learner to attend more closely to feedback, perhaps a new set of certitude measures is needed. Interactive videodisc instructional programs provide a whole new dimension of feedback which can be tied to rewards incorporating certitude. Although some of these strategies can be used in computer-based instruction, IVD offers the additional dimensions of motion visuals, audio, graphic overlays, text, or any combination of these. This allows for a more motivating form of feedback option easily attached to games, simulations, and real life-real time experiences.

Certitude measures integrated with a payback or rewards (points, privileges, recognition) may prove to have a greater effect on student learning and motivation. Games and simulations can easily provide excellent methods for measuring certitude. According to Keller and Suzuki (1988), three inclusions in the design of courseware can stimulate and increase a learner's motivation. These fall into the Relevance category of the ARCS motivation model (Attention, Relevance, Confidence, Satisfaction) and are built into games. The use of goal-oriented games, simulation, and fantasies can provide a sense of purpose for the learner. Games that provide a scoring system, use levels of challenges, and present feedback on performance can stimulate the need for achievement. In addition, games that allow for cooperative work can also increase motivation. By participating in games, learners are using and integrating information and skills learned in the lesson. Often they can be so absorbed in the game they do not realize they are working toward a learning goal. The learning goal can be the score they have achieved, the amount of time they have played the game, or number of objectives they have completed.

Anticipation of rewards increases motivation and self-efficacy and when goals are combined with rewards, students have two sources for gauging their learning progress (Schunk, 1990). It should be easy to link certitude measures to games and simulations in IVD programs. Several interactive videodisc situations illustrate this method of assessing certitude and using rewards.

• *Situation 1*
   In a training situation, learners (airline ticket agents) are presented

with numerous similar scenarios of personal interactions between a ticket agent and a customer. They are to stop the action by touching the screen when they feel the agent has not performed according to accepted company standards and justify their choice by choosing an answer. Their degree of certitude (e.g., 1–5) is chosen as a wager toward the correct answer. The higher the score, the more credit or special recognition they receive. Because they know the program will contain other examples of similar situations, they may tend to increase their feedback study time and retention for an incorrect response in order to score higher on subsequent examples.

- *Situation 2*
  Visual sequences of a patient treatment situation are presented for medical students to evaluate. Before prescribing a treatment, students can indicate how sure they are that their decisions are correct. A correct treatment linked with a high score can increase the patient's recovery time by a specified amount of time. It may allow them to avoid having to complete other similar instructional programs because they have performed well on this one.

- *Situation 3*
  Sixth-grade students view a call-in radio talk show between two so-called physics experts. A question is posed to the "experts." Each expert answers the question differently. Students select which expert they think is correct then indicate their level of confidence (1–10) as to which expert has given the correct answer. A correct answer gets all the points chosen as the level of confidence. An incorrect answer gets the confidence point deducted from the score. The team with the highest score wins. The information given by the experts will be used in other activities in the program so it will be to the students' advantage to not only score high but also remember the information they hear.

These three examples of certitude measure have several things in common:

1. Contain an element of chance.
2. Serve as information for subsequent activities or ways to avoid additional practice.
3. Are tied to a score which can be quantitative or qualitative.
4. Can be done by groups of students.
5. Are generally considered to be fun or entertaining for learners.

A problem that may exist in previous studies of certitude is that the instruction is presented as an isolated instance and not something that complements a series of integrated activities. This, of course, may simply be a function of print instruction as well as some CBI. Conversely, IVD by its very nature can be designed to be an integrated experience with activities that build on each other. With this type of instructional delivery system, it is easier to provide relevant rewards tied to certitude measures. As seen in the examples above, high certitude along with a correct answer was advantageous for the learner. Conversely, high certitude with an incorrect answer would result in a deduction of points or time and thus the learner may have to engage in additional activities in the program.

An important consideration of certitude measures in program-generated feedback in IVD instructional programs is that learners are aware of the relationship between their certitude estimates and the specific activity. They are also aware of the relationship with the rest of the program. When they understand the purpose of an activity and its integration into the rest of the program, they may be more apt to view it as an important component rather than an isolated part. Instead of simply playing a game or participating in a simulation, they should understand that this information will be of value somewhere else in the program—questions, another game, decision making, problem solving, or a final report.

Design features of interactive videodiscs have been evolving for about 10 years now. The primary interactivity in computer-based instruction is menu branches and feedback on individual answers. There are perhaps hundreds of well-used CBI programs that are educationally and instructionally sound. They are effective for what they are designed to accomplish. Hypertext and hypermedia cross over to the realm of IVD by allowing the learner to explore in many directions. With IVD, we can design truly integrated lessons and activities that are directly under a learner's control. As long as IVD programs can be designed in this totally interactive fashion, as much instructional interactivity as possible should be built into a Level III program. The most effective way to use a medium is often to integrate all of its capabilities.

Program-generated feedback which incorporates certitude measures is relatively easy to design and implement in IVD programs. It is most suitable for those programs addressing skill or procedural development. It can be used for a variety of situations and subject areas and can be a highly motivating way for students to learn material.

Restructuring the Classroom

It is a well-known lament in education today that students are not developing important thinking skills, and the blame has fallen on instructors, schools, textbooks, and instructional materials. The feeling is that all of these factors in the learning environment are too focused on lower-level skills. By far, the majority of schools operate the same now as they have for the past 100 years. Students are not encouraged to think independently. They are not guided to set goals, make decisions, think critically, and solve problems. They are not responsible for their own learning (Collins, 1991).

Many students sit in classrooms where instructors stand up and lecture—"the sponge syndrome." Education is similar to an hourglass—all the information must past through the instructor, which slows down everything. Education should be more like a sieve, where information comes from a variety of sources and in a variety of forms. Just by being in a classroom a student should be able to learn in a number of different ways. It is not sufficient to hear information. There must be action, reaction, production, involvement, thought, and reasoning.

These points are all too familiar to most educators. The numerous school reform reports have testified to the trivialization of schooling. They also point out the inordinate focus on low-level skills and information-dissemination. Also stressed is the inattention to using information and information technology tools to think, learn, and perform in and across the disciplines (Morton & Mojkowski, 1989). As a result of this recognized situation (some say crisis) in education, there have been several comprehensive programs and initiatives directed to alleviate these outdated practices. Science has received renewed attention with the works of Project 2061 (AAAS, 1989) and guidelines from the National Science Teachers Association. The National Council for Teachers of Mathematics has produced some sweeping guidelines for K-12 in their NCTM Standards (1991). Reading and social studies teaching and curricula also have begun to be revised.

A common thread in each of these restructuring guidelines for content areas is the inclusion of technology, thinking skills, and integration of content areas. Pea and Soloway (1987) identify several significant changes in education: the nature of learning and understanding, instructional materials, pedagogical strategies, and the social context of learning and work. Students can no longer be knowledge-absorbers. They need to be knowledge-producers. This production must be guided by technology and include interdisciplinary integration across content areas. By doing this, the nature of learning and understanding becomes one of reasoning and problem solving, where students are actively involved in their own learning. Instructional materials and pedagogical strategies must change to incorporate this global focus. By involving students in their own learning lessons, schools and instructors must begin to provide students with a wider range of instructional strategies and feedback about their progress.

The majority of computer programs designed for classroom use fall into the categories of tutorial and drill and practice. Generally these do not foster the development of higher-level cognitive skills (Litchfield & Dempsey,

1992). Now, with interactive videodisc programs, instructional materials are being developed to address higher-level skills. Level III IVD instructional programs (when designed to maximize the capabilities of the medium) provide students with opportunities to construct their own learning and feedback. These programs can focus on developing problem-solving, critical-thinking, evaluation, goal-setting, and organizational skills.

Carefully designed IVD programs require students to use a variety of higher-order cognitive processes. Activities can include numerous opportunities for students to construct their own knowledge. This is a different approach from the prevalent didactic practices that have a grip on the educational system. The constructivist view, which has been revived recently, has been around since John Dewey and Maria Montessori. It holds that teachers should be facilitators who help students construct their own understandings and capabilities in carrying out challenging tasks (Collins, 1991). This means that the student, not the teacher, is central to the learning effort.

This restructuring of the classroom from teacher-centered to student-centered is essential for the transformation of curriculum and instruction. Instructional activities and practices must be designed around the following requirements (Mojkowski, 1989):

1. Students must be viewed as knowledge producers as well as consumers.
2. Students must learn how to access and use a knowledge base outside themselves and their immediately available instructional materials.
3. Learning activities must be problem oriented and project organized and focused on an integrated set of knowledge and skills' outcomes.
4. Learning activities must require the application, as appropriate, of a variety of technology support tools, such as word processors, databases, and telecommunications.
5. Learning activities must promote and develop social interaction, including collaborative learning and peer coaching.
6. Learning activities must produce meaningful work.
7. The units must relate to a K-12 curriculum design or framework.

Without the change in focus in classrooms, it will be difficult to implement the type of requirements listed above. Certainly, wide-scale change will come slowly. Teachers can, however, begin to make changes in their own classrooms by using technology and programs that are designed to address these critical factors.

Inquiry-based programs appears to offer the best applications of student-centered instruction. In these programs students proceed at their own pace, receive a variety of feedback, construct their own knowledge, and often work cooperatively. These types of programs are becoming more widely available in all subject areas and grade levels. Just as the term interactive can be misleading, however, so is the designation of inquiry-based. What constitutes a good inquiry-based computer or IVD program is a combination of factors: (1) the nature of the investigation which sets the stage for the relative complexity of the program; (2) advantages over actual classroom or laboratory investigations; (3) number and types of inquiry skills incorporated; (4) concepts related to inquiry from low-end process skills to hypothesis and model formation; and (5) the level of inquiry from planning to application. See Figure 10.4 for a rating scale for evaluating inquiry-based science software and interactive multimedia programs (Litchfield, 1992).

It is the inclusion of IVD programs with components such as those listed above that can move students and teachers toward a more productive learning environment. When students can construct and make sense out of their own learning, then education becomes more relevant to them. They not only learn content, but also how to organize it into meaningful chunks that fit into a larger scheme of learning. In order to do this they must be able to monitor their own learning and move toward becoming self-regulated learners.

Self-Regulated Learning

The characteristics of self-regulated learning fit well into the types of IVD program discussed so far. In terms of metacognitive processes, self-regulated learners plan, set goals, organize, monitor, and self-evaluate their progress at points during their acquisition of new knowledge (Corno, 1986; Pressley & Ghatala, 1990). In addition, these learners also use the following strategies: structure their environment, rehearse and memorize information, seek social assistance, and review materials (Zimmerman & Martinez-Pons, 1988).

Many of the features and characteristics of self-regulated learning can be designed into Level III interactive videodisc programs because these programs require students to use a variety of higher-order cognitive processes. Well-designed programs facilitate the development of analysis, synthesis, and evaluation skills through self-paced individual and cooperative activities.

Feedback for self-regulated learners often takes the form of self-oriented feedback (Carver & Scheier, 1988; Zimmerman, 1989). In this process, students monitor the effectiveness of their learning methods or strate-

Directions - If program contains a feature, write the number in the blank.

Nature of investigation

_____1. Is the investigation a simulation of a
> _____ laboratory experiment? (1)
> _____ real-world situation (2)

_____2. Do students design the investigation? (3)

_____3. Do students retest, rethink, and ask what if? (3)

_____4. Do students generate a model ? (4)

Advantages of the investigation over actual lab investigation

_____5. Are there difficulties in actually performing the lab investigation? (1)

_____6. Can the lab investigation be dangerous to students? (1)

_____7. Would lab investigation be too expensive? (1)

_____8. Does lab investigation involve setting, supplies not available in school? (1)

_____9. Does the lab investigation require too much (regular classroom) time? (1)

_____10. Does the program investigation simplify and prevent conceptual (1)
> overload?

Inquiry skills

11. _Planning_. Does the student have the opportunity to:
> _____ a) define and formulate a problem? (1)
> _____ b) formulate an hypothesis? (2)
> _____ c) predict experimental results? (3)
> _____ d) plan an investigation? (5)
> _____ e) plan a control? (5)

12. _Performance._ Does the student have the opportunity to:
> _____ a) perform simulated activities? (1)
> _____ b) gather preset information or data? (1)
> _____ c) choose variables or method for investigation? (2)
> _____ d) generate own data? (3)
> _____ e) design the investigation? (4)
> _____ f) incorporate real lab activities along with (5)
> computer activities?

13. _Reporting, interpretation, and analysis._ Does the student have an opportunity to:
> _____ a) enter results into a ready made table? (1)
> _____ b) control the way results are reported? (2)
> _____ c) design a table and enter data? (2)
> _____ d) make a graph? (2)
> _____ e) other _____ (2)
> _____ f) interpret data to answer questions and draw conclusions? (2)
> _____ g) explain the nature of the control? (3)
> _____ h) synthesize data from other sources gathered during investigation? (3)
> _____ i) formulate generalizations of the investigation? (3)
> _____ j) determine mathematical relationships? (4)
> _____ k) define limitations of the investigation? (5)
> _____ l) compare results of previous predictions? (5)

14. _Application._ Does the student have to opportunity to:
> _____ a) apply ideas on the basis of the results obtained in the investigation? (1)
> _____ b) formulate problem/hypothesis on the basis of the results obtained in (3)
> the investigation?
> _____ c) plan a new investigation to continue the completed investigation? (5)

Figure 10.4. Evaluation of inquiry-based science software and interactive multimedia programs.

From "Evaluation of Inquiry-based Science Software and Interactive Multimedia Programs" B.C. Litchfield, 1992, *The Computing Teacher, 20*(3), p. 16.

Concepts related to inquiry

_____15. Does the investigation deal with process skills related to performance?   (1)
            (e.g. making prescribed dilutions, measuring,)
_____16. Does the investigation integrate concepts related to design of experiments?
            (e.g. hypothesis, control)   (3)
_____17. Does the investigation integrate concepts related to reporting and   (3)
            interpretation? (e.g. graphs, prediction, interpolation)
_____18. Does the investigation integrate concepts related to application of results?
            (e.g. extrapolation, synthesis, evaluation)   (5)

Level of inquiry

	Given	Directed	Open
Problem	__0	__1	__5
Procedure	__0	__1	__5
Solution	__0	__1	__5

TOTAL POINTS = _____

108 - 120 - (90%) Excellent, contains almost all of the inquiry-based investigation criteria
 97 - 107 - (80%) Good, contains most of the criteria
 85 - 96 - (70%) OK, contains a fair amount of inquiry-based criteria
 72 - 84 - (60%) Poor, contains very few of inquiry-based criteria

Figure 10.4. Evaluation of inquiry-based science software and interactive multimedia programs (continued).
From "Evaluation of Inquiry-based Science Software and Interactive Multimedia Programs" B.C. Litchfield, 1992, *The Computing Teacher, 20*(3), p. 16.

gies and react to it in a number of ways. They can review and revise or select an entirely different direction to investigate. The key is that they track their own feedback and use it as a basis for continued learning. Alterations in their strategies may range from covert changes in their self-perceptions to overt changes in their behaviors (Zimmerman, 1990). This covert evaluation of feedback and the student's actions as a result of it are highly related to self-esteem and self-concept (McCombs, 1984, 1989). Students will weigh the information obtained from the feedback to evaluate their internal learning progress and determine how satisfied they are with it. This feedback is also used to constitute more perceptible changes in outward processes related to the learning situation. Mace, Belfiore, & Shea (1989) see the overt actions as resulting in self-recording, self-instruction, and self-reinforcement responses.

It is these aspects of self-regulated learning that form the basis for learner-generated feedback. By creating their own feedback, students are able to monitor, evaluate, and revise their instructional progress. This entire process is essential for development of a student-centered learning situation where they become responsible for their own learning.

Learner-Generated Feedback

Feedback Characteristics

Learner-generated feedback (LGF) is a complicated process involving goal-setting and planning, self-initiation, self-evaluation, motivation, and certitude. Unlike program-generated feedback, LGF does not have a finite set of conditions from which to operate in providing feedback. Learner-generated feedback is suitable for inquiry and discovery-based IVD programs addressing problem-solving, critical-thinking, and decision-making. It allows learners to construct their own environment for creating feedback for a particular instructional experience. Students construct their own feedback showing individual or group understanding of a learning goal or task by using available resources in the IVD environment.

Within this feedback structure, self-instruction plays an important part. Self-instruction is self-speech or what we say to ourselves when analyzing, performing, or evaluating a task. Self-instruction may provide cues that guide behavior and may prompt, direct, or maintain behavior (Harris, 1990). When these self-instructions are exhibited as learner-generated feedback, it is possible to begin to examine the student's construction of cognitive processes. In this manner students are able to create an individual (or group) learning project to illustrate how they have learned the material.

Within this environment, variable pathways to an answer or conclusion exist for the learner.

Learner control is an important aspect of IVD progams promoting learner-generated feedback. Learner control is generally defined as the degree of control a learner has over his or her own learning. It can vary from selecting a particular lesson to study, to drawing up a student contract, to determining the pathway taken through a lesson. For IVD programs it would mean the learner is free to control what material is covered and in what order. There are numerous studies that have investigated learner control and have found positive as well as mixed effects on learning. For use in a feedback context, learner control relates to the freedom the learner has to choose how learning will be exhibited for evaluation. (No studies were found in this area.)

Learner-generated feedback can be looked at as feedback *for* the instructor rather than *by* the instructor. Also it is feedback *by* the learner rather than *for* the learner. This opens up a whole new way of measuring and evaluating certitude. In LGF, forms of student self-assessment such as scores, totals, or grades are not dependable. Expressions of certitude are linked to the outward exhibition of the way material has been learned and assimilated by students. The degree of learning can also be exhibited by expressions of certitude. Feedback by the learner may involve constructing a rationale to support the answer. To the degree learners are confident in their use of resources to construct a rationale, they are certain of their answers.

The format used by students in showing how much they have learned in a problem-solving IVD program is an integral part of their certitude because methods of LGF involve self-regulation. In order to foster self-regulated learning, two dimension needs to be considered: the learner dimension and the learning environment (McCombs & Marzano, 1990). In the learner dimension, the focus must be on helping students realize they are creative agents with the power of choice (will), and ensuring students that they have the metacognitive and cognitive information-processing strategies (skill) needed for meeting personal self-development and self-determination goals. Students confident in these areas will tend to produce feedback of a greater depth or show an understanding closer to what experts or developers intended. Along with this, it would be assumed that these students are also fairly sure they have mastered the material and feel confident they have met the criteria for evaluation or grading.

Program Requirements Necessary
for Learner-Generated Feedback

Interactive video programs which facilitate LGF are those providing students with interaction and situations to solve problems. Students need opportunities for choice and active anticipation in decision making as well as for autonomy and group problem solving (McCombs & Marzano, 1990). Learning activities need to provide students with choices to initiate and regulate behavior in a self-determined fashion (Deci & Ryan, 1986). Interactive learning is important in developing self-regulated learners (Graham & Harris, 1989; Meichenbaum, 1977; Stodolsky, 1985).

Program components necessary for students to produce learner-generated feedback can include the following:

- databases
- informational text
- video segments (procedural, informational)
- stills
- variable manipulation and experimental results
- microcomputer-based laboratory
- resources (maps, diagrams, graphs)
- human resources (experts, consultants)
- field guides, atlases
- references
- accompanying printed materials (workbooks, user guides)
- visual and still capture ability
- word-processing
- printing capability
- suggestions and directions for learner-generated feedback options

These components of a program will allow the learner to interact with a large number of sources. Deciding which ones have a direct relationship to the LGF product will be up to the learner. The learner should be required to choose what is most important, as well as plan and monitor how it is included in the final product. The motivation a learner has to initiate and complete an activity may depend on the number and quality of resources available. Having a good selection can influence the decision to exert more effort.

According to McCombs and Marzano (1990), it is important that motivation and the will component be addressed before the student can recognize the power of the self as agent. Increasing motivation depends on learner interventions that focus on the following: (a) metacognitive (self-assessment, planning, monitoring), (b) cognitive (problem solving, decision making, higher-order thinking skills), and (c) affective (goal-setting, managing effect, generating expectancies, self-images of success).

Some Level III interactive videodisc programs include a feature which allows students to create their own on-line programs using visuals, stills, text, and graphics in the program. They are in complete control of selection and integration of what they want to use to illustrate what they have learned.

Each of the above is an essential component in IVD programs designed to elicit learner-generated feedback from students. Students must be able to choose academic goals, select problem-solving strategies, and adjust their plans and efforts according to their success (Paris & Newman, 1990). These behaviors can be exhibited and measured only when students use IVD programs designed with these instructional strategies.

Measuring Certitude

Just how can students exhibit their certitude for a particular topic or subject area? This can be done via a chosen format (see list below), the amount of time spent on it, and the nature of the product. A final product can be short, long, detailed, or drawn from actual experience on the computer. An important measure can be the correspondence of the product to the material provided in the program. In a problem-solving IVD program, it is essential that an instructor be aware of how a particular problem was approached and solved. The tracking of these steps can provide additional insight into the learning process. Problem-solving interactive videodiscs include programs such as those listed below:

- medical diagnosis and treatment
- interviewing techniques
- teaching methods
- environmental issues, problems, and solutions—field activities
- science experiments and research
- classroom management
- legal issues, problems, and solutions—trials

Students can list their steps to a solution or steps can be tracked by the computer. A record of these steps can be used by an instructor to diagnose problems or low performance. It is important that students are provided with a variety of formats to use in this process in order to construct their personal divergent feedback options for the instructor.

Some examples of format (activities) for students to use to exhibit their certitude are listed below:

- journal notes
- case notes
- maps/charts
- protocols
- artwork
- photography
- games
- teaching a lesson
- surveys
- news articles
- graphs
- media slide shows
- treatment schedules
- database creation
- developing own ideas
- evaluations

Obviously, some activities are more complicated than others to accomplish in terms of effort, ability, and time. Selection of a format, however, could be considered an initial measure of confidence regarding the instructional material. Selection of a format is also related to personal interests and indirectly to learning style. If a student feels confident in the ability to write, a writing format will most likely be chosen to exhibit what was learned. The same holds true for artwork or mathematical calculations.

Measuring Certitude in Problem-Solving Instruction

We are now faced with the problem of measuring certitude in the problem-solving interactive videodisc environment. This instruction is not necessarily as precise and quantifiable because in problem-solving there can be variable pathways to an answer or answers. Because of this, evaluation becomes a bit more involved. The previous definition of certitude still applies; however, it needs some additional criteria when used in IVD programs. It is now integrated with self-regulation and self-efficacy. It is demonstrated during feedback construction and measured after a more involved product is completed rather than immediately after an answer to a specific question.

With learner-generated feedback, students have more time to think about and construct an answer or product that they do with program-generated feedback. Actually, with PGF they are not required to continue their learning by creating something else. They simply read, listen to, or view the program. Of course, they may use the information to adjust their answers, actions, or sequence, but the involvement usually stops there. With LGF, the learning process continues past the direct involvement with the program.

There appears to be a number of certitude measures that can be used in this environment:
- the type of product that is selected to complete—easy or difficult
- the way it will be accomplished—individual or group work
- time spent working on the product—planning, research, design, development
- depth of effort
- breadth of effort
- self-analysis measure—questionnaire

Many of these involve self-efficacy in that they are an indication of the choice of activities, the amount of effort expended, and the extent of persistence directed toward a task (Bandura, 1989). The question here becomes, how are learner-generated feedback and self-efficacy related and, more important, how are they measured? Admittedly, how to measure these is difficult. It involves qualitative and subjective judgments, which are time-consuming; however, they provide a more diagnostic way to evaluate learner progress. Getting a score of correct and incorrect answers can be of some value to instructors and students if matched to objectives. In contrast, learner-generated feedback can provide a much more detailed picture of student performance and understanding. Learner-generated feedback can also allow the learner to integrate concepts, processes, and procedures in any number of unique ways to capture the way content has been assimilated within each individual. Perhaps it is a combination of both types of feedback and certitude measures that provides the most complete picture of learning.

Redefining Feedback and Certitude for IVD

The same feedback and certitude measures cannot be applied equally to all IVD instructional programs because they vary considerably in design and presentation of materials. In those IVD programs in which simulations, games, and varied challenges are included, the familiar type of traditional feedback and certitude measures can be employed. Program-generated feedback seems to fit well. It may be more relevant to the learner if certitude measures are tied to rewards or payoffs—points, credits, high score, or exemptions. It is easy to design this type of feedback into an IVD program. Features such as these that gain and maintain the learner's attention generally increase motivation and learning (Keller, 1987).

On the other hand, in inquiry or discovery-based IVD programs similar to those addressing problem solving, critical thinking, and decision making, the usual feedback certitude measures do not work as well. Here is where learner-generated feedback is most useful. With variable outcomes in these learning situations, feedback is not precisely defined. In fact, in this environment, feedback shifts from instructor-centered to learner-centered and the pattern of exhibition and measurement changes. It takes longer and involves more components. It can be an individual or a group effort.

Well-designed and developed IVD technology affords learners a variety of experiences that closely mimic real-life situations. Often these situations and learning activities cannot be quantifiable and neatly packaged into groups of questions and answers. Certainly, if we are to use IVD to its fullest, the formats and instructional design methods and strategies of print-based and CBI instruction need to be carefully evaluated if included. In most cases, they should not be included. Many IVD programs end up looking like a race car with wagon wheels.

Feedback and certitude measures will evolve as IVD design and development becomes more refined. Currently, Level III interactive videodisc problem-solving programs are beginning to emerge in all areas. As expected, there is a wide variety of feedback options and few measures of certitude. It may be that certitude measures are just hiding waiting for redefinition. As we become more confident with IVD instruction and define its powers through research and development, our ability to accurately and thoroughly evaluate these components of this new technology will increase.

Areas for Research in IVD Programs

Research on feedback, certitude, and self-regulated learning in IVD is lacking. This could be attributed to the small number of educationally sound Level III programs on the market, along with the newness of the technology and sporadic availability in many school settings. In addition, the integration of these three research areas has not been examined. Some of the areas of research in IVD instructional programs that would seem to be worthwhile investigating are listed below:

- *Program-generated feedback*
  - Are learning and retention increased if certitude measures are tied to rewards?
  - Are learning and retention increased when learners are informed that a high score based on certitude will exempt them from additional work?
  - What is the relationship between motivation and program-generated feedback?
  - What effect does program-generated feedback have on certitude?
- *Learner-generated feedback*
  - What is the relationship between certitude and feedback in self-regulated learning using IVD programs?
  - Does certitude increase when learners set goals for learner-generated feedback construction?
  - What is the relationship between certitude and self-regulated learning in IVD programs?
  - What methods of evaluation accurately assess certitude levels in IVD programs?
  - What methods of evaluation accurately assess certitude levels in self-regulated learning?
  - What is the relationship between motivation and learner-generated feedback?

- What effect does learner-generated feedback have on certitude and self-regulated learning?

Implications for Practitioners

Where possible, when incorporating motivational sequences, include a confidence of response measure that is tied to a reward. Certitude measures integrated with payback or rewards tend to increase learning and motivation. Students see the activity as challenging and often do not realize they are applying what they have learned in an entertaining way. When students indicate the confidence of their response, they are providing information regarding their knowledge acquisition. Instructors can use this to diagnose learning problems or to adjust instructional strategies.

When designing Level III IVD programs, integrate true instructional interactivity rather than navigational interactivity. Students must interact intellectually with the program if meaningful learning is to take place. They must be actively involved in problem-solving and higher-level skills. Activities must be designed which require students to react to and integrate a variety of resources and receive varied feedback in order to reach a conclusion about a topic or subject area. Multiple sources of data and information should be provided for this to occur.

Provide numerous opportunities for students to plan, organize, monitor, and evaluate their own learning. Programs should guide students in self-directed learning and also require them to be responsible for a large part of their own learning. This can only be done in programs containing many open-ended activities, investigations, and challenges. Accompanying print materials, as well as on-line capabilities, can be an essential part of this process by including charts, diagrams, tables, and other mechanisms and spaces for recording and evaluating collected information and data. Extension activities should be provided with each program. These activities should get students out of the classroom and into life experiences to complete their learning.

Include inquiry-based activities which facilitate problem solving as a way of measuring certitude. When students are required to solve problems as an extension of an IVD program, they are providing the instructor with an indication of the degree of effort exerted toward completing a task. Programs should be designed where students can make choices regarding their approach to problem solution. These problem-solving approaches can be tracked and evaluated by the instructor as information about a student's progress and understanding of the material.

Design IVD programs which allow and encourage students to create

learner-generated feedback. These programs must include opportunities for goal setting and planning, self-initiation, self-evaluation, motivation, and certitude. Under these conditions, students can learn to construct their own environment for creating feedback for a particular instructional experience. Programs must provide visual, text, audio, and graphic resources that can be easily accessed and incorporated in students' efforts of feedback creation.

Summary

Program-generated feedback and learner-generated feedback present a wide range of design considerations for Level III interactive videodisc programs. Essential to the success of each type is the amount of *instructional* interactivity built into a program. This is entirely different from the navigational interactivity characterizing far too many of the programs on the market today that claim to be interactive. A true Level III IVD program provides activities and investigations for learners to manipulate variables, solve problems, think critically, and make decisions. In addition, students are actively involved with their own learning.

Certitude measures can be easily integrated into Level III programs. As program-generated feedback, it can take the form of games, simulations, and real-life, real-time experiences. Add to these activities a point system where students can indicate their confidence of response and receive additional points. Throw in an extra bonus of being able to be exempt from subsequent lessons if a high score is obtained—a guaranteed attention getter.

By assisting their own learning through planning, organizing, monitoring, and evaluating their progress, students move toward self-directed learning. As self-directed learners, they are more apt to use, as well as produce, feedback—allowing them to alter their learning strategies to build in more responsibility for their own actions and ideas. With the current teacher-centered educational system, employing these instructional strategies is difficult. Students must shift from knowledge consumers to knowledge producers by learning how to access knowledge bases through technology.

It is not enough to learn something; students must be able to do something with it. Learner-generated feedback is designed to allow students to do just this. Once they have learned the material, they are encouraged to plan, organize, and execute an activity or product showing their understanding of the material. IVD programs must include a number of resources to stimulate and aid their efforts. This means that programs must be designed with quite a bit more substance than many of the click-and-see programs designated as Level III.

It may be worthwhile to investigate building some models for interactive videodisc programs for incorporating appropriate feedback along with evaluations for self-regulated learning. At present, we are still primarily limited by designs of the past and leftovers from other modes of instruction (e.g., print or CBI). As an emerging method of instruction, IVD demands new types of feedback built on the best features of the past and integration of existing complementary ideas and theories. This evolution must be careful and deliberate, if we want to design systems to provide learners with meaningful instruction that supports, maintains, and maximizes this new learning technology.

References

American Association for the Advancement of Science. (1989). *Science for all Americans: Project 2061*. Washington, D.C.: AAAS Publishing.

Bandura, A. (1989). Human agency in social cognitive theory. *American Psychologist, 44*, 1179–1184.

Cameron, M. (1983). An interactive training environment for pilots. *Educational and Industrial Television*, 34–36.

Carnine, D., Englemann, S., Hofmeister, A., & Kelly, B. (1987). Videodisc instruction in fractions. *Focus on Learning Problems in Mathematics, 9*(1), 31–52.

Carrier, C.A., & Jonassen, D.H. (1988). Adapting courseware to accommodate individual differences. In D.H. Jonassen (Ed.), *Instructional designs for microcomputer courseware* (pp. 203–226). Hillsdale, NJ: Lawrence Erlbaum Associates.

Carver, C.S., & Scheier, M.F. (1988). *Attention and self-regulation: A control theory approach to human behavior*. New York: Springer-Verlag.

Collins, A. (1991). The role of computer technology in restructuring schools. *Phi Delta Kappan, 73*(2), 24–29.

Corno, L. (1986). The metacognitive control components of self-regulated learning. *Contemporary Educational Psychology, 11*, 333–346.

Cushall, M.B., Harvey, F.A., & Brovey, A.J. (1988, April). *Research on learning from interactive videodiscs: A review of the literature and suggestions for future research activities*. Paper presented at the annual meeting of the American Educational Research Association, New Orleans.

Deci, E.L., & Ryan, R.M. (1986). The dynamics of self-determination in personality and development. In R. Schwarzer (Ed.), *Self-regulated cognitions in anxiety and motivation* (pp. 171–194). Hillsdale, NJ: Lawrence Erlbaum Associates.

Gagné, R.M. (1977). *The conditions of learning*. New York: Holt, Rinehart, & Winston.

Gay, G., & Mazur, J. (1990). Navigating in hypermedia. In E. Berk & J. Devlin (Eds.), *Hypertext and hypermedia handbook*. New York: McGraw-Hill.

Gay, G., & Raffensperger, E. (1989, Sept.) Considerations and strategies in the design of interactive multimedia programs. *Academic Computing, 4*(1), 24–27.

Gery, G. (1989). Interactivity: The heart of the CBT matter. *Proceedings of the Seventh Conference on Interactive Instruction Delivery*, Society for Applied Learning Technology, Orlando, FL.

Graham, S., & Harris, K.R. (1989). A component analysis of cognitive strategy instruction: Effects on learning disabled students' compositions and self-efficacy. *Journal of Educational Psychology, 81*, 353–361.

Hannafin, M.J. (1986). Introduction to the special issue: Research and development in instructional interactive video. *Journal of Computer-Based Instruction, 13*(4), 101.

Hannafin, M.J., Gearhart, C., Reiber, L.P., & Phillips, T.L. (1985). Keeping interactive video in perspective: Tentative guidelines and cautions in the design of interactive video. In E. Miller & M.L. Mosley (Eds.), *Educational media and technology yearbook* (pp.13–25). Denver: Libraries Unlimited.

Harris, K.R. (1990). Developing self-regulated learners: The role of private speech and self instructions. *Educational Psychologist, 25*(1), 35–49.

Jost, K.L. (1990). Computer-based interactive video: The potential for effective instructional environments. *Instructional Developments, 1*(3), 16–21.

Keller, J.M. (1987). Strategies for stimulating the motivation to learn. *Performance and Instruction, 26*(9), 1–8.

Keller, J.M., & Suzuki, K. (1988). Use of the ARCS motivational model in courseware design. In D.H. Jonassen (Ed.), *Instructional designs for microcomputer courseware*. Hillsdale, NJ: Lawrence Erlbaum Associates.

Kinzie, M.B. (1990). Requirements and benefits of effective interactive instruction: Learner control, self-regulation, and continuing motivation. *Educational Technology Research and Development, 38*(1), 5–21.

Kisiah, M.A., & Litchfield, B.C. (1990). *Astrovision*. Level III interactive videodisc program. Boston, MA: Houghton Mifflin.

Kulhavy, R.W., & Stock, W.A. (1989). Feedback in written instruction: The place of response certitude. *Educational Psychology Review, 1*, 279–308.

Kulhavy, R.W., White, M.T., Topp, B.W., Chan, A.L., & Adams, J. (1985). Feedback complexity and corrective efficiency. *Contemporary Educational Psychology, 10*, 285–291.

Litchfield, B.C. (1990a). Criteria for evaluating videodisc interactivity. *Performance and Instruction, 29*(6), 23–26.

Litchfield, B.C. (1990b). ScienceQuest: A multimedia inquiry-based videodisc science curriculum. *Instruction Delivery Systems, 4*(3), 12–17.

Litchfield, B.C. (1992). Evaluation of inquiry-based science software and interactive multimedia programs. *The Computing Teacher, 20*(3), 15–18.

Litchfield, B.C., & Dempsey, J.V. (1992). The IVD equipped classroom: Integrating videodisc technology into the curricula. *Journal of Educational Multimedia and Hypermedia, 1*(1), 39–49.

Lynch, P. (1991). *Multimedia: Getting started*. Sunnyvale, CA: PUBLIX Information Products.

Mace, F.C., Belfiore, P.J., & Shea, M.C. (1989). Operant theory and research on self-regulation. In B.J. Zimmerman & D.H. Schunk (Eds.), *Self-regulated learning and academic achievement: Theory, research, and practice* (pp. 111–141). New York: Springer-Verlag.

Malby, C. (1987). Interactive video as a school resource. In D. Laurillard (Ed.), *Interactive media: Working methods and practical applications* (pp. 191–204). Chichester, West Sussex, UK: Ellis Horwood Limited.

Marlino, M.R. (1990). *A proposal for the utilization of a process modeling approach in the evaluation of interactive videodiscs.* Paper presented at the annual meeting of the American Educational Research Association, Boston.

McCombs, B.L. (1984). Processes and skills underlying continuing metacognition, cognitive, and affective learning strategies. In C.E. Weinstein, E.T. Goetz, & P.A. Alexander (Eds.), *Learning and study strategies: Issues in assessment, instruction, and evaluation* (pp. 141–169). New York: Academic Press.

McCombs, B.L. (1989). Self-regulated learning and academic achievement: A phenomenological view. In B.J. Zimmerman & D.H. Schunk (Eds.), *Self-regulated learning and academic achievement: Theory, research, and practice* (pp. 111–141). New York: Springer-Verlag.

McCombs, B.L., & Marzano, R.J. (1990). Putting the self in self-regulated learning: The self as agent in integrating will and skill. *Educational Psychologist, 25*(1), 51–69.

Meichenbaum, D. (1977). *Cognitive-behavior modification: An integrative approach.* New York: Plenum.

Milheim, W.D., & Azbell, J.W. (1988). *How past research on learner control can aid in the design of interactive video materials.* Paper presented at the annual meeting of the Association for Educational Communications and Technology, New Orleans, LA.

Mojkowski, C. (1989). *Transforming curriculum and instruction with technology.* Paper presented at the American Educational Research Association annual meeting, San Francisco.

Morton, C., & Mojkowski, C. (1989). *The dialog paradigm: A model for rethinking schooling.* Paper presented at the American Educational Research Association annual meeting, San Francisco.

National Council of Teachers of Mathematics (1991). *NCTM curriculum and evaluation standards.* Reston, VA: National Council of Teachers of Mathematics.

Nielson, J. (1990). *Hypertext and hypermedia.* San Diego: Academic Press.

Paris, S.G., & Newman, R.S. (1990). Developmental aspects of self-regulated learning. *Educational Psychologist, 25*(1), 87–102.

Osgood, D. (1987). The difference in higher education: Five colleges meeting the challenge! *Byte, 12* (2), 165–178.

Paris, S.G., & Newman, R.S. (1990). Developmental aspects of self-regulated learning. *Educational Psychologist, 25*(1), 3–17.

Pea, R.d., & Soloway, E. (1987). *Mechanisms for facilitating a vital and dynamic education system: Fundamental roles for education, science, and technology.* Office of Technology Assessment, Washington, DC.

Pressley, M., & Ghatala, E.S. (1990). Self-regulated learning: Monitoring learning from text. *Educational Psychologist, 25*(1), 19–33.

Schimmel, B.J. (1988a). *Patterns in students' selection of feedback in computer-based instruction.* Paper presented at the American Educational Research Association annual meeting, New Orleans.

Schimmel, B.J. (1988b). Providing meaningful feedback in courseware. In D.H. Jonassen (Ed.), *Instructional designs for microcomputer courseware* (pp. 183–195). Hillsdale, NJ: Lawrence Erlbaum Associates.

Schunk, D.H. (1989). Social cognitive theory and self-regulated learning. In B.J. Zimmerman & D.H. Schunk (Eds.), *Self-regulated learning and academic achievement: Theory, research, and practice* (pp. 1–25). New York: Springer-Verlag.

Schunk, D.H. (1990). Goal-setting and self-efficacy during self-regulated learning. *Educational Psychologist, 25*(1), 71–86.

Spock, P.A. (1988). *Feedback and confidence of response for a ruler-learning task using computer-assisted instruction.* Paper presented at the Association for Educational Communications and Technology annual meeting, New Orleans, LA.

Stodolsky, S.S. (1985). Telling math: Origins of math aversion and anxiety. *Educational Psychologist, 20*, 125–133.

Zimmerman, B.J. (1986). Development of self-regulated learning: Which are the key subprocesses? *Contemporary Educational Psychology, 16*, 307–313.

Zimmerman, B.J. (1989). Models of self-regulated learning and academic achievement. In B.J. Zimmerman & D.H. Schunk (Eds.), *Self-regulated learning and academic achievement: Theory, research, and practice* (pp. 1–25). New York: Springer-Verlag.

Zimmerman, B.J. (1990). Learning and academic achievement. *Educational Psychologist, 25*(1), 3–17.

Zimmerman, B.J., & Martinez-Pons, M. (1988). Construct validation of a strategy model of student self-regulated learning. *Journal of Educational Psychology, 80*, 284–290.

Chapter Eleven

Feedback and Emerging Instructional Technologies

Michael J. Hannafin
Florida State University

Kathleen McDermott Hannafin
Florida State University

and

David W. Dalton
Kent State University

The importance of feedback in interactive instruction, as detailed in other chapters contained in this text, hardly needs further elaboration. Yet, rapid advances in emerging, computer-based technologies require that we continually reassess our notions about lesson design, and feedback in particular. The nature of this reassessment, and the manner in which balance is attained among relevant considerations, is of special concern.

Many have argued for the uniqueness of emerging technologies, especially those incorporating optical storage technologies such as videodisc, CD-ROM, CD-I, and DVI. The gist of the argument is that newer technologies afford significant advantages not only in technological features such as mass storage and processing speed, but also in presentation features such as image quality, resolution, and fidelity of images. As a consequence, widespread and stirring endorsements of interactive video, hypertext, and hypermedia have been common (Engle & Campbell-Bonar, 1989; Paske, 1990; Phillipo, 1988).

It seems ill-advised, however, to attribute such effects to individual media, particularly due to the rapidly evolving nature of the technology. Emerging technologies are increasingly hybrid in nature, combining the features and capabilities of multiple technologies. It is not uncommon, for example, for hypermedia systems to support video, text, audio, and a variety of other presentation and management options previously associated with a particular medium. Instead, it may be more productive to assess how features and attributes can be extended and varied via current and future developments, and to build durable design guidelines for emerging technologies around the degree to which such features and attributes should be manipulated (Hannafin, 1989).

The purpose of this chapter is to present a framework for designing feedback by incorporating the powers of emerging instructional technologies. Emerging technologies are those computer-based systems that provide the technological capacity to present, manipulate, control, or otherwise manage educational activities (Hannafin, 1992). The phrase "emerging technologies" reflects an emphasis on enhanced functions and attributes likely to evolve through technological developments rather than specific, and largely transitional, technologies. Feedback has been defined elsewhere in this text, but for our purposes it is a technologically-mediated response which provides information or activities that are conditionally relevant to learning goals. The goals may be externally determined by teachers, organizations, or lesson designers, or internally assigned by the individual. The role of feedback is to clarify, strengthen, or extend knowledge, skills, or beliefs.

Emerging Technologies and Feedback Potential

Recent advances have led many to speculate on the unique instructional capabilities of emerging technologies (see, for example, Cooper, 1990; Engle & Campbell-Bonar, 1989; Paske, 1990; Phillipo, 1988; Wehrenberg, 1986). Others have argued that all delivery systems possess comparable attributes to varying degrees, and that the differences among technologies are often related to economic and pragmatic concerns versus unique effectiveness (Clark, 1983; Norman, Muzzin, Williams, & Swanson, 1985; Thorton & Cleaveland, 1990). Though partial toward the latter argument, we acknowledge that technological capabilities establish, in a very real sense, the limits of what **can be done** instructionally. While it may well be true that some form of feedback can be designed for all technologies, it is unlikely that truly comparable (or, in many cases, ideal) feedback can be provided across technologies. Emerging technologies provide the potential for varied feedback that is neither possible nor practical in conventional instruction

(Schimmel, 1988). What has changed with the advent of emerging technologies is not so much the functional role of feedback, but the dramatic range of ways in which feedback can be provided.

From an educational perspective, technologies vary according to their ability to orient students to learning tasks, present information, support encoding and retrieval, and sequence activities (Hannafin & Rieber, 1989a; 1989b). The ability to present information and support encoding is most closely associated with feedback design. Presentation options essentially provide stimulation to the learner, whereas encoding functions emphasize the capacity to invoke appropriate cognitive processing to support learning.

Consider the range of presentation dimensions available for feedback. Feedback can be provided through visual, verbal, sensory, or multiple modalities. These dimensions are shown in Table 11.1. Visual dimensions include those that can be visibly observed by the learner. Written text, for example, must be seen and is therefore initially a visual stimulus. Other visual stimuli include pictures and icons (in the form of static graphics and moving images). Verbal dimensions include stimuli of a semantic nature, including both the printed and spoken word. Sensory stimuli are physically or emotionally experienced by learners, while multiple dimension options include combinations of modalities.

To illustrate the range of feedback available through emerging technologies, consider an example illustrating the progressive nature of the dimensions shown in Table 11.1. When learning concepts related to resonance and load in structural engineering, different technological capabilities offer dramatically different options. In a traditional environment, such as in programmed- or self-study instruction, learners might be provided verbal information related to calculating load (e.g., tensile and compressive strength, formulas for calculating load) along with an opportunity to answer questions. Written feedback, in the form of simple knowledge of correct response, is the most likely form of feedback, since the printed materials restrict significantly the range of possible feedback. In a CAI version of the same lesson, an algorithm could be developed to permit feedback in the form of a response-differentiated statement. Individual variability in the response could be accommodated, and appropriate feedback could be adapted accordingly.

Using slightly more sophisticated technology, a recorded or synthesized human voice might be used in the response-differentiated feedback, minimizing the potentially confounding influence of reading and making the transactions between the student and the lesson more conversational. Feedback might be further supplemented by a combination of graphic and realistic video images depicting the widely studied demise of the Tacoma Narrows Bridge (Fuller, 1984). At the high end of the technology capability

Dimensions	Sample Forms	Examples
Visual	Written	Typed feedback within a lesson
	Pictorial	Photographs, graphics, visual metaphors
	Vicarious- Aural	Listening to the opinions of experts
	Dialog	Seek clarification, ask for specific types of information
	Text (Semantic)	Analogies, meaning from typed text
Sensory	Tactile	G-Force in aircraft, CPR on mannnequins
	Olfactory	Burning oil smell, scent detection
	Emotive	Arousing fear, nausea, concern, anger
	Text (Semantic)	Analogies, meaning from typed text
Sensory	Tactile	G-Force in aircraft, CPR on mannnequins
	Olfactory	Burning oil smell, scent detection
	Emotive	Arousing fear, nausea, concern, anger
Multiple	Pictorial- Textual	Superimpose text on graphics or pictures, windowing in CAI
	Oral-Motion	Narration while demonstrating a correct procedure
	Tactile-Pictorial	Two-dimensional medical emergency simulation
	Tactile-Emotive- Motion- Oral	Three-dimensional flight simulation, Trauma care simulations

Table 11.1. Dimensions and examples of feedback.

continuum, feedback might even be provided in the form of three-dimensional sensory consequences that mimic the actual consequences encountered, or by permitting the student to develop structural alternatives and test the structural limits of the design.

The point of this illustration is that technological capabilities influence directly the viability of various feedback activities. Emerging technologies provide the capability to deliver feedback by stimulating the various modalities, elevating both the sensory and performance aspects of learning tasks, and extending dramatically the notions of feedback beyond verbal information and low-level intellectual skills. Yet, while the availability of such capabilities provides a necessary condition for such high-level applications, it is, by itself, an insufficient condition for effective utilization.

Advances in both technological capabilities and pedagogical orientation offer potential to provide varied, realistic, intensive, and high-fidelity feedback. The relatively simple question, "Is feedback necessary?" is really not at issue. The issue is how to optimize concurrently both individual processing capabilities and technological potential. This requires that we extend rather than limit our notions of both feedback and technology. In an initial sense, the task is to understand how capabilities extend our notions of lesson design; in the final analysis, it is ultimately an issue of design.

The Evolution of Technology and Feedback

Skinner (1954) was among the most prominent learning theorists to emphasize an integral relationship between reinforcement and learning. More recently, others (e.g., Kulhavy, 1977) extended the notions of reinforcement theory to feedback by emphasizing the importance of information versus response confirmation. Research has underscored the importance of the nature of the information, response, and/or consequences provided via feedback.

Early efforts to automate feedback were reflected by Pressey's (1926) and Skinner's (1954) teaching machines. These systems provided preprogrammed, textual feedback following individual student responses. Such systems represented important conceptual advances in feedback, but significant operational problems. Feedback could be differentiated according to the distractors in embedded multiple-choice questions, but the activities of both the lesson and the feedback were exceedingly controlled. The methods were cumbersome, labor and cost intensive, and limited to textual information. In addition, as understanding of the role and design of feedback improved, certain assumptions were discredited. Research has consistently demonstrated that simple knowledge of correct response feedback for restricted multiple-choice response alternatives, a cornerstone of such systems, does little to deepen understanding of lesson concepts either correctly or incorrectly demonstrated (Gagné, 1985; Kulhavy, 1977; Rubin, Geller, & Hanks, 1977).

Attempts to incorporate feedback meaningfully also focused on programmed textbooks and programmed instruction (Crowder, 1963), personalized systems of instruction (Keller, 1974), and programmed individualized tutoring systems (Ellson, Barber, Engle, & Kampwerth, 1965). These systems provided not only feedback in the form of knowledge of correct answers, but also alternative elaborations (paraphrasing), recast model responses and lesson content, additional elaborations, and/or alternative solutions. Again, however, the available technology caused inherent limitations in the range of feedback options. Since the print format limited the capacity to elicit and verify student responses, as well as the capacity to monitor and adjust according to individual understanding, feedback provided "model responses" likely to be encountered and understood within the target student population. In effect, though feedback was available, the limited technological capabilities rendered impossible all but the most basic forms.

During the same period, technology evolved in extraordinary ways to expand the toolkit of lesson designers. Some attempts thrived momentarily, but most waned predictably. Initial enthusiasm was great, but interest declined as technological limitations overshadowed apparent pedagogical breakthroughs. In each case, limitations in the ability to support rich and varied learning activities contributed significantly to the demise of the movements. Many of these same patterns exist related to today's emerging, computer-based hypermedia systems. Enthusiasm and expectations are great, yet truly thoughtful and innovative applications are rare.

Will the current-day emerging technologies meet the fate of their predecessors? Though possible, it is highly unlikely, if the available resources are well managed. Unlike prior systems, emerging technologies possess the *potential* to overcome limitations in earlier-generation systems. The capacity to individualize learning, to access a broad range of learning tools and resources, to manage various aspects of student and class performance, and to "speak" and "hear" in human terms are distinct strengths. Indeed, many of the technological limitations of earlier generations have been overcome. It remains to be seen if the human limitations in *limited design vision* will be likewise overcome.

The Emergence of Emerging Technologies

Emerging technologies provide six major areas of improvement: adaptability, realism, hypermedia, open-endedness, manipulability, and flexibility.

Adaptability

Unlike prior systems, computer-supported systems can provide feedback of varied sorts based upon the uniquely evolved needs, responses, and histories of individual learners. Feedback, for example, need not be restricted to the lesson content immediately preceding a question, but can integrate response history from days or weeks prior to the current session, can adaptively provide one student a visual form of feedback and another text, or can access examples or explanations deemed most relevant to the interests of an individual student. In short, the capacity to adapt permits the integration of non-ritualized feedback options based upon the ongoing needs of students, lesson demands, or historical factors in a manner comparable to an expert teacher who possesses powerful pedagogical insights, a comprehensive historical background on all students, and highly organized, sophisticated, and refined grasp of relevant knowledge (see Tobias, 1991).

Realism

Dramatic advances have been made in the creation of realistic images and learning contexts. The available "image pool" is virtually unlimited, permitting the incorporation of live-action sequences—the in-depth study of the structure of an atom, detailed representations of the neurocircuitry of the brain, and so on. To the degree that realism and image fidelity are important to the learning task, images can be accessed and incorporated accordingly. Concerns related to crude graphic representations in early CAI, or the inability to study phenomena that existed only in isolated locations, have been addressed.

Hypermedia

Emerging technologies also allow learners to access and control varied media and information resources. Developments in hypermedia have emphasized the utilization of information in varied media, both extending the range of data available for lesson use and minimizing the costs associated with complete redesign. In a sense, the hypermedia movement has stimulated the creation of "pedagogical drivers"—empirically referenced computer programs that broker access among related resources. This has shortened dramatically the development time associated with converting the enormous domains of knowledge that already exist in various forms—a prospect that has daunted even the most enthusiastic of advocates.

Open-Endedness

Emerging technologies also offer the ability to create non-linear learning experiences. Though this feature affects all aspects of lesson design, it is possible for students to browse relevant concepts on their own terms, to sample activities at their own discretion, and to use the system to assist in clarifying individual learning needs. Once established, feedback becomes more integrally tied to the individual's need to know. Such systems emphasize the learner's role in determining and selecting relevant lesson activities rather than externally imposed lesson logic and sequence. That is, feedback can be responsive to student-directed learning paths.

Manipulability

Emerging technologies can provide feedback to learners through the creation and/or manipulation of elements provided within the system. In effect, such systems allow the development of living, testable learning environments where knowledge is not simply acquired but constructed. Perkins (1991) described "phenomenaria"—the creation of a microworld where relationships could be prescribed externally or assigned by the individual, and tested accordingly. Learners gain the capacity to manipulate important concepts, form and revise hypotheses about relationships, and observe the range of consequences associated with changes. Learners receive feedback based upon their manipulations of objects or elements in a learning environment, thereby enriching their understanding by active construction rather than simple assimilation.

Flexibility

Perhaps the greatest improvement has been in the diversity of applications—both in terms of lesson content and pedagogical orientation. Whereas early systems emphasized largely didactic, knowledge-centered approaches, influenced largely by behavioral approaches to instruction, recent activities have underscored the flexibility of emerging technologies. Diverse projects ranging from enabling constructivist views of middle school science (Tobin & Dawson, 1992), to building conceptual webs between and among authors in literature (Yankelovich, Hann, Meyrowitz, & Drucker, 1988), to simulating admissions and treatment plans for emergency room patients (Harless, 1986) have been reported. Designers espousing behavioral, cognitive, Piagetian, and constructivist pedagogical orientations have created exemplary learning systems featuring emerging technologies. In short, emerging technologies have shed the image of being relevant only for particular content or pedagogical orientations. They have become integral to the efforts of professionals with diverse views on the nature of learning and instruction.

A Conceptual Framework for Feedback Design

The overall framework for effective feedback centers on three lesson design foundations: psychological, technological, and pedagogical (Hannafin, 1989). A summary of this framework is shown in Table 11.2. Psychological foundations are based in learning theory and research, and emphasize the role of the individual in processing inputs, organizing and restructuring knowledge, and generating responses. Technological foundations focus on the capabilities of the hardware itself, the various devices

Lesson Design Foundation	Factors	Feedback Issues
Psychological	Processing Req'ts	How complex is the learning task, skills, or knowledge?
		How will students select and organize important info?
		How can knowledge be integrated with existing knowledge?
	Prior Knowledge	How can existing knowledge be employed to support new learning?
		How familiar is the individual with related concepts?
		How much lesson control can be given over?
		What kinds of adaptations can be incorporated in feedback design?
	Active Processing	How can feedback increase the quantity and quality of lesson processing?
		How can feedback engage the learners?
		What activities will help to vary how the lesson will be experienced?
	Encoding Strength	How does to-be-learned content relate to familiar?
		How sophisticated are learners in the domain?
		How can/should feedback be differentiated to help learners understand?
Technological	I/O Capabilities	How can/will the lesson be presented?
		What degree of image fidelity is possible?
		What unique capabilities are available for feedback?
	Symbol Manipulation	How can symbols be manipulated to amplify feedback value?
		Can symbols be controlled by student as well as designer?
	Management	Can the system "understand" human-like communication?
		Can the system "remember" student responses and paths?
		Can the system be "opened up" for student-centered query?
Pedagogical	Learner	How familiar are learners with the system employed?
		How motivated are they to perform in the lesson?
		How independently will they likely operate?
	Task	How complex is the learning task?
		Is sequence an important or necessary concern?
		Is reality/fidelity important in depicting consequences?
	Setting	What are the available resources? constraints?
		How will lesson fit within overall strategy?
		How much time is available for completion of lesson?

Table 11.2. Framework for feedback design.

available for providing output, receiving input, and processing appropriately the myriad of program code, data, and so forth. Pedagogical foundations are rooted in beliefs about how to organize lesson knowledge, to sequence lesson activities, and to support the learner in acquiring knowledge.

The goal of this framework, applied to feedback, is to address educational requirements while concurrently optimizing the capabilities of both learners and available technology. In this section, we describe the feedback implications for emerging technologies within this framework.

Psychological Foundations

A myriad of psychological factors warrant consideration, most of which cannot be presented in this chapter. However, several are especially relevant to the design of feedback: processing requirements, the role of prior knowledge, the role of active processing, and strength encoding.

Processing Requirements. The nature of the learning task and the manner in which learners make sense of the available stimuli influence directly the processing requirements of the learning task. Learners must select important information, organize relationships among lesson concepts, integrate new with existing knowledge, and restructure understanding accordingly (Hooper & Hannafin, 1991). Factors such as the amount of instruction, the conceptual density of information presented, the amount of detail available, and input from multiple modalities all influence the cognitive load associated with learning.

As suggested previously, emerging technologies vastly expand the number and type of resources available to support learning. One role for feedback, therefore, is to assist in metering the flow of information to ensure appropriate lesson pacing. This is accomplished, in some cases, by routinely embedding response-differentiated feedback to ensure that learners maintain satisfactory progress of essential lesson concepts. In other cases, the systems can assist the learner in constructing representations of knowledge (Scardamalia *et al.*, 1989), adapting presentations according to ongoing indicators of lesson success (Tennyson, 1984), or advising learners as to methods for speeding up or slowing down lesson rate (Ross, 1984).

Role of Prior Knowledge. Perhaps no learner variable influences learning as much as prior knowledge (Ausubel, 1968). Individuals who possess significantly related prior knowledge generally make better choices, draw conclusions more rapidly, and work faster than those with limited related prior knowledge. Such individuals have acquired not only a reserve of meaningful formal knowledge, but also important insights and associations. Obviously, not everyone will possess such knowledge.

Ideally, feedback will reflect differences in related prior knowledge. Novices likely benefit most from feedback that helps to simplify and clarify; experts likely profit most from feedback that promotes more evaluative, deeper processing. Emerging technologies permit individual differences in related prior knowledge to be accommodated by adapting the nature and type of feedback provided on a case-by-case basis. Novices, for example, might receive only direct visual feedback related to improper implantation of blood metering devices (e.g., reversal of valve, faulty suturing), since they lack the background knowledge needed to make sense of less apparent symptoms. Individuals with extensive background knowledge in related surgical procedures, on the other hand, can receive complex feedback illustrating secondary consequences (e.g., dizziness, stroke) due to their greater capacity to integrate new with existing related knowledge.

Role of Active Processing. Learners need to be actively engaged in learning. The mental effort learners exert is influenced directly by perceptions of the ease or difficulty of a given medium. Learners try harder using a medium they perceive as challenging than one they perceive as "easy" (Salomon, 1984). Instruction must engage the learners—procedurally, substantively, and affectively—if learners are to process knowledge purposefully. Further, they need to process knowledge purposefully if they are to fully integrate and reconstruct knowledge. Surface-level knowledge is rarely desired in most settings, yet feedback often fails to deepen processing of important concepts.

Emerging technologies are especially useful in directing, supporting, or otherwise facilitating engagement. Apart from the obvious capacity to elicit and manage responses, learning systems can encourage learners to generate hypotheses about relationships, make and test predictions, and otherwise manipulate directly the lesson content. Feedback, in this context, emphasizes elaboration—both supplied and generated by the learner—rather than simple confirmation. Learners actively mediate their understanding, and feedback is designed accordingly.

Strength of Encoding. Clearly, the extent to which lesson content is understood influences the retrievability and utility of knowledge (Klatzky, 1978). Understanding exists along a continuum ranging from minimal and superficial (novice knowledge) through authoritative and in-depth (expert knowledge). We have real potential to strengthen encoding across the full range of this continumm, but it is rarely exploited. Learning systems often emphasize feedback activities more akin to basic knowledge acquisition than to deepened understanding.

For novices, learning can be strengthened via feedback that relates new concepts to parallel concepts already known. For naive learners, for example, learning the human digestive systems might be a formidable task. There are levels of complexity that will either support or hamper the novice in understanding initial concepts. Presenting the metaphor of plumbing within a home and providing related feedback accordingly, however, provides a familiar framework for building basic understanding. Though the sophistication of this early learning might be modest, it is strengthened substantially by anchoring new within familiar concepts (Cognition and Technology Group at Vanderbilt, 1990, 1991, 1992).

At sophisticated levels, where advanced expertise is important, the complex nuances of the concepts are often critical. It becomes necessary to develop conditional knowledge rather than simplistic understandings. Feedback at this level needs to reflect important, often subtle distinctions. The plumbing metaphor might be of little value; in fact, it might actually promote oversimplification (Spiro *et al.*, 1991). Instead, systems that allow the learner to vary simultaneously aspects of the digestive system and examine via feedback the interplay among multiple factors might be of substantially greater value.

Technological Foundations

Hardware capabilities effectively define the "outer limits" of what is possible from a purely technological perspective. In certain cases, such as in reasoning, humans far exceed technological capabilities. In many cases, however, technological capabilities far exceed our meager human capacity to process. The issue, then, is how not only to understand the outer limits of technological capabilities, but also how best to utilize them. We emphasize three primary capabilities: input (response)-output (presentation), symbol manipulation, and management.

Input-Output Capabilities. Options for obtaining input have grown dramatically. Initially, the emphasis in computer-based learning was on textual input, comprising single letter or one- to two-word typed responses. More recently, however, devices such as the touchscreen, joystick, and mouse have supported direct responses as well as manipulation. With the advent of voice recognition technology, though painfully slow to evolve, users are able to communicate with the computer orally (though the range of computer "understanding" is clearly restricted).

On the output side, the varied symbols supported by emerging technologies are remarkable. Lessons that were historically text-based can include spoken words (e.g., digitized or synthesized), visual symbols (e.g., motion and still pictures, computer graphics, animation), and tactile (e.g., resistance, motion) elements. Instructional stimuli (including feedback) can be readily depicted to reflect the precision and detail warranted for feedback for a given task.

Symbol Manipulation. Apart from diversity in input-output symbols, we have evolved the capability to manipulate dynamically the symbols themselves. We can alter graphics dynamically, zoom to relevant features, superimpose images and symbols, construct phenomena, and organize computer responses dynamically within the computer itself. We can mimic a host of tactile sensations, and vary them in real time as circumstances evolve.

The implications for feedback are many. It is possible for children to hear the stories they write, and mix iconic and textual symbols through software such as *Story Writer*, thereby increasing the sensory stimulation associated with the writing process. Learners can also experience the physical sensation of G-force via flight simulators (Waag, 1981), mix potentially dangerous chemicals via interactive videodisc (Smith, Jones, & Waugh, 1986), or design, implement, and monitor ongoing simulated medical treatment plans using hypermedia (Harless, 1986). Clearly, the capacity to manipulate symbols provides extraordinary potential for feedback design.

Management. Though significant headway has yet to be made with regard to natural language processing (both in spoken and written forms), many other aspects have been improved greatly. Increasingly, the technology's capacity to manage hitherto troublesome aspects of instruction have been likewise improved. Systems now readily support user-designated (learner control) lesson paths, sometimes providing adaptive features which limit the confusion encountered in minimally structured systems. In addition, developments in connectivity have revolutionized our notions of emerging technologies. We can connect various computing devices, permitting communication between and among computers of various size, purpose, and sophistication. We can also manage information contained in other electronic resources in ways that have literally redefined notions of computerized access. It is no longer essential to convert all knowledge into computer code—a prospect that daunted even the most optimistic of computer advocates. We can now access available knowledge electronically via computers, both simplifying and extending the retrievability of extant knowledge.

Consider a few examples of how the management capabilities of emerging technologies have influenced our conceptions of feedback. Students can now pursue electronically, on demand and at the "teachable moment," relationships among literary themes. Yankelovich *et al.* (1988) developed a hyptertext system known as *Dickens Web*, within which learners both examine and build complex interrelationships among various themes in Dickens' writing. They can also examine as well as establish relationships to other authors of the period, as well as to authors who influenced, or were influenced by Dickens' work. The task remains literary and largely textual in nature, but the vehicles available for stimulating inquiry are vastly changed. Feedback, in such a system, is largely in response to student queries for related knowledge.

Pedagogical Foundations

Pedagogical factors are those typically identified during needs assessment or front-end analysis. They establish, in a very pragmatic sense, how the resources and constraints of a given environment influence the eventual design. They can be grouped into three categories: learner, task, and setting.

Learner. Differences in ability, motivation, and background are known to influence learning, but are often difficult to accommodate in non-computer learning environments. The goal of adapting to individual differences has been at the core of the computer-based learning movement. In some cases, the adaptations have been minimal and of little consequence; in others, the adaptations have been significant, resulting in both quantitative and qualitative improvements in learning.

A number of examples of noteworthy adaptivity have been reported. Tennyson's (1984) work emphasized adaptations of presentation content and rate, guidance and advice, and lesson sequence based on an algorithm which accounted for both current and historic indicators of learner performance. Ross (1984), on the other hand, emphasized adaptive methods that incorporated individual student data into mathematics lesson shells. Such adaptations increase the personal relevance of lesson content, making the learning more meaningful.

Task. There exists a wealth of research and theory indicating that task factors influence how instruction should be designed. Task considerations emphasize factors such as the nature of the task (e.g., verbal information, procedures, etc.), presumed hierarchical relationships, and conceptual density. In some cases, task variability can be accommodated by adapting lesson sequences and content; in others, the feedback activities themselves need to be differentiated.

Feedback related to appropriate medical procedures, such as cardiopulmonary resuscitation (CPR), is quite distinct from feedback on a verbal information task such as the learning of the parts of the circulatory system. In one case, a series of well-defined steps must be followed; in the other, integration with related knowledge might be desired. Emerging technologies permit the design of feedback with distinctive attributes, both in the nature of the accompanying activities and in the relative consequences. Inaccurate or poorly implemented procedures can cause further injury or death, which can be simulated in real-time via computer-managed CPR mannequins. Fidelity, in both temporal and tactile senses, is important for the resulting feedback.

Setting. Examination of the implementation setting(s) reveals important information in the design of feedback. Apart from important concerns such as hardware configurations and compatibility, we gain a sense for the "fit" of instructional units and modules within real-life learning settings. We acquire notions about how technology is perceived and used, which aspects of a project are most valued, and how such projects will be implemented in practice. Analysis of the setting, in effect, helps to clarify the context in which our efforts will be placed and the "climate" within which learning systems will operate.

This is perhaps most evident in projects that call for significant restructuring of teaching methods. Settings where "live" teachers have been employed during instruction or where the content is perceived as "human" content, for example, may require feedback of a more familiar nature. Computerized counseling and guidance systems, for example, often frustrate users by their abruptness and directness. Users may be accustomed to asking questions, or wanting more information of one type than another; systems must capture the essence of the settings in which they will be installed.

Emerging Technologies and Feedback Design

Prior to the emergence of contemporary technologies, feedback was conceptualized largely as single-stimulus and domain-specific (Newell, 1974; Trowbridge & Carson, 1932). In the past, typical feedback ranged from textual statements, to modeling of correct procedures, to presentation of graphical examples/non-examples (Kulhavy, 1977). Emerging technologies support not only these applications, but also the design of multisensory elaborate feedback.

Three types of feedback will be discussed: task, strategic, and affective, each of which has several variations.

Task Feedback

Task-based feedback emphasizes information and activities that clarify or reinforce aspects of the learning task itself. Task feedback may be consequential, contextually-referenced, content, or sensory.

Consequential feedback. Consequential feedback is used to clarify cause and effect relationships between learner actions and the associated implications. In medical education, the decision to render treatment to a trauma victim, for example, requires consideration of the implications of possible alternatives. Each may have particular consequences in isolation, and collectively they might have further implications. The role of consequential feedback is to amplify key causal relationships involved in such a decision.

RESUSCI-ANNIE, a computer-based CPR simulator, and HARVEY, a computer-based cardiac stimulator (Gordon, 1981) are examples from medical education where emerging technologies provide consequential feedback to assist learners in clarifying the relationships between actions and consequences. In these simulations, feedback is provided through a computer-mediated mannequin. In the CPR simulator, for instance, the learner hears the patient's obstructed breathing, sees the effects of treatment or procedures on the patient, and feels the mannequin's lungs fill with oxygen as the student administers CPR. The computerized mannequins are effective because the feedback is consistent with the consequences of treatment, diagnoses, and intervention procedures.

Contextual feedback. Contextual feedback illustrates implications of learner responses, actions, or choices in a relevant context. It provides credible and believable information or reactions within a situation closely aligned with a particular learning task or goal. The role of contextual feedback is to establish relationships between the content or concepts under study and the circumstances in which the content is to be internalized by the student.

During the past 20 years, business education programs have used various simulations to study the complexities of management training. Many of the newer computer-based simulations focus on decision-making skills (Thorton & Cleaveland, 1990), management strategies (Prohaska & Frank, 1990), leadership, quality decision making, negotiation style, and evaluation of management potential. The simulations themselves have expanded from simple role-playing scenarios to highly complex high-fidelity activities where both the content and context of learning are emphasized. Thorton and Cleaveland (1990) suggest a hierarchy of simulations where student response requirements are intensified by varying both the evolving conditions and contextual feedback provided. For example, simple scenarios call for the demonstration of simple skills (e.g., direct communication, timely decisions), whereas complex simulations require learners to develop decision-making strategies and understand the effects in relation to an entire organization.

Content feedback. This type of feedback is perhaps the most commonly used in learning settings. Content feedback supports the acquisition of particular knowledge presented within a given lesson or module. The focus is largely on building the verbal information or intellectual skills requisite to a well-articulated knowledge base.

Examples vary from feedback given in simple computer-based drills to more sophisticated applications where textual feedback is combined with audio and visual feedback. For example, in the *Teacher Survival Skills* interactive videodisc (Caswell, 1989), content feedback is provided by both knowledge of correct response and through "live" models. In the *Employ-*

ability Skills videodisc series (Tribble-MacDonald, 1989), students are presented information on effective interviewing techniques, appropriate business apparel, and social behavior. Students practice this information and receive feedback regarding correct answers, while simultaneously receiving additional vicarious models of correct behaviors and speech. These lessons converge on specific sets knowledge and information.

Sensory feedback. Sensory feedback supplies physical consequences— often in intense, vivid forms—to the learner. Typically, this is provided in circumstances emphasizing relevant psychomotor or related events, such as the physical sensations associated with a particular learning task. Sensory feedback that is integral to the learning task simulates realistic sensations, including visual, aural, tactical, and olfactory stimulation.

Intensive sensory stimulation can be a powerful feedback tool, especially when learning task requirements are complex (Norman *et al.*, 1985; Thorton & Cleaveland, 1990; Wehrenberg, 1986). For example, in many flight-training simulators, sensory feedback is designed to simulate real-life consequences of pilot decisions and cockpit crew interactions (Ayres *et al.*, 1984; Semple *et al.*, 1981; Waag, 1981; Wehrenberg, 1986). Pilots and flight crews participate in various flight scenarios where immediate, consequential, and contextually-based feedback directly relate to their flight decisions. Sensory feedback is provided via variations in visual, verbal, and tactile sensations, such as realistic noises, turbulence, conversations between crew and ground support, and real-time three-dimensional cockpit motion.

Strategic Feedback

Strategic feedback is also a powerful feedback tool (Abrahamson, Denson, & Wolf, 1969; Gordon, 1981; Hansen, 1990; Norman *et al.*, 1985; Shortliffe, 1976). Strategic feedback often emphasizes the learner's lesson decision making. Strategic feedback includes diagnostic-prescriptive, performance, management, and process feedback.

Diagnostic-prescriptive feedback. Diagnostic-prescriptive feedback allows the learner to determine systemic trends in performance and prescribe further action. Such feedback might include analyses of error patterns, identification of systematic versus random errors, and recommendations for ameliorating deficiencies.

Medical interns, for example, use trauma unit simulators covering such topics as shotgun wounds to the abdomen, stab wounds, and chest trauma. These multimedia simulations are used to hone emergency room medical and decision-making skills. Often interns receive feedback via simulated medical apparatus or by accessing simulated medial reports and data to assess a patient's condition. Interns invoke strategic feedback from on-line experts who "consult" on diagnosis, dosage, and type of medicine to be administered, and consult regarding required medical procedures.

Performance feedback. Performance can be described using variables such as time on task, unit or overall score, performance rank within class by task, and so forth. As such, it provides no information related to the content per se. Instead, the role of performance feedback is to characterize the individual's status on some criterion dimension or dimensions which can be used metacognitively by learners to make choices or invoke individual strategies.

Performance feedback is often provided at the end of computerized lessons in the form of lesson summaries. Students might be advised of the total number of correct and incorrect responses and the criteria for successful performance. Students might then be advised as to recommended actions or alternatives, such as repeating particular sections or which units to select next.

Management feedback. Management feedback emphasizes tactical information related to the learner's use of lesson features and components. In some cases, the management feedback informs learners as to lesson sections completed, performance history during, lessons completed, or objectives mastered.

Management feedback may also assist learners in locating particular information in a comprehensive learning system or providing advice on how a learning task might be approached. Again, however, the role is to provide supporting tactical information versus content knowledge.

Intermedia (Yankelovich *et al.*, 1988) provides hypermedia links for students among literary resources. This assists students in finding, reading, analyzing, and understanding literary resources. Feedback is provided by expediting the processes of locating resources on the system, developing tactical knowledge of system navigation, and allowing users to view knowledge "webs" of others to share opinions or collaboratively solve problems.

Process feedback. Process feedback is information that relates to learner decision making or logic. The focus is to develop supporting methods or strategies to be used by the learner. In some cases, process feedback provides information that might help students better utilize the components of a lesson, examine effective or faulty methods and alternatives, or to the review the methods of experts.

One variety of process feedback focuses on lesson navigation. Navigational feedback is often provided to help students to maneuver through vast amounts of information, resources, tools, and available options. Navigational feedback might take the form of a lesson map showing completed units or sections, guidance as to recommended lesson sequences, or advice about lesson activities that provide related information.

Affective Feedback

Affective feedback engages learners primarily through eliciting, then sustaining, interest and engagement. Unlike other forms, motivational feedback seeks to influence beliefs, willingness to participate, and interest in engaging the lesson content.

A striking example of affective feedback is provided in an interactive videodisc system emphasizing the complexities in ethics and morality, titled *"A Right to Die? The Case of Dax Cowart"* (Covey, 1990). Using actual footage and interviews, a severe burn victim expresses the desire to be permitted to die rather than to exist in a state of prolonged agony. His treatments are expensive and his injuries largely irreparable, yet he is in apparent control of his mental faculties. Learners are moved through a progression of treatments where his pain is clearly evident, as well as interviews with family, friends, and medical personnel. Varied perspectives are presented, but the learner is affectively engaged through both graphic depiction of the circumstances and the complexity of the crisis.

Summary

The range of emerging technology feedback applications that can be supported is potentially overwhelming. The decision to integrate these applications into instruction is also a significant one. Designers must consider how, when, and why emerging technologies can be used to promote meaningful learning in a given learning task.

Implications for Practitioners

Utilize the feedback capabilities of emerging technologies selectively to optimize the individual's capacity to process information and activities. Overstimulation is a common problem associated with emerging instructional technologies. If the purposes of application are entertainment-related, then perhaps massive stimulation is warranted. If, however, the purposes are learning-related, then the capabilities must be utilized selectively in order to amplify particular aspects, information, and activities. Selectivity must be based upon the nature and processing requirements of the learning task, not simply the available capabilities of the technology.

Design feedback activities that parallel the features, attributes, and consequences of the learning context when such activities and features are integral to the learning task. One of the principal advantages of emerging technologies is the ability to represent, or simulate, performance contexts in more or less real form. This is true both for presentation and interaction activities. It is possible to create learning environments that closely approximate the physical, psychomotor, and emotional demands and attributes of actual performance settings. In many cases it is unnecessary to strive for high-fidelity, high-realism activities; in others, however, it is essential. Where important, utilize the capabilities to approximate the learning context.

In tasks where multiple, simultaneous consequences are naturally embedded, utilize emerging technologies to provide concurrent, but differentiated, feedback. In many complex learning environments, feedback is both multidimensional and concurrent. When executing a landing in a flight simulator, for example, it is of little use to simply indicate that the airplane has crashed or landed successfully, when the various dimensions of performance are not identified. It is possible, for example, that crashes occurred due to a severe angle of approach. Successful landings might have resulted from a combination of bad decisions that unintentionally self-corrected the aircraft. It is important that the aggregate consequences across various dimensions be provided, but it is also important that the various factors contributing to the feedback are effectively isolated. This will both help the learner to identify consequences of individual critical actions and permit the learner to examine multiple adjustments dynamically.

Where physical sensation or affective arousal are important, elevate the sensory aspects of feedback. In many learning settings, it is important that strong messages accompany encoding. Reactions to physical (e.g., turbulence) as well as emotional (e.g., panic surrounding a natural disaster) sensations mediate how well individuals are able to respond in crisis settings. These sensations invoke conditions of performance that are often more critical than simple knowledge of proper responses. Properly designed feedback allows learners to develop both the sensory as well as intellectual capacities to respond.

In cases where image fidelity or realism are integral, utilize emerging technologies to elevate feedback acuity. Much of what must be learned can be successfully accomplished through very portable, low-cost media such as pamphlets and workbooks. Often, image fidelity and resolution are comparatively unimportant, and certainly do not warrant the cost and sophistication of elaborate learning systems. On the other hand, at times it is essential that images be represented precisely. Videodiscs depicting microsurgery simulations, where various lesions are made among clusters of similar objects, require that high-fidelity images be provided. Feedback reflecting true aspects of blood flow and brain trauma, for example, must be represented in ways that closely approximate their live surgery counterparts.

During initial learning, simplify feedback to ease the decoding-encoding burden of the learner; during advanced learning, design feedback

which approximates task complexity and elicits both complex mental processes and physical behaviors. Feedback must be differentiated according to the learner's facility with lesson content. Principal among these concerns is the learner's related prior knowledge. Where little background exists, elaborate responses and feedback do little to clarify the nature of the various components to be learned. Simple response requirements and focused feedback are likely to be more readily understood and enable the learner to acquire foundation knowledge for more sophisticated learning and feedback.

Do not underestimate the motivational impact of feedback via emerging technologies, but do not rely on motivation to ensure lesson success. Initially, learners often react positively to the uniqueness and sophistication of emerging technologies. They will frequently explore, attempt tasks that are not fully understood, and attribute confusion to their limited understanding rather than to limitations in the learning environment itself. They are often eager to engage new content and persist in their learning in the near term. However, novelty invariably wanes. Activities that are inherently confusing and unclear will be perceived as such; users will attribute shortcomings to the technology rather than to themselves. The moral is that, even with emerging, high-profile technologies, "good instruction, bad instruction" distinctions hold. Emerging technologies can do impressive things to elicit and maintain attention and motivation, but these capabilities must be understood and applied sensibly if they are to support learning.

References

Ausubel, D. P. (1968). *Educational psychology: A cognitive view.* New York: Holt, Rinehart, & Winston.

Abrahamson, S. Denson, J. S., & Wolf, R. M. (1969). Effectiveness of simulators in training anesthesia residents. *Journal of Medical Education, 44,* 515–518.

Ayres, R., Hays, R., Singer, M. J., & Heinicke, M. (1984). *An annotated bibliography of abstracts on the use of simulators in technical training.* Research Product Number 84–21, U.S. Army Research Institute, Alexandria, VA.

Caswell, D. (1989). Surviving day one. [interactive video program] *Florida Vocational Journal, 14*(6), 14.

Clark, R. E. (1983). Research on student thought processes during computer-based instruction. *Journal of Instructional Development, 7*(3), 2–5.

Cognition and Technology Group at Vanderbilt (1990). Anchored instruction and its relationship to situated cognition. *Educational Researcher, 19*(6), 2–10.

Cognition and Technology Group at Vanderbilt (1991). Technology and the design of generative learning environments. *Educational Technology, 31*(5), 34–40.

Cognition and Technology Group at Vanderbilt (in press). The Jasper Experiment:

An exploration of issues in learning and instructional design. *Educational Technology Research and Development, 40*(1), 65–80.

Cooper, R. (1990) From fun and game to effective learning. *CBT Directions, 3*(10), 12–17.

Covey, P. (1990, April). *A right to die? The case of Dax Cowart.* Presented at the Annual Meeting of the American Educational Research Association, Boston.

Crowder, N. (1963). The rationale of intrinsic programming. *Programmed Instruction,* (1), 3–6.

Ellson, D., Barber, L., Engle, T., & Kampwerth, L. (1965). Programmed tutoring: A teaching aid and a research tool. *Reading Research Quarterly, 1,* 77–127.

Engle, D., & Campbell-Bonar, K. (1989). Using videodiscs in teacher education: Preparing effective classroom managers. *Canadian Journal of Educational Communication, 18*(3), 221–228.

Fuller, R. G. (1984). The Tacoma Narrows Bridge videodisc: A personal history (pp. 87–92). In R. Daynes & B. Butler (Eds.), *The videodisc book: A guide and directory.* New York: John Wiley & Sons.

Gagné, E. D. (1985). *The cognitive psychology of school learning.* Boston: Little, Brown.

Gordon, M. (1981). HARVEY: The cardiology simulator. *Journal of Practice, 13,* 353–357.

Hannafin, M. J. (1992). Emerging technologies, ISD, and learning environments: Critical perspectives. *Educational Technology Research and Development, 40*(1), 49–64.

Hannafin, M. J. (1989). Interaction strategies and emerging instructional technologies: Psychological perspectives. *Canadian Journal of Educational Communication, 18*(3), 167–180.

Hannafin, M. J., & Rieber, L. P. (1989a). Psychological foundations of instructional design for emerging computer-based instructional technologies: Part I. *Educational Technology Research and Development, 37*(2), 91–101.

Hannafin, M. J., & Rieber, L. P. (1989b). Psychological foundations of instructional design for emerging computer-based instructional technologies: Part II. *Educational Technology Research and Development, 37*(2), 102–114.

Hansen, J. (1990). *A trauma room simulator for emergency room physicians.* Paper presented at SALT Conference, Fall, 1990.

Harless, W. (1986). An interactive videodisc drama: The case of Frank Hall. *Journal of Computer-Based Instruction, 13,* 113–116.

Hooper, S., & Hannafin, M. J. (1991). Psychological perspectives on emerging instructional technologies: A critical analysis. *Educational Psychologist, 26,* 69–95.

Keller, F. (1974). Ten years of personalized instruction. *Teaching of Psychology, 1,* 4–9.

Klatzky, R. (1978). *Human memory* (2nd ed.). San Francisco: Freeman.

Kulhavy, R. (1977). Feedback in written instruction. *Review of Educational Research, 47,* 211–232.

Newell, K. M. (1974). Knowledge of results and motor learning. *Journal of Motor Behavior, 6,* 235–244.

Norman, G. R., Muzzin, L. J., Williams, R. G., & Swanson, D. B. (1985). Simulations in health science education. *Journal of Instructional Development, 8*(1), 11–17.

Paske, R. (1990). Hypermedia: A progress report (Part 3): CD-ROM, CD-I, DVI, etc. *T.H.E. Journal, 17*(9), 93–97.

Perkins, D. (1991). Technology meets constructivism: Do they make a marriage? *Educational Technology, 31*(5), 18–23.

Phillipo, J. (1988). An educator's guide to interactive videodisc programs. *Electronic Learning*, 70–75.

Pressey, S. L. (1926). A simple apparatus which gives test and scores—and teaches. *School and Society, 23*, 373–376.

Prohaska, C. R., & Frank, E. J. (1990). Using simulations to investigate management decision making. *Simulation and Gaming, 21*(1), 48–58.

Ross, S. (1984). Matching the lesson to the student: Alternative adaptive designs for individualized learning systems. *Journal of Computer-Based Instruction, 11*, 42–48.

Rubin, H., Geller, J., & Hanks, J. (1977). Computer simulations as a teaching tool in biology. *Journal of Computer-Based Instruction, 3*(3), 91–96.

Salomon, G. (1984). Television is "easy" and print is "tough": The differential investment of mental effort in learning as a function of perceptions and attributions. *Journal of Educational Psychology, 76*, 647–658.

Scardamalia, M., Bereiter, C., McLean, R.S., Swallow, J., & Woodruff, E. (1989). Computer-supported intentional learning environments. *Journal of Educational Computing Research, 5*(1), 51–68.

Schimmel, B. (1988). Providing meaningful feedback in courseware. In D. H. Jonassen (Ed.), *Instructional designs for microcomputer courseware* (pp. 183–196). Hillsdale: NJ: Lawrence Erlbaum Associates.

Semple, C.A., Hennessey, R.T., Sanders, M., Bross, B.K., Beith, B.H., & McCauley, M.E. (1981). *Aircrew training device fidelity features.* AFHRL-TR-80-36. Brooks AFB, TX: Air Force Human Resources Laboratory.

Shortliffe, E. H. (1976). *Computer-based medical consultations: MYCIN.* New York: Elsevier.

Skinner, B. F. (1954). The science of learning and the art of teaching. *Harvard Educational Review, 24*, 86–97.

Smith, S., Jones, L., & Waugh, M. (1986). *Journal of Computer-Based Instruction, 13*(4) 117–121.

Spiro, R., Feltovich, P., Jacobson, M., & Coulson, R. (1991). Cognitive flexibility, constructivism, and hypertext: Random access instruction for advanced knowledge acquisition in ill-structured domains. *Educational Technology, 31*(5), 24–33.

Tennyson, R. (1984). Application of artificial intelligence methods to computer-based instructional design: The Minnesota Adaptive Instructional System. *Journal of Instructional Development, 7*(4), 17–22.

Thorton, G. C., & Cleaveland, J. N. (1990). Developing managerial talent through simulation. *American Psychologist*, February, 190–199.

Tobias, S. (1991). Adapting instruction to individual differences among students. *Educational Psychologist, 16*, 111–120.

Tobin, K. G., & Dawson, G. (in press). Constructivism: A framework for science curriculum. *Educational Technology Research and Development, 40*(1), 81–92.

Tribble-MacDonald, L. (1989). Laserdisc: One solution to the problem of adult literacy: A closer look at available hardware and generic software. *Instructional Delivery Systems, 2*(5), 14–18.

Trowbridge, M.H., & Carson, H. (1932). An experimental study of Thorndike's theory of learning. *Journal of General Psychology, 7,* 245–258.

Waag, W. L. (1981). *Training effectiveness of visual and motion simulation* (AFHRL-TR-79-7). Brooks AFB, TX: Air Force Systems Command.

Wehrenberg, S. B. (1986). Simulation: Capturing the experience of the real thing. *Personal Journal, 65*(4), 101–103.

Yankelovich, N., Haan, B. J., Meyrowitz, N. K., & Drucker, S. M. (1988). Intermedia: The concept and the construction of a seamless information environment. *Computer, 21*(1), 81–96.

Chapter Twelve

Feedforward

DeLayne R. Hudspeth
The University of Texas

Introduction

The phenomenon described by General Systems Theory, using such terms as input, process, output, boundaries, and homeostasis, provides us with expectations of any open system. Because of the isomorphic nature of systems, we can identify the flow of energy into, through, and out of an assemblage of functions that serves some defined purpose. Feedforward is one of the generalized aspects of systems that has received little theoretical attention even though, like many system functions, the use of feedforward techniques may seem to be common sense, once implemented.

Feedforward, like feedback, relates to the flow of material or energy within a system that constitutes the essential purpose of the system. We discuss feedstock when fattening cattle or producing steel. Or, we state that feeder roads provide access routes for highway transportation systems. The concept of *feed* as input refers to the materials or energy being acted upon for which the system was designed, and is therefore functionally different from other forms of input, such as might be used for operation or maintenance of the system.

This chapter will first describe and contrast the operational principles of feedforward (FF) and feedback (FB) as simple system functions, describe the conditions needed to use these, and then discuss the merits and problems of combining both functions. This discussion draws upon a wide range of system types, including learning systems. The issue of systematic research for the design of learning systems which separate feedback from feedforward is discussed. Finally, recommendations for research are out-lined.

Theoretical Overview

Feedback

From a theoretical perspective feedback is a process whereby we take part of the *feed* (or input) which has been processed by a system to become output and compare this output to system standards. This comparison creates an information base that serves either to accept the output or to create an information flow which loops back to the input for the purpose of changing the input. For example, Considine (1989) defines feedback as ". . . the transfer of energy from the output to the input of a system, or from one part of a system to another in a direction opposite to the main flow of energy" (p. 1115). When discussing feedback as a basic control principle, Murrill (1981) notes the value of feedback in that "The beauty of feedback control is that the designer does not need to know in advance exactly what disturbances will affect the process and, in addition, the designer does not need to know specific quantitative relationships between these disturbances and their ultimate effects on the controlled variables" (p. 15).

Within instructional settings, this fundamental principle can be illustrated by imagining a learner who is engaged in drill and practice with flash cards to learn 10 new words. Feedback control is provided by flipping a card to see if the correct word is recalled. The designer of this system need not know what might cause the mind to wander and the person to become distracted from this memory task.

Systems which rely on feedback loops as the primary means of error correction or quality control function best when the range of input is within narrow standards. Excessive fluctuation in the characteristic of the input either reduces the efficiency of the system or causes it to malfunction. In the case of the above example, entry reading skill, motivation, and time available for study are presumed to be much the same for all learners as-signed to use the flash cards.

Feedforward

Feedforward is the process whereby we assess the characteristics of the feedstock *before* it enters the system. This information serves to ascertain whether feedstock should enter the system (so that the input feed variations do not exceed what the system can handle) and serves to provide a feed-forward loop to cause the system to configure itself to meet variable input requirements. Considine (1989) notes that feedforward control is "an auto-matic control action in which information concerning one or more conditions that can disturb the controlled variable [input] is converted into corrective [system] action to minimize deviations of the controlled variable" (p. 1118). Parker (1984) defines feedforward control more simply as "Process control in which changes are detected at the process input and an anticipating correction signal is applied before process output is affected" (p. 356). In discussion of feedforward, Murrill (1981) notes:

> Feedforward control is much different in concept than feedback control. . . . Feedback control worked to eliminate errors but feedforward control operates to prevent errors from occurring in the first place. The appeal of feedforward control is obvious. Feedforward control does escalate tremendously, however, the requirements of the practitioner. (p. 16)

Systems which rely primarily on feedforward as a means of quality output have two generalizable characteristics. First, the feedstock is valued or judged essential to the function of the supra-system. (For example: water cooled to a given temperature in a cooling stack is essential for the operation of a plant.) Second, well-defined relationships are known about the nature of the feedstock and the operation of the system. Or, stated in different terms, the qualities of feed input that affect output are known and can be measured, and this data can be used by the operation of the system to achieve output standards.

Summary of Theoretical Overview

In summary, the theories of feedback and feedforward both assume that a system receives input that is transformed by the system to become output. Feedback is the process of output error detection which collects information about output, to either reject output or to provide a feedback loop which serves the purpose of re-processing input so that it meets system output standards. In contrast, feedforward assesses input before it enters the system or a sub-system to determine if the input is within the limits for which the system was designed. If input is appropriate, then assessment information creates a feedforward loop to cause the system to adapt to input characteristics.

Generally, systems which rely primarily on feedback are comparatively easy to construct and efficient to operate, and provide consistent output as long as the feed input remains homogeneous and little value is placed on discards. Systems which rely on feedforward are more difficult to construct, because well-defined relationships between input and system operation must be known, input must be monitored, and the system must be able to act on this data. Feedforward-based systems typically place high value on whatever is being processed, which subsequently results in investment of dynamic systems designed to process systematically variable input.

Problems of Feedback Research

Because the rest of this book is devoted to feedback, relatively little discussion is provided in this chapter about the specific role and function that feedback plays in learning systems. Suffice it to note that one difficulty in delineating the principles of feedback is that relatively few authors carefully define this function, even when it is the basis for their own research. For example, between 1980 and 1985, Tsai reviewed 16 articles on feedback in six major journals, and found that "In general, the term feedback was not specifically defined in the reviewed studies" (p. 7). In discussing the dynamics of feedback in training, Kowitz and Smith (1985) point out that, although feedback is frequently treated as an integral part of every training program, ". . . workable definitions and specifications of feedback are rare" (p. 4).

Even in many instructional design texts, discussion of how to provide feedback, which would seem to be an essential element of planning instruction, is treated in a dilatory fashion. For instance, Gagné, Briggs, and Wager (1988) provide two paragraphs, which state that ". . . as a minimum, there should be feedback concerning the correctness or degree of correctness of the learner's performance" (p. 188). They fail, however, to go past simple error-detection as a design criteria and conclude simplistically that ". . . the important characteristic of the communication [feedback] is not its content but its function: providing information to the learners about the correctness of their performance" (p. 189). Other purposes that feedback can serve such as process or status information are not even mentioned.

Even 20 years ago the differential effects of feedback to support knowledge acquisition versus higher level outcomes were indicated. In looking at feedback needed to teach medical diagnostic skills, Hammond (1971) found, "As expected, this task was too difficult to be learned by means of outcome feedback alone" (p. 905). However, by providing computer-based graphics as a form of *process* feedback Hammond concludes that "human beings can exercise sufficient control over their cognitive processes to rapidly modify them in the direction intended. In other words, good judgment can be learned rapidly" (p. 907).

Cybernetics

A rich source of precise definitions (and discussion of the different types and effect of feedback) can be found in the largely ignored field of cybernetics, such as documented by Smith and Smith (1966). "By sensory feedback, we mean the pattern of afferent stimuli (visual, auditory, tactile, and so on) which result from a specific response pattern in a particular environmental situation'' (p. 177). Smith and Smith discriminate between dynamic sensory feedback and knowledge feedback, place the issue of reinforcement in perspective, include motivation and perception in their models, examine issues of communication feedback and group behavior, and generally (and specifically) provide useful foundations for virtually all research in feedback during the last three decades. They also include recommendations for the study of cognition.

Elements of Feedforward

Feedforward is defined as the process of assessing input before it enters a system or sub-system to (a) determine whether the input meets system process requirements, and (b) provide a feedforward information loop which serves to modify the functions of the system to meet input requirements. The purpose of feedforward is to maintain efficient and consistent output of the system, given variable input. The design of feedforward systems presumes that necessary relationships between feed and process are known, that the essential characteristics of feedstock can be measured, and that the system can be responsive to feedforward information.

To illustrate, presume that a computer-based social studies simulation exists that is designed to teach relationships between geography and transportation. Lee, a seventh grade student, is assigned to this unit in the Local Area Network (LAN) computer lab. One type of feedforward information could be reading level that has been determined with a standardized test. Based on information provided through the LAN, the level of vocabulary used in the social studies simulation is automatically adjusted for Lee's reading level. Where new terms are introduced, extra information and practice is provided by the system. These are based on Lee's reading ability.

Presume further that one instructional strategy used in this lesson (which was designed to teach relationships) relies heavily on charts, histograms, and other highly symbolic (graphic) representation. A short quiz is administered within the lesson, specific to the type of graphics used in this lesson. With a low score, Lee could be advised to sign off and to seek his teacher, or the system could branch Lee to a graphic skills program designed to teach the specific skills needed in the lesson. If criteria with the graphic skills program were met, Lee could proceed. However, the simulation program might still display graphics of more or less sophistication based on Lee's ability to extract meaning from graphics. Another system response might be to provide additional aural explanation if Lee's perceptual preference test indicated this medium would be useful.

In a highly automated classroom management system, the graphic skills diagnostic data (collected for this one lesson) could be forwarded to the classroom management system and might become feedforward for other lessons that relied on these specific graphic comprehension skills. Whether a more comprehensive standardized assessment of symbol and graphic *literacy* would be useful is problematic. Such tests tend to rely on central tendency and seldom have sufficient specificity, or sub-scales, to provide direction for individual learner pathways.

The above example illustrates the following points: feedforward information was used to modify the system to suit the characteristics of the feedstock (Lee). This information may be standardized (as with reading skills) or unique to sub-system process needs (ability to understand certain types of graphics). The relationship between Lee (in terms of reading and graphic comprehension skill levels) and lesson content were known and could be measured, and this data could be used by the system to respond to Lee as an individual.

Characteristics of Input

When determining what should be assessed, in terms of individual learner input, at least three different types of characteristics could be considered. The first type consists of relatively fixed traits such as general reasoning ability. Instructional systems could respond to high/low reasoning ability with variable pacing, information density, or a review of previous material. A second type of input might be that of information-processing preference. Some folks, for example, like to read, while others prefer a verbal description. Systems can respond to these differences with multiple and perhaps overlapping media and parallel message design.

The third type of input is entry knowledge that is based on the task or content to be learned. The criteria for assessing content-specific entry knowledge can be drawn from the specific curriculum as well as terms and processes needed, given the instructional strategies employed. For example, if object-driven CAI is assigned, then an input characteristic that could be assessed might be recognition of the icons used for navigation through the lesson.

Conceptually, another view of learner input characteristics can be drawn from mechanical systems wherein we think of processing requirements such as the *temper* of feedstock. For example, a steel rolling mill requires metal of known properties. Subsequently, metals of known temper are specified as raw stock; or materials may be tempered further as part of the production process. In the case of individuals, their temperament might be equated to thinking skills, perceptual learning styles, capacities to reason logically, and other intrinsic factors. This type of process-oriented feedforward information is distinct from requisite knowledge of the subject or content being taught.

Another aspect of feedforward is that of sensing how input can *flow* through the system. In the case of metal processing, lubrication of raw stock may be needed. Or, in humans, we may be able to create a potential for processing information through such devices as advanced organizers, statements of performance objectives, reviews of previous experiences, or perhaps flags for learners when a specific thinking strategy might be appropriate. In his studies of human learning and cognition, Bjorkman (1972) limits the use of feedforward to this flow enhancement function: "By definition feedforward is the transmission of task information directly to the subject" (p. 156). Within his discussion he notes that:

> Feedforward and feedback have the same function, namely to reduce uncertainty about the task. Both can be varied with respect to amount of information, and have a compensatory relationship to each other. There is less to gain from feedback when feedforward contains much information and vice versa. There is at present an almost complete lack of data on the interplay between feedback and feedforward . . . . (p. 156)

Early references to feedforward also dwell on the unknown relationship between feedforward and feedback. In a philosophical discussion, Richards (1968) notes that "Feedforward, as I see it, is the reciprocal, the necessary condition of what the cybernetics and automation people call 'feedback'" (p. 14). His muse considers feedforward to be a product of a past experience which causes us to anticipate cause and effect. In discussing instructional design considerations he states that:

> Meanwhile, however, constancy and attachment to the *principles* of the design (as opposed to the minutiae of its implementation) are required. For these principles have (or should have) governed the choice of the detail; it is these principles which are really under trial (not some one of a number of possible embodiments), and unless the principles stay constant, fertile interplay between what is looked for (feedforward) and what actually happens (feedback) is precluded. The experimentation will not lead to the strengthening or weakening or emendation of the principles, which should be its main purpose. (p. 16)

Separation of Feedforward and Feedback?

Both theoretically and practically, combining the two effects of feedforward and feedback would seem to make sense. As we acquire a more sophisticated database about learning and about specific interactions between learner and task, and as we acquire tools and toys such as sophisticated authoring languages and interactive media, both the reasons and opportunity to combine FF and FB will seem apparent. However, I submit that we currently lack both taxonomies (or some agreed-upon structure) and a database to support any but the broadest principles of feedback as a design feature. With the exception that feedback can serve as an error-correction function, little consistency exists in published research as to why and at what level feedback is appropriate. The critical variable of type and level of question used to elicit a response is usually ignored. The issue of level of learning and type and timing of feedback is seldom addressed adequately. One study will find significant results, a similar study will not.

For example, Shulman and Elstein (1975) discuss different forms of feedback such as outcome feedback (the traditional knowledge of results) and process feedback. They also discuss the role of feedforward as defined by Bjorkman (1972). In discussing the role of feedback for different levels of learning, they note, "Studies conducted by Hammond (1971) and others have demonstrated that simple outcome feedback is practically worthless for improving judgments, since it does not aid learning the ecology of relations among cues and criteria. On the other had, lens model [process] feedback and feedforward are powerful and dramatic aids to learning" (p. 27).

Comparison Research

Prudence suggests we learn as much about feedforward and feedback as possible, as separate functions, before we begin to combine their effects. In theory, each of these design approaches can produce the same output. We can design feedforward instructional systems capable of handling some range of entry skills which are so responsive to individual differences that the output is certain. Computer software allows us to branch (based both on ability assessment and achievement) to provide dynamic and interactive instruction appropriate for a specific learner. No feedback to the learner need to be provided.

A parallel system which presumes the entry skills described above, but which does not interact with the student based on this information, could be constructed. This lesson could provide a variety of feedback based both on the how well the learner used a process and for the more traditional use of feedback for error detection (to send the learner back through some part of the system to relearn).

Comparing separately both the design and outcome effects of these two systems (each designed with different control principles) should yield valuable insight into the phenomena of feedforward and feedback.

Feedforward Combined with Feedback

Although the need for research which examines FF and FB separately can be argued, a number of factors indicate the advantages of using FF combined with FB. For researchers, the synergistic effect of FF and FB represents a challenge that has both practical (publishable) and marketable (consulting) outcomes. For designers and automation folks, the systematic and integrated use of FF and FB represents justification of increased development costs and elaborate software and hardware. For educators and trainers who face the task of selling learning systems based on return of investment, the (yet to be proven) assertion that learner time spent on systems which include both FF and FB might be cut in half, while dramatically increasing learning outcomes, is important. Finally, a quantum jump forward in effective software will help industry in its attempt to sell interactive work stations.

The potential of synergy using combined functions can be found in research with Intelligent Tutoring Systems (ITS), which includes, but is not limited to, feedforward. In describing the characteristics of ITS Shute (1990a) notes that:

> Some aspects of the tutor making it "intelligent" are the ability to: (a) adapt instruction to the particular learner (e.g., Sleeman & Brown, 1982; Wenger, 1986); (b) solve the same problems as presented to the students; and (c) dynamically analyze solution histories, using *principles* to decide what to do next rather than preprogrammed responses (e.g., Clancey, 1986). (p. 2)

Shute (1990b) examined whether ITS meet their potential in terms of what Bloom (1984) calls *the two sigma problem*. In an evaluation of four different Intelligent Tutoring Systems, Shute found consistent and promising results that typically cut learning time in half while increasing learning outcomes. She notes that "although this represents a significant improvement of ITS over traditional instruction, it falls short of attaining '2 sigma status' " (p.5).

The point, however, is that research with ITS and evaluations of the kind described above do not factor out feedforward as a separate function. It may be that with the principled use of feedforward and feedback, a two sigma increase in learning outcomes is possible without having instructional systems that can solve the same problems that are presented to the students, or which use complex algorithms to analyze solution histories. Instead, the achievement of significant outcomes by using a simpler model of branching routines based on individual learner differences may be possible.

Broad Design Guidelines

As a model for research, the general findings of cognitive learning theories can be used. Elaboration Theory, for example, summarizes the instructional design guidelines of a general-to-detailed sequence approach. Reigeluth and Stein (1983) note, "Progressively more detailed, specific, and complex ideas can then be acquired more easily as derivations or elaborations of the more general content. The use of a general-to-detailed sequence of content thus provides the learner with a progression of anchoring knowledge that subsumes, integrates, and organizes the more detailed or complex knowledge" (p. 376).

Within this general design model, the specifics of assessing learner as input can be viewed as a systems problem. For example, the need for vocabulary assessment can be derived both from the task being learned and from the teaching strategies employed. Requisite subject knowledge can be derived for each unit within the lesson from the key points of previous lessons. Both general and specific tests of message characteristics can be determined (i.e., the ability to obtain meaning from graphics). Criteria for future research should be prioritized by the potential for designing responsive systems based on these types of input characteristics which are both relatively easy to determine and which might provide high yield in terms of achievement.

The Promise of ATI/TTI

The possibility of assessing basic learner traits and using this data for the design of responsive systems is seductive. For instance, trait and aptitude-treatment interaction data could well be important building blocks for the design of feedforward. It would be useful if a relatively simple measure such as the Hidden Figures Test could be used for design guidelines. Unfortunately, being able to use scores from most aptitude and trait instruments is problematic in terms of reliable assessment and effective prescription.

Gehlbach (1979) raises the issue of whether our basic theories have been adequate, and suggests we examine the strategy of trying to move from broad theory to specific questions. Snow (1977) is much more specific in that he suggests that general theory construction be dropped and we proceed with specific *local* theories. According to Snow, it may be useful to develop theories that apply to teaching in certain schools within a city that may not even be useful for other schools in the same city.

In short, although the general construction of aptitudes and treatments interacting in a systematic way seems useful, the history of ATI/TTI research provides few dependable guidelines for feedforward-based design. What seems to hold more promise than such abstract measures as field dependence-independence (Goodenough, 1976) are the more direct measures of perceptual preferences (e.g., auditory, visual or kinesthetic; see Dunn, 1981) and the role that dual modalities can play (such as documented by Fleming & Levie, 1978). ATI research may still hold promise but reliable cause/effect relationships may well depend upon a situational triangulation of learner traits, type of learning as dictated by the task and instructional strategy.

Another issue that needs debate and good supporting research involves learner control. The principle of feedforward is based on the premise that the system will provide alternatives based on learner characteristics. However, if the learner is skilled at thinking and can reflect on whether a chosen learning strategy was effective, the options selected by the system are a much different order of magnitude than if the system must provide a learning strategy for an unskilled learner. Unfortunately, most learner control research has not included learner training, particularly of cognitive skills, so that control could be maximized.

Elements of Feedforward Research

Shute (1990a) provides the basic rationale for Intelligent Tutoring System (ITS) research, which can also apply to feedforward systems:

> An ITS can increase its effectiveness and progress . . . by adapting to individuals' strengths and weaknesses. To optimize learning, additional structure and guidance . . . could be provided to subjects with certain characteristics (e.g., less exploratory behaviors). Learning environments are much more easily modified than basic cognitive abilities in humans. So, these data can provide a point of departure for building more adaptive learning environments. (p. 6)

Certainly cognitive abilities are an important factor. However, other learner characteristics may also play an important role in the design of adaptive systems. An extended list of these characteristics might include:
- basic academic skills (reading comprehension, general reasoning ability, problem-solving skills);
- lesson-specific entry knowledge (vocabulary, symbols, recall of procedures, use of formulas and equations);
- ability to engage in instructional strategy (team skills, rote vs. didactic, prepare a specimen, matrix or graphic);
- processing mode (audio/visual/kinesthetic preference, ability to monitor self, holistic vs. serial thinking, procedural vs. exploration); and
- motivation (internal vs. external, self-imposed vs. peer or teacher imposed).

Each of the factors can be a strength, weakness, or preference which represents design considerations for the ideal instructional system for one individual. Some factors are less malleable (i.e., general reasoning ability) than others. Data indicating basic or intrinsic skills such as reading ability can be measured at infrequent intervals and retrieved from a central source. Other data, such as content-specific entry skills, need to be collected at the beginning of each lesson. Some learners are flexible in terms of preferred processing mode and can learn equally well from either audio or visual materials while others would benefit from a selected medium. Holistic thinkers might benefit from the big picture presented first followed by detail whereas the serial learner may be more efficient if detail is followed by picture. Each of the above factors can be measured and used to create systems which respond, at different points within the system, to satisfy individual differences.

Summary

Feedforward is a General Systems phenomenon that has considerable potential for the design and development of instructional systems which are highly responsive to individual differences. Using data which reflect both intrinsic and situational differences of individuals, feedforward control can be used to create learning environments that seem tailored for each person and which capitalize on the different cognitive, perceptual, and processing abilities of different learners.

Ideally, well-reasoned models and a sound and comprehensive research base would be established for feedforward and feedback separately before we begin to combine these two control functions. It is difficult if not impossible to factor out and understand the significant effects of two different control elements within a dynamic learning system that include both FF and FB.

Feedforward is one control factor in Intelligent Tutoring Systems, and a great deal can be learned about FF in this environment. However, the specific results of FF are seldom factored out in analysis of ITS results. Further, the synergistic results of systematically combining FF and FB may be such that the more complex design elements of a full ITS are not needed, and satisfactory systems can be developed without the complexity of an ITS. Intuitively, a two sigma gain in the effect of instructional systems which combine FF and FB, that may use no more than a dozen learner status indicators, seems reasonable during the next half-dozen years. Although considerable investment will be needed to create both the research base and to specify effective design principles, the benefits of having instructional systems that can respond to a wide range of individual differences will soon make this investment worthwhile.

References

Bjorkman, M. (1972). Feedforward and feedback as determiners of knowledge and policy: Notes on a neglected issue. *Scandinavian Journal of Psychology, 13*, 152–158.

Bloom, B.S. (1984). The two sigma problem: The search for methods of group instruction as effective as one-to-one tutoring. *Educational Researcher, 13*(6), 4–6.

Clancey, W.J. (1986). *Intelligent tutoring systems: A tutorial survey.* Report No. KSL-86-58. Stanford, CA: Stanford University.

Considine, D. (1989). *Van Nostrand's scientific encyclopedia* (7th ed.). New York: Van Nostrand Reinhold.

Dunn, R. (1981). *Productivity environmental preference survey.* Lawrence, KS: Price Systems.

Fleming, M., & Levie, W. H. (1978). *Instructional message design: Principles from the behavioral sciences.* Englewood Cliffs, NJ: Educational Technology Publications.

Gagné, R.M., Briggs, L.J., & Wager, W.W. (1988). *Principles of instructional design.* New York: Holt, Rinehart, & Winston.

Gehlbach, R. (1979). Individual differences: Implications for instructional theory, research and innovation. *Educational Researcher, 8*(4), 8–14.

Goodenough, D.R. (1976). The role of individual differences in field dependence as a factor in learning and memory. *Psychological Bulletin, 83*, 675–694.

Hammond, K.R. (1971). Computer graphics as an aid to learning. *Science, 172* (3986), 903–908.

Kowitz, G.T., & Smith, J.C. (1985). The dynamics of successful feedback. *Performance and Instruction Journal, 24*(8), 4–6.

Kyllonen, P.C., & Shute, V.J. (1988). *Taxonomy of learning skills* (Technical Report AFHRL-TP-87-39). San Antonio: Air Force Human Resources Laboratory.

Murrill, P. (1981). *Fundamentals of process control theory.* Research Triangle Park, NC: Instrument Society of America.

Parker, S. (1984). *McGraw-Hill dictionary of science and engineering.* New York: McGraw-Hill.

Reigeluth, C., & Stein, F. (1983). The elaboration theory of instruction. In C. Reigeluth (Ed.), *Instructional design theories and models: An overview of their current status* (pp. 339–381). Hillsdale, NJ: Lawrence Erlbaum Associates.

Richards, I.A. (1968, February). The secret of "feedforward." *Saturday Review, 51*, 14–17.

Shulman, L., & Elstein, A. (1975). Studies of problem solving, judgment, and decision making: Implications for educational research. *Review of Research in Education* (pp. 3–42). Itasca, IL: Peacock.

Shute, V.J. (1990a, April). *A comparison of inductive and deductive learning environments: Which is better for whom and why?* Paper presented at the meeting of the American Educational Research Association, Boston.

Shute, V.J. (1990b). Rose garden promises of intelligent tutoring systems: Blossom or thorn? *Proceedings from the Space Operations, Application and Research Symposium* (pp. 1–8). Albuquerque, NM.

Sleeman, D., & Brown, J.S. (1982). *Intelligent tutoring systems.* New York: Academic Press.

Smith, K.U., & Smith, M.F. (1966). *Cybernetic principles of learning and educational design.* New York: Holt, Rinehart, & Winston.

Snow, R. (1977). Individual differences and instructional theory. *Educational Researcher, 6*(10), 11–15.

Tsai, Y. (1985). *Feedback in educational studies: A preliminary study.* Unpublished manuscript, University of Texas, College of Education.

Wenger, E. (1986). *Artificial intelligence and tutoring systems.* Los Altos, CA: Morgan-Kaufmann.

Chapter Thirteen

Evaluation as Feedback in Instructional Technology: The Role of Feedback in Program Evaluation

Susan A. Tucker
University of South Alabama

Other chapters in this book have argued the import of feedback and its influence on emerging intructional technologies. This chapter will attempt to add one more component to the discussion—the role of feedback in the evaluation of interactive technologies. Evaluation will be examined from a comprehensive or macro-level perspective of program evaluation.

This chapter has three main purposes. The first purpose is to analyze the strengths and weaknesses of three prevailing evaluation models, with special attention to the role of feedback (overt or covert) in each paradigm. The second is to present a framework for analyzing feedback issues faced by evaluators of interactive instructional technologies. Finally, the implications of applying this framework will be discussed.

Evaluation and Feedback

Professionals in the business of affecting human performance cannot escape evaluation. When making program decisions, a systematic process of judging must be used. Compound the pressure of instructional decision-making with ever-changing interactive technology delivery systems, and the inherent problems surrounding evaluation expand into an exponential migraine.

With these problems come a wave of questions. Where do you start? Who are your real clients? How do you decide upon the major questions to structure your study? How do you address hidden agendas? How sufficient are objectives-based evaluations when working with innovative programs? How do you balance quantitative and qualitative data-collection methodologies? Sure, it's cheaper than hiring outsiders—but does formative internal evaluation really work? How do you decide the evaluation is complete? Most importantly, after you have conducted this study, how do you feed back your hard-earned evaluation results to critical audiences? Call them what you will—trainers, instructional designers, course developers, instructional technologists, curriculum planners, teachers, program evaluators— these professionals have not yet reached consensus about how to answer these questions.

Since the late 1960s, authors have addressed the need for systematic program evaluation models. Undoubtedly, the use of models to order educational processes facilitates the conception of problems and the perception of interrelationships within these problem contexts. While each model may view the same set of interrelationships, it is inevitable that certain concerns of the model builders will differ due to personal frames of reference (Alkin, 1968). Dillon (1981) extends this personal dimension of modeling to include "prefabricated configurations of concepts" or "patterns of coherence that we expect to find."

The modeling of social systems involves another potential danger. Education's use of analog models drawn from the "hard" sciences is troublesome to the extent that empirical models represent only "observable" realities. The human dimension in instruction requires models which represent both observable and subjective realities. This dilemma of inherent change is further compounded in evaluation when the evaluator threatens to question existing structures, make covert values visible, and test commonly accepted myths (Tucker & Dempsey, 1991).

In 1971, Daniel Stufflebeam raised several issues of concern to evaluators. These issues have yet to be addressed adequately by prevailing evaluation models. He notes four problems in the application of experimental designs to evaluation. First, selection of experimental designs conflicts with the principle that evaluation should facilitate continuous program improvement. According to a colleague of Stufflebeam, "experimental design prevents rather than promotes changes in the treatments because . . . treatments cannot be altered if the data about differences between treatments are to be unequivocal" (Guba, 1969, p. 34). Second, traditional research methodologies are useless for making decisions during the planning and implementation of a project. Rather, the stress on controlling operational variables creates a contrived situation and blocks the collection of natural and dynamic information. Third, the typical research design does not apply to the "septic" conditions of most evaluation contexts. The evaluator is not interested in establishing highly controlled conditions within which universally true knowledge can be generalized. Instead, "one wishes to set up conditions of invited interference from all factors that might ever influence a learning (or whatever) transaction" (Guba, 1969, p. 33). As a final point, internal validity is gained at the expense of external validity. Clearly, equating evaluation models with empirical models is limiting to dynamic program development concerned with credibility (Lincoln & Guba, 1985), particularly in largely undocumented areas like instructional technology programs.

Feedback appears to be one variable that can contribute toward resolving some of these evaluation dilemmas. In essence, this chapter considers the role of feedback in the evaluation process as well as the resultant changes that ensue. The implications of feedback in evaluating dynamic, continuing instructional programs are particularly important because the presence or absence of feedback can dramatically affect the accuracy required of human judgment and decision making.

Diversity of Major Evaluation Models

The current practice of evaluation relies heavily on three models developed over twenty years ago: (1) Tyler's (1942) objectives-based model, (2) the decision-making approaches exemplified by Provus' discrepancy model (1969, 1971) and Stufflebeam's (1983) CIPP model, and (3) values-based approaches such as Stake's responsive schema (1967, 1983) and Scriven's goal-free model (1967, 1972).

Model diversity emerges from the various emphases placed on each of these tasks. Another source of variance is how the evaluator relates to the client system. For example, Pace's (1968) analysis of evaluation models indicates that large, complex, and longitudinal evaluations may require a different model—one that considers a broad range of social and educational consequences. Holistic judgments require assessing more than program objectives. Instead, expand the evaluation to question other program dimensions, such as expected and unexpected consequences, cultural characteristics of the setting, and the processes of program delivery. Evidence gathered to answer these questions should be both quantitative and qualitative, including the systematic collection of personal perceptions.

There are strengths and weaknesses in each approach which have emerged over the ensuing years. Rather than focus on their well-publicized strengths, the rest of this section will summarize some inconsistencies or areas which have not been addressed by each model. This critique is motivated by the need to understand why evaluation of interactive instructional technologies has been fraught with difficulties and is often a dissatisfying experience for both the evaluator and the evaluated.

To demonstrate the different emphases placed in various evaluation concerns, Figure 13.1 compares three prevailing evaluation approaches: Tyler's instructional objectives (IO) model, Stufflebeam's decision-making (DM) approach, and the values-based (VB) approaches of Scriven and Stake. Special attention is given to the following criteria: a systematic methodology which utilizes a combination of quantitative and qualitative data sources to portray a more holistic reality; helpfulness toward program improvement; and the evaluator's openness to make values overt and to facilitate the planning of probable futures for a program. The rest of this section analyzes the strengths and weaknesses of each model in more depth.

1. Instructional Objectives Approaches

Tyler (1942) is known for an evaluation model which stresses measuring student progress by means of instructional objectives. Originating over 50 years ago, he conceives evaluation as the process of assessing the degree to which a program is achieving its predetermined objectives. Tyler's model concentrates on spelling out the objectives behaviorally rather than judging the value of these objectives. Ideally, measurement is broad in scope and continual.

Tyler's model has several merits. It provides valid, reliable, and objective data for an evaluation. It allows the evaluator to indicate attained and unattained objectives. On the other hand, strict application of the Tyler Model creates difficulties. It ascertains student outcomes but ignores the contexts and processes that lead to these final outcomes. The statement of objectives in behavioral terms is a long and often tedious procedure which limits sources of evidence to purely quantifiable data. In essence, it is too easy to avoid questions about the worth of the objectives themselves. This is especially true if the evaluation is conducted after the objectives are formulated. When this happens, the evaluation is often limited to making superficial revisions of performance objectives.

In response to these difficulties, more flexible "neo-Tylerian" models have emerged (Taba & Sawin, 1962; Cronbach, 1963; AAAS Commission on Science Education, 1965). Taba and Sawin propose an evaluation model that focuses on the collection of information in order to determine why some learners failed to achieve stated objectives. Tyler's data sources have been expanded to include observations on teaching method, patterns of

MODEL CRITERIA	OB	DB	VB
1. intended outcomes documented	•	•	?
2. unintended outcomes documented		x	•
3. document contexts leading to outcomes		•	•
4. document processes leading to outcomes		•	•
5. client standards overt		•	•
6. evaluator standards overt			•
7. client-evaluator negotiation			
8. program improvement-oriented			•
9. hard & soft data balanced			

key: • denotes criterion being met in a model

x denotes criterion being inconsistently met in model

Figure 13.1. Summary of criteria for three evaluation models: objectives-based (OB), decision-based (DB), and values-based (VB).

classroom interaction, physical facilities, and student motivation. "Neo-Tylerian" ideas have contributed to the field's shift from a terminal focus to one which synthesizes both process and product elements. The emphasis of evaluation is on facilitating instructional improvement. Two major limitations persist. One, the evaluators do not incorporate client feedback into the proposed evaluation. Second, futures planning is neglected.

2. Decision-Making Approaches

A second group of evaluation theorists, notably Provus and Stufflebeam, believe the evaluator's task is one of delineating information to be collected, planning a data-collection methodology, and helping decision makers to use the information collected. It is the responsibility of the decision maker, not the evaluator, to make judgments from this information. Four questions are basic to this approach:

• What should the objectives be?
• How should the program be designed to meet these objectives?
• Is the program design being carried out effectively and efficiently?
• Was the program worth what was invested in it, considering the products achieved? (Reasby, 1973, p. 23)

The Discrepancy Model, developed by Provus (1969, 1971), emphasizes the discrepancy between the ideal standards in a program and the real performances. Provus assumes that there can be no evaluation without a standard. The explicitness of the standard generally determines the precision of the evaluation. Special attention is paid to training the staff in three tasks: (1) delineating and agreeing on program standards; (2) awareness of political and scientific considerations; and (3) determining whether a discrepancy exists and using this information in a feedback loop to identify program weaknesses. According to Provus, education programs must be evaluated in stages relative to the development and stability of the program being investigated. Five stages of evaluation have been posited in the Discrepancy Model: design, installation, process, product, and cost. At each stage, comparisons are made and discrepancies sought between operational reality and some ideal standard derived from the values of the program staff and the client population it serves.

Larger in scope than objectives-based models, the discrepancy model has been widely used, particularly with federal programs. While advancing the field by specifically addressing standards, Provus (1971) identified several weaknesses in his model. He concludes that the major weakness with the discrepancy model seems to stem from failure to understand the limits on institutional behavior set by field conditions, the intricacies of the decision-making process, and the origin and use of criteria in that process. Context evaluation is not addressed, and the exhaustive use of behavioral standards may limit the creative, adaptive responsiveness of program staff. Provus's approach does not clearly identify the type and ultimate use of information to be collected at each stage. The model could also be faulted for being incapable of evaluating rapid, large-scale changes characteristic of early instructional technology projects. Decision makers are not always rational, yet the model assumes such behavior. Finally, the Discrepancy Model does not address how evaluators are recruited, trained, and supported in the system.

The Phi Delta Kappan Committee on Evaluation, chaired by Daniel Stufflebeam (1971), has perhaps exerted more influence than any group in attempting to lead the educational profession away from excessive reliance on classical research models. Instead, an evaluation model is offered which assists decision makers in pinpointing their values so that they can best be served by the decisions made. This model, known as CIPP, specifies four types of evaluation: Context, Input, Process, and Product (Stufflebeam, 1983). The procedure for the four evaluations mentioned is basically the same. First, identify the type or decision to be served. Second, delineate the information needed. After the relevant decision makers have been identified, develop techniques to obtain and collect this desired information. The final step involves providing the information to relevant decision makers and audiences.

Though mechanically total, the CIPP model excludes overt values in its schema. According to Stufflebeam, the evaluator's role is one of collection, organization, and analysis of "relevant" data for "relevant" decision-makers. Overt judgment of the intrinsic worth of the program's objectives is not considered by the evaluator or the clients. The entire question of values is kept tacitly in the decision-makers' domain. Another limitation of the CIPP model is its inability to answer two basic questions. How do evaluators and/or clients know which standards are operant? Furthermore, what processes are necessary to enable the decision maker to apply value criteria?

3. Values-Based Approaches

Two major examples of values-based approaches to program evaluation are considered: Scriven's Goal-Free Model and Stake's responsive schema.

Scriven's (1967, 1972, 1978) Goal-Free Model is in definite contrast to those evaluators advocating objectives-based or decision-making approaches. According to Scriven, the distinction between the roles and goals of evaluation are often intentionally blurred. Whatever its role, the goals of evaluation are always the same—to estimate the merit, worth, or value of the thing being evaluated. Scriven goes on to point out that the subversion of goals to roles is very often a misguided attempt to allay the anxiety of those being evaluated. The consequence of this type of distorted evaluation could be much more undesirable than the anxieties evoked. As an alternative, Scriven (1972) declared that both summative and formative evaluations will increasingly become "goal-free." Scriven stresses the evaluation of actual effects against a profile of demonstrated needs. One of the many roles of the evaluator is to examine the goals of the educational program and judge the worth or value of these goals against some standard of merit. From the data he has collected, the evaluator can determine whether these objectives are being met.

One of the great strengths of this model is addressing the role and values of the evaluator. In spite of the model's strengths, several questions remain unanswered. How can a client insure that external evaluators properly judge actual effects of a program, whether planned or not? What standards are there to judge whether a goal-free evaluator is not arbitrary, inept, or unscrupulous in his or her actions? How does one judge how well a goal-free evaluator has interpreted the "demonstrated needs" of a project?

The theme throughout many of Stake's writings (1967, 1970, 1972, 1973, 1982, 1983) is that an evaluator must do his or her best to reflect the nature of the program and not focus on what is most easily measured. Furthermore, he writes less about the link between evaluation and decision making than other evaluation theoreticians. Like Scriven, Stake believes that both descriptions and judgments are essential and basic acts of any evaluation and should be combined to portray an educational program. He believes that the evaluator's task is one of identifying outcomes or "intents." These intents are contingent upon particular antecedent conditions and instructional transactions, which occur on two levels: first, what was intended; second, what is observed. In addition to contingencies, the evaluator examines the congruence of these intents and observations in terms of antecedents, transactions, and outcomes. Thus, the evaluator is a technician who can provide both relative and absolute judgments. In this respect, Stake takes a more conservative stance than Scriven. Stake (1973) recommends that the evaluator not take an absolutist position regarding the program's goals because this is likely to make clients less willing to cooperate in the evaluation.

The Stake model exceeds most models in attempting to describe and judge the entire educational enterprise. In terms of process and scope, the Stake model deals more comprehensively with a number of evaluation needs. The assessment of evaluation procedures in the descriptive matrix is unclear, as it appears that procedures would be described with transactions. However, procedures are selected prior to the learning experience. An effective method for analyzing the role of values in the program can be found in this model, as can a methodology for discovering which values are being served. On the critical side, Stake's approach does not appear to provide for evaluating decision alternatives during the structuring of the learning experience. Furthermore, he does not provide for systematic feedback in program development. While the instructional program is looked at in terms of antecedents, transactions, and outcomes, underlying the whole approach is a perspective that looks at evaluation from the terminus.

Polemics in Program Evaluation

Evaluation is ever-present and continues to operate, both overtly and covertly. Furthermore, evaluation is only as good as the environment that the evaluator is able to coalesce and share among all significant players. Approaching this cooperative state can be facilitated by Polanyi's (1962, 1966, 1975, 1978) constructs of collecting multiple perceptions in order to approach a shared reality. He also advocates trying to make tacit perceptions overt rather than being unconsciously controlled by these perceptions, and including extended dwelling in an evaluation to experience more than the surface and first-impression phenomena. In essence, out of these diverse perceptions we can identify critical polemics as signposts which expand but do not fix our capability to describe and judge. That is, we can use these polemics to avoid a closed view of evaluation and open our perspective to the variety of factors which can influence evaluator's and client's judgments. Figure 13.2 summarizes some of these major polemics and their continua.

```
Questions:  To what degree should they be...

 1.(   )      (   )      (   )      (   )      (   )
client helpful                          field helpful

 2.(   )      (   )      (   )      (   )      (   )
formative                               summative

 3.(   )      (   )      (   )      (   )      (   )
objectives-based                        holistic-based

 4.(   )      (   )      (   )      (   )      (   )
independent                             negotiated


Sources:  To what degree should they be...

 5.(   )      (   )      (   )      (   )      (   )
descriptive                             judgmental

 6.(   )      (   )      (   )      (   )      (   )
quantitative                            qualitative

 7.(   )      (   )      (   )      (   )      (   )
in-dwelling                             one-shot

 8.(   )      (   )      (   )      (   )      (   )
deductive                abductive      inductive


Standards:  To what degree should they be...

 9.(   )      (   )      (   )      (   )      (   )
tacit                                   overt

10.(   )      (   )      (   )      (   )      (   )
proactive                               reactive

11.(   )      (   )      (   )      (   )      (   )
self-initiated/internal                 imposed/external

12.(   )      (   )      (   )      (   )      (   )
elitist or parochial                    subordinate
```

Figure 13.2. Evaluation polemics concerning the questions asked, the sources of evidence collected and the quality criteria used to judge the program in question.

The Need for a Different Model
to Evaluate Instructional Technologies

As summarized in Figure 13.2, the three prevailing approaches possess similarities and differences. Special attention is directed to the presence or absence of several criteria: (1) using a sytematic methodology which combines quantitative and qualitative data sources to portray a more holistic reality; (2) helping others move toward program improvement; (3) providing the evaluator's feedback to make values overt; and (4) facilitating program planning regarding probable futures. To varying degrees, the instructional objectives approach, the decision-making approach, and the values-based approaches all lack methods for systematizing the feedback of both the evaluated and evaluators.

Given the aforementioned variance in evaluation models as well as diversity in clientele and program purposes, it is apparent that judgments about program worth can vary accordingly. It is the contention of this chapter that feedback of both the evaluated and the evaluators need to be made as overt as possible. This feedback process will enable the acts of informed judgment-making and program improvement. Support for this position has been persuasively advanced by Weckworth:

> First, there is no one way to do evaluation; second, there is no generic logical structure which will assure a unique "right" method of choice. Third, evauation ultimately becomes judgment and will remain so, so long as there is no ultimate criterion for monotonic ordering of priorities; and fourth, the critical element in evaluation is simply: who has the right, i.e., the power, the influence, or the authority to decide. (1969, p. 48)

It is the purpose of this section to offer an interactive evaluation model (Kunkel & Tucker, 1983; Tucker & Dempsey, 1991) which addresses some of the weaknesses of the aforementioned models and strives for credible synthesis of their strengths. This is especially difficult to achieve in contexts reflecting diverse client and audience values such as instructional technology programs. An evaluation model is therefore perceived as a body of interrelated criteria. These criteria help determine major questions, sources of evidence, and standards for judging the findings and making recommendations. Finally, it is informed by the research base of recent developments in cognitive psychology. Figure 13.3 summarizes the cognitive complexity of this process as a series of:

- contextually relevant exchanges between information inputs and feedback messages beween the evaluation and clients;
- perceptual representations of this data; and
- resultant actions, responses and/or judgments regarding the data.

By making overt the vulnerable judgments of both evaluators and those being evaluated, a synthetic picture of what the evaluation intends to focus on can be negotiated. Through cycles of feedback between the evaluator and clients and negotiation using the feedback information, operative values can be embodied in the major evaluation questions asked. In addition, these values can serve as judgment criteria for decision making. On the other hand, if the operative values are not known, distortion results in terms of what is questioned, how evidence is gathered, and how judgments are made.

In the model of evaluation proposed, certain value criteria are non-negotiable in the sense that along with accepting the evaluator personally, the primary audience must be made aware of and accept five criteria. That is, the model embodies holism, negotiation, evaluator vulnerability, multiple data sources, and is improvement-oriented and futuristic.

A Holistic Model of Program Evaluation: Integrating Feedback into Evaluation

The proposed model of evaluation relies greatly on developments in cognitive psychology. Cognitivism helps us understand the processes behind two evaluation truisms: "Information is power only in the hands of those who know how to use it" and "Evaluation is only as good as the information it is based upon." It is helpful to view evaluation as a complex activity which involves sequences of: gathering information within situations or contexts, representing this information in idiosyncratic perceptions, and then using this data for some sort of judgment, decision, or action.

Evaluators and decision-makers are required to integrate information from many sources when forming an initial judgment, reviewing recommendations, and ultimately making a choice among alternative strategies. The quality of the decision hinges upon how well the rater is able to encode, store, retrieve, and integrate information from these multiple sources into a judgment. Unfortunately, this process is not easy. A piece of information must pass through many filters before it is recorded or retrieved. More than informational, feedback can also serve motivational functions (Kopelman, 1986). It can provide information about the correctness, accuracy, and adequacy of the program. It encourages developing, revising, and refining task strategies, thereby laying the foundation for program improvement (Earley, 1988). Not surprisingly, decision makers use only a subset of available information in evaluating a program. In fact, information can delay and complicate decision making for many. When confronted with a problem, the decision maker brings his limited information and limited cognitive strategies and arrives at the best solution possible under the circumstances. Simon (1978) calls this "satisficing."

As described in the next section, research suggests that decision making is both a rational and irrational process. Decision makers rely upon simplifying strategies or heuristics when judging complex environments. While these strategies can be helpful in avoiding cognitive overload, if applied inappropriately heuristics can provide a significant source of bias and error in decision outcomes.

To counter this potential bias, an evaluation model (see Figure 13.3) is proposed that:

- is interactive and negotiated between the clients, evaluators, and participants;
- is based on the perceptions and values of many participants to capture a holistic rather than positivistic reality;
- involves significant players throughout all four phases, not just at the beginning and at the end; and
- systematically uses feedback to serve informational and motivational functions.

Phase 1: Generating Questions and Setting Standards

As depicted in Figure 13.3, Phase 1 has two levels of feedback loops. These loops consist of perceptual exchanges between the clients, evaluators, and relevant audiences. These exchanges involve the perception of the task demand of the client and major questions synthesized by the evaluator to focus on the evaluation.

Consider the first feedback loop in Figure 13.4. Here, the client introduces the task demand to the evaluator. The client's presentation can be influenced by both overt and covert factors, how stable the client's organizational environment appears to be, prior history of experiences with evaluation, and general belief structures. It becomes readily apparent that evaluation serves many functions besides error reduction. For example, it can provide evidence of the client's competence, signal impending action, and can protect the client politically.

Next, the evaluator perceives the task. This perceptual representation is shaped by a variety of factors. These factors include the evaluator's prior work experiences, his ability to decode semantic and semiotic messages, the perceived priority or strength of demand of the task, recognition of political forces, confidence, and stakeholder boundaries.

The first output of the evaluator is an attempt to identify the program's operational questions and standards expressed by the client. This could be done at any phase of the instructional process (e.g., analysis, design, devel-

INPUTS WITHIN CONTEXTS	PROCESSES	OUTPUTS
PHASE 1: QUESTIONS		

INFORMATION	PERCEPTUAL REPRESENTATION	ACTION, RESPONSE, AND/OR JUDGMENT
1. Client's Task Demand • surface and depth factors • stable vs unstable contexts • past performance of clients • client belief structures	**2. Evaluator's Perceived Task** • prior experience of evaluator • semantic/semiotic content priority • confidence, politics, resources, audiences, purposes, boundaries	**3. Evaluator sets Questions and Standards** • phases: analysis, design, development, implementation
4. Client feedback Message to Evaluator • client-helpful • field-helpful • audience-helpful • expectations • spontaneous vs. systematic	**5. Evaluator Represents Feedback** • effort, rapport • match mismatch • objectives, management, or perception-based • changes between task & feedback: overt/covert • formative vs. summative • internal vs. external	**6. Negotiate Paradigm and Schema Setting** • negotiated vs. independent • response certitude, framing • self-set vs. assigned standards

PHASE 2: DESCRIPTIONS

7. Evaluator collects data • qualitative vs. quantitative • stable vs. changing • indwelling vs. 1-shot • intuitive vs. analytical • maximal/optimal/actual • disjunctive vs. conjunctive • additive vs. dicretionary	**8. Evaluator analyzes data** • information load • description vs. judgement • anticipated vs. unanticipated • analysis model • audience analysis	**9. Evaluator Reports Initial Descriptions** • feedback time: simultaneous vs equential prove/improve
10. Client Feedback Message to Evaluator • initial certitude • credibility of Evaluator • match-mismatch • selective perception	**11. Evaluator Represents Client's Feedback** • prove/improve • quantitative, qualitative or holistic • overt vs. covert • subjective, intersubjective, objective • balance of positive/negative feedback	**12. Evaluator Edits Descriptions and Reports Alternatives** • feedback time • framing • heuristics vs. algorithyms • implications

Figure 13.3. Four phases of evaluation: asking questions, gathering descriptions, making judgments, and making decisions and choices.

PHASE 3: JUDGMENTS

INFORMATION	PERCEPTUAL REPRESENTATION	ACTION, RESPONSE, AND/OR JUDGMENT
13. Client's Feedback Message to Evaluator	**14. Evaluator's Editing of Alternatives**	**15. Evaluator Rates Alternatives**
• expect gains or losses • truth vs utility • Client's certitiude • purposes & resources • selective perception • strategic myopia	• concrete vs abstract • duration of events • display format • self efficacy	• feedback processing time
	16. Evaluator/Client Judgment	**17. Delivery Matrix & Recommendations**

	• inductive, deductive, abductive
	• heuristic vs normative;
	• confidence of Evaluator,
	• expectations:
	  internal vs external
	• overt vs covert;
	  proactive vs reactive
	• uncertainty of decision:
	  cognitive dissonance
		• time and format of delivery

PHASE 4: DECISIONS & CHOICES

INFORMATION	PERCEPTUAL REPRESENTATION	ACTION, RESPONSE, AND/OR JUDGMENT
	18. Decision Mechanism	

	• satisfice
	• self-initiated vs imposed
	• role of Evaluator and Client in
	  decisions
	• risk taking vs risk seeking:
	  error penalties
	• novice vs exper	

	19. Choice Mechanism	**20. Outcomes & Implementation**

	• perceived self-efficacy
	• environmental demands
	  (closed, open or optimizing
	    system)
	• elitist vs subordinate
	• attractiveness of alternatives/
	  incentives
	• past expenditures of effort
	• performance valence:
	  short & long term
	• press/compensate/integrate/
	  inaction	

Figure 13.3 (Continued). Four phases of evaluation: asking questions, gathering descriptions, making judgments, and making decisions and choices.

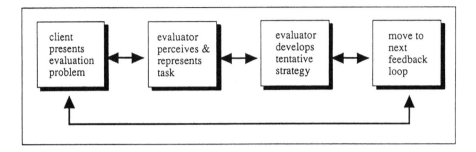

Figure 13.4. Three cognitive events that occur in the first cycle of determining questions to ask during the evaluation.

opment, implementation, or dissemination). This completes the first cycle of information outputs.

If an evaluator uses only the first feedback loop to develop questions and set standards, the risk of perceptual misunderstandings between the evaluator and client are still present. Recognizing this risk, experienced evaluators often confirm their identification of the major questions by seeking feedback from the client (see Figure 13.5). Clients are asked how relevant these questions are to their interests and needs (versus a more research-oriented perspective, which would give the evaluator sole authority to determining what is valuable and relevant). Factors which can influence the client's feedback message include: the client's expectations about short- and long-term program outcomes, the personal significance of the questions, penalty costs of whether to gather the information, the client's perception of the evaluator's degree of expertise, and rapport established between the client and evaluator.

When feedback is readily available, the risk of serious initial judgment errors is not as high because feedback provides information upon which to base corrective adjustments. Consider Hogarth's (1981) likening this process to aiming at a target. The evaluator may engage in a series of exchanges

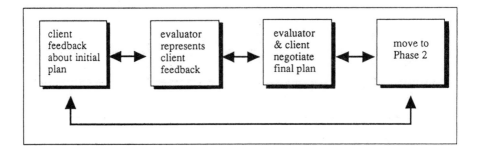

Figure 13.5. Three cognitive events that occur in the second cycle of negotiating questions for inclusion in the final evaluation paradigm.

with the client. The intent of these exchanges is to focus the evaluator's perception of the task or "target." Then the evaluator forms a mental representation of the perception. For example, in the first phase of evaluation, this representation serves to eliminate, substitute, or strengthen the evaluator's perceptions about the questions being asked. For example, perceptions of any hidden agendas emerging from the first cycle of information inputs are considered. Given the prior experience of the evaluator, the task may be encoded as objectives-based, management-based, values-based, or a composite of all three.

Finally, this cycle ends with the evaluator negotiating an evaluation plan. This plan or paradigm serves as a blueprint to guide the ensuing evaluation. Three components make up this paradigm: questions, evidence, and standards. Questions to guide the study are framed, potential sources of evidence clarified, and standards or qualities by which to judge the findings are made overt. Negotiation of the paradigm allows for the systematic participation of all relevant stakeholders. By stakeholders we mean ensuring all important perspectives are represented, including those most negative and positive about the program. This negotiation should be done during the first phase of the evaluation, thereby reducing some of the perceptual errors inherent in models such as Scriven's goal-free approach. It has been the experience of the author that negotiation serves as the first step in co-opting even the most negative stakeholders. This is accomplished by being open to their critical questions and emerging perceptions. Walsh and Fahey's (1986) notion of a negotiated belief structure seems to be viable here, as does the implications of recent work on third party negotiations (Harris & Carnevale, 1990) for external evaluators.

Implications of Phase 1. Helping stakeholders generate questions affected by one's capacity and motivation to generate alternative hypotheses for a given question. (For more thorough discussions of hypothesis generation, refer to the work of Higgins & King, 1981; Eco, 1983; Eco and Sebeok, 1983; Fisher, Gettys, Maming, Mehle, & Baca, 1983; Mayseless & Kruglanski, 1987.) For example, in situations where time pressures are great, a client or evaluator may be tempted to focus solely on addressing pre-defined objectives. In settings where formative evaluation provides useful feedback for product development and revision, its design is often constrained by available resources such as time, money, personnel, and facilities.

Extending the example of formative evaluation to interactive instructional technology further, it appears that two major questions are posed. One deals with the content and technical quality of the product, and the other deals with its learnability within authentic contexts. More specific questions generated by these two foci could deal with product initiation, design, content development, media development, production, testing, and maintenance (Foshay, 1984). Geis (1987) suggests that feedback is needed regarding the content and sequencing of instructional events as well as the nature of learner control of the content or message as sent.

Besides the two major questions, each stakeholder appears to have idiosyncratic questions of interest. Rather than reaching consensus on the questions, an effort is made to solicit the complete realm of questions and then synthesize them into broad questions which allow multiple perspectives. Fifteen years of evaluation field narratives suggest this is a viable strategy, and management research seems to support this as well. The research of Walsh and his associates (1988) argues that increased coverage and decreased consensus are important early in the decision-making process to help define the problem or task. Once the group comes to understand the information environment, however, a consensus around a narrower view (i.e., evaluation paradigm negotiated during feedback loop 2) is beneficial. The ability to read a decision environment and capture the major evaluation questions and the belief structures behind these questions is the essence of shared veridicality.

Questions are also influenced by an individual's capacity to see the values or standards that are behind the questions. Why was the question asked in the first place? Standards describe the results that are desired or should be achieved upon satisfaction of a task. To facilitate performance, researchers contend that standards need to be specific as well as identify qualities and quantities of output expected (Baird, 1986). Specific standards serve as motivational devices for individual performance (Locke *et al.*, 1981; Taylor, 1983) and can anchor future decisions of the client (Huber & Neale, 1986). This phenomenon may explain the evolution of "building block" evaluations which focus on lower level, fragmented tasks which are more easily identified and documented.

Instructional designers lack consistent formative evaluation guidelines regarding products that aim at interactive, integrative skill development. It is difficult (but not impossible) to evaluate situations which allow learners to practice multiple skills. Compounding this complexity is the presence of unpredictable navigational paths and a need to assess variable performance standards. In fact, interactive instructional design seems fraught with many aversive prior learning experiences. For starters, many managers expect cost overruns and schedule slippage. Another fear involves the losses attributed to the new product's possible failure spreading to established products. Finally, while many designers recognize that prevailing linear and iterative strategies result in "piecemeal" products, they lack alternative design methods peculiar to this technology.

Program and product performance is compared to a norm or standard. Usually, the norm is the maximum achieved by an optimal allocation policy. Invariably, performance is found wanting (Busemeyer, Swenson, & Lazarte, 1986). Optimal policies cannot be specified without perfect knowledge of the goal state. For many real-life decisions, however, only imperfect and vague information about the objective and solution is available. Even if specifications exist, management may not have made it clear whether the intent is to meet specifications or exceed them. Hence, there is a perceived need for evaluation. This seems to be particularly true of interactive technologies, such as instructional hypermedia, where the operant criteria have yet to be defined. In fact, this issue seems to be compounded where the product's instructional and business goals may not be clearly communicated to the technicians and instructional designers. What often results is loyalty to functional standards versus the total plan, because immediate functional rewards upstage measures of organizational performance. For example, in university environments where product development is almost exclusively driven by external funding, the product can have high priority within the grant but low priority throughout the rest of the institution.

Standards are often very difficult to calculate, and it seems unreasonable to expect that the typical client knows the optimal solution *a priori*. For example, developers' and users' judgment of product quality extends beyond hardware and software. Quality involves technical, educational, and financial attributes; installation issues; low maintenance; high reliability; compatibility with other equipment already in place; ease of upgrading; and multi-platform access. These are standards that are typically not incorporated into questions asked by developers. However, it is reasonable to expect that program managers and designers can improve their standards and rules for optimal policies after training with informative feedback (Busemeyer, Swenson, & Lazarte, 1986). And the corollary is that while this rational explanation may be possible, the evaluators must be prepared for instances where the client intends the evaluation to serve functions other than an error-reducing role. For example, clients may want the evaluation to give evidence of a key player's competence, signal impending action, or "cover their tracks."

Expectations about future outcomes strongly affect one's decisions (Abelson & Levi, 1985; Feather, 1982). Developers often devote much time (and worry) examining the implications of alternative designs and the adequacy of the likely reward in view of the risks incurred. Because of the importance of such expectations, much research has been devoted to understanding how individuals estimate probabilities of future events. Evidence has accumulated that individuals use a general cognitive strategy, the "availability heuristic" (Tversky & Kahneman, 1973). In using this heuristic, individuals estimate the probability of events by the ease with which they can recall or cognitively construct relevant instances. Specifically, questions can serve as a valuable heuristic or cognitively simplifying strategy for participants in the evaluation process.

The strategies of cognitive feedback and negotiation can vary in their impact on the client. For example, the Nominal Group Technique and the Delphi method appear to be significantly less helpful in facilitating individual learning, in reducing intragroup conflict, and in building consensus. These circumstances were more enhanced when no method of structuring was imposed on group members. Groups were thought by their members to perform more satisfactorily in situations where individual informative feedback was provided to each member, freely exchanged, and fully discussed with focus groups (Zemke & Kramlinger, 1982). In fact, these studies suggest shared cognitive feedback will result in significantly better performance than either of the reduced feedback treatments.

Not surprisingly, our field experience indicates that decision makers use only a subset of available information in evaluating a program. Rather, managers seem to rely on heuristics to simplify complex environments. While serving to avoid information overload, inappropriately applied heuristics can provide a significant source of bias and error for decision outcomes. For instance, people seem inclined to overweigh certainty in their decisions (Kahneman & Tversky, 1979). As evaluators, we should anticipate this heuristic when clients generate evaluation questions—and strive for questions that capture the task's complexity rather than satisfy predetermined decision making. The systematic use of shared cognitive feedback and negotiation to "cleanse" the questions is seen as an effective strategy to minimize this bias.

Finally, framing a question can lead to a perceptual bias which may potentially be elicited by either task or context characteristics. Kahneman and Tversky (1979) suggest that decision makers treat the prospect of gains much differently than the prospect of losses. Often, whether the decision maker is evaluating the prospect of gains or losses is simply a matter of the way a question is presented or phrased. Thus, the way questions as well as findings are framed (in terms of losses or gains) can influence decision makers' risk propensity and thereby their decisions (Bazerman, Magliozzi, & Neale, 1985; Fischoff & MacGregor, 1982; Huber & Neale, 1986; Neale & Bazerman, 1985).

Phase 2: Description of Data Sources and Analysis of Alternatives

The quality of the ultimate choices made hinges upon how well the clients and evaluators are able to attend to, encode, store, retrieve, and integrate information from multiple sources into a judgment. Ilgen, Fisher, and Taylor (1979) identified feedback source as a particularly critical determinant of feedback utilization. They go on to warn that individual differences often influence feedback receptivity, credibility, and use.

Unfortunately, this process is not easy. A piece of information must pass through many filters before it is recorded or retrieved. Decision makers have a propensity to use only a subset of available information when judging a program's worth. This irregular (and often irrational) process may be more systematic if feedback loops are used. This loop or cycle consists of: (1) information inputs; (2) perceptual representations; and (3) outputs regarding the evidence gathered to answer the questions posed in phase one. Two feedback loops appear to operate during this second phase.

The first feedback loop in this phase is depicted in Figure 13.6. The evaluator collects data. This process is affected by: the stability of the organizational environment; the length of the time the evaluation has committed to dwelling in the system; and the nature of the balance between qualitative and quantitative evidence. Acquiring information prior to a decision has two major risks. First, a tenuous evaluator could overacquire information and incur excessive costs. Second, an overconfident evaluator might underacquire information and incur excessive risks of decisional error. In any event, the costs of gathering additional information may be immediate and easy to estimate,

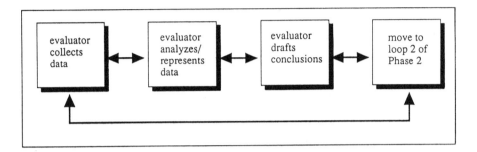

Figure 13.6. Three cognitive events that occur during the first cycle of collecting and describing the data.

but the benefits of doing so can be unclear and often long delayed (Connolly & Thorn, 1987).

Next, the evaluator analyzes the obtained data. This representation is affected by a myriad of factors such as: the evaluator's information load capacity; his or her audience analysis; the amount of anticipated versus unanticipated information revealed; audience and client analysis; and whether a compensatory or noncompensatory data synthesis model is being used (Einhorn & Hogarth, 1981; Billings & Marcus, 1983). Noncompensatory models minimize the criticisms and divergent data. Compensatory models allow the representation of cognitively complex and sophisticated strategies for information integration.

After the data receives its initial analysis, the evaluator reports initial data findings to the client. This reporting procedure must consider many factors. Some crucial variables include: the amount of feedback processing time available to the client; the client's relative emphasis on program documentation versus program improvement; and whether the evidence can be shared with the clientele all at one time or presented over a period of time.

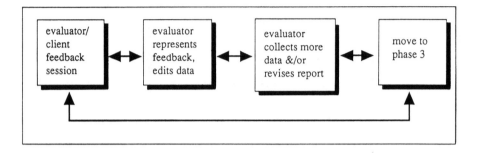

Figure 13.7. The second cognitive cycle which occurs when the evaluator receives feedback from the client about the data collected.

Perceptual errors can result if the evaluator does not receive a feedback message from the client regarding the accuracy of this initial data report. By scheduling a regular feedback session (see Figure 13.7), the client's initial certitude about the original evaluation plan (as well as hidden agendas) can be ascertained. In the process, a sort of error-checking occurs about the perceived accuracy of the data thus far collected, as well as an early measuring of the evaluator's credibility (Northcraft & Earley, 1989; Podsakoff & Farh, 1989). This is also the time to assess the client's tunnel vision and blind spots (i.e., selective perception).

The evaluator cognitively represents the client's feedback messages in light of commitments (sometimes complementary and sometimes competing) between the client and evaluator. This representation takes the form of either improving or simply documenting the program. A choice point also involves the balance between qualitative and quantitative data. Obviously, this takes skill in balancing positive and negative feedback. This perceptual recycling of data perceptions is necessary in light of research showing that human information acquisition is often weakly guided by normative, cost-minimizing considerations. This occurs even when serious efforts are made to simplify the task, provide high motivation, and focus attention on balancing information costs and benefits. Clients consistently underpurchase "good" information, and "bad" information is consistently overpurchased. One part of the explanation is client difficulty in discerning the validity of different information sources, even after repeated exposure. Another possible explanation is the certainty of the cost involved in acquiring information as against the uncertainty of its benefits in reducing decision errors. A risk-adverse client will tend to overpurchase, a risk seeker to underpurchase.

Finally, the evaluator edits the initial data analysis and reports the revisions along with the implications of preliminary judgments given the evidence. Once again, influencing variables include the amount of time available to the evaluation for information feedback to the client, the kind of heuristics which accompany the data, the way information is "framed," and the form of information display.

Implications of Phase 2. Let's continue the example of formative evaluation of interactive technology products and/or projects. The actual process of data collection can generate as many questions as it answers. Just consider the following issues:

- How continuously should data collection be conducted: during rapid prototyping, draft form testing, final testing, or during each stage of the developmental process?
- What qualitative and quantitative methods should be used: self-evaluation, expert review or student review (Montague *et al.*, 1983); try-out, revision testing sessions (Geis, Burt, & Weston 1985); draft, revise and field-test (Dick & Carey, 1985); one-to-one testing; group testing; extended testing (Stolovitch, 1982; Komoski & Woodward, 1985); peer debriefing; triangulation; focus groups (Morris & Smith, 1988); negative case analysis; and/or audit checks?
- Who should be included as data sources: learners (expert versus novice), developers, subject area experts, teachers and trainers, native informants, audience specialists, gatekeepers, sponsors, former learners, editors?
- How many people should be involved—what is an "adequate" size?
- What are desirable characteristics of the data sources: representative versus select (e.g., highly verbal or high aptitude), active versus passive, internal versus external to project, continuous versus one-time involvement?
- Where should data be collected: in-house versus field, using simplified versus progressively more complex and less familiar systems?
- When should data collection stop? For example, should evaluation

continue until redundancy of learner comments occurs? When is the criterion performance level reached? (Jolliffe, 1990)

The client may accept the evidence "as is," request additional evidence, or even seek to reject the evaluation. For example, the use of user feedback in instructional materials development tends to be supported in research (Baker, 1974; Andrews & Goodson, 1980; Stolovitch, 1975; Stolovitch, 1982; Wager, 1983; Weston, 1986). In general, there does not seem to be an indication that one method of gathering feedback is superior to another. Rather, findings suggest that materials that have undergone formative evaluation with users were superior to original versions. While there is agreement that user feedback promotes product improvement, few clear guidelines exist regarding how to build this feedback systematically into the development process.

Knowledge of client expectations *and* behavioral characteristics is essential for evaluators when gauging the receptivity to their activities and ultimately to the information gathered. Available research in this area suggest that decision-makers are:

- only weakly responsive to various normative considerations such as information quality and cost (Pitz, 1968; Wendt, 1969);
- substantially responsive to normatively irrelevant factors such as total information available (Levine, 1975);
- slow to show learning in repeated decision situations (Lanzetta & Kanareff, 1962; Wallsten, 1968; Busemeyer, 1985); and
- not consistent in their need for either overpurchasing or underpurchasing information (Pitz et al., 1969; Hershman & Levine, 1970) though risk seekers show a tendency to underpurchase information.

A two-tiered approach to data sharing is important for both cognitive and political reasons. The data is most likely to be heard and used by clients if they believe it is true and has utility. This satisfaction index seems to rise when client feedback about data accuracy is sought before presenting data of a judgmental nature. Additionally, the form of information display can encourage or discourage certain methods of cognitive processing, given the propensity of humans to adopt strategies which minimize their effort. For example, organizing data into a table makes quantitative information easier to use, increasing its impact upon choices (Russo, 1977, 1978). Similarly, when data is described in words instead of numbers, decision makers abandon strategies that use mental arithmetic (Huber, 1980). As Slovic (1966, 1975) has indicated, the more effort required, the more likely it is that clients will ignore or misuse information. Cognitive strain may cause decision makers to resort to simplifying strategies or heuristics, many of which lead to biased responses, such as preference reversals and violations of transivity. They take information as presented and change the strategy to suit the display rather than transform the data to fit the strategy. When evaluators recognize this process and the impact of framing, they can design information feedback displays which passively encourage better information processing (Levin *et al.*, 1985).

Consider Snyder and Swann's (1978) proposal that in the testing of questions and hypotheses (about themselves or other people or events), people predominantly seek to confirm their pre-existing notions. This implies a pervasive insensitivity to disconfirming evidence, and (presumably) a reluctance to generate alternatives. The implications for how evaluators can feed back information to clients are profound. If the evaluation uncovers data which contradicts the client's prevailing views, this discordant information should be fed back at several stages, not all at once, or it will probably be rejected. Another variable which evaluators may be able to manipulate is client motivation. The tendency to confirm one's expectations could depend on the client's motivational state. According to Mayseless and Kruglanski (1987), the motivation to respond to a problem may be affected by three needs:

- those needing high cognitive structure tend to base their judgments on early information, so be careful what information you first release;
- those with a high fear of invalidity are more open to alternatives, and if this value can be tapped, it promotes unfreezing of existing perceptions; and
- those needing specific conclusions will reject unrelated, albeit important, information.

Phase 3: Making Judgments

Many evaluators neglect to address their role in the act of judging, preferring to perceive themselves as untainted by values issues. This is counterintuitive. Judgment pervades the total process, from the selection of questions and data sources to the ultimate decisions reached and choices made. Figure 13.8 presents a series of informational inputs, perceptual representations, and actions in order to generate judgments about program worth.

After receiving the evaluator's final descriptions, data analyses, and tentative alternatives, the client reacts in the form of another feedback message. The nature of this feedback will be tempered by the client's perceptions of certitude about the findings and expected gains versus losses. Many researchers are pessimistic about managers' abilities to interpret accurately information from complex environments accurately. Managers are thought to suffer from selective perception (Dearborn & Simon, 1958), strategic

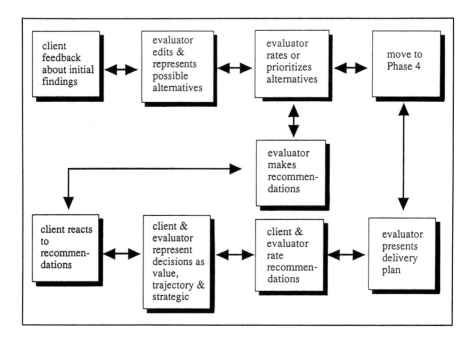

Figure 13.8. The cognitive events that occur during the judgment phase of an evaluation.

myopia (Lorsch, 1985), tunnel vision (Mason & Mitroff, 1981), blind spots (Murray, 1978), and uneven levels of confidence (Sharp, Cutler, & Penrod, 1988).

Given the client's reactions, the evaluator itemizes and begins to edit the pool of possible alternatives in preparation for generating judgments. Variables that seem to influence this editing process include the evaluator's capacity to visualize a continuum of concrete and abstract instances, the duration of events, and the client's self-efficacy status.

Editing results in the evaluator rating or valuing alternatives against the standards specified in Phase One. Besides the amount of processing time available for the evaluation, what is at stake is the quality of the alternatives envisioned as well as the heuristics used for conveying these alternatives to the client (for example, availability, adjustment, anchoring, and representativeness).

It appears that some decision strategies are used more than others. Recent research suggests expectation models over-intellectualize the cognitive processes people use when choosing alternative actions (Schwab, Olian-Gottlieb, & Heneman, 1979; Fischhoff, Goitein, & Shapira, 1983; Mitchell & Beach, 1990). For example, formal analytic strategies are seldom used, even by people who know about them. Isenberg (1984) adds that even when they use these logical strategies, they seldom accept the results that run counter to their intuition. In certain cases, intuition turns out to be more accurate than analytic strategies (Hammond, Hamm, Grassia, & Pearson, 1987). Mitchell and Beach (1990, p. 3) capture this concept well with the following statement: "Formal analytic strategies require a great deal of concentration, time, effort, and skill, and very few decisions are worth all that. Moreover, for even very important decisions, the formal strategies often seem too coldly intellectual."

Observations of professional decision-makers making on-the-job decisions also support the notion that few decisions involve explicit balancing of costs and benefits, let alone the use of behavioristic probability models (Peters, 1979). Mintzberg (1975) reported that most decisions involved only one option rather than many. The decision was whether to go with that option rather than a choice among competing options.

Simultaneously, the evaluator and the client develop judgments. Their ability to form sound information-based judgments appears to be grounded upon many factors, including:

- the ability to reason on three levels: deductively, inductively, and abductively;
- the ability to manipulate overt and covert information normatively and heuristically;
- the clarity of expectations, both internal and external; and
- the amount of cognitive dissonance and uncertainty of the decision to be reached.

Out of the judgments represented in the prior step, the evaluator synthesizes a delivery strategy and accompanying recommendations. Besides dealing with the standard variables of determining the timing, written and/or oral formats, and the framing of the delivery matrix, the evaluator needs to weigh the impact of priming. Priming is a process through which particular information becomes activated or more readily accessible to recall (Wyer & Srull, 1980). Priming has been found to impact the type of action plan developed by an individual. In fact, those individuals who were faced with pressures imposed by a difficult goal relied more heavily on the plan they had been provided than those with more general goals (Earley & Perry, 1987). Furthermore, recommendations are more likely to be maintained if the outcomes are positive and more likely to be changed if the outcomes are posed negatively.

Implications of Phase 3. Given the fact that decision makers are required to integrate information from numerous sources when forming a judgment, the quality of the resultant judgments relies on the value each stakeholder places on this information. For example, Foshay (1984) suggests three criteria of interest to training vendors:

- cost-effectiveness (such as reliability and validity of measurement, return on investment, corporate reputation, and contractual expectations for project);
- compatibility with project management systems in terms of yielding timely, useful project status information and impacting employee morale and productivity;
- compatibility with the design systems such as generating information specific to design and development decisions.

While the research base is limited, our experience suggests that clients judge situations as instances of types with which they are familiar (pattern recognition). They tend to respond best where their own prior successful solutions are presented as the recommended strategies. This can be a problem when trying to enhance an already effective operation with a novel strategy. In addition, there seems to be a difference in whether the "client" making the judgments is an individual or a collective. Fischhoff *et al.* (1983) suggest that while individual clients may adapt to recommendations and judgments that will further their gains more easily than their losses, a group of clients is influenced by social consensus. Team members who have been recently successful are more responsive to the needs of others and are less likely to make independently serving judgments.

Self-esteem seems to be a related variable as well. Recent research (Weiss & Knight, 1980; Knight & Nadel, 1986) suggests that low self-esteem people gather more information about possible solutions before implementation and perform better on tasks where the one best solution must be identified (i.e., optimizing). High self-esteem people seem to search for less information before trying a solution, performing better on tasks with obvious solutions, strict time constraints, or where information search is costly. Knight and Nadel (1986) suggest that high self-esteem managers would be less likely than managers low in self-esteem to experiment with new policies or solutions when confronted with negative performance feedback.

While Fischhoff's findings bode well for cohesive teams, many interactive development projects consist of several (sometimes competing) teams. This specialization can give rise to functional managers who begin to insist on making all decisions pertaining to their respective stages, and inputs from other teams are not welcomed. The longer the development cycle, the greater the possibility of communication rifts. A compounding problem concerns accountability and receptivity to evaluation feedback in competing environments. If functional managers know they will be held accountable for anything that goes wrong, there is a tendency to hold up work on the new product pending written notice (Foshay, 1984). This sign-off process can dramatically affect the openness to risk-taking.

People's cognitive representation of judgmental tasks may conceive of "probabilities" as indices of belief intensity rather than as ratios of favorable chances (Cohen, 1982). They also might conceive of events as nonrandom (Cohen, 1982) and fail to take into account all the potentially relevant information or all the potentially relevant alternatives (Hintikka & Hintikka, 1983). It appears that the motivation to respond to judgmental questions may be affected by at least two needs: the need for cognitive structure and the fear of invalidity. Preliminary research by Mayseless and Kruglanski (1987) suggests that revision of judgments might be slower under a high fear of invalidity but faster under a high need for structure. "In short, fear of invalidity might induce a tendency to be conservative, whereas need for structure might induce a tendency to be excessive" (p. 180). For example, in novel, open-ended environments such as instructional hypermedia projects, designers may often experience an acute need for guiding structure, to which they might respond by adopting inappropriately high levels of self-assurance and a closed-mindedness to alternative points of view.

This heightened need for cognitive structure is assumed to promote an early closure on a solution—this is referred to as "cognitive freezing" (Freund, Kruglanski, & Schpitzajzen, 1985). For evaluators, this suggests the many risks inherent in how early to give client feedback as well as the nature of the information's significance. Get to know your client cognitively! Even for evaluators this poses a risk. For example, high-structure evaluators who rely on checklists for interactive instructional materials revision risk neglecting some critical components, since little prescriptive documentation exists at this juncture. It seems more defensible to involve a diverse set of leaders and opinion makers as reviewers, if the goal is to trend acceptance of materials. There is still little to guide us in deciding how to choose experts (as well as evaluators) and how to guide their task or structure their output (Geis, 1987).

A person with a high need for cognitive structure is likely to inhibit the generation of competing alternatives to a given recommendation, because such alternatives might appear to threaten his existing schema. Previous research manipulating the need for structure in such ways found that individuals in which this need was aroused tended to base their judgments more on (1) early information, rejecting subsequent data, thereby exhibiting "primacy effects," and (2) on pre-existing stereotypes, in this sense being theory rather than data driven. Furthermore, high versus low "need for structure" individuals tended more to seek comparison with similarly minded others likely to support their views and opinions (Mayseless & Kruglanski, 1987). High "need for structure" individuals were characterized by: higher initial confidence in their judgment; more confidence in early information provided by the search; fewer requests for information; and high final confidence in their judgment.

Functionally opposite to the need for structure is the fear of invalidity. This motivation has to do with the desire to avoid mistakes in judgment in terms of their perceived costliness. Where high need for structure promotes a freezing of the judgmental process, fear of invalidity may often promote unfreezing; that is, an increased tendency to respond positively to alternative solutions to the existing situation and/or an increased sensitivity to information inconsistent with the prevailing order and negative feedback. Previous research manipulating the fear of invalidity found that high fear of invalidity individuals suppressed the magnitude of primacy effects. Instead, they had a tendency to translate stereotypes into discriminatory judgments (Kruglanski, 1980; Kruglanski & Freund, 1983). High fear of invalidity individuals had lower initial confidence, less confidence in early information, requested more information, and had higher final confidence. Overall, fear of invalidity might induce a tendency to be conservative.

Priming constraints are not to be ignored (Tversky & Kahneman, 1974, 1981). For example, when presenting negative feedback about the effectiveness of interactive technology in a training program, individuals who are provided with negatively framed recommendations (i.e., taking an action to prevent losses) are more open to questioning the status quo and considering risky alternative strategies, while those provided with positively framed recommendations (judgments to protect gains) are more likely to choose safer, more predictable outcomes. Individuals who have experienced recent losses are more likely to accept informative feedback and are more open to risky alternatives than usual (Fischhoff, Goitein, & Shapira, 1983).

Finally, little research has been conducted concerning the effects of standards on client and evaluator judgment. It seems plausible that standards might anchor rater judgments by providing a natural starting point against which to evaluate performance outcomes. It also seems logical that performance-based priorities (weighting) would simplify the rating process

(Naylor, Ilgen, & Pritchard, 1980) but would exacerbate anchoring effects for low priority standards. Consequently, the validity of performance ratings would be highest when standards are specific and highly weighted (Neale, Huber, & Northcraft, 1987). Results of the Neale *et al.* study suggest that performance standards do not influence raters' performance-related judgments. As they suggest, it would be instructive to test whether evaluators and clients are capable of incorporating differential weighting into their appraisal judgments.

Finally, the recent work on image theory (Beach & Mitchell, 1987; Mitchell & Beach, 1990) seems very promising, particularly the compatibility test. The notion is that intuitive, automatic decision making (and even some deliberative decision making) relies on a simple comparison of each alternative of interest with a limited set of relevant standards called images. Images serve as informational representations and consist of: (1) value images such as the decision-makers' ethics, imperatives, and vision of what is appropriate; (2) trajectory images such as future aspirations, goals, and agendas; and (3) strategic images such as plans, tactics, and forecasts used to attain the desired goals. If a decision alternative is incompatible with these images, it is rejected. If it is not incompatible, it is accepted as the final decision or as one of the alternatives that is passed on to a more complex mechanism that selects the "best" among them. The concept of image is related to cognitivists' "schemata" and "scripts" (Graesser, Woll, Kowalski, & Smith, 1980; Anderson, 1983) and control theory's "template" (Lord & Hanges, 1987). Feedback is matched to the image (i.e., standard or template or scripts) and an alarm sounds if a discrepancy exceeds some threshold. This alarm engages the deliberative process and problem solving commences (Lord & Hanges, 1987).

Phase 4: Arriving at Decisions and Choices

The final phase of this evaluation model deals with decision and choice mechanisms. Decisions consist of presenting clients with alternatives packaged in a certain form, such as a set of outcomes and probabilities. After searching a perceptual representation of options, the decision maker edits and evaluates these alternatives. Alternatives are compared with each other by rationally calculating the degree of preference or using intuitive tests of compatibility and profitability. Choosing the "best" alternative involves strategies such as elimination by aspects (Tversky, 1972) and prospect theory (Kahneman & Tversky, 1979) and profitability test (Mitchell & Beach, 1990). In addition, affective variables such as mood and the context of the alternatives of a choice can be important in making decisions. As discussed earlier, we know that people tend to avoid risk when alternatives are gains and seek risks when alternatives are losses. This is known as a "reflection effect."

The context in which decisions occur appears to give them meaning. In addition, past successes and failures in similar contexts seem to provide guidance about what to do about the current decision. If the current decision is virtually identical to a past decision stored in memory, it is considered to be recognized and automatic (Beach, 1964). Framing results when the contexts of prior similar decision memories are used to go beyond the information that is presented by the current situation alone and interpret new contexts. Thus, we might expect that manipulating the framing process could have a significant effect on decision making and choosing a final behavior (Rachlin, 1989). In novel contexts, where the exceptional is encountered, it seems that the process becomes much less automatic.

The decision mechanism is influenced by whether the client is a novice decision maker or expert, whether the decision environment is self-initiated by the client or imposed from above or pressured from below, and the degree to which the client is risk-taking or risk-seeking. The selection among decision strategies is often seen as a trade-off between the amount of cognitive resources (effort) required to use each strategy and the ability of each strategy to produce an "accurate" effect (Beach & Mitchell, 1978; Brehmer & Hagafors, 1986; Russo & Dosher, 1983).

The choice mechanism is an outgrowth of the decision mechanism. Its efficiency is contingent upon: the client's perceived self-efficacy; the environmental demands of the client's situation; the attractiveness of the alternatives and incentives for change; past expenditures of effort; short- and long-term performance valences; and the type of delivery strategy required by the decision.

Finally, the outcome and implementation of the ultimate choice results. As can be seen by the prior sequences, decision and choice are complex, cognitive operations of which evaluators must be more cognizant if genuine implementation of evaluation findings and recommendations is desired.

Implications of Phase 4. Two major types of decision strategies described in the literature are compensatory and noncompensatory models. Compensatory models represent cognitively complex and sophisticated strategies for information integration (Einhorn & Hogarth, 1981), which are indicated by the absence of the interactive use of cues (Billings & Marcus, 1983). Noncompensatory models are indicated by the interactive use of information cues in which a low score on one dimension cannot be compensated by a high score on another dimension (Billings & Marcus, 1983).

Compensatory strategies refer to either the linear model or the additive difference model. The linear model assumes that each dimension for a decision alternative is given a value for each alternative. Comparisons among alternatives are then based on these overall values, and the alternative with the greatest value is selected. The additive difference model implies that decision makers compare alternatives on each dimension and then sum the differences between dimensions. The summation of differences results in a preference for one decision alternative (Olshavsky, 1979). With both linear and additive difference models, a high value on one dimension "compensates" or counteracts low value on another dimension for the same decision alternative. Noncompensatory strategies involve the use of simplifying rules to reduce the complexity of the decision. The major noncompensatory models identified by Payne (1976) and others include conjunctive, disjunctive, lexicographic, and elimination by aspects strategies.

Frequently, clients must make choices under less than ideal conditions. Uncertainty results when people have incomplete information about the task, and doubt is typically generated in a crisis situation when time is restricted for decision-making and unanticipated choice points have been presented. Increasing uncertainty is often associated with a decentralization of an organization's communication structure (Tushman, 1979) whereas increasing the threat often leads to a centralization of structure (Staw, Sandelands, & Dutton, 1981).

A related factor appears to be the complexity of the task. Decentralized structures were found to be more efficient and resulted in fewer decision errors for complex and uncertain tasks (Shaw, 1981). Faucheaux and Mackenzie (1966) found that groups performing simple tasks evolved toward a centralized structure, while those performing complex tasks did not. Recent researchers have generally supported these findings but caution that the relationship between uncertainty and structure is a complicated one that depends on additional factors such as the quality of feedback a client receives from individuals versus groups, insiders, and outsiders like contracted evaluators; the skill of its leaders; commitment to a course of action; and the particular sources of uncertainty (Argote, 1982; Argote, Devades, & Melone, 1990; Fry & Slocum, 1984; Schoonhoven, 1981).

Empirical results concerning the effects of threat upon structure are fairly consistent throughout the literature. Increasing threat is associated with reduction in the number of information channels used and with an increase in structural centralization (Isenberg, 1981; Johnson & Payne, 1985; Smart & Vertinsky, 1977). Threat leads to an erosion of general cognitive abilities, including the ability to process novel information, and to a reliance upon formal, established procedures and centralization (Milburn, Schuler, & Watman, 1983; Staw *et al.*, 1981).

This tendency toward centralization can be dysfunctional, given centralized structures perform more poorly than decentralized structures for complex and uncertain tasks (Snadowsky, 1972). This appears to occur because members at the hub of centralized networks experience overload under high-uncertainty conditions, and centralized structures are very vulnerable to this increased overload. As more group members perceive that the information needed to reach a decision and make a choice resides throughout the group, rather than one member, we expect decentralized structures to emerge.

Carnevale and Conlon (1988) discuss four basic mediator strategies which have implications for evaluators: press, compensate, integrate, and inaction. Press refers to efforts to reduce disputant stakeholders' aspirations, and occurs when evaluation mediators do not value client aspirations and they perceive that there is little common ground. Compensation deals with efforts to entice client disputants into agreement. For example, this occurs when evaluators value each stakeholder's aspirations, agreement appears likely, and there is little chance that integration will be successful. Integration occurs when there are efforts to discover options that satisfy the disputants' aspirations, or when mediating evaluators value parties' aspirations and perceive that there is common ground. Integration is used when there is a good chance of achieving a mutually acceptable solution. A final choice is inaction, by which the mediating evaluator lets the parties handle the dispute on their own.

Summary

The systematic combination of evaluation and feedback processes can guide the decision-maker in a direction that continually improves his or her performance. This chapter has presented a cognitively grounded framework for evaluating interactive instructional technology programs that addresses three criteria: a systematic methodology which uses a combination of quantitative and qualitative data sources to portray a more holistic reality; helpfulness toward program improvement; and feedback to make values overt and to facilitate the planning of probable futures for a program. To varying degrees, the instructional objectives approach, the decision-making approach, and the values-based approaches all lack consistent methods for systematizing the feedback of both the evaluated and evaluators.

This chapter describes an evaluation framework consisting of four sequential phrases: (1) negotiating a paradigm to focus the evaluation and specifying major questions, sources of evidence, and standards by which to judge the findings; (2) collecting and analyzing data sources and reporting the emerging implications of various alternatives; (3) judging the alternatives and synthesizing a delivery matrix of recommendations; and (4) helping the client to process decision and choice mechanisms instrumental in delivering an improved program.

Recent cognitive research suggests that the presence of feedback in evaluation can dramatically affect the accuracy required of human judgments, decisions, and choices. Evaluation is viewed as a way of monitoring programmatic progress via a series of perception-representation-action feedback loops. In summary, successful evaluation depends upon: (1) availability of feedback; (2) receptivity to feedback; and (3) the opportunity for taking corrective action based on that feedback.

References

AAAS Commission on Science Education. (1965). *An evaluation model and its application.* Publication 65/9. Washington, DC: American Association for the Advancement of Science.

Abelson, R.P., & Levi, A. (1985). Decision-making and decision theory. In G. Lindzey & E. Aronson (Eds.), *Handbook of social psychology* (3rd ed., Vol. I, pp. 231–309). New York: Random House.

Alkin, M.C. (1968). *Towards an evaluation model: A system approach.* CSE Working Paper No. 4. Los Angeles, CA: Center for the Study of Evaluation.

Anderson, C.A. (1983). Imagination and expectation: The effect of imaging behavioral scripts on personal intentions. *Journal of Personality and Social Psychology, 45,* 293–305.

Andrews, D.H., & Goodson, L.A. (1980). A comparative analysis of models of instructional design. *Journal of Instructional Development, 3*(4), 2–16.

Argote, L. (1982). Input uncertainty and organizational coordination in hospital emergency units. *Administrative Science Quarterly, 27*(3), 420–434.

Argote, L., Devades, R., & Melone, N. (1990). The base-rate fallacy: Contrasting processes and outcomes of group and individual judgment. *Organizational Behavior and Human Decision Processes, 46,* 296–310.

Argote, L., Seabright, M.A., & Dyer, L. (1986). Individual versus group use of base-rate and individuating information. *Organizational Behavior and Human Decision Processes, 38,* 65–75.

Baird, J.R. (1986). Improving learning through enhanced metacognition: A classroom study. *European Journal of Science and Education, 8,* 263–282.

Baker, E.L. (1974). Formative evaluation of instruction. In W.J. Popham (Ed.), *Evaluation in education* (pp 531–585). Berkeley, CA: McCutchan.

Bazerman, M.H., Magliozzi, T., & Neale, M.A. (1985). Integrative bargaining in a competitive market. *Organizational Behavior and Human Decision Processes, 35*(3), 294–313.

Beach, L.R. (1964). Recognition, assimilation, and identification of objects. *Psychological Monographs, 78,* 22–37.

Beach, L.R., & Mitchell, T.R. (1978). A contingency model for the selection of decision strategies. *Academy of Management Review, 3,* 439–449.

Beach, L.R., & Mitchell, T.R. (1987). Image theory: Principles, goals, and plans in decision making. *Acta Psychologica, 66,* 201–220.

Billings, R.S., & Marcus, S.A. (1983). Measures of compensatory and noncompensatory models of decision behavior: Process tracing versus policy capturing. *Organizational Behavior and Human Performance, 31*(3), 331–352.

Brehmer, B., & Hagafors, R. (1986). Use of experts in complex decision making: a paradigm for the study of staff work. *Organizational Behavior and Human Decision Processes, 38*, 181–195.

Busemeyer, J.R. (1985). Decision-making under uncertainty: A comparison of simple scalability, fixed sample, and sequential sampling models. *Journal of Experimental Psychology of Learning, 11*(3), 538–564.

Busemeyer, J.R., Swenson, K.N., & Lazarte, A. (1986). An adaptive approach to resource allocation. *Organizational Behavior and Human Decision Processes, 38*, 318–341.

Carnevale, P.J.D., & Conlon, D.E. (1988). Time pressure and strategic choice in mediation. *Organizational Behavior, 42*(1), 111–133.

Carroll, J. (1984). Analyzing decision behavior: The magician's audience. In T.S. Wallsten (Ed.), *Cognitive processes in choice and decision behaviors* (pp. 69–76). Hillsdale, NJ: Lawrence Erlbaum Associates.

Cohen, L.J. (1982). Are people programmed to commit fallacies? Further thoughts about the interpretation of experimental data on probability judgments. *Journal for the Theory of Social Behavior, 12*, 251–274.

Connolly, T., & Thorn, B.K. (1987). Predecisional information acquisition—effects of task variables on suboptimal search strategies. *Organizational Behavior, 39*(3), 397–416.

Cronbach, L.J. (1963). Course improvement through evaluation. *Teachers College Record, 64*, 672–683.

Dearborn, D.C., & Simon, H.A. (1958). Selective perception: A note on the departmental identification of executives. *Sociometry, 21*, 140–144.

Dick, W., & Carey, L. (1985). *The systematic design of instruction* (2nd ed.). Glenview, IL: Scott Foresman.

Dillon, G. (1981). *Constructing texts: Elements of a theory of composition and style.* Bloomington, IN: Indiana University Press.

Earley, P.C. (1988). Computer-generated performance feedback in the magazine subscription industry. *Organizational Behavior and Human Decision Processes, 41*(1), 50–64.

Earley, P.C., & Perry, D. (1987). Work plan priming. *Organizational Behavior and Human Decision Processes, 39*, 279–302.

Eco, U. (1983). Horns, hooves, insteps: Some hypotheses on the types of abduction. In U. Eco & T.A. Sebeok (Eds.), *The sign of three* (pp. 198–220). Bloomington, IN: Indiana University Press.

Eco, U., & Sebeok, T.A. (Eds.) (1983). *The sign of three.* Bloomington, IN: Indiana University Press.

Einhorn, H.J., & Hogarth, R.M. (1981). Behavioral decision theory: Processes of judgment and choice. *Annual Review of Psychology, 32*, 53–88.

Faucheaux, C., & Mackenzie, K. (1966). Task dependency on organizational centrality: Its behavioral consequences. *Journal of Experimental Social Psychology, 2*, 361–375.

Feather, N.T. (1982). *Expectations and action: Expectancy-value models in psychology.* Hillsdale, NJ: Lawrence Erlbaum Associates.

Fischhoff, B., & Bar-Hillel, M. (1984). Diagnosticity and the base-rate effect. *Memory & Cognition, 12*, 402–410.

Fischhoff, B., Goitein, B., & Shapira, Z. (1983). Subjective expected utility: A model of decision making. In R.W. Scholz (Ed.), *Decision-making under uncertainty* (pp. 96–115). Amsterdam: North Holland.

Fischhoff, B., & MacGregor, (1982). Judged lethality: How much people seem to know depends upon how they are asked. *Risk Analysis, 13*(4), 229–236.

Fisher, S.D., Gettys, C.F., Maming, C., Mehle, T., & Baca, S. (1983). Consistency checking in hypothesis generation. *Organizational Behavior and Human Performance, 31*(2), 233–254.

Foshay, W.R. (1984). QA and QC: A training vendor's view of the formative/summative distinction. *Performance and Instruction, 23*(10), 15–17.

Freund, T., Kruglanski, A.W., & Schpitzajzen, A. (1985). The freezing and unfreezing of impressional primacy: Effects of the need for structure and fear of invalidity. *Personality and Social Psychology Bulletin, 11*(4), 479–487.

Fry, L.W., & Slocum, J.W. (1984). Technology, structure, and workgroup effectiveness: A test of a contingency model. *Academy of Management Journal, 27*(2), 221–246.

Geis, G.L. (1987). Formative evaluation: Developmental testing and expert review. *Performance and Instruction, 26*(4), 1–8.

Geis, G.L., Burt, C., & Weston, C.B. (1985, April). *Instructional development: Developmental testing.* Paper presented at the Annual Meeting of the American Educational Research Association, New Orleans.

Graesser, A.C., Woll, S.B., Kowalski, D.J., & Smith, D.A. (1980). Memory for typical and atypical actions in scripted activities. *Journal of Experimental Psychology, 6,* 503–515.

Guba, E.G. (1969). The failure of educational evaluation. *Educational Techology, 9* (5), 29–38.

Hammond, K.R., Hamm, R.M., Grassia, J., & Pearson, T. (1987). Direct comparison of the efficacy of intuitive and analytical cognition in expert judgment. *IEEE Transactions on Systems, Man, and Cybernetics,* SMC-17, 753–770.

Harris, K.L., & Carnevale, P. (1990). Chilling and hastening: The influence of third-party power and interests on negotiation. *Organizational Behavior and Human Decision Processes, 47,* 138–160.

Hershman, R.L., & Levine, J.R. (1970). Deviations from optimum information-purchase strategies in human decision-making. *Organizational Behavior and Human Performance, 5*(4), 313–329.

Higgins, E.T., & King, G. (1981). Accessibility of social constructs: Information processing consequences of individual and contextual variability. In N. Cantor & J. Kihlstrom (Eds.), *Personality, cognition and social interaction* (pp. 69–121). Hillsdale, NJ: Lawrence Erlbaum Associates.

Hintikka, J., & Hintikka, M.B. (1983). Sherlock Holmes confronts modern logic: Toward a theory of information seeking through questioning. In U. Eco & T.A. Sebeok (Eds.), *The sign of three* (pp. 154–169). Bloomington, IN: Indiana University Press.

Hogarth, R.M. (1981). Beyond discrete biases: Functional and dysfunctional aspects of judgmental heuristics. *Psychological Bulletin, 90,* 197–217.

Huber, O. (1980). The influence of some task variables on cognitive operations in an information processing decision model. *Acta Psychologica, 45*(1–3), 187–196.

Huber, V.L., & Neale, M.A. (1986). Effects of cognitive heuristics and goals on negotiation performance and subsequent goal setting. *Organizational Behavior and Human Decision Processes, 38*(3), 342–365.

Ilgen, D.R., Fisher, C.D., & Taylor, M.S. (1979). Consequences of individual feedback on behavior in organizations. *Journal of Applied Psychology, 64*(4), 349–371.

Isenberg, D.J. (1981). Some effects of time pressure on vertical structures and decision-making accuracy in small groups. *Organizational Behavior and Human Performance, 27*(1), 119–134.

Isenberg, D.J. (1984) How senior managers think. *Harvard Business Review, 62*(6), 80–90.

Johnson, E.J., & Payne, J.W. (1985). Effort and accuracy in choice. *Management Science, 31,* 395–414.

Jolliffe, S.D. (1990). Formative evaluation of interactive training materials. In B.L. Flagg (Ed.), *Formative evaluation for educational technologies* (pp. 99–112). Hillsdale, NJ: Lawrence Erlbaum Associates.

Kahneman, D., Slovic, P., & Tversky, A. (1982). *Judgment under uncertainty: Heuristics and biases.* Cambridge: Cambridge University Press.

Kahneman, D., & Tversky, A. (1979). Prospect theory: An analysis of decision under risk. *Econometrica, 47,* 263–291.

Kleinmuntz, D.N., & Thomas, J.B. (1987). The value of action and inference in dynamic decision making. *Organizational Behavior and Human Decision Processes, 39,* 341–364.

Knight, P.A., & Nadel, J. (1986). Humility revisited: self-esteem, information search, and policy consistency. *Organizational Behavior and Human Decision Processes, 38*(2), 196–206.

Komoski, P.K., & Woodward, A. (1985). The continuing need for the learner verification and revision of textual material. In D.H. Jonassen (Ed.), *The technology of text* (volume two, pp. 231–264). Englewood Cliffs, NJ: Educational Technology Publications.

Kopelman, R.E. (1986). *Managing productivity in organizations: A practical, people-oriented perspective.* New York: McGraw-Hill.

Kruglanski, A.W. (1980). Lay epistomo-logic: Process and contents: Another look at attribution theory. *Psychological Review, 87,* 70–87.

Kruglanski, A.W., & Freund, T. (1983, March). The freezing and unfreezing of lay inferences: Effects ofimpressional primacy, ethnic stereotyping, and numerical anchoring. *Journal of Personality and Social Psychology, 46,* 503–518.

Kunkel, R.C., & Tucker, S.A. (1983). *Critical evaluation skills at a time of retrenchment.* Paper presented at the annual meeting of the Association for Supervision and Curriculum Development, Houston, TX.

Lanzetta, J.T., & Kanareff, V. (1962). Information cost, amount of payoff, and level of aspiration as determinants of information seeking in decision-making. *Behavioral Science, 7,* 459–473.

Levin, J. P., Johnson, R.D., Russo, C.P., & Deldin, P.J. (1985). Framing effects in judgement tasks with varying amounts of information. *Organizational Behavior and Human Decision Processes, 36,* 362–377.

Levine, M. (1975). *A cognitive theory of learning: Research on hypothesis testing.* Hillsdale, NJ: Lawrence Erlbaum Associates.

Lincoln, Y.S., & Guba, E.G. (1985). *Naturalistic inquiry.* Beverly Hills, CA: Sage.

Locke, E.A., Shaw, K.N., Saari, L.M., & Latham, G.P. (1981). Goal setting and task performance: 1969–1980. *Psychological Bulletin, 90,* 125–152.

Lord, R.G., & Hanges, P.J. (1987). A control system model of organizational motivation: Theoretical development and applied applications. *Behavioral Science*, *32*, 161–178.

Lorsch, J.W. (1985). Strategic myopia: Culture as an invisible barrier to change. In R.H. Kilmann, M.J. Saxton, & R. Serpa (Eds.), *Gaining control of the corporate culture* (pp. 84–102). San Francisco, CA: Jossey-Bass.

Mason, R., & Mitroff, I. (1981). *Challenging strategic planning assumptions.* New York: John Wiley & Sons.

Mayseless, O., & Kruglanski, A.W. (1987). What makes you so sure? Effects of epistemic motivations on judgmental confidence. *Organizational Behavior and Human Decision Processes*, *39*, 162–183.

Milburn, T.W., Schuler, R.S., & Watman, K.H. (1983). Organizational crisis. 2. Strategies and responses. *Human Relations*, *36*(12), 1161–1179.

Mintzberg, H. (1975). The manager's job: Folklore and fact. *Harvard Business Review*, *53*(4), 49–61.

Mitchell, T.R., & Beach, L.R. (1990). "'. . . Do I love thee? Let me Count . . .'" Toward an understanding of intuitive and automatic decision making. *Organizational Behavior and Human Decision Processes*, *47*, 1–20.

Montague, W.E., Ellis, J.A., & Wulfeck, W.H. (1983). Instructional quality inventory: A formative evaluation tool for instructional developers. *Performance and Instruction Journal*, *22*(5), 11–13.

Morris, J.D., & Smith, A.B. (1988). Using focus groups to evaluate instructional media: A case study. *Educational Technology*, *28*(3), 27–32.

Murray, E.A. (1978). Strategic choice as a negotiated outcome. *Management Science*, *24*, 960–972.

Naylor, J.C., Ilgen, D.R., & Pritchard, R.D. (1980). *A theory of behavior in organizations.* New York: Academic Press.

Neale, M.A., & Bazerman, M.H. (1985). The effects of framing and negotiation overconfidence on bargaining behaviors and outcomes. *Academy of Management Journal*, *28*, 34–49.

Neale, M.A., Huber, V.L., & Northcraft, G.B. (1987). The framing of negotiations: Contextual versus task frames. *Organizational Behavior and Human Decision Processes*, *39*, 228–241.

Northcraft, G.B., & Earley, P.C. (1989). Technology, credibility, and feedback use. *Organizational Behavior and Human Decision Processes*, *44*, 83–96.

Olshavsky, R.W. (1979). Task complexity and contingent processing in decision making: A replication and extension. *Organizational Behavior and Human Performance*, *24*(3), 300–316.

Pace, R.C. (1968, December). Evaluation perspectives: 1968. Los Angeles, CA: UCLA Center for the Study of Evaluation. (ERIC ED 037828.)

Payne, J.W. (1976). Task complexity and contingent processing in decision making: An information search and protocol analysis. *Organizational Behavior and Human Performance*, *16*, 366–387.

Peters, T. (1979). Leadership: Sad facts and silver linings. *Harvard Business Review*, *57*(6), 164–172.

Pitz, G.F. (1968). Information seeking when available information is limited. *Journal of Experimental Psychology*, *76*, 25–34.

Pitz, G.F., Reinhold, H., & Geller, E.S. (1969). Strategies of information seeking in deferred decision-making. *Organizational Behavior and Human Performance*, *4*, 1–19.

Podsakoff, P.M., & Farh, J. (1989). Effects of feedback sign and credibility on goal setting and task performance. *Organizational Behavior and Human Decision Processes*, *44*, 45–67.

Polanyi, M. (1962). *Personal knowledge*. Chicago, IL: University of Chicago Press.

Polanyi, M. (1966). *The tacit dimension*. London, UK: Pergamon Press.

Polanyi, M. (1975). *Meaning*. Chicago, IL: University of Chicago Press.

Polanyi, M. (1978). *Phenomenology of perception*. London, UK: Routledge & Kegan Paul.

Provus, M. (1969). Evaluation on ongoing programs in the public school system. In R.W. Tyler (Ed.), *Educational evaluation: New roles, new means* (pp. 242–283). Chicago, IL: N.S.S.E.

Provus, M. (1971). *Discrepancy evaluation*. Berkeley, CA: McCutchan Publishing.

Rachlin, H. (1989). *Judgment, decision and choice*. New York: W.H. Freeman.

Reasby, H. (1973). *Application of multiple evaluation strategies to comprehensive and innovative middle school programs*. Unpublished Doctoral Dissertation, University of Washington.

Russo, J.E. (1977). The value of unit price information. *Journal of Marketing Research*, *14*(May), 193–201.

Russo, J.E. (1978). Eye fixations can save the world: A critical comparison between eye fixations and other information processing methodologies. In H. Keith Hunt (Ed.), *Advances in consumer research* (Vol. 5, pp. 561–570). Chicago, IL: Association for Consumer Research.

Russo, J.E., & Dosher, B.A. (1983). Strategies for multi-attribute binary choice. *Journal of Experimental Psychology: Learning, Memory & Cognition*, *9*, 676–696.

Schoonhoven, C.B. (1981). Problems with contingency theory: Testing assumptions hidden within the language of contingency "theory." *Administrative Science Quarterly*, *26*(3), 349–377.

Schwab, D.P., Olian-Gottlieb, J.D., & Heneman, H.G. (1979). Between-subjects expectancy theory research: A statistical view of studies predicting effort and performance. *Psychological Bulletin*, *86*, 139–147.

Scriven, M. (1967). The methodology of evaluation. In R. Tyler *et al.*, *AERA Monograph series on curriculum evaluation*. Chicago, IL: Rand McNally.

Scriven, M. (1972). Prose and cons about goal-free evaluation. *Evaluation Comment*, *3*(4), 1–8.

Scriven, M. (1978, April). *Goal-free evaluation in practice*. Paper presented at the fourth annual meeting of the American Educational Research Association, Toronto, Ontario.

Sharp, G.L., Cutler, B.L., & Penrod, S.D. (1988). Performance feedback improves the resolution of confidence judgments. *Organizational Behavior and Human Decision Processes*, *42*, 271–283.

Shaw, M.E. (1981). *Group dynamics: The social psychology of small group behavior*. New York: McGraw-Hill.

Simon, H.A. (1978). Information processing theory of human problem-solving. In W.K. Estes (Ed.), *Handbook of learning and cognitive processes*. (Vol. 5, pp. 261–309). Hillsdale, NJ: Lawrence Erlbaum Associates.

Slovic, P. (1966). Cue consistency and cue utilization in judgment. *American Journal of Psychology*, *79*, 427–434.

Slovic, P. (1975). Choices between equally valued alternatives. Journal of Experimental Psychology: *Human Perceptions and Performance*, *1*, 280–287.

Smart, C., & Vertinsky, I. (1977). Designs for crisis decision units. *Administrative Science Quarterly, 22*(4), 640–657.

Snadowsky, A. (1972). Communication network research: An examination of controversies. *Human Relations, 25,* 283–306.

Snyder, M., & Swann, W.B., Jr. (1978). Hypothesis-testing processes in social interaction. *Journal of Personality and Social Psychology, 36,* 1202–1212.

Stake, R.E. (1967). The countenance of educational evaluation. *Teachers College Record, 68* (7), 523–540.

Stake, R.E. (1970). Objectives, priorities, and other judgment data. *Review of Educational Research, 40*(2), 181–212.

Stake, R.E. (1972). Focus or portrayal. *Evaluation and Measurement Newsletter, 14,* 1–2.

Stake, R.E. (1973). Measuring what learners learn. In E.R. House (Ed.) *School evaluation, the politics and process* (pp. 193–223). Berkeley, CA: McCutchan.

Stake, R.E. (1983). Program evaluation, particularly responsive evaluation. In G.F. Madaus, M.S. Scriven, & D.L. Stufflebeam (Eds.), *Evaluation models: Viewpoints on educational and human services evaluation* (pp. 287–310). Boston, MA: Kluwer-Nijhoff.

Staw, B.M. (1981). The escalation of commitment to a course of action. *Academy of Management Review, 6,* 577–587.

Staw, B.M., Sandelands, L.E., & Dutton, J.E. (1981). Threat-rigidity effects in organizational behavior: A multilevel analysis review. *Administrative Science Quarterly, 26* (4), 501–524.

Stolovitch, H.D. (1975). Formative evaluation of instructional games. *Improving Human Performance Journal, 4* (3), 126–141.

Stolovitch, H.D. (1982). Applications of the intermediate technology of learner verification and revision (LVR) for adapting international instructional resources to meet local needs. *NSPI Journal, 21*(7), 16–22.

Stufflebeam, D.L. (1983). The CIPP model for program evaluation. In G.F. Madaus, M. Scriven, & D.L. Stufflebeam (Eds.), *Evaluation models: Viewpoints on educational and human services evaluation* (pp. 117–143). Boston, MA: Kluwer-Nijhoff.

Stufflebeam, D.L., Foley, W.J., Gephard, W.J., Guba, E.G., Hammond, R.L., Merriman, H.O., & Provus, M.M. (1971). *Educational evaluation and decision-making.* Itasca, IL: F.E. Peacock Publishers.

Taba, H., & Sawin, E. (1962). A proposed model in evaluation. *Educational Leadership, 20*(1), 57–71.

Taylor, S.E. (1983). Adjustment to threatening events—a theory of cognitive adaptation. *American Psychologist, 38*(11), 1161–1173.

Tucker, S.A., & Dempsey, J.V. (1991). An evaluation semiotic. *American Journal of Semiotics, 8*(4), 73–103.

Tushman, M. (1979). Work characteristics and subunit communication structure: A contingency analysis. *Administrative Science Quarterly, 24,* 82–98.

Tversky, A. (1972). Elimination by aspects: A theory of choice. *Psychology Review, 79,* 281–299.

Tversky, A., & Kahneman, D. (1973). Availability: A heuristic for judging frequency and probability. *Cognitive Psychology, 4,* 207–232.

Tversky, A., & Kahneman, D. (1974). Judgment under uncertainty: Heuristics and biases. *Science, 185,* 1124–1131.

Tversky, A., & Kahneman, D. (1981). The framing of decisions and the psychology of choice. *Science, 211*(4481), 453–458.

Tyler, R.W. (1942). General statement on evaluation. *Journal of Educational Research, 30,* 492–501.

Wager, L.C. (1983). One-to-one and small group formative evaluation: An examination of two basic formative evaluation procedures. *Performance Improvement Quarterly, 22*(5), 5–7.

Wallsten, T.S. (1968). Failure of predictions from subjectively expected utility theory in a Bayesian decision task. *Organizational Behavior and Human Performance, 3,* 239–252.

Walsh, J.P., & Fahey, L. (1986). The role of negotiated belief structures in strategy making. *Journal of Management, 12*(3), 325–338.

Walsh, J.P., Henderson, C., & Deighton, J. (1988). Negotiated belief structures and decision performance: An empirical investigation. *Organizational Behavior and Human Decision Processes, 42,* 194–216.

Weckworth, V.E. (1969). A conceptual model versus the real world of health care service delivery. In C.E. Hopkins (Ed.), *Outcomes conference: Methodology of identifying, measuring and evaluating outcomes of Health Service programs, systems and subsystems.* Rockville, MD: Office of Scientific and Technical Information, NCH SRD, 39–62.

Weiss, H.M., & Knight, P.A. (1980). The utility of humility: self-esteem, information search, and problem solving efficiency. *Organizational Behavior and Human Performance, 25*(2), 216–223.

Wendt, D. (1969). Value of information for decisions. *Journal of Mathematical Psychology, 6*(3), 430–443.

Weston, C.B. (1986, Winter). Formative evaluation of instructional materials: An overview of approaches, *Canadian Journal of Educational Communications, 15*(1), 5–11.

Wyer, R.S., Jr., & Srull, T.K. (1980). The processing of social stimulus information: A conceptual integration. In R. Hastie, T.M. Ostrom, E.B. Ebbesen, R.S. Wyer, Jr., D.L. Hamilton, & D.E. Carlson (Eds.), *Person memory: The cognitive basis of social perception* (pp. 227–300). Hillsdale, NJ: Lawrence Erlbaum Associates.

Zemke, R., & Kramlinger, T. (1982). *Figuring things out: A trainers' guide to needs and task analysis.* Reading, MA: Addison-Wesley.

About the Authors

David W. Dalton

David W. Dalton is Associate Professor in the Department of Educational Psychology and Leadership Studies at Kent State University. He previously was on the faculty at Indiana University and Florida State University. He is the author of many research publications on the subjects of interactive videodisc design, feedback, and instructional development.

John V. Dempsey

John V. Dempsey is Assistant Professor of Instructional Design and Development at the University of South Alabama. Prior to joining the faculty at South Alabama, Dr. Dempsey worked in the evaluation and testing section of the Florida Department of Education. Before that he worked for the Center for Educational Technology at Florida State University as a senior instructional designer and programming production coordinator. His interests include the design, development, and evaluation of interactive instructional technologies with a particular emphasis on variables involving feedback, concept learning, automaticity, gaming, quality control, and photo-interviewing. In addition to a number of articles in the area of instructional technology, Dempsey is co-author of the *Learner's Guide to the Principles of Instructional Design*. He received his Ph.D. in Instructional Systems from Florida State University.

Marcy P. Driscoll

Marcy P. Driscoll received her Ph.D. in Educational Psychology from the University of Massachusetts at Amherst in 1978. Prior to joining the faculty at Florida State University in 1980, she worked as an Instructional Design Consultant for Educational Radio & Television of Iran and the New York Department of Mental Health, and as a Project Director for National Evaluation Systems, Amherst, MA. She is currently Associate Professor in the Division of Psychology in Education at Arizona State University. Her interests encompass learning and instructional theory, feedback, and alternative paradigms for research. On these topics, she has published numerous articles and, with co-author Robert M. Gagné, a book entitled *Essentials of Learning for Instruction*. She is Editor of the Research Section of *Educational Technology* magazine.

Kathleen McDermott Hannafin
Kathleen McDermott Hannafin earned her Ph.D. in Instructional Systems from the Pennsylvania State University. Her research interests focus on technology, school restructuring, and applications of technology in teacher education. Presently, she is Research Associate at Learning Systems Institute at Florida State University.

Michael J. Hannafin
Michael J. Hannafin is Professor of Instructional Systems at Florida State University. Dr. Hannafin earned his Ph.D. in Educational Technology from Arizona State University in 1981. Since that time he has held academic positions at both the University of Colorado and The Pennsylvania State University prior to joining Florida State in the summer of 1989. His research has focused on the psychological underpinnings of computer-mediated learning, and has emphasized emerging instructional technologies such as interactive video, voice recognition, and so forth. During his career, he has published more than 50 journal articles, and has more than 90 research and theory presentations both domestically and in the former Soviet Union and Canada. He has authored an award-winning textbook entitled *The Design, Development, and Evaluation of Instructional Software*, and has written four chapters contained within edited texts.

Dorothy M. Hoska
Dorothy M. Hoska is a PhD candidate in Curricular and Instructional Systems at the University of Minnesota. Over the last twelve years, she has concentrated on developing technical and managerial instructional materials for businesses, with an emphasis on multimedia curricula that include computer-based instruction. She is currently the senior training specialist for Delta Environmental Consultants, Inc.

DeLayne R. Hudspeth
DeLayne R. Hudspeth, Associate Professor and Area Coordinator of Instructional Technology in the College of Education at the University of Texas at Austin, is President of the National Society of Performance Instruction chapter in Austin, gives papers, is active in two other national organizations, has published in the area of systems design and telecommunications, and consults widely for business, education, and health organizations.

John W. Jacobs

John W. Jacobs is a human resource consultant with Electronic Selection Systems Corporation, a company that specializes in combining simulation technology with other technologies (e.g., video, computer, or interactive videodisc) to develop employee selection instruments. Prior to this position, Jacobs was awarded a Department of Energy Fellowship and conducted a meta-analysis of flight simulation training literature for the U.S. Navy. He received his doctorate in Psychology from Florida State University. While at FSU, Jacobs oversaw production of a "learning strategies" curriculum for a large CBI project. He has remained active in the continued development of instructional systems that promote reading strategy use. Jacobs' research interests are in the area of human cognition, including cognitive skills training and attentional factors in learning.

David W. Johnson

David W. Johnson is Professor of Educational Psychology with an emphasis on Social Psychology at the University of Minnesota. His master's and doctoral degrees are from Columbia University. Dr. Johnson is the author of 15 books, including an educational psychology textbook. He has published over 200 research articles in leading psychological journals. In 1972, Johnson received a national award for outstanding research from the American Personnel and Guidance Association, and in 1981 he received a national award for outstanding research on intergroup relationships from Division 9 of the American Psychological Association. He is currently listed in Marquis' *Who's Who in the World*. For the past 20 years he has served as an organizational consultant to schools and businesses in such areas as management training, team building, ethnic relations, conflict resolution, and the evaluating of affective outcomes of school systems. In addition, Johnson is an authority on experimental learning, a practicing psychotherapist, and a recent past editor of the *American Educational Research Journal*.

Roger T. Johnson

Rogert T. Johnson is Professor of Curriculum and Instruction with an emphasis on Science Education at the University of Minnesota. He has an M.A. from Ball State University and an Ed.D. from the University of California at Berkeley. His public school teaching experience includes teaching in kindergarten through eighth grade in self-contained classrooms, open schools, non-graded situations, cottage schools, and departmentalized (science) schools. While teaching in the Jefferson County schools in Colorado, he received an award for outstanding teaching. He has taught in the Harvard-Newton Intern Program as a Master Teacher and was curriculum developer with the Elementary Science Study in the Educational Develop-

346   *Interactive Instruction and Feedback*

ment Center. For three summers he has taught classes in the British primary schools at the University of Sussex near Brighton, England. He is the author of numerous articles and coauthor of *Learning Together and Alone* and *Circles of Learning*.

Raymond W. Kulhavy

Raymond W. Kulhavy is Regents Professor of Psychology in Education at Arizona State University. After receiving a doctorate in Educational Psychology from the University of Illinois at Champaign-Urbana, Kulhavy began a distinguished career which included stints as a Visiting Research Scientist with the U.S. Navy Research Center, a Fulbright Research Scholar at the Institute for Psychology at the University of Rome (Italy), and a Visiting Lecturer at the University of Newcastle (Australia). In addition to his numerous articles and chapters in the area of feedback and educational psychology, Kulhavy serves on the editorial and review boards of a dozen major educational psychology and research journals. Dr. Kulhavy is Editor of *Contemporary Educational Psychology*.

Brenda C. Litchfield

Brenda C. Litchfield is Assistant Professor of Curriculum and Instruction at the University of South Alabama. She earned her Ph.D. in Instructional Systems at Florida State University. Prior to joining the faculty at USA she was director of a large level III interactive videodisc project funded by the National Science Foundation, which produced a science curriculum for middle-grade students. She also has working experience as an instructional designer and quality control specialist on a large military development project. Dr. Litchfield serves as consultant to school districts and state and private agencies in the areas of instructional technology and environmental science education. She taught elementary school and middle and high school science for 11 years. Her research interests include feedback and motivational design factors, interactive videodisc design and development, and teacher education.

Gary R. Morrison

Gary R. Morrison is an Associate Professor in the Department of Curriculum and Instruction at Memphis State University. Before joining the faculty at MSU in 1984, Morrison worked as a project manager or instructional designer for Tenneco Oil Company, General Electric Company, Solar Turbines International, and the University of Mid-America. Dr. Morrison has conducted research and published extensively in the area of personalizing interactive instruction and screen design factors.

Edna Holland Mory

Edna Holland Mory received her Ph.D. in Instructional Systems from Florida State University. Her dissertation focused on the effects of feedback and employed a model of response certitude upon student performance and efficiency within both verbal information and concept tasks. She has also completed research in the area of teacher planning. She wishes to continue research in these areas as well as expand her line of inquiry to such areas as student motivation, creative imagery and illustrations, and design factors in the use of CAI. She recently completed work on a project for the Florida Department of Health and Rehabilitative Services as an instructional designer and programmer for a mainframe simulation.

Tillman J. Ragan

Tillman J. Ragan is currently Professor and head of the Instructional Psychology and Technology Program at the University of Oklahoma. He received his Ph.D. in Instructional Technology from Syracuse University in 1970. Ragan is the author of five books and numerous journal articles. He has been active in professional organizations, including the International Visual Literacy Association, of which he has been Vice President. His area of research and teaching interests is in applications of computer technology to instruction, learner characteristics, and visual literacy.

Stephen M. Ross

Stephen M. Ross is Professor of Educational Psychology and Research at Memphis State University. During the past 14 years he has published over 60 articles in professional journals and written three textbooks. His current research interests are in computer-based instruction, with primary emphasis on personalization and screen design. He is also working on a grant sponsored by Apple Computer to examine distance learning and CBI interventions with at-risk children.

Gregory C. Sales

Gregory C. Sales is an Associate Professor of Instructional Systems at the University of Minnesota. His research investigates individual differences and design variables that influence the effectiveness of feedback in technology-assisted instruction. He has authored or co-authored more than 50 articles, chapters, technical reports, and commercial products. In addition to his work on this book, Dr. Sales' recent efforts have included the design of *Beyond Words*, a forty-one disc interactive multimedia curriculum on adult basic skills, and *FacTrac*, an award-winning software program to facilitate school performance disclosure.

Patricia L. Smith

Patricia L. Smith is Assistant Professor of Instructional Technology at the University of Oklahoma. Her area of focus is instructional design, and she teaches courses in instructional design, computer-based instruction design, computer-based instruction authoring, computer literacy, instructional text design, and instructional research. She received her B.S. and M.S. degrees from Texas Tech University, and her Ph.D. in Instructional Systems from Florida State University. She is the author of two books and numerous articles in the area of computer-based instruction and instructional design.

Linda K. Swindell

Linda K. Swindell's current research interests include the role of post-response information in monitoring comprehension and transfer of learning. Prior to joining the faculty at the University of Mississippi, she worked at the Instructional Science Research Facility at Arizona State University. There her responsibilities included supervising graduate research assistants as well as designing and implementing studies in research and instruction.

Susan A. Tucker

Susan A. Tucker, an educational psychologist, teaches in both the Instructional Design and Behavioral Studies programs at the University of South Alabama. Tucker recently completed a national study for the U.S. Office of Technology Assessment on training teacher technologists and a cross-national study for the U.S.-Japan Foundation. Using perception-based models, she has been conducting research in both education and business environments and has used this data to enhance program improvement. Her primary areas of interest include perception-based program evaluation, developing qualitative evaluation tools such as photo-interviewing, interactive media, feedback, automaticity, and semiotics.

Walter Wager

Walter Wager received his doctoral degree in Instructional Systems Design from Indiana University in 1972. Since then he has taught at Florida State University and is Professor and program leader of the Instructional Systems and Educational Psychology Program in the Department of Educational Research. Dr. Wager's areas of specialty are instructional materials development, design models, and the design of computer assisted instruction. Dr. Wager is co-author with R.M. Gagné and L.J. Briggs of the text *Principles of Instructional Design*, as well as *The Handbook of Procedures for the Design of Instruction* with L.J. Briggs. Wager has contributed chapters to a half-dozen texts, and published numerous articles in educational journals and magazines. He is senior author of a recently-published text entitled *Computers in Teaching and Learning: A Systems Approach,* and *Learner's Guide to the Principles of Instructional Design* with co-authors John V. Dempsey, Jim Applefield, and Rodney Earle.

Author Index

Bjorkman, M., 293, 294
Blaiwes, A. S., 210, 213
Bloom, B. S., 295
Boekaerts, M., 119
Borg, W. R., 32
Borgida, E., 136
Borkowski, J. G., 124
Boyle, C. F., 12
Brackbill, Y., 14, 23
Braden, W., 28
Bradway, K., 112
Bradwell, R., 14
Bransford, J. D., 178
Braskamp, D. H., 202
Bravos, A., 23
Bredemeier, M. E., 201, 202
Brehmer, B., 332
Briggs, L. J., 21, 27, 56, 58, 80, 290
Brit, A., 9
Brophy, J., 135
Brovey, A. J., 234
Brown, A. L., 213
Brown, F. J., 5
Brown, J. S., 12, 185, 295
Bruner, J. S., 112
Bull, S. G., 58
Burger, J. M., 122
Burt, C., 323
Burton, R. R., 12, 185
Busemeyer, J. R., 318, 319, 324
Buss, A. H., 28
Buss, E., 28
Butkowsky, I. S., 123
Butler, J. T., 220
Buttrey, T., 115, 169, 184, 193
Byham, W. C., 200, 206, 207

C

Cameron, M., 232
Campbell-Bonar, K., 263, 264
Campione, J. C., 213
Cantor, N., 149
Carey, L., 323
Carlson, W. S., 56, 70

Carnevale, P. J. D., 317, 334
Carnine, D., 12, 232
Caro, P. W., 210, 213
Carpenter, J., 185
Carrier, C. A., 169, 235
Carson, H., 277
Carter, J., 159
Cartledge, N., 28
Cartwright, D., 145
Carver, C. S., 246
Cason, H., 5
Caswell, D., 278
Chan, A. L., 12, 29, 31, 36, 81, 239
Charles, R., 185
Chase, D. H., 5
Chase, W. G., 92
Chatelier, P., 201
Chi, M. T. H., 92
Clancey, W. J., 295
Clariana, R. B., 26, 180, 183, 192, 200, 211, 212
Clark, H. J., 201
Clark, R. E., 147, 151, 264
Cleaveland, J. N., 264, 278, 279
Cocchiarella, M. J., 34
Coella, A., 37
Cohen, L. J., 329
Cohen, M. P., 185
Cohen, V. B., 159
Coleman, J. S., 200
Collins, A., 244, 245
Collins, M., 12
Conlon, D. E., 334
Connolly, T., 321
Considine, D., 288
Cooney, J. B., 168
Cooper, R., 264
Corbeil, P., 200
Corbett, A. T., 12
Corley, W. E., 210, 213
Corno, L., 246
Coulson, J. E., 4, 11
Covey, P., 280
Covington, M. V., 113, 118, 122
Crandall, R., 136

Subject Index

A

Ability
  feedback to focus attention on, 116
  learner view of, 121-122
  misjudged by learners, 119
Accretion, 66
Achievement
  as criterion variable, 168
  effect of adapted and adaptive feedback on, 169
Acquisition and avoidance goals, 107, 109
Adapted and adaptive feedback, 163-168, 172-173
  and achievement, 169
  and attribution, 171
  increasing effectiveness of instruction, 168
  and motivation, 170-171
  recommendations and guidelines, 172-173
  variables on which to adapt, 166-168
Adapted feedback, 163, 165-166
Adaptive feedback, 163, 166-168
  See also Personalized feedback
  computer-based, 184-186
  computer-based, compared with conventional feedback, 185-186
  design and development of, 166
  dynamic nature of, 166
Adaptive instruction

bases for designing, 172
  suggestions for designers, 172-173
Adaptive instructional modeling (AIM), 184
Adaptive instructional strategy, personalization as, 178-179
Adaptive structures, and feedback, 34-36
Adaptive systems, role of learner characteristics in design of, 297-298
Adjunct questions, 64-65. *See also* Questions
Advance organizers, 61
Affective feedback, 281. *See also* Feedback
Affective component of attitudes, 99
Answer until correct (AUC) feedback, 180-184
  See also Feedback
  advantages of, 180
  compared with other types, 183-184
  disadvantage of, 182
Anticipated wrong answer (AWA) feedback, 185. *See also* Feedback
ARCS model of motivation, relevance for simulation and gaming, 214-216
Assessment, link with feedback, 198
Asymmetrical transfer, 213
Attitudes
  components of, 99

P

Part-task trainers, 199. *See also* Simulation
Past-performance discrepancy feedback, 37. *See also* Feedback
Performance assessment, link with feedback, 198
Performance comparisons, learners' reactions to, 116
Performance evaluation, learner self-evaluation, 214, 216
Performance feedback, 280. *See also* Feedback
Performance-goal orientation, 122. *See also* Goal orientation
Performance in the learner's environment, role of questions and feedback, 59, 69
Performance-orientation feedback, 171. *See also* Feedback
Performing goals, and learner success or failure, 108-110
Personal feedback, 135. *See also* Feedback
Personalization strategies, 178-179 implications for feedback, 179
Personalized feedback, 170
See also Adaptive feedback; Feedback
advantages of, 191
opportunities for, 192-193
Personal performance, as a source of self-efficacy, 118
Positive interdependence, in cooperative learning, 139-140
Post-questions, 64
Practice
for cognitive strategies, 95-96
for components of procedural rules, 88-89
for concept learning, 83
for declarative knowledge learning, 81

design considerations, 78-79
as an instructional event, 78-79
levels of, for relational rules, 85-86
for problem solving, 92-93
for psychomotor skills, 97
Praise, potential for misinterpretation, 114-115
Praise or blame feedback
blame more effective than praise, 115
factors affecting, 114-115
ignored by learners using computer-based instruction, 115
Pre-questions, 61-62
affecting rehearsal, 65
Priming, 327-328
Probabilities, estimating, 319-320
Problem solving
differing from rule learning, 91
practice for, 92-93
prerequisites for, 91-92
simulations as practice format, 93
stages in, 92
strategies required by, 92
Problem-solving instruction, measuring certitude in, 253-254
Problem-solving interactive videodisc, tracking of students' steps in, 252
Procedural rules, 87-91
feedback for learning, 89-91
information processing analysis for, 88
pattern for productions for procedures, 87-88
practice for components of, 88-89
Procedural simulation, 199. *See also* Simulation
Process feedback, 280. *See also* Feedback
Process simulation, 199. *See also* Simulation

S